Mixtape Nostalgia

Critical Perspectives on Music and Society

Series Editor: David Arditi, University of Texas at Arlington

This book series produces books that present a critical perspective on popular music and the music industry. Two dominant strains of thought exist for the study of popular music. First, many texts in the popular culture tradition celebrate the artists, fans, and cultures that arise from popular music. Second, Music Industry Studies texts give students a "how-to" perspective on making it in the music industry. In both cases, texts rarely address the way that the music industry produces and reproduces power. The purpose of this book series is to provide a platform for authors who explore the social production of music; as such it is broadly interdisciplinary.

The series invites submissions by scholars from the fields of cultural studies, American studies, history, sociology, literature, communication, media studies, music, women's studies, ethnic studies, popular culture, music industry studies, political science, economics, and history.

Specific topics addressed:

- Musicians as Labor
- Identity (Sex, Gender, Race, Ethnicity, Disability, and Sexuality)
- Critical Representations
- Music Industry Studies
- Music in the Global South
- Production of Genres
- New/Old Technologies
- Sound Studies
- Access inequalities to music production and consumption
- Spaces of music production, creation, and consumption

Mixtape Nostalgia: Culture, Memory, and Representation by Jehnie I. Burns

iTake-Over: The Recording Industry in the Streaming Era, Second Edition by David Arditi

Cruisicology: The Music Culture of Cruise Ships by David Cashman and Philip Hayward

"This Is America": Race, Gender, and Politics in America's Musical Landscape by Katie Rios

Mixtape Nostalgia

Culture, Memory, and Representation

Jehnie I. Burns

Enjoy!

LEXINGTON BOOKS
Lanham • Boulder • New York • London

Published by Lexington Books
An imprint of The Rowman & Littlefield Publishing Group, Inc.
4501 Forbes Boulevard, Suite 200, Lanham, Maryland 20706
www.rowman.com

6 Tinworth Street, London SE11 5AL, United Kingdom

British Library Cataloguing in Publication Information Available

Library of Congress Cataloging-in-Publication Data on File

ISBN 978-1-7936-1679-1 (cloth : alk. Paper)
ISBN 978-1-7936-1680-7 (electronic)

♾™ The paper used in this publication meets the minimum requirements of American National Standard for Information Sciences—Permanence of Paper for Printed Library Materials, ANSI/NISO Z39.48-1992.

This book is dedicated to bb who made me my first best mixtape and my most recent playlist.

Contents

List of Figures

Acknowledgments

When I started this project, I never guessed it would turn into a book. It would not exist without the help of my community. I would like to thank my coworkers, friends, and family for their patience and support. Bob Ross read the introductory chapters and offered invaluable advice to better construct my arguments. Kendra Ross read everything related to hip hop, recommended incredibly useful sources, and helped me make sense of the world of hip hop. Kwame Harrison patiently answered my questions about the hip hop mixtape. Ed Traversari tracked down contacts in the music industry. Missa Haas and my mom Pam Burns read full drafts and encouraged me at every stage. Tom Parkin knows everyone and made connections so I could conduct an interview. My late-advisor Lenard Berlanstein taught me everything I know about writing cultural history, but he never would have expected this to be the book I completed.

A big thanks to the entrepreneurs, authors, and creators who have made mixtapes in the past five years and let me interview them about their work: Bailey Allegretti, Joel Johnson, Brendan Leonard, Steve Lowry, Owen Murphy, and Alexander Olson.

My colleagues at Point Park University have supported me and kept me sane. Sarah Perrier has listened to me whine, worry, and think out loud over coffees—both on Teams and in person. Sera Mathew, Brendan Mullan, Tracey Brent-Chessum, the members of COAC and ORC have encouraged and supported me throughout. The University librarians (Liz Evans, Mel Kirchartz, Phill Harrity, and Lauren Irvin) tracked down sources for me with good grace and patience. The University administration gave me the opportunity to teach Music History and a sabbatical to write the book. Jonas Prida shared my love of pop culture and music, taking over my class when I went to conferences. The students in my History of American Music class, Spring

2018, Spring 2019, Fall 2019 and Spring 2021 listened to me work through ideas that became part of this book. I appreciate your enthusiasm for the final project. The mixtapes you made, complete with cover art, Spotify playlists, and themes you had to justify to the class, were fun but also helped me to think more coherently about what made a mixtape a mixtape.

The colleagues at the conferences I have attended since I started this project who asked questions and shared stories have helped me hone my story. Panelists and section chairs at the Southwest Popular/American Culture Association, the Popular Music Books in Progress talk, and the Popular Culture Association offered feedback and insight when I presented. Those conference papers became the foundation for this book. My editors at Lexington Books Courtney Morales and especially David Arditi have answered tireless questions, offered advice, support, and feedback, and kept me moving forward.

On a personal note, I owe a debt of gratitude to my boys for understanding when I needed to work and when my mind was far away in the land of music and analog technology. Matthew has kept me updated on young people today, read sections, asked me lots of questions, and listened to me talk. Andrew takes me away from my work and makes me think. My mom and dad Pam and Bill Burns taught me to read, to write, and to love music. You are the two best editors and biggest supporters I've had since I first put pen to paper. Most importantly, this book would not exist without my partner Brian, who has always shared his love of music with me. Aside from being my tech support, he has listened to me ruminate, offered his limitless insight on music and fandom, understood when my mind was a million miles away, worked remotely beside me, shared links with me tirelessly, and expanded my musical world with concerts, CDs, and of course mixtapes.

Introduction

I am a Gen X music fan: I attend concerts regularly, I still buy new music on CDs because I like to have a tangible copy, I rarely use streaming apps. I am a Gen Xer: I grew up with cassette tapes and remember getting my first CD player in junior high; there was no internet; and I only got a smartphone when I needed to track my children's social schedules. Five or six years ago, I noticed a resurgence of interest in the quirky niche world of mixtapes. The more I observed, the more I discovered. Eventually, I had family members mentioning mixtapes they had seen in pop culture. My mom informed me both television series, *Grace and Frankie* and *Yellowstone*, had discussed mixtapes. My teenage son bought me a flash drive shaped like a cassette tape called "Mashtape" to keep digital copies of my conference papers. What started as a curiosity turned into a viable academic project; mixtapes have a lot to say about nostalgia, the past, and how we understand ourselves in relation to the music we share.

The more I thought about mixtapes the more they appeared. While on vacation I walked into any number of tourist stores in the western United States where vinyl stickers are all the rage. While attending concerts, I always check out the merch table. Walking through the parking lot at the local public library, I observe bumper stickers on cars. In each of those cases mixtapes, which represent viable, fun products, appeared as memorabilia of events and travels. Among the vinyl cassette-shaped stickers in my collection are: "Rocky Mtn. Mix/Boulder, CO," "House of Blues Remix '92," "Live Local Music," purchased in Cleveland, Ohio, and "Welcome to your Tape" by a zentangle artist. I have seen stickers for small unknown punk bands on bumpers and bought a shirt with a mixtape emblazoned across the front at a merch tent at Red Rocks in Colorado. At the Rock & Roll Hall of Fame I found an enamel cassette pin, and a sterling charm shaped like a cassette.

While browsing in young adult apparel stores, I have seen lacquer pins with cassette tapes, a two-piece pin with a chain connecting a Walkman with a pair of headphones, and a greeting card with a hand-drawn pink and red cassette tape titled "Love Songs" and a matching pin. I walked past a woman's clothing store in downtown Pittsburgh where I spied a handbag shaped like a boombox. In Chicago, I took a picture of a bejeweled clutch purse shaped like a cassette with the word "party mix" emblazoned in glitter as the accessory to a red evening dress. At a well-known New York City bookstore, I found refrigerator magnets shaped like mixtapes and a pair of black and white socks with woven cassette tapes for sale. In Antwerp, Belgium a store had a coin purse for sale with a blue and red cassette and the phrase "free to be mix/87" as the label. A restaurant in the same Antwerp neighborhood had made a pen holder out of four cassette tapes and the front of the checkout counter consisted of a mosaic of various cassette tapes, including many hand-labeled mixtapes. Target sold a black and white shower curtain with images of outdated music paraphernalia like boomboxes, Walkmans, and reel-to-reel players. I have seen planners and blank notebooks with a cassette-tape-drawn cover and phrases like "mixed messages" on the spine. There are "mixtape greetings" notecards and tote bags with cassette tapes on the side, the handle of the bag representing spooling tape. Walking through flea markets I have seen yoga pants emblazoned with cassette tapes. Jeopardy has used mixtapes in their clues. The podcast *Mark and Sarah Talk About Songs* reminisce about their youthful mixtapes with regularity. Radio stations have created murals on their walls of cassette tapes. The local yoga studio hosted a special "I ♥ Mixtapes" class. If it is possible to create a product and emblazon it with a mixtape, it exists. When I typed mixtape into Etsy, I found everything from t-shirts to coffee mugs, to personalized, etched, retro money clips. As with the money clip, many of these products add wording to clarify this item is not merely a cassette tape, it is self-consciously a mixtape. In 2019, the popular dystopian television show *Handmaid's Tale* featured a mixtape as a connection between characters. June opens a box full of tapes, with titles like "A Mixtape Miasma," "Ocean Swimming Mix," and "Shower Thoughts," picks one, and listens to it on a boombox, sitting on the basement floor.[1] In 2020 the K-Pop band Stray Kids released an EP called *Mixtape* from the reality TV show which launched them.

I had to wonder why. What about the mixtape has captured the imagination of the pop culture world that no longer owns, sells, or plays cassette tapes as a viable outlet for music? How did an icon of the 1980s anti-consumer, self-consciously emotive youth generation become so ubiquitous in the 2010s? One could argue it remains a small, retro kitsch niche, not nearly as common as I think. Because I looked for them, I found them. However, when chain stores like Urban Outfitter and international brands like Kipling Bags have added the imagery to their products, it is not only niche. When blockbuster comic book films like *Guardians of the Galaxy* release a billboard-charting soundtrack called "Awesome Mix, Vol.1" it is not only niche. When Nick Hornby's novel *High Fidelity*, which centers mixtapes as a plot point, becomes a film, remains a cult classic, and gets a 2019 TV reboot, it is not only niche.

Alongside the physicality of the artifact as a cassette is the vocabulary surrounding the mixtape. There is no cognitive difference between the terms: "mix, mix tape, mix-tape, mixtape, mixed tape, and compilation tape." Dictionaries define "mix tape, mix-tape, and mixtape" as the same term. A mixtape is a compilation of songs, which may account for the term "compilation" (tape). Compilation encompasses a broader definition because it also includes commercially released albums with various artists. At times individuals and pop culture references use "mixtape" when referring to a compilation on a CD or a digital playlist; there is no "tape" involved. "Compilation," as a synonym for mixtape, appears more often in British texts, possibly because it was the term Nick Hornby chose for *High Fidelity*.

Among the first to use the term "mix tape" were hip hop artists creating compilations of live performances for fans. Mix tape simultaneously appeared in the late 1970s referring to personally crafted compilations to be shared between individuals. Over time the single word mixtape predominated, but some individuals continue to use the other variations. Hip hop culture has used "mixtape" continually since the 1970s to refer to noncommercially created products, regardless of the medium on which the music is recorded. Current hip hop mixtapes might only appear on Soundcloud, for example. Throughout the book I use "mixtape," a single, nonhyphenated word, for clarity and "hip hop mixtape" for the artist-produced items borne out of hip hop culture.

Those definitions are straightforward, but as time progressed people continued to use the term "mixtape" even if the final product appeared on a CD or digitally. By the late 1990s the term "mixtape" stuck, regardless of the recording medium. In contemporary interviews people often clarify and state if they made their mixtape as a CD or a digital playlist, acknowledging their awareness of the technological nuance. Creators make stylistic choices based on the stories they want to tell. Yvonne Prinz's 2009 *Vinyl Princess* incorporates a mix CD which is relevant for the characters in her story. David Nicholl's characters in *One Day* make both cassette and CD mixes, which reflects the passage of time from 1989 to 2009. Authors illustrate if the mixes are cassette tapes by mentioning the tape outright, describing the cover art on a J-Card, or discussing the type of stereo on which the mixtape can be played. I refer to all compilations of music as mixtapes but clarify if the product was a CD or a digital playlist.

When contemporary artists use mixtape, it encompasses the technology as well as the emotional appeal. Visual representations of mixtapes are overwhelmingly images of cassette tapes. In these instances, the rhetoric confirms the image is a mixtape and not merely a cassette. Artists signify the distinction in their descriptions of their merchandise or through visual cues like hand-written titles including the word mix. Digital playlists also use the term "mixtape" even though there is not an analog product to accompany the music. This use of the term builds on the legacy of the personally crafted compilation mixtape, the continued appeal, and the growth of the hip hop mixtape, and is a self-referential acknowledgment of the history of these products.

In this book, I will argue that mixtape represents a point of nostalgia which combines auditory memory and kitsch retro appeal. The current interest in the medium of cassettes demonstrates a culture invested in music, emotional ties to the past, and artistic and material representations of those products. While the mixtape is not solely responsible for current reinvestment in cassette culture, there is a link with the subculture invested in analog technology.[2] The boom in vinyl and the nostalgic appeal of the mixtape in shows like *High Fidelity* suggest a growing investment in retro material culture. The personal mixtape represents a reflective nostalgia of the recent past; it suggests an idealized, middle-class, consumer-culture-driven, mainstream world. The term also represents an independent album release outside of consumer culture, particularly, but not exclusively, in the hip hop community. The commodification of the mixtape highlights the appeal of kitsch and the use of nostalgic material culture to appeal to a generation who appreciates the opportunity to harken back to a simpler, younger time. The appeal of retro crosses generations and musical communities. It reflects those who lived through the mixtape period themselves and are nostalgic for their own past: Gen X and the elders of Gen Y (more commonly referred to as millennials). However, it also integrates a younger generation who are invested in a past steeped in analog technology they never experienced. And it incorporates those individuals involved in the contemporary, often digital, hip hop mixtape. This book is structured around the many means through which the mixtape has become a representation of a larger idea. It will cover discussions of music, movies, memoirs, and novels and explain how the mixtape moved from a tangible item to a nostalgic idea, to a conceptual thought piece.

To understand the role of the mixtape, it is relevant to see the mixtape as evolving over four distinct periods. In the 1980s and 1990s a mixtape was a tangible technological norm. It began as an inexpensive opportunity to own a recording of a live hip hop, punk, or rock show. Early on, hip-hop DJs curated recordings to create an idealized listening experience. For many young people, the mixtape existed as a piece of youth culture that allowed individuals to create compilations of music on a simple, inexpensive medium which they could play in cars and on personal stereos. Mixtapes created personal ways of using music as an expression of identity and connection. By the end of the 1990s with a shift to streaming and the growth of digital technology, the mixtape became a passé outdated media of Gen X culture. Neither innovative nor the easiest means of compiling and sharing music, the mixtape became a topic of discussion largely among music aficionados telling stories of their own lives using the mixtape as a sign of their age and community-identity. In hip hop it became a promotional item, vetted by independent DJs and sold in independent stores. By the 2010s the mixtape had diverged even further depending on which definition one used. The mainstream Gen X mixtape moved into the realm of nostalgia, in part because of the stories written in the previous decade. By this period, the mixtape represented a nostalgic idea of an analog past. The mixtape became identified with relationships and emotion, but it no longer required the physical artifact to express it as an idea. However, the mixtape in hip hop transformed as well-known artists used the medium to showcase new styles and grew fans independent of major label releases. The mixtape exploded into digital rap lingo as an independent EP. The contemporary reappearance of the mixtape in pop culture imagination pulled pieces from both the nostalgic Gen X understanding and the contemporary non-commercial hip hop definition. Blockbuster products incorporated mixtapes in their stories and benefitted from the word's familiarity across pop culture subcultures. Mixtapes no longer only meant a physical artifact on which individuals shared music; for many it is synonymous with compilation, independent of its relationship to music. Benefitting from the continuous use and redefinition of the term, the "mixtape" has become a metaphor and an image for organizational structure, a shortcut idea for nostalgia, and an emotive link. The term "mixtape" resides as a site of cultural memory which speaks to individuals across demographics.

Starting with the definition of a mixtape, chapter 1 explores the history of the cassette tape and the burgeoning youth cultures of the same era. Magnetic recording, which grew out of World War II technology, significantly shifted sound technology and the music industry. It allowed for novel ways of recording, making, and playing back music. The creation of the compact cassette in the mid-1960s was a sea change for the music industry. The cost of recording, producing, and releasing music shifted. For the consumer, the ability to make music portable changed how music intersected with peoples' lives. In this era, a new young generation came of age who resisted the experiences of their elders. Known for their disgruntlement with commercial society, Generation X craved new ways of interacting with culture which dovetailed with the music technology, grounding the importance of the cassette tape.

Chapter 2 begins with an analysis of the importance of musical identity and its connection to youth culture. The solidification of the cassette as the main means of listening to music, coinciding with the release of the Walkman and the boombox led to a burgeoning musical self-production. Punk and hip-hop benefitted from cassette technology and the ability to self-release music. These genres appealed to the Gen X generation who disliked the hype of commercialism and wanted a more real connection to their musical heroes. The music industry pushed back against these noncommercial releases, fighting a losing battle against bootlegging and piracy which continued throughout the mixtape era.

Chapter 3 picks up with young people recognizing their own power in artistic creation as a result of the personal stereo and the cassette tape. The DJ curated hip hop mixtape foregrounded the self-made personalized mixtape. Young people discovered they could self-curate albums with the best of their music to listen to in the car, through their headphones, or to share with friends. It allowed young people to shape their emotional outlet in a personalized way while still paying homage to the music of their communities. In this generation, authors began writing stories, like *Less than Zero* and *High Fidelity*, which incorporated mixtapes, not as sites of cultural memory but as a fundamental aspect of the lived experience of a young person in the late 1980s and 1990s.

Chapter 4 shows the quickly shifting landscape in the role of technology and music. The move to CDs and computers left the cassette tape and the personally curated mixtape as icons of the past. By the turn of the new millennium, the mixtape became a piece of nostalgia. Storytellers wrote memoirs framing their experiences around the mixtape, musicians released music singing about their favorite mixtapes, and Broadway playwrights wrote stories reflecting on the mixtape as a fun moment in the past. In the world of hip hop, a crackdown on copyright infringement shifted the mixtape away from the DJ set and moved it to a new uncertain digital medium. Not yet an intangible idea, the mixtape shifted in this decade to a quaint icon of the past generation, reflected in individuals writing and singing about their younger days.

Chapter 5 coincides with a growth in fascination with analog products. By this generation, the personal mixtape had become a beloved artifact of the past that emphasized close connection, tangibility, and the appeal of taking time to make someone a gift. Musicians incorporated the mixtape in lyrics to feature shared memories, lost loves, and idealized pasts. In hip hop, the DJ-curated mixtapes ended with a crackdown against sampling. At the same time, hip hop mixtapes gained a new life as the self-released EPs of independent rappers. Authors incorporated "mixtape" as reflective nostalgia connecting characters through the music they shared. The renewed interest in vinyl highlighted a public who disliked commercial media and the limitations of digital.

Chapter 6 emphasizes a fascination with retro technology and a shift away from the mixtape as music-centered. Novelists geared young adult plots around the emotionality of physically sharing music on an analog medium. Memoirists used the mixtape as an organizing principle or a conceptual idea about friendship. Mainstream media seized this idea in two record-breaking releases: *Guardians of the Galaxy* and *Hamilton*. The Hollywood film solidified the nostalgic emotive appeal of the physical artifact. The Broadway musical connected the hip hop mixtape and the personal mixtape, reframing them as a single concept. The notion of the mixtape which had moved in two parallel tracks over the past thirty years became reconnected through Broadway fame.

Chapter 7 explores the shift in the terminology as the mixtape became a metaphor rather than an object. Fiction, memoir, academia, and podcasts incorporated the mixtape into their vocabulary, but no longer connected the physicality of a cassette tape to the idea of a playlist tied to personal connection. Moving closer to the present, the technostalgia of the current era finds a fascination with, if not a desire to return to, the technology of the past. Rather than purchasing old cassette players, entrepreneurs are creating digital cassette-inspired music players. Podcasters are using mixtape as a word to mean a list of tangentially connected ideas combined in a curated way. And Questlove, a hip hop DJ famed for his ability to create dynamic playlists for well-known superstars, has written a cookbook called *Mixtape Potluck*.

Chapter 8 brings the story full circle to the "stuff." It is an analysis of the consumer culture around the mixtape and how it has become a name and an idea. The mixtape has become an intangible representation of an era, an idea, and a feeling which no longer needs to be held in a cassette. The choice of graphics and colors help situate the visual mixtape as reflective of the Gen X personal mixtape or the hip hop self-produced, self-released mixtape. This chapter examines, among other products, a board game, a bar, and a marketing campaign for a college musical that has touched on the idea of a mixtape to bring people together. It covers the marketing world from coffee and beer to public radio. The creators who have invested their work in their ideas often talk about music, yes, but also the link music creates between people. The nostalgia of the cassette era remains part of the story, as does the marketability of cassette culture, but the investment in interconnectedness makes the mixtape worthy of recreation.

When I have told people I write about mixtapes, the responses range from incredulity to excitement. Rarely are people bored by my area of research, but often they are surprised there is enough to write about. Most commonly when I mention mixtapes to my colleagues and friends, they have a story about the mixtapes they made, received, or remember from their youth. I have heard about boxes of mixtapes tucked away in the attic, about driving old cars that only play cassette tapes, about the first, the last, the goofiest mixtape people received. My own mixtapes sit on a shelf next to my desk, and no, I do not have a cassette player where I can play them. While the technology has shifted and cassettes, albeit more popular than ten years ago, will not become a mainstream technology again soon, the mixtape remains in the collective imagination. There is something about holding the DIY, sharpie-d, Maxell 90 cassette, with hand-written title tracks to bring a giddy reflection. The small smile of reminiscence made this a book worth writing.

NOTES

1. *Handmaid's Tale*, Season 3 episode 5, "Unknown Caller," directed by Colin Watkinson, written by Marissa Jo Cerar and Lynn Renee Maxcy, aired June 19, 2019 on Hulu.

2. Peter Manuel coined the phrase "cassette culture" for his book *Cassette Culture: Popular Music and Technology in North India*. Today it has grown to include the role of the cassette and tape recording internationally as cited in Andre Millard, *America on Record: A History of Recorded Sound*, Second ed. (Cambridge: Cambridge University Press, 2005), 327.

Chapter 1

Birth of the Cassette

WHAT IS A MIXTAPE?

How does one define "mixtape"? One website asked, "What is a mixtape? Is it a group of songs given away for free? Is it a gathering of songs from multiple artists? Is it all of the above? Or is it none of the above? The term 'mixtape' has become so generic in some circles that it either means too many things or nothing at all (since we don't really even use 'tapes' anymore)."[1] In simple terms, it is a compilation of carefully chosen songs, often by various artists, primarily recorded onto a cassette tape by an individual. However, this straightforward definition undermines the long-standing emotional element associated with the mixtape. Thurston Moore credits *Village Voice* critic Robert Christgau with the first public discussion of a mixtape in a 1978 article.[2] The mixtape has become a musical cultural icon which reflects youth who listened, created, and shared music on analog technology. Los Angeles writer Matias Viegener defined the role of the mixtape in youth culture stating,

> The mix tape as a form of American Folk Art: predigested cultural artifacts combined with homespun technology and magic markers turn the mix tape to a message in a bottle. I am no mere consumer of pop culture, it says, but also a producer of it. Mix tapes make the moment of consumer culture in which listeners attained control over what they heard, in what order and at what cost. [...] A mix tape can never be perfect. My taste as a mixer tells you even more about me than my taste as a consumer already does. No mix tape is accidental.[3]

Viegener's definition encapsulates the importance of a youth-created cultural artifact that helps to define an aspect of musical culture at the end of the twentieth century. This acknowledgment of a mixtape as a cultural artifact gives better depth of understanding to the role it has played in representing youth culture and identity tied to music and analog creations. Judith Peraino, a music professor who analyzes social identity and musical expression expands her definition, underlining the technological and emotive communication inherent in a mixtape. She affirms the mixtape is usually intended for a single recipient.

> The analog mixtape—that is, a homemade compilation of music—always records and enacts a closet drama. In contrast to the instantaneous drag-and-drop process of digital compilations, the analog mixtape drama unfolds in the real time of planning and playing a song sequence, and splicing together songs from different sources. [. . .] The splice that marries songs on a dubbed mixtape represents the moment of greatest physical labor. This involves changing or flipping records and tapes, adjusting volume levels, synchronizing stat times, fading out (to avoid sudden cuts in sound or machine noise), adding silence, pressing pause or rewind to erase mistakes or cue-up the next song. With this embodied and durational experience of each song in sequence, mixtape creators embed themselves within the tape and prefigure the tape's future listeners.[4]

For her, the act of creating and giving a mixtape is a participatory performance, which enhances the meaning of individual songs because of their inclusion. Even a history of intellectual property has acknowledged the importance of the mixtape when discussing the ideological role of copyright. Robin Wright wrote,

> With an audiotape cassette, fans could change the order of play, add sounds and effects, draw or write on the label, and take and play the tape anywhere. Most importantly they could create an individualized expression of their own musical experience that could be shared with others. The homemade mix tape became a standard trope of musical communication, connecting with friends and family at home, in the car, at a party, or on the beach. The choice of what would go onto a tape was a matter of serious import for romantics across the globe. As they recognized that every mix tape is a love letter.[5]

The idea of mixtapes as love letters grounds the nostalgic mixtape while the importance of song choice overlaps with the other key mixtape of the late 20th century: the hip hop mixtape. Regan Sommer McCoy, the founder of the digital archive, The Mixtape Museum, views mixtapes primarily through the lens of hip hop. Her first mixtapes were bootleg recordings of DJ sets bought in Harlem and the Bronx.[6] For her mixtapes are the shared foundation of both the nostalgic mixtape and the hip hop mixtape. In a 2020 interview with Tape Op she stated, "If you ask me what a mixtape is, the answer would be very different from some of my mixtape and hip hop purist friends. My first entry point to mixtapes were the first ones that I made in my bedroom, recording off the radio. But in high school I started buying the mixtapes that I cover in The Mixtape Museum. Those were the mixtapes that were curated and dubbed by these DJs."[7] Her work shows the continued growth and expansion of hip hop through the guise of the mixtape.

These four well-thought-out definitions give mixtapes a gravitas which might strike mixtape recipients as overladen. However, it is the amount of time and effort people put not only into creating these artifacts, but preserving, reflecting, and writing about them. A simple item originally created to share music for a portable playlist or between two individuals has become a demarcation of a middle-class youth experience at the end of the 20th century.

In their study about cultural practices related to music, Dutch scholars distinguished between three types of "mixtapers": the reference person, the self-referential mixtaper, and the mixtape recipient.[8] A mixtape reference person is an individual with musical knowledge who has a desire to dispense knowledge either as an analytical introduction to new and unfamiliar styles of music or the personal, emotive mixtape created to share feelings. The hip hop DJ falls into this category. The self-referential mixtaper is the individual who records music for themselves and creates playlists based on the music they may already have. This type of mixtape remains emotive, but it is often about how musicians and other artists use music as a tool to help them increase their own skill or understanding of sound. The third individual is the recipient of the mixtape. For this individual, the mixtape creates a bond, either emotive or mentor-driven, with the mixtaper who made the artifact. In either case, the recipient of the mixtape is the focus of the mixtape story. They are the person for whom the nostalgic tie to the artifacts remains prescient. Having kept a cassette tape through multiple moves and across time, knowing they no longer have the ability to listen to the music via cassette, the connection they feel to a physical object remains more important than the sounds it creates.

Authors, musicians, and artists have used mixtapes to help tell their stories and define their life experiences. However, no overarching themes are represented on mixtapes.[9] No one genre predominates. There is no right way to construct a mixtape. Mixtapes are deeply personal, deeply quixotic, and defy easy identification. The lack of structure to the mixtapes, despite what well-known adages in pop culture and novels suggest, is more important than if every mixtape, fictional or real, followed a pattern. To understand the mixtape, one must understand the people who made them. One must look at the social world in which mixtape creators and mixtape recipients lived, loved, and listened. Up to now, the mixtape was "never upheld as a creative practice in its own right that deserved protection as a form of original media production."[10] However, to understand the people and the artistry, the technology which allowed self-creation needs acknowledgment.

THE COMPACT CASSETTE

The cassette tape is a fundamental feature of the mixtape. The simplicity of recreation via cassette both expanded the music industry and transformed the relationship fans had to music. The role of the mixtape resides in an understanding of the background of the cassette and how it reflected musical ideals. The ease of recording music changed with cassette technology which had an impact both within the music industry and among music fans. What had been the realm of specialists became quotidian for anyone who could purchase a tape player.

A history of the cassette tape is one part engineering, one part commercial advertising, and two parts musical involvement. Although cassettes predominated the music industry for a relatively short era, the tape industry changed recorded music. In 1928 German engineer Fritz Pfleumer invented magnetic tape. It was a technological breakthrough built on the difficult-to-use wire recording. Magnetic tape allowed individuals to record and play back sound in a new format. Pfleumer, and Hermann Bucher, Chairman of the Board of Directors of Allgemeine Elektrizitatsgesellschaft (AEG), debuted the Magnetophone K1 at the Berlin Radio Fair in August 1935.[11] The cost, reliability, and portability of this model gave it advantages over the steel recording models being developed in other nations. Over the next thirty years these two men revised, perfected, and standardized the first-generation, industry-standard tape and recorder. BASF, a German chemical company made the magnetic tape for the AEG product. In 1936 BASF recorded Sir Thomas Beecham and the London Philharmonic while on tour in Germany. The recorded performance was broadcast on the radio, showcasing how the new technology could change radio play and performance. Music performances no longer had to rely on live broadcasts. The event solidified the eventual focus of magnetic tape to record and playback music.[12]

During World War II magnetic tape was the purview of military broadcasters. Much of this generation of magnetic tape technology transitioned into data storage capability for early computers. However, key advancements made during the War advanced the viability of tape moving forward: the ability to splice tape without hearing the break, the ability to erase and use tape repeatedly, and the ability to copy tape without significant quality deduction.[13] In 1944 American soldiers found an AEG Magnetophone in a liberated bunker. They sent it to the United States where it became the model for engineers at Ampex who in 1947 made the first magnetic tape recorder for American studios.[14]

With Ampex working on this technology, magnetic tape recording acquired a different trajectory. Ampex developed a playback head; Audio Devices and 3M developed new tape. Together, this new postwar American product advanced sound quality. In May 1946 American soldier and engineer, Jack Mullin, demonstrated the new recorder at an Institute of Radio Engineers (IRE) show in San Francisco highlighting the improved audio. This new technology was introduced to Bing Crosby, musician and owner of Crosby Enterprises, who was struggling with radio networks' debate between live and recorded shows. Mullin did a test recording of Crosby's first tape delay radio broadcast of the Bing Crosby show in 1947–1948.[15] Impressed by the outcome of the test, Crosby purchased multiple new Ampex 200-As and had them sent to branches of ABC television.[16] These machines allowed radio stations to move towards pre-recorded shows, which over time became an industry standard. The collaboration between Crosby, Mullin, and Ampex foreshadowed the "first major commercial production of tape recorders in the United States and, by extension, anywhere in the post-war economy."[17] Motion picture studios began using reel-to-reel tape recording for ease of editing during production. Recording studios also embraced Ampex tape technology because it was easier to edit than master discs.[18] This incorporation encouraged new independent companies which expanded the industry.[19] Both Capitol and Decca records purchased Ampex 200As to record songs like Bill Haley's "Rock Around the Clock" and Nat King Cole's "Unforgettable."[20] Magnetic reel-to-reel tape had entered the mainstream American entertainment industry by 1950.

Crosby gifted one of the early Ampex 200-As to Les Paul, musician and inventor of the solid-body electric guitar. This reel-to-reel tape machine was the foundation for Paul's first-generation, well-known multitracking system.[21] Paul and his wife Mary Ford recorded multiple tracks of the same song on the same loop of tape. They created a depth of music with only two musicians, they could overdub, and they could bounce tracks. Paul saw the recorder as a way to overdub without degradation of quality and with greater fidelity to his sound.[22] Equally important, they did not have to record the tracks live in a single take. By 1954 Ampex produced the first eight-track machine for Paul to have greater diversity in his tracks.[23] Multi-tracking revolutionized the music industry and allowed for experimentation in the studio.

Tape technology offered a variety of innovative functions. Phil Spector's Wall of Sound utilized multi-tracking. Musicians could use the original dictation function of a tape recorder to record ideas. Keith Richards claimed he created "Satisfaction" in his sleep using the tape recorder next to his bed.[24] The Beatles Abbey Road studios created novel, complex, nuanced music using magnetic tape. Reel-to-reel recording made music production less expensive, allowing small recording studios to compete with the major labels. Music could be recorded one musician or instrument at a time, and if they made mistakes, they could rerecord an individual layer.[25] This generation of Ampex machinery not only changed radio stations; it also changed how music was made. Reel-to-reel recording coincided with the growth of rock and roll and a general diversification in musical genres.

Reel-to-reel recorders became consumer products in the 1950s. Music listening was a secondary function of this new consumer technology although one guide book declared users could create an "'up-to-date reel of the latest hits' by collecting musical selections on tape for a party."[26] More often advertisements compared a recorder to an audio family photo album; it included the ability to record important moments in family life or to record and share audio with family members.[27] Samuel Beckett built on this version of tape recording when he published the one-act play *Krapp's Last Tape* in 1958.[28] The play, which revolves around a sixty-nine-year-old man listening to recordings he made of himself over the previous thirty years, reflects the first generation of personal recording as an audio diary. Beckett used a brand-new format to tell a story of personal reflection and remorse centered on recorded memory.

For the average user, *Literary Guidebooks* emphasized the skills for a sound hobbyist with phrases like, "Tape recording is fun!"[29] The mid-century magazine, *Tape Recording*, advertised new products, answered users' questions about the newest technology, and showcased stars, like Doris Day and Rosemary Clooney, using tape in their work.[30] A 1958 article titled "Teen Tapers" suggested candidly recording friends for laughs later was a fun use for the new machines. It encouraged placing a microphone in "the ladies powder room" where they "congregate and discuss the merits of their dates for the evening."[31] The author advised waiting until the dates left to listen to the playback.[32] *Tape Recording* held a reoccurring contest called, "Why My Recorder is Important to Me" in which readers could win a reel of tape. In the November 1961 issue a contestant, named Randy Galloway, stated, "My tape recorder is my only means of income. [. . .] I am a local disk jocky (sic) in the Fort Wayne area. I record top hits from the radio and television and use this music for my record hops." Galloway confirmed local stations had permitted this which he verified with a lawyer.[33] His admission acknowledges copyright and fair use of music. Galloway's recordings also offer an insight into the future mixtape. In the same contest, another contestant stated,

> To tell such a story, I must admit to being hep on rock and roll and admit that there's nothing like tape to store it on. This is an economical way of obtaining an abundant supply of this trend, and a sure way to be the main source of dance entertainment at teen-age dance parties.
>
> Secondly, I must admit to being sly and even sneaky. By this I mean; you borrow a jazz, classical, or folk music album that you like, and you copy it. In doing so, your collection grows.[34]

These two contestants had the foundation of mixtapes; they recorded music off the radio and copied music from other commercial releases. Another described using the music as samples behind his poetry. These personal accounts of the appeal of tape recording are among the earliest examples of mixtapes in all but name.[35] With no editorial commentary, they evoke an innocent, personal, creative way individuals engaged with the new recording technology.

A variety of artistic endeavors expanded tape recording outside of the merely consumer applications. Andy Warhol, intrigued by tape technology, tinkered with recording throughout his career. After he recorded and transcribed a taped conversation in his art studio, The Factory, he released the verbatim recording as the book *a, A Novel*: a piece of unexpected pop art.[36] John Cage and Steve Reich, avant-garde musicians, both used magnetic recording to create innovative works in the 1960s. Reel-to-reel technology also helped formalize the concepts of musique concrète in which recorded sounds, often found in the natural world, become the raw material for new compositions. A reader comment in a 1958 British edition of *Tape Recording* was among the first to use the term "compilation" to describe recording ostensibly musical sounds together. However, he argued musique concrète "is neither music nor art."[37]

In 1966 Any Warhol judged a contest in *Tape Recording* called "Pop Sounds" which offered over 10,000 dollars in prizes and the opportunity to have the tape placed at a prominent New York art gallery.[38] Playing on the popularity of the newly released Batman television show, the article opened, "'POW!' 'BAM!' 'ZONK!' 'ZAM!'" and encouraged contestants to think broadly about everyday sounds.[39] The only limitation was "since many people associate 'Pop Sounds' with popular music—no music tapes, please."[40] This contest showcased how diverse tape recording was viewed in the 1950s and 1960s as an artistic medium in its own right, used to record countless sounds not limited to music. While these types of interactions with tapes reflected a professional and narrow tape enthusiast subset in the 1960s, it acknowledges the diverse ways consumers engaged with magnetic recording. This avant-garde movement represents a side of the new technology which encouraged a broader cultural perspective on the myriad uses of tape.

The Cassette Cartridge

Commercially, tape technology became a more viable option outside the niche reel-to-reel enthusiasts which spurred continued research and development into the 1970s. In 1958 RCA created a "closed system reel-to-reel design" four-track tape cartridge.[41] Although this proprietary product did not flourish, it highlighted the desire for a smaller more compact version of the reel-to-reel. The challenge with the first generation of technology was creating an easily playable format which conformed to the desired recording characteristics. A variety of options were produced over the next twenty years.[42] Radio stations began developing their own tape cartridges. By the end of the 1960s, these products led to the 8-track, a new technology almost exclusively for use in cars. William P. Lear, Sr. assembled a consortium of individuals from Motorola, Victor, RCA, 3M, and Ford to collaborate on a player to work with preexisting radio systems when the cartridge was inserted. In 1966, the first year of production, Ford installed 65,000 Motorola produced 8-track cartridge players as a luxury option in cars. The next year General Motors and Chrysler added 8-track players as well, increasing the number to more than two-million players by the end of 1967. RCA agreed to market pre-recorded tapes for these players.[43] The new 8-track revolutionized both the car and the music industry because of the low cost, the ease of use, and the portability of the item.[44] The technological shift coincided with the rise of a large youth culture generation. In 1966 Baby Boomers, in their late teens, represented the ideal market for these new products. The ability to play music in a car reflected the era's independence and increased standard of living.

While Lear worked on the 8-track for cars, scientists in Europe still considered the reel-to-reel an office machine for dictation. Their goal was to reduce the size of the magnetic recording devices, reduce the cost, and increase the quality. In the late 1950s, American companies CBS and 3M worked on advancing this technology. Building on this work, Lou Ottens, technical director of the audio division at Philips, a Dutch company, created the first audio cassette, originally called the Pocket-Cassette.[45] Like the consumer products of the era, Philips intended to create an updated dictation machine. They had five goals for the new product: a simple construction, reliability, protection of the tape, low energy consumption, and the smallest dimension able to play thirty minutes.[46] Music was not a consideration in their development. Philips introduced the "compact cassette" at a radio conference in Berlin on August 30, 1963. Ottens and his team aimed to create a new "cheap, small, [. . .] low battery consumption, together with an appropriate reproduction quality" product for the recording market.[47]

Ottens and his team traveled to Japan and worked with Norio Ohga, section manager of the Tape Recorder Division at Sony. Akio Morita and Masuru Ibuka had created Sony in 1946 to make a variety of devices, but they had a specific interest in music and therefore concentrated on audio products.[48] Their previous experience creating the first Japanese open-reel tape recorder gave them an insight when working with Philips.[49] Sony and Philips created and released a new medium to conform to a single worldwide standard.[50] By shrinking the width and the thickness of the tape, Philips compromised on the audio quality produced by a cassette but allowed for a portable product. The appeal for the new technology lay in the size; touted as "smaller than a pack of cigarettes," the cassette was instantly more appealing than the large reel-to-reel technology.[51] Philips created the compact cassette for its portability and not to replace the higher-quality reel-to-reel. They began production of blank audio cassettes in Hanover, Germany in 1964.[52]

By creating a royalty-free product which could be widely and freely licensed, Ottens' model standardized the new generation of reel-to-reel magnetic recording in the body of the cassette tape. Because the "basic structure of all tapes is absolutely uniform in order to ensure they are compatible with every kind of tape player," it became an international product.[53] Technology could continue to improve the sound and the quality of the tape, but the designers did not have to redevelop the hardware at every stage. From the first cassette tapes in the 1960s until the current day, their basic size, shape, and format have not changed. Unlike the early magnetic recording technology, the cassette tape standardized the technology and solidified what became one of the foundational ways of listening to and sharing music for half a century. Standardization of the compact cassette allowed for a standard format for tape players. Panasonic and Norelco sold the first cassette players in the United States, but more than eighty manufacturers had joined the industry by the end of the 1960s.[54] One of the unique features of this technology compared to other audio formats was the ability to rewind. Most players incorporate a "push-button interface" which has remained consistent across time and remains an appealing feature for the technostalgic crowd.[55] They usually comprise play, stop, fast-forward, and rewind buttons. Most also include a record button, a fundamental function of magnetic recording. This fifth button is key for mixtapers.

Although music had not been the original focus for Philips, the designers recognized the appeal of replicating record albums and worked to create cassettes that could record thirty minutes per side, the length of a long-play (LP) record. To cross-market their product, they standardized the technology for recording and playback of cassettes to ensure a cassette tape would sound the same regardless of the player on which it was played.[56] Cassettes became a less-expensive way to hear music than LPs, but the technology sacrificed sound quality. "Musicassettes," the first cassettes to have pre-recorded music, first appeared in late 1965.[57] By the summer of 1966 Mercury, an American company owned by Philips, had released forty-nine albums in cassette format which sold for $4.95 per album.[58] A December 1966 advertisement in *Tape Recording* advertised "EMI Musicassettes [. . .] star studded first issue" with twenty songs including Shirley Bassey and Eartha Kitt.[59] The ad stands out for its image of a cassette tape in a magazine primarily still discussing reel-to-reel technology. Sony began mass production of cassette tapes and tape recorders that year.[60] In the summer of 1966 cassette players for cars emerged, costing around 150 dollars.[61] The durability, portability, and lower cost than records were appealing to consumers. In 1968 Philips placed ads in magazines like *Autocar* and *Motor* for the "Philips Cassette Car Radio," a Phils RN582 advertised as "a quality car radio. And a cassette-player too."[62] The ad defined the new product: "Musicassettes are quality recordings on tapes sealed in slim cassettes. No scratches, no dust. Music can't be erased."[63] By the end of the decade the cassette tape had become a standard in music listening, in no small part because of its inclusion in cars. Lou Ottens, the creator of the cassette tape stated, "The biggest surprise was the worldwide revolution it caused in the individual availability of music. But that surprise came into being only very gradually, which is not normal for a surprise."[64] His tongue-in-cheek assertion underscores the lasting appeal of the cassette tape. Writing in 1966 about the technological shifts in music, classical pianist Glenn Gould stated, at the centre of the technological debate, then, is a new kind of listener—a listener more participant in the musical experience. [. . .] It means we decide which tracks to play and in which order. And it means we decide how loudly to play them.[65] A career musician, Gould understood the changing dynamics of how individuals listened to, and expected to listen to, music.

However, cassette players had limitations compared to other means of listening to music. The small size of the player meant small speakers which resulted in poor sound quality. Companies had to overcome tape hiss before serious audiophiles would consider switching to tape. Incorporation of magnetic materials, and the use of equalization and compression, borrowed from the film industry, reduced noise in recording and increased sound fidelity in tape technology.[66] Technological shifts in the size and quality of speakers and in the creation of Dolby sound multiplied the popularity of the cassette. The new Dolby noise-reduction technology was patented in the United States in 1969. A 1971 *Popular Science* article explained the Dolby system "is doing a remarkable job of eliminating background hiss on audio cassettes" and companies like Fisher and Harman Kardon announced production of Dolby decoders later that year.[67] Panasonic and JVC prototyped a four-channel player which raised the quality of playback. Norelco worked on the cassette standards to meet the quality of the machines. They allowed for four channels to be "crammed onto each half of the tape."[68] The creation of Dolby sound and four-track playback increased cassette quality over the previous mono or stereo options, making it similar to the LP record, which boosted the marketability of the products. In the mid-1970s Maxell and TDK released high-end blank cassette tapes which also enhanced the audio quality.[69] These changes ensured the sound quality of the cassette tape had equaled if not surpassed the 8-track. High-fidelity equipment incorporated cassette players by the end of the 1970s underlining how far the audio quality had shifted.[70] Within ten years, record labels abandoned the 8-track but maintained the cassette tape to simplify production. Recording artists and labels chose cassettes over 8-tracks or LPs for demos and promos.[71] The cassette had become a world-wide standard by 1980.

Personal Stereos

The most profound shift in the popularity of the cassette was the creation of a personal stereo.[72] In 1979 Sony released the first Walkman, which made music portable and personal in a new way; it created an "individual sonic space."[73] The 14-ounce Soundabout, a proto-Walkman, retailed for 199 dollars.[74] Ibuka, one of the founders of Sony, requested a hi-fi portable pocket-sized player. To enhance the sound, unlike transistor radios, his engineers created dynamic loudspeakers in headphones. The Walkman no longer needed a speaker on the body of the machine.[75] The idea of hearing music privately was a completely new concept in the 1970s, an era in which only those with hearing impairments or for work purposes used earphones.[76] Nearly 50,000 Walkmans sold in the United States in the first two months, underscoring its wide appeal.[77] A cheaper lighter Walkman II made by Sony engineer Kozo Ohsone debuted in 1981.[78] It had 50 percent fewer moving parts and was 25 percent smaller.[79] The ability to listen to music privately while in public had a profound impact on music and youth culture.

> The Walkman is generally credited with making recorded music portable in a new way, allowing its users to immerse themselves in private worlds of entertainment in public—on the metro, in the bus, or on the beach, for instance. It was regarded as shifting the boundaries between the public and the private, and it helped spark new consumption patterns that challenged some of the traditional practices of the music industry.[80]

When it first appeared, critics viewed the ability to shut out society as isolating. Headphones signaled a desire to be left undisturbed, but they also helped to shield out the sounds of the city.[81] The new gear quickly became a status symbol, appearing in Bloomingdales and being discussed by Andy Warhol.[82] The Walkman became a billion-dollar industry which sold 50 million units in its first ten years, surpassing 220 million units sold over its lifespan.[83] Within three years Matsushita, Toshiba, and Aiwa had created competitor personal stereos. Twenty- to thirty-million personal stereos were sold per year in the early 1990s underscoring Andre Millard's argument, "The universal popularity of the Walkman ensured that the tape cassette would become the dominant form of sound recording in the last quarter of the twentieth century."[84]

Released in the same decade as the personal stereo, the boombox became an icon of a new generation of young people. First developed by Philips in the late 1960s, they took the qualities of the tape recorders and added high-quality speakers. While Walkmans were personal, boomboxes became social. Technology scholar Mark H. Clark codified that idea stating, "The boombox was a more social instrument, allowing owners to share music with others (regardless of whether they were willing listeners)."[85] Boomboxes became particularly popular in urban areas and were a fixture in the hip hop generation of dancers and musicians.[86] A 1979 *Billboard* article discussing hip hop mentioned the "countless portable tape players carried through the city streets."[87] This technology and this 1980s urban subculture used cassettes and social performances in the birth and rise of rap music. Sharing live events, recorded on boomboxes defined first-generation hip hop mixtapes.

The rise of the compact disc shifted the predominant medium on which people purchased music away from the cassette. Developed by Philips in the 1970s and released in the early 1980s, the CD became the principal product for music sales in the 1990s.[88] The new technology encouraged music sales as fans purchased classic albums they already owned on vinyl or cassette.[89] One appeal of the CD was its lack of deterioration on repeat listening. However, CDs scratch and therefore remained less durable than the cassette.[90] The basic tenet of music listening was comparable between a cassette Walkman and a portable CD player. The portable CD player replicated the functions of a Walkman. The boombox replaced a tape player with a CD player. For the 1990s youth generation, the CD allowed for a new way to create mixtapes. The burgeoning shift to digital allowed mixtapers to burn CDs which sped up the process, eliminated the challenges of timing on cassettes, and created near-perfect copies.[91] This technology represented a middle step on the road to fully digital music.

The next major leap in audio listening technology was the iPod, created by Apple in 2001.[92] The ability to upload music digitally began at the end of the 1990s which shifted how people engaged with music, no longer requiring an analog product. The same year the iPod appeared Apple also introduced iTunes which redefined how consumers accessed music. The digital player and the digital market reinvigorated the music industry in an era when peer-to-peer sharing had significantly undermined music sales.[93] Smaller than a tape deck, the iPod had a larger storage capacity than other MP3 players available at the time.[94] Marketed at 399 dollars, the high cost of an iPod did not deter consumers who appreciated the sleek design and ease of use.[95] Over the next ten years, Apple continued to upgrade and improve on the iPod design, releasing more than ten distinct models, varying in size, capability, and storage capacity.[96] By 2010 Apple integrated the features of the iPod into iPhones and how consumers listened to music shifted again. Like the Walkman a generation earlier, the iPod reopened discussions about using music to remove oneself from social interaction. One 2011 analysis stated, "often it involves the use of music to screen out the outside world and avoid unwelcome social interactions."[97] With the rise of the iPod and the ability to shuffle entire music collections, the move from the personalized mixtape to the generic shuffled playlist could have been complete. Yet, the power and idea of the mixtape never disappeared, even if it waned in the hype of Apple merchandise.

Before the rise of digital music, the Walkman and the boombox reveal shifts in the recording industry. On the one hand, the Walkman was a regressive technology: it removed the record function and the speaker from a cassette player. Dictation was no longer a conversation. On the other hand, it was sleeker, slimmer, and it adhered to a high-quality reproduction of sound. The personal stereo served a single purpose to transform music technology for consumers, products, and artists. Music could now be an exclusively private experience.[98] Portable music listening became the purview of the Gen Xers. Whether in cars, with a boombox or with personal stereos, the cassette became the icon of music on the go. Recorded music became portable but more importantly, personal. Listening to the radio or the jukebox, as would have been the case in earlier generations, was not the only means of hearing recorded music outside the home. The Walkman, especially, signified a personal relationship to listening to music. On the boombox, the record function remained a key aspect of tape recorders. Anyone could use them to make music and with the birth of the dual cassette deck, share music. It was only a small step from the creation of the cassette to a generation that created personalized cassettes: the mixtape.

GENERATION X

The quintessential youth generation of MTV, cassettes, and the mixtape is Generation X. Generation X, the name of Billy Idol's band, became cemented in culture through the title of Douglas Coupland's novel, *Generation X: Tales for an Accelerated Culture*.[99] While generational definitions speak to a small percentage of the entire population, "Generation labels capture something about how the *Zeitgeist* is reflected in the kind of people coming to young adulthood."[100] The definition of Gen X used throughout this book includes those individuals, regardless of class, race, or demographic details, born between 1965 and 1980.[101] A member of Gen X born in 1965 would have been fourteen when mixtapes and the Walkman made their debut. A young Gen Xer born in 1980 would have been fourteen in 1994 the last year cassette sales peaked before being replaced by CDs.[102] While generational definition remains a fluid designation, media continues to use the term "Gen X" to describe creators born in the 1960s and 1970s. The self-referential description of Gen Xers in mass media does not imply a simple bookend in which mixtapes and Gen X coexisted exclusively. Nonetheless this pop culture distinction is a useful moniker because cassette technology corresponds neatly with the generational boundaries.

Generation X's pop culture experiences overlapped with those of older millennials born in the 1980s (aka Generation Y). In the book *X vs. Y: A Culture War, A Love Story*, Gen Y sister Leonora Epstein describes her relationship to her older sister, a Gen Xer, "Millennials have a capacity for feeling nostalgic for things we can't actually lay claim to, and so we steal heavily from Gen X's pool of awesomeness, cultivating extensive vinyl collections and obscure Pixies trivia knowledge. [. . .] The point is that Gen Y couldn't exist without Gen X because we've (selectively) made their nostalgia our nostalgia."[103] The mixtape, in technology and in name, does not belong exclusively to Gen X. Family and peer relationships confirm a continuation of cultural ideas across generational divide. Tape players remained constant in cars until the 1990s ensuring older millennial familiarity with the medium. While siblings shared mixtapes on cassette, for many millennials mixes existed on burned CDs. They continued to use the term "mixtape," regardless of the media on which they listened. Epstein continues her introductory analysis, "As our generation began bridging the gap from physical to digital, we realized that we'd also be the last group to experience a predigital music industry."[104] The tangibility of the music connected certain millennials with members of Gen X.

Coming of age between the counterculture-baby-boom generation and the digital millennial generation, members of Gen X experienced a relatively coherent worldview. Gen Xers grew up in an era of globalization which led to an increased perception of the wider world. Christine Henseler states, "What distinguishes 'Generation X' as a way of looking and perceiving the world, no matter which demographic or culture this term is applied to, is an awareness of the global and immersive influence of technologies on everyday life."[105] For Gen X, education was paramount, through the TV with shows from *Sesame Street* to *Schoolhouse Rock*, and through the message that hard work and education would allow anyone to achieve their dreams.[106] More than half of Gen Xers have college experience and statistically women have more education.[107] Yet, they came of age in a period when the economy had declined which created a growth in anxiety and aimlessness.[108] Authors like Bret Easton Ellis and singers like Kurt Cobain and his band Nirvana highlighted a generation seen as sarcastic, cynical and negatively impacted by consumer society and mass media.[109] These elder statesmen of Gen X became the representative voice in pop culture moving forward.

The representation of a typical Gen Xer in pop media emphasizes the white, suburban, middle-class male. This expectation undermines the diversity born in this decade. Sociologists exploring the American demographics incorporate disparate populations in their studies, clarifying, "Gen Xers are a diverse segment of the population, with minorities accounting for a large share of the whole."[110] Henseler's expanded definition of Gen X allows for a wider understanding of racial, demographic, and gender diversity that expands Gen X beyond this narrowly defined cross section. A shared, global Gen X community exists.[111] Understanding the diversity inherent in this term allows for a recognition that mixtapes existed for young people across demographic boundaries. The Gen X mixtape was not exclusively made by white men, nor was the hip hop mixtape exclusively purchased by African American men. Author Hanif Abudurraqib exemplifies this reality, describing his interest in diverse music as emerging out of his high school experience.

> Everyone that I rolled with was so curious about hearing more from wherever they could find it. Mixtape, mix CD era a lot of people were willing to be surprised, ya know, to have one song bleed into another song that was nothing like the song that came before it.[112]

Musical diversification has always permeated the mixtape conversation, allowing a song by Grandmaster Flash to appear next to a Billie Holiday track or a Lenny Kravitz song to play before a Chris Isaak one.[113]

While not exclusively male-dominated, the quintessential media-described Gen Xer in the 1990s was male. By the end of the 1980s, American mass media suggested second-wave feminism had succeeded and the fight for women's rights was complete. This simplistic argument undermined the lack of diversity inherent in the movement, not yet acknowledging intersectionality and the rise of third-wave feminism. The riot-grrrl movement, started by Gen X female musicians, brought younger, less-economically advantaged millennials into the fold with discussions about sexual harassment and female empowerment. Their movement repudiated claims of attained gender equality. A musical subculture, which functioned as an outlet for young women's frustrations, used gender dynamics to codify membership. Nonetheless, the most well-known Gen X music writers remain men. Josh Harmon, Nick Hornby, Rob Sheffield, and Jim Walsh wrote most of the Gen X-authored mixtape memoirs. As with the familiar image of Rob in *High Fidelity*, men are viewed in pop culture as the primary consumers of music; they collect, learn, and obsess over music in a way that becomes unconsciously gendered. Books like *Old Records Never Die: One Man's Quest for His Vinyl and His*

Past, Sonata for Jukebox: Pop Music, Memory, And the Imagined Life, and *Vinyl Freak: Love Letters to a Dying Medium*, all have male authors.[114] The majority of mixtapers included in Thurston Moore's *mix tape: the art of cassette culture* are men while those in Jason Bitner's *Cassette from My Ex* are divided between male and female creators.[115] The novels about mixtapes written by women, such as Celia Pérez, Rainbow Rowell, and Jane Sanderson, are the emotive, often young-adult stories which examine interconnections between people. The gendering of music consumption collectively affords men an obsessive, collective experience and women a personalized, sensory relationship.[116] The media representation of Gen X gender dynamics as aggressively male undermines the nuanced reality of how this youth culture navigated courtship and emotional outpouring and confirms the necessity of recognizing a multiplicity of youth cultures and experiences.

This diversity and the economic realities for Gen Xers led to discussions about how to reach this audience. A mid-1990s analysis of how to market to Gen Xers, stated, "Generation X doesn't dislike advertising. They dislike *hype*. They dislike overstatement, self-importance, hypocrisy, and the assumption that *anyone* would want to be disturbed at home by a salesman on the telephone."[117] Instead, they preferred peer-to-peer interactions and feedback from their friends. Many Gen Xers found alternative ways to express themselves outside of the negative mainstream descriptions given to them. Music, videos, and the DIY (do-it-yourself) culture of zines created those social spaces of expression.[118] Certain subcultures rejected the consumer, *Billboard*-recognized artists and worked to create a sound that felt more authentic and less commercial. This integration of music in youth cultures and the attempt to reject the commercial sales of music defines the growth of the mixtape era. The mixtape was a clear-cut product within this anti-corporate world; it allowed young people to express themselves independent of corporate involvement and share their expertise freely.

Many young people who grew up in the era of cassette technology shared a perspective on pop culture and mass media because of the global, commercially aware, analog world they inhabited. Generational designations show a generalized continuity of worldview which makes this classification a useful tool. The definition however is fluid; individuals on either side interacted with, learned from, and shared technology with members of Gen X. Individuals underrepresented by media perceptions engaged with this technology and these products. Nonetheless, the self-referential overlap between Generation X, nostalgia for the analog past, and cassette culture remains a cognizant aspect of understanding mixtape culture.

The birth of the cassette, coinciding with a generation tied to consumer culture iconography like MTV, produced the mixtape generation. Using cassette technology, young people found ways to interact independently of mass media marketing. Whether hip hop or punk and alternative communities, the opportunity to share music and connection on cassette defined a generation.

The cassette, a fundamental consumer product, defined the musical world from the 1960s through the 1990s. The recording industry shifted significantly because of the new capabilities magnetic recording offered. Musicians engaged with their music in more dynamic ways with the introduction of multi-tracking and layering. But the biggest impact of the cassette is how it changed consumers' relationship to music. Cassettes were less expensive than records, portable, and easily accessible. Magnetic recording led to the creation of new techniques like 8-track and cassette players in cars, the personal stereo, and the boombox. Emerging in the same eras as the rise of diverse musical genres, these new instruments expanded musical fandom and equalized individuals' ability to engage with music on their own terms.

Over time cassettes signaled a novel way consumers could engage with music by creating their own versions of playlists. Analyzing the shifting understanding of recording technology, Andrew Millard described mixtapes in all but name,

> Recording onto a cassette involved learning a new set of skills—timing the recording, editing it, and adjusting the recording level—which soon supplanted the old craft of playing a revolving disc. Combined radio/phonograph/cassette units made it possible to record customized tapes from radio programming or prerecorded music on disc. Every collection of records and tapes soon contained personalized recordings on cassettes.[119]

Fans no longer had to listen to albums in order. The cassette gave consumers an innovative way of interacting with recorded music, creating "an object that reflected their own personal media identity."[120] Genres of music outside the recording industry and the radio broadcast world could create music and disseminate it inexpensively on cassette. By definition, the mixtape is a cassette-based culture. The wax and wane of the cassette as a format for creating, sharing, and listening to music led to the shifting role of the mixtape in pop culture.

NOTES

1. theDAWstudio, "What Really Is a Mixtape?", 2017. https://www.thedawstudio.com/what-really-is-a-mixtape/. (Accessed September 21, 2017).

2. Moore's attribution has been cited in multiple sources including, Thurston Moore, ed. *Mix Tape: The Art of Cassette Culture* (New York: Universe Publisher, 2004), 9., Judith A. Peraino, "I'll Be Your Mixtape: Lou Reed, Andy Warhol, and the Queer Intimacies of Cassettes," *The Journal of Musicology* 36, no. 4 (2019): 407,

and Brandon Stosuy, "High Fidelity," *The Village Voice* (June 7, 2005), https://ww w.villagevoice.com/2005/06/07/high-fidelity/. (Accessed September 10, 2020). The Christgau article Moore mentions remains uncited.

3. Moore, 34.

4. Peraino, 406.

5. Robin Wright, "Audiotape Cassette," in *A History of Intellectual Property in 50 Objects*, ed. Claudy Op Den Kamp and Dan Hunter (Cambridge: Cambridge University Press, 2019), 289–90.

6. Larry Crane, "Regan Sommer Mccoy: The Mixtape Museum," *TapeOp*, no. 138 (July/August 2020), https://tapeop.com/interviews/138/regan-sommer-mccoy/. (Accessed May 12, 2021).

7. Ibid.

8. Karin Bijsterveld et al., "Sound Technologies and Cultural Practices: How Analogies Make Us Listen to Transformations in Art and Culture," in *Contemporary Culture: New Directions in Art and Humanities Research,* ed. Judith Thissen, Robert Zwijnenberg, and Kitty Zijlmans (Amsterdam: Amsterdam University Press, 2013).

9. I constructed a spreadsheet of 2,400 songs taken from 108 mixtapes including photographs in art books, chapter headings in memoirs, fictional mixtapes in novels, and compilations made for a radio contest.

10. Andrew J. Bottomley, "'Home Taping Is Killing Music': The Recording Industries' 1980s Anti-Home Taping Campaigns and Struggles over Production, Labor and Creativity," *Creative Industries Journal* 8, no. 2 (2015): 140.

11. Steven Schoenherr, "The History of Magnetic Recording," presented at *IEEE Magnetics Society Seminar* (University of San Diego November 5, 2002). http: //www.aes-media.org/historical/html/recording.technology.history/magnetic4.html (Accessed July 8, 2020)

12. Barry Kernfeld, *Pop Song Piracy: Disobedient Music Distribution since 1929*, (Chicago: University of Chicago Press, 2011), https://ebookcentral.proq uest.com/lib/pointpark-ebooks/detail.action?docID=3038271. 149. and Museum of Magnetic Sound Recording, "Beginnings," http://r2rtx.org/node/12.

13. Museum of Magnetic Sound Recording, "Beginnings."

14. Kernfeld, 149.

15. Peter McMurray, "Once Upon Time: A Superficial History of Early Tape," *Twentieth-Century Music* 14, no. 1 (2017): 42–43; Bob Phillips, "Bing Crosby and the Tape Revolution," The Audiophile Man, https://theaudiophileman.com/bing-c rosby-tape-revolution/.

16. Museum of Magnetic Sound Recording, "Beginnings."

17. McMurray, 43.

18. Andre Millard, *America on Record: A History of Recorded Sound*, Second ed. (Cambridge: Cambridge University Press, 2005), 225.

19. Ibid., 289.

20. Museum of Magnetic Sound Recording, "Beginnings."

21. Ibid.

22. Albin J. Zak, *The Poetics of Rock: Cutting Tracks, Making Records* (Berkeley: University of California Press, 2001), https://ebookcentral.proquest.com/l ib/pointpark-ebooks/detail.action?docID=223044. 11.

23. National Museums Liverpool, "Emergence of Multitrack Recording," https:/ /www.liverpoolmuseums.org.uk/emergence-of-multitrack-recording (Accessed June 1, 2021).

24. Lily Rothman, "Rewound: On Its 50th Birthday, the Cassette Tape Is Still Rolling," *Time*, August 12, 2013.

25. Mark H. Clark, "Product Diversification," in *Magnetic Recording: The First 100 Years*, ed. Eric D. Daniel, C. Denis Mee, and Mark H. Clark (New York: The Institute of Electrical and Electronics Engineers, Ic., 1999), 94–97.

26. Wallace S. Sharps, Tape Recording for Pleasure (London: Fountain Books, 1961), 7. as quoted in Alex Sayf Cummings, *Democracy of Sound: Music Piracy and the Remaking of American Copyright in the Twentieth Century* (New York: Oxford University Press, 2013), 71.

27. Bijsterveld et al., 142. and John Z. Komurki and Luca Bendandi, *Cassette Cultures: Past and Present of a Musical Icon*, English Edition 2019 Benteli ed. (Switzerland: Deutsche Nationalbibliothek; Braun Publishing AG, 2019), 11–13.

28. Peraino, 407.

29. Cummings, 71.

30. *Magnetic Film & Tape Recording* (Severna Park, MD: Mooney-Rowan Publications, Inc. April 1954), http://thehistoryofrecording.com/Magazines/Tape%20 Recording%20Magazine/Tape-Recording-1954-04.pdf Accessed (Accessed August 26, 2020).

31. Jerry Heisler, "Teen Tapers," *Tape Recording*, March, 1958. http://thehisto ryofrecording.com/Magazines/Tape%20Recording%20Magazine/Tape-Recording -1958-03.pdf

32. The article concludes this type of recording should only be in fun and should not hurt anyone's feelings. Furthermore, it acknowledges legally one must get permission to use someone else's voice. Ibid.

33. "'Why My Recorder Is Important to Me' Contest," *Tape Recording*, 1961. http://thehistoryofrecording.com/Magazines/Tape%20Recording%20Magazine/Tape -Recording-1961-November.pdf

34. Ibid.

35. The information in this paragraph came from: Bijsterveld et al., 143. Komurki and Bendandi., 9–19. James D. Livingston, "100 Years of Magnetic Memories," *Scientific American* 279, no. 5 (1998), and Schoenherr. np.

36. Grove Atlantic, "a: *a Novel* by Andy Warhol," https://groveatlantic.com/ book/a-a-novel/. and Peraino, 407–08.

37. In the world of tape recording, compilation usually referred to collection of recorded voices like sermons or school lessons. David Harding, "This Isn't Music: 'The Ideas Pool . . . ,'" *Tape Recording and Hi-Fi Magazine*1958. https://worldra diohistory.com/hd2/IDX-UK/Technology/Technology-Modern/Archive-Tape-Re cording-UK-IDX/IDX/50s/Tape-Recording-UK-1958-09-OCR-Page-0044.pdf#sea rch=%22compilation%22 (Accessed August 27, 2020).

38. Richard Ekstract, "Pop Sounds," *Tape Recording*, January 1966.

39. Peraino, 408.

40. Ekstract, 95–96.

41. Kernfeld, 141.

42. Andrea F. Bohlman and Peter McMurray, "Tape: Or, Rewinding the Phonographic Regime," *Twentieth-Century Music* 14, no. 1 (2017): 13–14.

43. Millard, 316.

44. Kernfeld, 152–53.

45. David Byrne, *How Music Works*, 1st ed. (San Francisco: McSweeney's, 2012), 109. Clark, 102. Bob Dormon, "Compact Cassette Supremo Lou Ottens Talks to *El Reg*," *The Register* (2013), https://www.theregister.co.uk/2013/09/02/compact_cassette_supremo_lou_ottens_talks_to_el_reg/. and Schoenherr.

46. Clark, 102.

47. Dormon.

48. Andre Millard, "Personal Stereo," in *Encyclopedia of 20th-Century Technology*, ed. Colin A. Hempstead (New York: Routledge, 2004), 579.

49. Clark, 97.

50. Sony Corporate Info, "Chapter 5 Promoting Compact Cassettes Worldwide," https://www.sony.net/SonyInfo/CorporateInfo/History/SonyHistory/2-05.html (Accessed June 1, 2021).

51. Rothman.

52. Bob Dormon, "Happy 50th Birthday, Compact Cassette: How It Stuck a Chord for Millions," *The Register* (September 2, 2013), https://www.theregister.co.uk/2013/08/30/50_years_of_the_compact_cassette/. and Kernfeld. 155.

53. Komurki and Bendandi, 134.

54. Millard, *America on Record: A History of Recorded Sound*, 317.

55. Bohlman and McMurray, 15.

56. Dormon, "Happy 50th Birthday, Compact Cassette: How It Stuck a Chord for Millions."

57. Ibid. and Kernfeld, 155.

58. Kernfeld, 154.

59. Advertisement for EMI Musicassettes. *Tape Recording*, December, 1966. Page 6. https://worldradiohistory.com/Archive-Tape-Recording-UK/60s/Tape-Recording-UK-1966-12.pdf (Accessed August 26, 2020).

60. Sony Corporate Info, "Chapter 5 Promoting Compact Cassettes Worldwide."

61. Kernfeld, 154.

62. Philips, *Never before Has a Car Radio Done This!* (*Autocar* August 1968), Advertisement.

63. Ibid.

64. Dormon, "Compact Cassette Supremo Lou Ottens Talks to *El Reg*."

65. Gould "Prospects of Recording" quoted in Simon Frith, *Performing Rites: On the Value of Popular Music* (Cambridge, MA: Harvard University Press, 1996), 230–31.

66. Millard, *America on Record: A History of Recorded Sound*, 317–18.

67. C. P. Gilmore, "Look and Listen . . . What's New in Electronics for Your Home Entertainment," *Popular Science*, September 1971.

68. Ibid.

69. Anthony Kwame Harrison, "'Cheaper Than a CD, Plus We Really Mean It': Bay Area Underground Hip Hop Tapes as Subcultural Artefacts," *Popular Music* 25, no. 2 (2006), https://www.jstor.org/stable/3877563.

70. Millard, *America on Record: A History of Recorded Sound*, 319.

71. Ibid., 320.

72. Clark, 100.

73. The Oxford English Dictionary added the word "Walkman" in 1986. Millard, "Personal Stereo," 580. Karin Bijsterveld and José van Dijck, eds., *Sound Souvenirs: Audio Technologies, Memory and Cultural Practices* (Amsterdam University Press, 2009), 115.

74. Mark Coleman, "Can Cassette Tapes Be Cool Again?", *CNN* (September 30, 2013), https://www.cnn.com/2013/09/06/opinion/coleman-cassette-day/index.html (Accessed July 9, 2020).

75. Millard, "Personal Stereo," 579–80.

76. Matt Alt, "The Walkman, Forty Years On," Cultural Comment, *The New Yorker* (June 29, 2020), https://www.newyorker.com/culture/cultural-comment/the-walkman-forty-years-on (Accessed March 20, 2021).

77. Meaghan Haire, "A Brief History of the Walkman," *Time* (July 1, 2009), http://content.time.com/time/nation/article/0,8599,1907884,00.html.

78. Coleman.

79. Millard, "Personal Stereo," 580.

80. Paul du Gay et al., *Doing Cultural Studies: The Story of the Sony Walkman* (London: Sage Publications Ltd, 2003), xi.

81. Alt.

82. Ibid.

83. Harry Wallop, "Why I Will Mourn the Death of the Walkman," Telegraph, October 27, 2010, http://www.telegraph.co.uk/comment/personal-view/8088232/Why-Iwill-mourn-the-death-of-the-Walkman.html, accessed May 12, 2012. quoted in Richard Burgess, The History of Music Production (Cary: Oxford University Press, 2014), https://ebookcentral.proquest.com/lib/pointpark-ebooks/detail.action?docID=1696420. 70.

84. Millard, *America on Record: A History of Recorded Sound*, 325–26.

85. Clark, 108.

86. Anna Jane Grossman, *Obsolete: An Encyclopedia of Once-Common Things Passing Us By* (New York: Abrams Image, 2009), 39–40.

87. *Billboard Magazine* (1979), 3 as quoted in Harrison, 287.

88. Philips Research, "The History of the CD—The Beginning," https://www.philips.com/a-w/research/technologies/cd/beginning.html (Accessed September 29, 2020).

89. David M. Arditi, "Freedom, Music and the RIAA: How the Recording Industry Association of America Shapes Culture by De-Politicizing Music" (master's thesis,Virginia Polytechnic Institute and State University, 2007), 49.

90. Harrison, 296.

91. Arditi, 47–48.

92. Alt.

93. There is a conversation about copyright, digital music, and the rise of streaming services which are outside the scope of this research. See Greg Kot, *Ripped: How the Wired Generation Revolutionized Music* (New York: Simon & Schuster, Inc., 2009), 48.

94. Inc Apple, "iPod," https://apple-history.com/ipod (Accessed June 1, 2021).

95. Ibid.

96. Nate Lanxon and Andrew Hoyle, "The Complete History of Apple's iPod," c|*net* (October 25, 2011), https://www.cnet.com/pictures/the-complete-history-of-a pples-ipod/.

97. Simon Reynolds, *Retromania: Pop Culture's Addiction to Its Own Past* (New York: Faber and Faber, Inc, 2011), 117.

98. Burgess, 71–72.

99. Jennie Bristow, *Stop Mugging Grandma: The "Generation Wars" and Why Boomer Blaming Won't Solve Anything* (New Haven: Yale University Press, 2019), 62.

100. All italics in quotations throughout the book are in the original source. While generational identification can be a problematic characteristic because it oversimplifies and assumes qualities for its membership, its self-referential use in mainstream media and pop culture make it a valid analytical category. Ibid., 66.

101. Peter J. Whitehouse and Candace Steele Flippin, "From Diversity to Intergenerativity," *Generations: Journal of the American Society on Aging* 41, no. 3 Generation X: From Fiction to Fact, and Still a Mystery (2017), 8.

102. RIAA, "U. S. Sales Database," https://www.riaa.com/u-s-sales-database/?fbclid=IwAR2IuPU0w989pz0nuGsZflTrF3BFdK1C9FhpD3PfHg1CJTt4bs86UzP OvY (Accessed June 1, 2021).

103. Eve Epstein and Lenora Epstein, *X vs. Y: A Culture War, a Love Story* (New York: Abrams Books, 2014), 11.

104. Ibid., 17.

105. Christine Henseler, ed. *Generation X Goes Global: Mapping a Youth Culture in Motion* (New York: Taylor & Francis, 2012), 7.

106. American X: The Ironic History of a Generation Dan Leidl in ibid., xiv–xvii.

107. The New Strategist Editors, ed. *Generation X: Americans Born 1965 to 1976*, The American Generation Series (Amityville: New Strategist Press, LLC, 2015), Introduction & 33; Henseler, 1–4.

108. Bristow, 62–63.

109. Henseler, 10.

110. The New Strategist Editors, 1.

111. The novelty of cassettes to share information is not a specifically English-speaking phenomenon, but the extended understanding of cassette history in the wider world is outside the scope of this book. The editors of *Generation X* argue Gen Xers are diverse with a large population of minorities. But this description, while statistically relevant, is not always represented in mass media.

112. Hanif Abdurraqib. "The Intersection of Black Performance, Joy & Pain." By Arun Venugopal. *Fresh Air* (April 6, 2021) (Accessed May 12, 2021).

113. Jason Bitner, ed. *Cassette from My Ex: Stories and Soundtracks of Lost Loves* (New York: St. Martin's Press, 2009), 71–73 and 164–65.

114. John Corbett, *Vinyl Freak: Love Letters to a Dying Medium* (North Carolina: Duke University Press, 2017), Geoffrey O'Brien, *Sonata for Jukebox: Pop Music, Memory and the Imagined Life* (New York: Perseus Books Group, 2004), and Eric Spitznagel, *Old Records Never Die: One Man's Quest for His Vinyl and His Past* (New York: Plume, 2016).

115. Bitner and Moore.

116. This analysis of *This is Not A Love Song* solidifies the debates around gendering and consumption of music. The novel is not part of the analysis because expanding into German works exceeds the focus of this research. Alison Lewis and Andrew W. Hurley, "Love, Popular Music, and 'Technologies of Gender' in Karen Duve's 'Dies Ist Kein Liebeslied (This Is Not a Love Song),'" *New German Critique* 115, Winter (2012), https://www.jstor.org/stable/23259392.

117. Karen Ritchie, *Marketing to Generation X* (New York: Lexington Books, 1995), 159) cited in Ryan Moore, *Sells Like Teen Spirit: Music, Youth Culture, and Social Crisis* (New York: New York University Press, 2010), 132.

118. Henseler, 11.

119. Millard, *America on Record: A History of Recorded Sound*, 327.

120. Wright, 289.

Chapter 2

Musical Self-Production

By the late 1970s, musical diversification led to a growing number of genres geared exclusively at young people. Emerging genres like punk and hip hop aimed to create an authenticity on stage to which audiences could relate. The growth of the cassette industry meant that bands could sell live recordings of shows, they could make their own albums without the expense of studio time, and they could encourage fans to dub and distribute shows amongst themselves. Fans wanted to feel the emotions and the experience of their favorite bands rather than listen to the polished, major label–produced albums. Bootlegs of live performances defined the music of these bands.

The dominance of the cassette had led to technological innovations in the creation of the Walkman and the boombox. These two products took what had been a social experience and personalized it. Individuals could now listen to music through headphones, solo, or in groups. With these new products and the flexibility of cassettes, the mixtape became a fundamental personalization of music listening. It was no longer necessary to wait for a music professional to curate music. Instead, it became a personal experience. The growth of the mixtape in these early years created a new way for young people to communicate through music, creating playlists to introduce friends to music or to share feelings with one another.

YOUTH CULTURE

For young people music is more than just a pastime. According to music scholar Simon Frith, "Music, according to sociologists, is an aspect of peer-group organization. It is in their peer groups that teenagers learn the rules of the social game [. . .] all adolescents use music as a badge and a background, a means of identifying and articulating emotion."[1] Young people can build relationships and develop friendships based on their music. They attend shows, discuss music, and share songs to solidify their relationships. In the last seventy years, music has become a fundamental aspect of identity formation. Music is not a consumable product. It is not tangible and cannot be exhausted. However, certain aspects of musical culture are physical products, such as mixtapes. Young people poured their emotions into these objects, cemented their connections, and shared themselves with others to develop and strengthen communities. Past a certain age, people become nostalgic for mixtapes as a representation of youth identity.[2] The mixtape, a physical representation of network building and community development via music, remains cogent because it became a shorthand way of expressing identity building via music. The songs on a mixtape verify credibility because an individual's choices highlight the depth and nuance of their knowledge of a particular subculture's music. As Mike Watt, bass guitarist for the bands Minutemen and Firehose stated, "People tell a little bit about themselves by showing you what they listen to."[3] The diversity of music on single mixtapes shows that individuals do not exclusively function within a single musical community.

In the post–World War II era the birth of a consumer youth culture dovetailed with a rise in a new style of music aimed at that youth. Shifting social and cultural norms in England and North America changed young peoples' expectations, deferred adulthood, and extended adolescence.[4] The revolution from blues and jazz to the quintessential sounds of Elvis Presley and the Everly Brothers reflects a self-referentially white postwar society invested in leisure time with money to spend on luxury and surplus. From the 1950s, marketing forces engaged with a population with increased disposable income to whom they could advertise. While there has never been a single universal English-speaking youth culture, mass media crafted a simple model geared at white, middle-class males. Economic stability and an increased standard of living expanded a consumer culture for the new demographic by creating products marketed specifically to them. With the rise of the jukebox, listening to recorded music became more of a social rather than a family pastime. The rise of TV culture and shows like American Bandstand, which premiered in 1952, solidified the role of music in the creation of a teen culture and a community tied to musical affinity. For Frith, "Rock is often analyzed as a contemporary folk music—a music made for young people, by young people, and thus an organic part of young people's culture."[5] In a 2012 speech at SXSW Bruce Springsteen described his introduction to musical identity,

Television and Elvis gave us full access to a new language, a new form of communication, a new way of being, a new way of looking, a new way of thinking; about sex, about race, about identity, about life; a new way of being an American, a human being; and a new way of hearing music.[6]

Rock and roll created a new mass-media-driven youth culture. Recording industry executives capitalized on the commercial appeal of rock music and targeted music at teen audiences who had money to spend on records and could now afford their own record players.[7]

The postwar music culture created a shared community, much like the ones described by Benedict Anderson's *Imagined Communities.* This racially homogenous community became defined around generational affiliation to music as opposed to language or national ties. Frith stated, "Pop music has been an important way in which we have learned to understand ourselves as historical, ethnic, class-bound, gendered, national subjects. [. . .] What music does (all music) is put into play a sense of identity that may or may not fit the way we are placed by other social forces."[8] As he pointed out, "The novelty of rock 'n' roll was that its performers were the same age as their audience, came from similar backgrounds, had similar interests."[9] The rise of the television shifted the dynamic again. Young people could listen to recorded music and watch musicians on the TV; these music-based shows defined a new rock and roll community.

Between the 1950s and the 1980s the single trajectory of popular music splintered into a wide variety of genres which allowed for a more nuanced identity constructed around a community that understood and reflected the specific cultures of particular musical genres. Jennifer Lena describes, "systems of orientations, expectations, and conventions that bind together industry, performers, critics, and fans in making what they identify as a distinctive sort of music. In other words, a genre exists when there is some consensus that a distinctive style of music is being performed."[10] Both Frith and Lena have defined sociological concepts within American youth culture using music and affinity to genres as a way of categorizing and building identity. The shift from a single popular-culture music to a variety of popular genres in the second half of the twentieth century exemplifies the role of music as an important facet of cultural identity. Diversity, defined by gender, race, language, economic, or regional difference obviously existed, but mainstream media rarely acknowledged it. These large differences, alongside more nuanced localized distinctions, led to the creation of subcultures: specific groups of people within a culture who defined themselves in opposition to or a subversion of the dominant paradigm.[11] Subcultures created an alternative hierarchy outside of mainstream society to create new group norms, often defined by feelings of disillusionment and outsiderness.[12] Walter Benjamin claimed, "youth subcultures are said to make their own meanings, to *create* cultures in their acts of consumption."[13] Hearing music as a transcendent experience and knowing others may feel the same helps to solidify the imagined cultural community around a specific genre, band, or type of music.[14]

Access to music products and communities frequently developed through peer interactions. Siblings and friends introduce one another to subcultures, often through the exchange of literature and music. This shared information diversifies a person's taste and allows for musical and literary eclecticism. The fluidity of young people allows them to navigate multiple simultaneous identities including families, peer groups, and extended social networks.[15] Throughout adolescence music and literature function as both public markers of social status and private ways to navigate feelings. Young Adult literature, which focused on literary realism aimed at readers aged between 12 and 18, became a codified marketable genre in the 1960s and 1970s.[16] Television shows and music geared towards adolescents flourished in these decades.

Popular music became a community-building structure for American baby boomers, reflecting Theodor Adorno's idea of an audio mass culture.[17] Music became entertainment and young people became consumers of a commercial marketplace. The young generation flocked to music that gave them a sense of community, crossed socioeconomic boundaries, and allied young people together.[18] Radio DJs like Alan Freed attempted to unify young people across racial boundaries, highlighting a shared sense of attachment to music in a world divided by political segregation. The popular perception of the 1950s as an optimistic, simple, conservative era, as portrayed in music lyrics and shows like American Bandstand, gave way to a more complicated narrative in the 1960s.

The rise of a simplistic consumer youth culture eventually led to a revolt against mainstream culture. As the social and political debates of the United States in the 1960s became harder to ignore, members of this young generation used their affiliation to music to showcase their cultural and political protest. Fashion, literature, and music connected individuals to specific communities through a shared knowledge of insiderness. These subcultures allowed for a deeper understanding of myriad diversities while they simultaneously established the growth of commercial diversity in music.[19] For consumer marketing, youth culture became a key analytic to help define a growing pop culture. Marketing agencies, recording companies, and television shows concentrated on this new demographic. This population, 15–25 years old, affluent, often suburban, white, not yet heads of households, became the target audience for new products.

Not everyone conformed. Some individuals pushed against this unified marketing and targeted the corporate consumer ideology of mainstream pop music. As Springsteen continued his homage to the musical past, he perfectly encapsulated the social and generational discord of the era,

If you were young in the sixties and fifties, everything felt false everywhere you turned. But you didn't know how to say it. [. . .] Bob [Dylan] came along and gave us those words. He gave us those songs. [. . .] And if you were a kid in 1965, you were on your own, because your parents, God bless them, they could not understand the incredible changes that were taking place. You were on your own, without a home. He gave us the words to understand our hearts.[20]

Part of what Springsteen aptly describes is the allegiance this 1960s audience felt with the musicians. Audiences felt a connection to the artists, a part of the larger community who understood the music and the language. This idea of connectivity and authenticity in the music grew during the counterculture which led to increased identity building around particular styles of music like folk and psychedelic rock. By the mid-1970s young people could choose between different types of music that appealed to their needs. In schools, adolescents could find friendship around shared musical interests. Traveling to shows and festivals created subgroups who defined themselves around their fandom. Rather than a universal youth culture music, diversification around regions, race, and socioeconomic strata blossomed.

Subcultures strove to create a diversification in mainstream pop culture. They looked for music making to integrate their own cultures and identities. The music industry had to grapple with how to both meet the needs of the corporate masses and appeal to the growing diverse styles of music. Certain genres, which the mainstream recording industry rejected, created, and released their own music. Teenage rebellion defined the difference of opinion and style against commercially approved pop culture. Whether greased-back hair in the 1950s, flared jeans in the late 1960s, or safety-pin earrings and mohawks in the 1970s, youth subcultures found ways to resist societal expectations until the commercial world embraced the resistance and created products for sale which mimicked corporate resistance.[21] Music intertwined with this movement; songs and lyrics, fashion, and fandom articulated the trials of adolescence.[22] The cassette tape assisted the growth and diversification of these new genres because musicians could interact directly with their fans, creating and selling music locally. In the 1960s, mainstream culture splintered into the counterculture movement, defined in response to the mainstream political and economic norm. Since the 1970s youth culture has highlighted social change and a diversification of subcultures to reflect the production and consumption of cultural markers.[23] Mod and punk culture showcased an urban distinction separate from the more commercially palatable suburban ideal. Hip hop culture embraced and added both an economic and a racial categorization which again highlighted the lack of universality of the youth culture. New television channels, like MTV in 1981 and VH1 in

1985 reified the idea of a streamlined pop music identity geared at the simplified media-defined predominant young audience.

Debates emerged in the late 1960s about the authenticity of musicians: did
singers sell out to corporations to make money? Audiences began to debate an
artist's legitimacy and genuine link to the music they performed. Meanwhile,
the counterculture movement waged an anti-consumer, anti-capitalist war
against mainstream America. A community of baby boomers increasingly
disliked consumerism and greed which coincided with the rise of the anti-
war, anti-establishment, hippie movement and the burgeoning urban punk
and hip hop movements. How one consumed music defined this cultural distinction. Because cassette tapes had started as dictation machines, live recording was a fundamental aspect of the new technology. Companies created the
first consumer reel-to-reel machines as tools to record voices. Prerecorded
music was a secondary market. This function as a recording device had a
profound impact on the music industry, however, because it allowed for
secondary market recording and the rise in bootlegging and piracy. In the
1970s tape piracy overshadowed phonograph bootlegging exponentially and
became a fight between the industry, musicians, and consumers. Amongst
certain musicians and hip hop fans, the ability to access music without having
to work through the conventional sales of record producers and stores grew.

Within the context of new technology, combined with the social climate
of anti-establishment identities, bootlegging and piracy became a facet of
youth culture and music.[24] The magazine *Tape Recording* discussed copying
records onto tape to maintain the audio fidelity because of the degradation
of LPs over time.[25] They advocated "splicing the tunes together," to create
appealing background music which fell outside any concerns about bootlegging.[26] There was no suggestion this idea was an inappropriate use of tape
technology. As the number of musicians grew and the idea of music festivals
boomed, fans became more concrete in their fandom. They believed record
companies only released what they thought people wanted to hear, rather than
everything available. Fans wanted to hear live recordings. Bootlegging in this
venue was less about sales and money.

The rise of the Deadhead, the super fan of the Grateful Dead, highlights
this fandom best. The band began to release live bootleg recordings which
fans flocked to hear. For the Dead, more than about making their music
available, bootlegs reflected a commitment to a "noncommercialism," taking control over their art and removing it from the capitalist power of the
industry.[27] Fans used tape players to copy and share those recordings amongst
themselves.[28] Bootleggers in the late 1960s recorded live shows, selling copies for a profit. These sales reflected a capitalism which worked against the
non-consumerism the Dead espoused; they encouraged fans to trade their
recordings instead. Fans could release cassette recordings faster than the

music industry could create them.[29] Bootlegging became a mass model that created a market for music outside of commercial sales. This model has remained a quintessential aspect of jam bands like the Grateful Dead, Phish, and The String Cheese Incident where fans are not only allowed to record and disseminate a show, they are encouraged to do so.[30] What had begun as rebelliousness by fans in the 1960s became the foundation of underground collecting by the 1970s.[31] Rather than commercial competition, bootlegs became alternative versions and unreleased material to supplement commercial sales. For some musical subcultures, live recordings are more important than the recorded catalog. By the 1980s, bootlegs became part of mainstream sales when labels officially released recordings of live shows from bands like Bon Jovi and Guns & Roses.[32]

In the late 1960s and early 1970s unauthorized compilations of "party tracks, dance mixes, platter packs" appeared in the market. The early days of piracy involved unapproved compilations of musicians represented by different labels who could not legally appear on an album together. Pirates created these compilations to sell "best of" singles of popular songs and introduce fans to new bands they would not have heard otherwise.[33] However, these tapes existed outside of corporate boundaries and reduced the sales of albums. A 1970 *Billboard* article explained, "You can't buy a legitimate product with songs by all the top artists, because they have exclusive contracts with different companies. So the illegal operator picks selections from several leading albums, puts them together on a tape and offers all the hits in one."[34] Distributors found a way to appeal to their customers by putting popular songs together or making a compilation of songs in a new and appealing order. Alex Sayf Cummings explains, "The history of bootlegging contains many examples of pirates who imprinted their own sense of humor or critical perspective on records that contained live performances or merely rearranged previously released tracks in a new context."[35] This type of piracy aimed for profitability and wresting control from record labels. Customers could purchase these unapproved cassettes to hear songs they knew.[36] While this appealed to the consumers and to the distributors, it angered record labels because piracy was illegal and undercut official record sales.

Ampex Corporation, the largest tape duplicator in the United States led a campaign in Congress claiming they lost $100 million in cassette sales in 1970 as a result of piracy.[37] That year the Federal District Court for the Southern District of New York filed a suit against "Eastern Tapes, Cartridge Counter, Inc" for clandestine bootlegging.[38] This began a decades-long debate about copyright infringement and the role of piracy in the music industry. New copyright laws appeared in New York and California which made it a misdemeanor to,

knowingly transfer or cause to be transferred any sounds recorded on a phonograph record, disc, wire, tape, film, or other article on which sounds are
recorded, with intent to sell, or cause to be used for profit through public performance, such article on which sounds are so transferred without the consent
of the owner.[39]

Cases appeared in courts throughout the 1970s as bootleggers tried to push
copyright boundaries. Courts closed loopholes while distributors continued
to push their agenda.

This concern about music sales outside of commercial mediums arose
because of the new technology and as a result of the youth culture resistance to commercialized sales and culture. Young people no longer wanted
the single corporate-approved music promoted through radio stations and
Billboard charts. The ability to share music individually emerged from the
new technology and the new ideology about the freedom of music. By the
1970s when individuals wanted to share music with friends, they now had the
ability to make a copy on a cassette tape. This version of music sharing is the
direct ancestor of the mixtape.

Music subcultures diversified the music scene in the 1970s. The technology of this generation allowed for individuals outside the corporate world of
music producers and recording studios to create music they loved.[40] A new
generation recognized formal music training was not a requirement. These
musicians created punk and hip hop music which significantly shifted how
audiences consumed and interacted with music. Some members of Gen X
eschewed mass culture, seeing it as corrupt and counterfeit. They moved
away from Adorno's perception of individuals as willing consumers of mass
culture. They desired an identity independent of radio play, TV shows, and
Billboard charts.[41] The birth of a DIY culture led to a desire to share music
apart from the consumer mainstream. With the rise of cassette culture in the
1970s, recording music outside of a studio became possible. Musicians who
could not get recording contracts with major record labels found new ways to
make and share their music. In the world of hip hop and punk, sharing music
via bootleg or pirated tapes became a norm.

HIP HOP

Hip hop culture emerged in the South Bronx in the 1970s as an artistic
response to the economic crisis, cultural oppression, and racism residents felt.
Defined as "the music, arts, media, and cultural movement and community
developed by black and Latino youth in the mid-1970s on the East Coast of
the United States," it embraces "an identity, a worldview, and a way of life."[42]

In the late 1960s the Black Panther Party had become a visible protest group; Black power leaders joined anti-war protestors; and cops in the Bronx battled with locals.[43] A new young culture coalesced around "crews" as a source of group identity. These adolescents engaged in graffitiing, b-boying, DJing, and MCing as social expression and artistic outlets for their frustrations.[44] Rappers used DJing and MCing to create an authentic music that expressed their frustration with society. These artists did not have formal musical training; instead, they used technology to create a new musical style. Playing turntables like instruments, DJs sampled beats and extended rhythms, much like looping capabilities in contemporary music. Sampling was a fundamental part of music making; it paid homage to foundational genres from funk and soul to classical jazz.[45] It allowed digital duplication of existing sounds to create the break beat.[46] Rap emerged at the hands of artists like DJ Kool Herc, Grandmaster Flash, and Afrika Bambaataa, all New York City residents in the 1970s. Herc grew up listening to American jazz, gospel, and country in Jamaica. When he moved to New York in 1966 he brought his music and the tradition of Sound Clash culture with him.[47] Herc took this foundation, used the music of his childhood, and debuted at a Bronx house party in 1973.[48] His style relied on preexisting musical tracks which DJs mixed to create a new sound. He originated a method known as the "Merry-Go-Round" which allowed him to lengthen a song by playing it simultaneously on two turntables, alternating the passage from one record to the other.[49] As other DJs copied Herc's techniques, they began to tape their performances, heralding the first generation of hip hop mixtapes. As early as 1981 Afrika Bambaataa helped to desegregate rap by performing in punk-rock clubs in lower Manhattan.[50]

The burgeoning era of the hip hop mixtape developed out of the live recordings of shows in New York City. As the music and the community spread, regional hip hop communities had their own unique set of DJs and live recordings. The earliest mixtapes, called "customized tapes" began in the late 1970s with live recording of rappers in New York City parks. By the early 1980s these shows moved from parks to indoor clubs.[51] Recording a show on tape, making copies, and sharing it defined the first generation of the hip hop mixtape. Brucie B, a DJ from the Bronx, began marketing and selling live audio recordings of sets at The Rooftop, a disco roller rink. People paid upwards of one hundred dollars to have a live recording of the evening's set.[52] Orpheus "Justo" Faison, a rap record promoter, described these tapes saying, "[attendees] were buying the night" to prove they were at the party and to "pay for their shoutout."[53] Distinguishing this type of mixtape from the personal mixtape, Cummings describes how hip hop DJs "combined sounds from various records to create a new type of sound collage that gradually became an underground commodity and a vital part of the hip hop music industry in New York, Atlanta, and elsewhere."[54] "Rapper's Delight," released in 1979 captured a pivotal moment for rap, compressing hours-long DJ performances into a single tape. It showed that rap could move from live music to a recorded format.[55] In the early 1980s the informal sound collage with a DJ playing tracks and a rapper performing over them defined the genre before rap became a mainstream music industry genre. These early shows often included DJs sampling various songs to create a dance track. Rappers defined their strength by rapping over the music, "[producers] redefined what the word mixtape meant. Rhyming over other rappers' instrumentals in an uncanny fashion. [. . .] Back then tapes were a flare gun shot by up-and-coming artists trying to paint their name on the day's rap mural."[56] These live recordings, dubbed on cassette tapes, hastened the growth of hip hop.[57] According to DJ Drama, a mixtape producer, "mixtapes were the main form of distribution in [the rise of rap]. They were the currency that kept things in rotation as the culture evolved."[58] The first generation who owned mixtapes took their tapes to college, spreading the idea and the sounds of hip hop.[59]

Rap became a political music that highlighted black marginality in American culture and allowed Black urban youth to vent their grievances and speak to their generation.[60] Their voices had power *because* they existed outside commercial reach.[61] Rapper and Producer, Chuck D called rap "Black Folk's CNN" because the lyrics focused on the realities of ghetto life which many people chose to ignore.[62] As Michael Eric Dyson stated, "hip hop music is important precisely because it sheds light on contemporary politics, history, and race. At its best, hip hop gives voice to marginal black youth we are not used to hearing from on such topics."[63] Rap paid homage to the musical forefathers of jazz, funk, and soul. DJs often sampled instrumental tracks over which an MC could rap.[64] Like Herc, artists borrowed records from their parents which they used as the foundation for their new sound, blending recorded music and live performance.[65]

Hip hop culture expanded out of the east coast and traveled, via cassette, to various regions of the United States (and eventually internationally). From its earliest days in the Bronx, hip hop was never an exclusively African American art form. It has always been a multicultural artistic movement which incorporated Hispanic communities and expanded to other voiceless marginalized populations.[66] As hip hop achieved commercial popularity, its audience became increasingly white, which for some performers undermined its authenticity. In *Hip Hop Underground*, Kwame Harrison demonstrates the sociocultural and racial diversity of underground hip hop in part as a response to mainstream media's representation of it as a predominantly Black art form.[67] The Bay Area in California built a resilient underground hip hop scene which has continued to define itself around the cassette tape as the medium of exchange.[68] The cassette maintains an ad hoc quality and "In the case of Bay Area underground cassette tapes, their antiquated technology gives a nod to nostalgic sentiments of local tradition, upholds the democratic priorities of DiY movements, and serves as a technological barrier to mainstream co-optation."[69] Cassettes have played a key role in hip hop identity building as well as in defining the genre's technological needs.

The diminishing cost of technological equipment in the 1980s increased access to copying, dubbing, and mixing equipment for aspiring artists.[70] Good quality microphones became key to the success of rappers who needed to maintain the audience's attention with their performance skills and verbal dexterity.[71] As these artists became more popular, the size of shows grew, and awareness of their acumen traveled. Fans and artists recorded live shows and members of the hip hop underground distributed or sold the recordings to fans on cassette tapes. These artists did not envision their shows as albums; they recorded live sets not individual songs.[72] These hip hop mixtapes were the foundation for the contemporary commercial mixtapes which remain an essential aspect of hip hop culture.[73] Because this generation remained independent of the recording industry, musicians could pick and choose which sounds to sample.[74] In the mid-1980s when rap became commercially viable, a debate about sampling emerged. In the recording industry, sampling equaled copyright infringement and musicians were required to pay to rap over other artists' samples. The cost was so prohibitive hip hop artists had to rethink music production.[75] The hip hop mixtape with samples continued to prosper independent of the recording company, "Traditionally, mix tapes formed part of a street economy with DJs blending the latest hits, punctuated by the occasional freestyle verse or unreleased track."[76] The debate between the recording industry and artists continued to plague hip hop and eventually shifted the understanding of a hip hop mixtape.

Bootlegging defined hip hop and expanded the genre into multiple localized subcultures. Bootleg cassette tapes of hip hop's forefathers circulated outside of the Bronx to other New York neighborhoods in the 1980s. The next generation used these underground mixtapes as the foundation to formalize hip hop into a more sophisticated commercial genre.[77] Underground hip hop in California's Bay Area built their circulation from the late 1970s to the 1990s through bootlegged material. Circulating cassettes with radio shows, live recordings, and DJ mixtapes allowed for a growth and documentation of this local hip hop scene.[78] In the 1990s go-go music defined Black youth cultures in the Washington D.C. area. Never a mainstream crossover, popular concert bootleg releases sold locally, reaffirming the importance of local scenes and the role of the bootleg.[79] Circulation of tapes enhanced a local scene which continued to thrive into the twenty-first century. The localized, relatively small circulation of these hip hop mixes kept them out of the eye of copyright holders. While they were commodities, they were not the genre focused on in copyright debates of this decade. Copyright debates in hip hop revolved not around the relatively small-scale bootlegs but around the larger debates with sampling.

PUNK

Like hip hop and jam bands, punk musicians also encouraged their fans to exchange bootleg tapes to widen their membership. Punk existed largely outside the mainstream corporate recording industry. Also similar to hip hop, punk musicians often sang about local political frustrations, highlighting their disaffection with the world around them.[80] A genre originally defined by one's working-class roots, punk distanced itself from middle-class suburban values as seen in mainstream media. Sociologist Ryan Moore states, "Punk made a huge splash in the late 1970s in part because it seemed to symbolize a particular moment in history characterized by the death of idealism."[81] Punk musicians did not require formal musical training; raw emotion and a willingness to express oneself defined the genre in the 1970s. The provocative attitude and lyrics of bands, like The Dead Kennedys' "Holiday in Cambodia," proved too confrontational for mainstream radio.[82] At the outset, recording industries did not consider punk a marketable style of music. This genre relied on live performances and community building. Punk musicians did not see themselves as separate from their fan base. They dressed like their fans and preferred to perform in small venues rather than separating themselves with lights, a removed stage, and excessive production.[83] Fashion became a fundamental facet of the punk scene. The Sex Pistols, dressed by Vivienne Westwood and Malcolm McLaren, aimed to create an outside-the-box outrageousness to push social boundaries.[84] Musicians like the Ramones created a long-standing association between punk and Converse All Stars.[85] Punk became as much a social movement as a genre of music. It encouraged people to take control of their own identity and not conform to the mainstream attitude. Punk fashion expanded notions of what is acceptable.[86] All of these aspects of punk created a world in which DIY culture became a fundamental tool for the genre. Like hip hop, recording live shows and selling tapes was the main mode of sharing the music.

Punk developed a regionally specific subculture community defined around musical style and the concerns of a given location. British punk differed from the counteraesthetic punk of east coast bands like The Velvet Underground and from the counterculture response on the West coast with bands like X or Black Flag, with lead singer Henry Rollins.[87] With the rise of a group like Minor Threat, punk fans could associate themselves with a straightedge movement and a resistance to drugs. Fans felt connected to the music and the musicians because they participated, rather than a separate and removed scene. Individuals could become invested in the lyrics of local bands because they resonated socially and politically. They could emulate the fashion of the bands, defining themselves as a member of the group. They could record a show and share it with their friends.

Like with hip hop artists, many punk bands relied on a DIY aesthetic because they could not, or did not want, to work with mainstream recording labels. Releasing albums on cassettes was an inexpensive way to get their music to their audience directly at live shows, which remained the most important facet for punk musicians. For Henry Rollins, it allowed him to make music with his bands without having to afford the cost of a studio.[88] For Ian MacKaye, lead singer of Minor Threat, hearing unfamiliar bands on a mixtape introduced him to a whole new way of thinking about music. "[He] was being schooled in a way that [he] had never been schooled before about the possibilities about a medium."[89] The ability to work directly with technological medium allowed punk musicians to create their own music, on their own terms, without the funding needed for a studio or the approval of a recording label. It also took music and put it in the hands of the artists rather than the producers. The aesthetic of punk, which made no distinction between the band and the fans, allowed fans to think about making music themselves. Many of the foundational mixtape stories start with punk fans turned musicians. Postpunk artist Thurston Moore and metal musician Jason Bitner used their experiences within the punk scene as the foundations for their artistic works about the mixtape in the years after the end of the cassette era.

A specific feminized outgrowth of punk, interwoven with the emerging West-coast grunge movement, was the creation of riot grrrl. The quintessential band of this genre, Bikini Kill, created a place for young women to express themselves through punk music and communicate with each other about systemic sexism.[90] Creating their own cultural products, they used a DIY aesthetic, both in the production of the music and the expansive use of zines. The music and the social message of riot grrrl brought to light the sexual abuse and sexual harassment of young women in the United States, an issue the musicians felt the public had chosen to ignore. By consciously exaggerating their femininity, wearing baby doll dresses paired with combat boots, the riot grrrl artists created a visible identity to unify and distinguish them.[91] MacKaye produced the first Bikini Kill record, introduced their sound to the D.C. punk world, and co-supported fundraisers for abortion clinics and self-defense training.[92] As with punk, the riot grrrl musicians rejected consumer culture and actively resisted being commodified and labeled by marketers. They refused to be seen as a fad that society could dismiss over time.[93] The ideas of riot grrrl perpetuated the mid-1990s and intersected with the next generation of feminism.

Women who identified with riot grrrl used those ideals as they moved into their own careers. While there are mixtapes that pay specific homage to the punk stylings of riot grrrl bands from Sleater-Kinney to L7,[94] there are also authors who have taken the adages of riot grrrl and used them as a model for writing fiction geared at a new generation of young women. A handful of young adult books, like *Vinyl Princess* and *The First Rule of Punk*, in the 21st century have borrowed imagery, songs, and the DIY aesthetic, including mixtapes, to tell stories geared towards a new generation who can benefit from the female empowerment introduced in the 1990s.

THE DOMINANCE OF CASSETTES

By circumventing the recording industry and the recording companies, musicians could create inexpensive tapes to sell to their audience and multiply their fanbase through word of mouth. This gorilla style of marketing and selling music was incredibly important in punk and rap. Punk music was not seen as commercially marketable. And punk musicians who tried to record in traditional recording studios found them limiting. The free-form appeal of punk music was lost in the sterile, click-track world of the recording industry. Cassettes, which incorporated the idiosyncrasies of live performance, appealed to fans who wanted a dynamic feel. For fans of hip hop, cassettes were the sole means of sharing the music from a live show. According to Robert "Bobbito" Garcia, "Cassettes *were* hip hop."[95] Like punk, rap was not seen as a marketable, mainstream music in the 1970s and early 1980s. Therefore, individuals recorded live shows, made multiple copies, and distributed them to friends and fans. Without cassettes, the music could not have expanded out of its supra-local scene. The long-standing correlation between these genres of music and cassettes diminished with the rise of the internet, but it never stopped completely. Cassettes have remained a subculture means of sharing non-mainstream music.

The music industry viewed the 1980s as the decade of the cassette as sound engineers continually improved the quality to align more closely to records. By 1983 cassettes had surpassed vinyl record sales.[96] Philips claimed to have sold three billion compact cassettes between 1963 and 1988.[97] In 1987 recording companies created a new type of cassette: the cassingle. Companies intended these inexpensive cassettes, which played two to three songs in a short ten minutes, to compete with vinyl 45s. They filled a niche in an era in which CD singles remained expensive.[98] One of the first cassingles, Whitney Houston's "I Wanna Dance with Somebody Who Loves Me," was released a month before her album, much the same way rap artists release mixtape EPs digitally today.[99] These economical cassette singles appealed to a younger audience who no longer owned turntables. The cassingle survived until the mid-2000s but was replaced by the CD and soon the shift to digital.

In 1986 Personics manufactured a novel device to produce personalized cassette tapes. Their company sold their kiosk, "a device that resembles a large jukebox equipped with headphones" to a record store, like the chain Sam Goody.[100] The kiosks first appeared in Los Angeles, San Francisco, and New York City. Record companies licensed their songs to Personics, which then created a catalog of 15,000 songs to browse. A customer would select several songs and create a personalized cassette. The audio quality of a Personics tape was higher than what a consumer could have crafted at home. Each track cost between twenty-five cents and two dollars, which meant a full cassette could total upwards of twenty-eight dollars, but it was one of the only available ways to buy a single in the 1980s. A 1988 newspaper review of the device highlighted the appeal of the machine,

> For an individual to make a 90-minute tape at home would require finding all the selections, buying a blank cassette, spending more than an hour and a half making the tape and having the persistence to type the cassette label. Even then, the sound quality of the finished tape probably wouldn't compare favorably to the Personics version. [101]

Figure 2.1 Cassette and J-Card. Image Courtesy of the Author

A J-Card with the track listings, including all copyright information, a title, and the name of the person who bought the item, came with the tape. Unlike the cassingle, a consumer could have a single cassette full of songs by different artists which took up less room than the equivalent number of cassingles. According to *Popular Music*

> In 1990, the company will pay out some $8.5 million to the record industry and will open up in Canada and Britain [. . .] it has the potential to revolutionise the whole organisation of buying and selling pre-recorded sound-carriers.[102]

However, this product had already disappeared from stores and filed for bankruptcy in 1991. Aside from the rise of the CD, the licensing of songs caused the company's demise. BMG had never agreed to license their music and individual artists like Bruce Springsteen and Michael Jackson had not agreed to license their songs to Personics.[103] A dearth of well-known artists plus the high cost for a full album turned off consumers who continued to find other means of creating self-made tapes. Despite the Personics commercial which claimed, "You could pick the songs you want and put them in any order you want [. . .] all with amazing quality sound on a one-of-a-kind, custom made cassette," consumers chose to make their own mixtapes.[104]

While magnetic recording technology transformed the recording industry, and consumer power changed because of the availability of cassettes, cassette technology also impacted how artists made music on their own terms. For musicians outside the commercial recording industry, cassettes offered a new opportunity. Simon Reynolds clarifies, "Tape was the ultimate in do-it-yourself, because it could be dubbed-on-demand at home, whereas vinyl required a heavier financial outlay and a contractual arrangement with a manufacturer."[105] Cassette technology had moved out of the realm of scientists and experts and into the world of young entrepreneurial artists who wanted to share their music independent of corporate labels. Musicians no longer had to rely on professional recording studios with access to the type of technology needed to create albums. Unsigned musicians could record tracks inexpensively using a simple tape recorder or boombox. Creating a modest demo allowed musicians to get their music to record labels. Without having to pay for session time, they could focus on making music.

For two decades the cassette tape dominated the music industry. Albums released by labels were sold on both vinyl and cassette. An analysis of the Recording Industry Association of American (RIAA) music sales by volume data shows from 1985 to 1990 cassettes accounted for more than 50 percent of all units sold. Cassette sales grew as record sales declined. The cassette single, measured separately by the RIAA, added to cassette sales totals between 1987 and 1999. Although the cassette era overlapped with the creation and growth of the CD, cassettes remained at least 25 percent of all music sales revenue through 1994.[106] According to Nielsen SoundScan, in 1993 the sale of cassettes and CDs was comparable.[107] By the mid-1990s however, cassette sales dwindled substantially. Napster, one of the first mainstream companies to create peer-to-peer file sharing, started in 1999. Despite significant debate in the recording industry about the legitimacy of streaming music, streaming predominated in the 2000s. When Apple released iTunes in 2001 it signaled the end of analog format dominance. By 2004 cassettes accounted for only 5 percent of music sales volume. In 2011 the RIAA stopped including cassettes in their sales chart.[108]

Outside of commercial distribution, cassettes had also allowed individuals to tape music directly at home. Mentioned in publications as early as 1958, anyone could record songs from the radio to a tape recorder. This genre of mixtape persisted throughout the era of the cassette. With the right cables, consumers could also make personal copies of records they had borrowed from friends or from the library. The release of the double-deck cassette machine took self-recording one step further, allowing individuals to make inexpensive recordings at home. Although corporate record labels condemned these copies as piracy, private, non-commercial copying was protected, "under the doctrine of first sale in the USA, which says that once you buy a record, it is yours."[109] A decline in recorded music sales in the late 1970s led trade associations like the RIAA, the British Phonographic Industry (BPI), and the International Federation of the Phonographic Industry (IFPI) to claim a loss of one to three billion dollars as a result of home taping.[110] Musicians discouraged blaming customers, forcing the companies to contend with the consumer electronics section. The associations encouraged governments to add levies to blank tapes, asserting people would use blank tapes to record music illegally rather than purchase it commercially. They wanted to allocate the proceeds from these levies to various agencies that they believed deserved the profit. While some versions of this legislation passed in parts of Western Europe, the proposals failed in the United States, the United Kingdom, and Canada.[111] It was difficult to prove individuals purchased blank cassettes only for illegitimate purposes.

By 1981, BPI had had enough. In 1980 The British new wave band Bow Wow, under manager Malcolm McLaren, had released an album with a blank B-side so fans could record their own music.[112] This move highlighted the appeal of home taping and the disconnect between corporations and musicians. BPI began the "Home Taping is Killing Music. And It's Illegal" campaign.[113] The logo, "featuring a Jolly Roger-style cassette tape and-crossbones image," appeared on the sleeves of vinyl British album releases.[114] British imports like Culture Club and Duran Duran brought the logo to the United States.[115] In the States, the RIAA began a "Home Taping: copyright Killer" campaign suggesting home tapers were "poachers."[116] Largely a moral argument, home taping remained protected by fair use. Bands, pushing against industry control, mocked the campaign and allied with their fan base. In 1981 The Dead Kennedy's released the EP *In God We Trust, Inc*. The phrases "Home Taping Is Killing Record Industry Profits!" and "We Left This Side Blank So You Can Help" appeared in lieu of track names on the B-side.[117] Bootleg cassette stalls crowded London's Camden Lock Market throughout the 1980s. Even after a BPI raid in 1987 the trade continued, albeit less overtly.[118] In 1988 BPI took legal action against Amstrad Consumer Electronics because their double cassette deck recorded from one tape deck to another at double speed allowing consumers to copy music onto blank audiotapes. Amstrad successfully argued they were not liable for how consumers used their equipment, again defeating BPI.[119] Billy Bragg's 1988 album took more direct aim at the recording companies. The cover included the phrase, "Capitalism is killing music—pay no more than £4.99 for this record."[120] These bands highlighted the correlation between the anti-consumerism of the counterculture era, and the desire to connect to their fans on their own terms. This aggressive morality campaign remained unsuccessful because the musicians themselves did not have a problem with how their music was being shared. The passage of the Audio Home Recording Act of 1992 confirmed home taping was a "non-infringing activity."[121]

Cassette's dominance coincides with increased music piracy because of the ease of copying magnetic tape. Cassette culture revolves around creating and sharing music outside of the recording industry. Punk, metal, and hip hop remain reliant on tape sharing. The bootlegger who wants to make money by undercutting legitimate sales of a full album is separate from the individual who wants to make a playlist to share with friends or to listen to on a personal stereo or in the car. This private copying of recorded music for personal use—a mixtape—is not illegal. These are copies made for enjoyment and sharing. The mixtape, as a concept, exists outside of the legal definition of piracy.

As members of the analog generation became voices in media, they began to write about their own experiences with youth culture and music in many artistic formats. Whether it is analyzing how mixtapes are used in Bret Easton Ellis' *Less Than Zero* or understanding the song Mixtape in the Broadway Musical *Avenue Q*, the engagement of Gen X and older millennials as adolescents in the 1970s, 1980s, and 1990s creates the story of mixtapes. As David Byrne, musician turned theorist wrote,

> The mixtapes we made for ourselves were musical mirrors. The sadness, anger, or frustration you might be feeling at a given time could be encapsulated in the song selection. You made mixtapes that corresponded to emotional states, and

they'd be available to pop into the deck when each feeling needed reinforcing or soothing. The mixtape was your friend, your psychiatrist, and your solace.[122]

Byrne's passionate evocation of the role of mixtapes solidifies the position of a cassette-based piece of art as a fundamental aspect of understanding analog generations' youth cultures. Coinciding with technological shifts in how music is made and heard, the mixtape took the idea of counterculture experiences and personalized them and eventually made them a site of nostalgia.

NOTES

1. Simon Frith, *Sound Effects: Youth, Leisure and the Politics of Rock 'N' Roll* (New York: Pantheon Books, 1981), 217.

2. A British study suggested people stop listening to new music around the age of 30 because they are focused on jobs and family. Lindsay Dodgson, "We Stop Discovering New Music at Age 30, a New Survey Suggests—Here Are the Scientific Reasons Why This Could Be," *Business Insider* (June 7, 2018), https://www.business insider.com/why-we-stop-discovering-new-music-around-age-30-2018-6.

3. Zack Taylor, "Cassette: A Documentary Mixtape" Documentary. (Gravitas Ventures, 2018). DVD 88 mins.

4. Sunaina Maira, "Youth," in *Keywords for American Cultural Studies, Second Edition*, ed. Bruce Burgett and Glenn Hendler (New York: NYU Press, 2014), 246.

5. Frith, 75.

6. Bruce Springsteen, "Exclusive: The Complete Text of Bruce Springsteen's SXSW Keynote Address," *Rolling Stone* (March 28, 2012), https://www.rollingstone.com/music/music-news/exclusive-the-complete-text-of-bruce-springsteens-sxsw-keynote-address-86379/ (Accessed July 16, 2019).

7. Ben Yagoda, *The B Side: The Death of Tin Pan Alley and the Rebirth of the Great American Song* (New York: Riverhead Books, 2015), Chapter VII "The Big Beat."

8. Simon Frith, *Performing Rites: On the Value of Popular Music* (Massachusetts: Harvard University Press, 1996), 276–77.

9. *Sound Effects: Youth, Leisure and the Politics of Rock 'N' Roll*, 203.

10. Jennifer C. Lena, *Banding Together: How Communities Create Genres in Popular Music* (New Jersey: Princeton University Press, 2012), 6.

11. Ryan Moore, *Sells Like Teen Spirit: Music, Youth Culture, and Social Crisis* (New York: New York University Press, 2010), 25.

12. Ibid., 29.

13. Frith, *Sound Effects: Youth, Leisure and the Politics of Rock 'N' Roll*, 57.

14. *Performing Rites: On the Value of Popular Music*, 275.

15. Dan Laughey, *Music and Youth Culture* (Edinburgh: Edinburgh University Press, 2006), www.jstor.org/stable/10.3366/j.ctt1r1zxm. 11–12.

16. Young Adult literature had existed since the 1800s but became a larger marketable genre in the mid-20th century. Erin Blakemore, "A Brief History of Young

Adult Fiction," Website (April 10, 2015), https://daily.jstor.org/history-of-young-adult-fiction/.

17. Theodor W. Adorno, *Introduction to the Sociology of Music*, trans. E. B. Ashton (New York: The Seabury Press, 1976), Chapter 2 Popular Music.

18. Frith, *Sound Effects: Youth, Leisure and the Politics of Rock 'N' Roll*, 43.

19. The commercial musical diversity continued to cater to specific populations as defined by marketing and industry paradigms based on what they believed would sell. Questions of national identity, race, sexual identity, and gender expression have again forced creators of consumer culture to acknowledge greater nuance in how they engage with youth culture.

20. Springsteen.

21. See Brian MacGabhann, "Marketing Youth Culture," *Studies: An Irish Quarterly Review* 94, no. 374 (2005). 134–136. and Monica Sklar, *Punk Style* (New York: Bloomsbury, 2013), Chapters 2 and 3 for more details about these movements.

22. Moore, 209.

23. Ibid., 25.

24. In this book I use bootlegging and piracy synonymously. There is a difference in larger contexts which are not necessary to detail here.

25. "33 Things You Can Do with a Tape Recorder," *Tape Recording*, January 1966. https://worldradiohistory.com/Archive-All-Audio/Archive-Tape-Recording/60s/Tape-Recording-1966-01.pdf (Accessed August 26, 2020).

26. Ibid.

27. Alex Sayf Cummings, *Democracy of Sound: Music Piracy and the Remaking of American Copyright in the Twentieth Century* (New York: Oxford University Press, 2013), 159.

28. Ibid., 152–56.

29. Ibid., 99–102, 09.

30. Greg Kot, *Ripped: How the Wired Generation Revolutionized Music* (New York: Simon & Schuster, Inc., 2009), 102–08.

31. Cummings, 154–59.

32. Ibid., 163.

33. Barry Kernfeld, *Pop Song Piracy: Disobedient Music Distribution since 1929* (Chicago: University of Chicago Press, 2011), https://ebookcentral.proquest.com/lib/pointpark-ebooks/detail.action?docID=3038271. 142.

34. Robert A. Rosenblatt, "Tape Pirates: Industry Fights Bootleg Music," *Los Angeles Times*, Feb. 28, 1970, 23 as quoted in Cummings, 112.

35. Ibid., 206.

36. Kernfeld, 160.

37. David Morton, *Off the Record: The Technology and Culture of Sound Recording in America* (New Brunswick: Rutgers University Press, 2000), 162.

38. Kernfeld, 160.

39. "N.Y. Disk Piracy Bills Stir Industry," Variety, March 30, 1966, 1, 94; Sparkman, "Tape Pirates," 119–23; Towe, "Record Piracy," 259–60 as quoted in Kernfeld., 162. 2.

40. Moore, 23–25.

41. Ibid., 29.

42. The article continues by analyzing the hip hop nation as an international "imagined cultural community." Marcyliena Morgan and Dionne Bennett, "Hip-Hop & the Global Imprint of a Black Cultural Form," *Daedalus* 140, no. 2 (2011), https://www.jstor.org/stable/23047460.

43. Jeff Chang, *Can't Stop Won't Stop: A History of the Hip-Hop Generation* (New York: Picador, 2005), Chapter 3.

44. Ibid., Chapter 6. Tricia Rose, *Black Noise: Rap Music and Black Culture in Contemporary America* (Hanhover, NH: Wesleyan University Press, 1994), http://search.ebscohost.com/login.aspx?direct=true&AuthType=sso&db=nlebk&AN=45315&site=ehost-live. 34.

45. Rose. 79.

46. Ibid., 73.

47. Sound Clashes were musical competitions in which DJ crews brought speakers turntables, and microphones to perform over one another. Genius, *The History of Sound Clash Culture* (YouTube 2017). https://youtu.be/aASQlbktGkc (Accessed August 18, 2020).

48. Chang, Chapter 4.

49. Cummings, 165.

50. Chang, Chapter 5.

51. Mr. Davey D, *Breakdown* FM, podcast audio, Interview with Justo Faison: The History of Mixtapes, 2005, https://soundcloud.com/mrdaveyd/breakdown-fm-intv-w-justo (Accessed May 12, 2021).

52. "Brucie B," Mixtapedia, http://www.mixtapedia.org/brucie-b (Accessed May 15, 2021).

53. Faison died in 2005, before the shift to the commercial mixtape. His reflections describe the mixtape from its earliest incarnation until the shift to digital. Cummings, 165; Mr. Davey D.

54. Cummings, 151.

55. Ibid., 166.

56. Michael Kawaida, "Mixtapes: A Brief History of Hip-Hop's Ever Evolving Tool," *Hot New Hip Hop* (Feb. 25, 2020), https://www.hotnewhiphop.com/mixtapes-a-brief-history-of-hip-hops-ever-evolving-tool-news.103882.html.

57. Ibid.

58. *The Day the Mixtape Died: DJ Drama*, podcast audio, Louder Than a Riot, 1 hr 5 mins 2020, https://www.npr.org/2020/10/27/928307301/the-day-the-mixtape-died-dj-drama (Accessed Oct. 29, 2020).

59. Mr. Davey D.

60. Rose 3.

61. Afrika Bambaataa and DJ Kool Herc were members of the Baby Boom generation but the artists who came after them were all younger. Christine Henseler, ed. *Generation X Goes Global: Mapping a Youth Culture in Motion* (New York: Taylor & Francis, 2012), 11.

62. Lena, 49.

63. Michael Eric Dyson, *Know What I Mean?: Reflections on Hip-Hop* (New York: Basic Books, 2007), http://ebookcentral.proquest.com/lib/pointpark-ebooks/detail.action?docID=530375. xvi.

64. Adam Bradley and Andrew DuBois, eds., *The Anthology of Rap* (New Haven: Yale University Press, 2010). 3.

65. Jack Denton, "A Generation of Hip-Hop Was Given Way for Free. Can It Be Archived?", Pacific Standard, https://psmag.com/social-justice/a-generation-of-hip-hop-was-given-away-for-free-can-it-be-archived (Accessed July 8, 2020).

66. Anthony Kwame Harrison, *Hip Hop Underground: The Integrity and Ethics of Racial Identification* (Philadelphia: Temple University Press, 2009), 89; Rose. Chapter 2.

67. Harrison.

68. These artists use "underground" specifically to define music that circulates outside major labels. "'Cheaper Than a CD, Plus We Really Mean It': Bay Area Underground Hip Hop Tapes as Subcultural Artefacts," *Popular Music* 25, no. 2 (2006), https://www.jstor.org/stable/3877563.

69. Ibid., 298.

70. Rose, 7.

71. Ibid., 55.

72. Bradley and DuBois, 5.

73. DJ Semtex, "Street Dreams: How Hip-Hop Mixtapes Changed the Game," *Hip-Hop Raised Me* (Medium: Thames & Hudson, 2016), https://medium.com/cuepoint/street-dreams-how-hip-hop-mixtapes-changed-the-game-40af79e8d953 (Accessed July 15, 2020).

74. Cummings, 164.

75. Kot, 11.

76. Bradley and DuBois, 566.

77. Chang, 142–43.

78. Harrison, "'Cheaper Than a CD, Plus We Really Mean It': Bay Area Underground Hip Hop Tapes as Subcultural Artefacts," 287.

79. Chang, 423.

80. Theo Cateforis, *Are We Not New Wave? Modern Pop at the Turn of the 1980s* (Ann Arbor: University of Michigan Press, 2011), 22.

81. Moore, 59.

82. Cateforis, 1.

83. Lena, 12.

84. Avery Trufelman, *Articles of Interest*, podcast audio, Punk Style, MP3 Audio, 32:42 2018 (Accessed October 18, 2018).

85. Sklar, Chapter 2.

86. Trufelman.

87. Moore, 44–53.

88. Taylor.

89. Ibid.

90. Stevie Feliciano, "The Riot Grrrl Movement." New York Public Library, June 19, 2013, https://www.nypl.org/blog/2013/06/19/riot-grrrl-movement. and Moore, 130.

91. Sara Marcus, *Girls to the Front: The True Story of the Riot Grrrl Revolution* (New York: Harper Perennial, 2010), 59.

92. Moore, 127.

93. Marcus, Chapter 7.

94. Jason Bitner, ed. *Cassette from My Ex: Stories and Soundtracks of Lost Loves* (New York: St. Martin's Press, 2009) and Thurston Moore, ed. *Mix Tape: The Art of Cassette Culture* (New York: Universe Publisher, 2004).

95. Taylor.

96. Cummings, 85.

97. Bob Dormon, "Happy 50th Birthday, Compact Cassette: How It Stuck a Chord for Millions," *The Register* (August 30, 2013), https://www.theregister.co.uk/2013/08/30/50_years_of_the_compact_cassette/ (Accessed July 15, 2019).

98. Jon Pareles, "Cassette Singles: New 45's," *The New York Times*, September 2, 1987.

99. Ibid.

100. Stephen Holden, "The Pop Life," ibid., 1989.

101. Harry Somerfield, "Music Gets Personal with New Tape Idea," *Orlando Sentinel*, March 19, 1988.

102. Dave Laing, "Record Sales in the 1980s," *Popular Music* 9, no. 2 (1990), http://www.jstor.org/stable/853504.

103. Holden.

104. "Personics commercial" YouTube video, :30 posted by "reallyreel" July 26, 2007. https://youtu.be/NPJemnDK3FY (Accessed June 1, 2021).

105. Simon Reynolds, *Retromania: Pop Culture's Addiction to Its Own Past* (New York: Faber and Faber, Inc, 2011), 349.

106. RIAA, "U. S. Sales Database," https://www.riaa.com/u-s-sales-database/?fbclid=IwAR2-IuPU0w989pz0nuGsZflTrF3BFdK1C9FhpD3PfHg1CJTt4bs86Uz POvY. (Accessed July 8, 2020). Discogs, "The Cassette Comeback, by the Numbers," Discogs, https://blog.discogs.com/en/the-cassette-comeback-by-the-numbers/. (Accessed July 8, 2020).

107. Lily Rothman, "Rewound: On Its 50th Birthday, the Cassette Tape Is Still Rolling," *Time*, August 12, 2013.

108. RIAA.

109. Andrew J. Bottomley, "'Home Taping Is Killing Music': The Recording Industries' 1980s Anti-Home Taping Campaigns and Struggles over Production, Labor and Creativity," *Creative Industries Journal* 8, no. 2 (2015) 126.

110. Ibid.

111. Kernfeld, 161.

112. Ted Mills, "Home Taping Is Killing Music: When the Music Industry Waged War on the Cassette Tape in the 1980s, and Punk Bands Fought Back," *Open Culture* (April 5, 2019), http://www.openculture.com/2019/04/home-taping-is-killing-music.html (Accessed July 9, 2020).

113. Ibid. Moore.

114. Bottomley. 124; Annie Zaleski, "35 Years Ago: The U.K. Launches the 'Home Taping Is Killing Music' Campaign," *Diffuser* (October 25, 2016), https://diffuser.fm/home-taping-is-killing-music-uk/ (Accessed July 9, 2020).

115. Bottomley, 129.

116. Ibid.

117. Zaleski.

118. Jude Rogers, "Total Rewind: 10 Key Moments in the Life of the Cassette," *The Observer*, August 30, 2013.

119. Robin Wright, "Audiotape Cassette," in *A History of Intellectual Property in 50 Objects*, ed. Claudy Op Den Kamp and Dan Hunter (Cambridge: Cambridge University Press, 2019), 290–91.

120. Mills.

121. Bottomley, 131.

122. David Byrne, *How Music Works*, 1st ed. (San Francisco: McSweeney's, 2012), 109.

Chapter 3

The Mixtape Generation

MAKING A MIXTAPE

By the mid-1980s mixtapes were a fundamental aspect of mainstream American youth culture. Creating a mixtape had become an artistic experience. The time spent crafting the label, choosing the music, and perfecting the track length demonstrated a tangible investment in the music, the art, and the person the mixtape was intended for. Music, an emotional artform, became a venue for sharing emotionality wordlessly. Discussing mixtapes and sharing them with friends was not a novelty or a concern about bootlegging, it was a normal aspect of life. Novels and music of the era reflected this reality. Authors, from Alan Warner to Stephen Chbosky incorporated mixtapes into plots of their novels as unremarkable aspects of lived youth experience. They helped to ground life and allow characters to express themselves without words. In music, songwriters like Ben Folds sang about mixtapes as aspects of everyday life. The music discussed in these novels and the artists singing about mixtapes mirrored a consumer, middle-class, "all-American" culture. Rock, punk, and new wave predominated the discussions. In this same time period, the hip hop world continued to engage with mixtapes, but not only as self-curated, personal creations. In urban centers, New York remaining the cultural apex, DJs dubbed songs, recorded a set, and sold the tapes to local stores. Like they had in the previous decade, the hip hop mixtape remained tied to expanding and growing the world of hip hop outside the commercial mainstream. These two types of mixtapes ran parallel through the 1990s and only intersected with crossover groups like The Beastie Boys who had toes in both worlds.

The time, energy, and thought put into making mixtapes indicate their cultural importance. Individuals who made mixtapes viewed them as labors of love. Road trip mixtapes had a different feel than break-up mixes which were distinct from declaration-of-a-crush tapes. A Music Psychology Professor grants these tapes even more power stating,

> The [compilation] cassette suddenly became a representation of your whole personality, a tool to make someone else feel the emotions that you feel. It also helped people create new narratives out of the music they liked, and by extension, of their lives.[1]

Mixtapes allowed consumers to become producers and DJs; they could infuse their personality into their creations, inexpensively without technological experience.[2] In musician Damon Krukowski's view a mixtaper plays a crucial role: "When there is too much music to be able to sort through it all and find something new and interesting, it is useful to have a curator to help navigate the minutiae."[3] Individuals could spend hours contemplating not only the songs to include but the technology to use. From the first step, mixtape creation took forethought. A litany of decisions went into crafting the perfect mixtape: who it was for, what emotion it was intended to evoke, where it would be played. From the choice of tape to the technology used, every step took time and thought. By the late 1980s stores sold a wide variety of blank cassettes. Practical tapes, like the classic black Philips CRX 90 had an old-school corporate feel. The clear plastic with fuchsia and yellow highlights Memorex dBS 90 had a youthful, trendy appearance. The Maxell 90 packages included the image of "the Maxell blown away guy" sitting in a plush chair literally blown away by the quality of sound on the tape.[4] Tapes were available in 60-, 90-, and 120-minute lengths. They could be purchased in packs between one and twenty cassettes. A music journalist describing his quest for cassettes in 1981 stated, "a box of 10 high-quality Maxell 90-minute tapes cost something like $40 at Tapeville USA, in Nanuet, N.Y. That was a lot, for me. But I found a wholesale store across the street from there which sold packages of BASF Studio 2s—not very good, but good enough—for about half that price."[5] Cost, quality, and availability all played into what brand one purchased.

Cassette choice was the simple technological step. More important was the equipment needed to make the recording. In the early days of mixtapes, a common process was to call a radio DJ, request a song, wait by the radio, and press record when the song played. This version always risked the DJ talking over the first few seconds of the song, destroying the perfection of the recording. Jay Sweet, Executive Producer and Organizer of the Newport Folk and Jazz Festivals described his earliest mixtape creations, "I would hold my Fisher Price tape recorder up to a boombox and I would hit play and record." To get the song he wanted he would, "Call and make the request and wait 40 mins to see if [my] request was played just so [I] could capture that song."[6]

For those individuals with the appropriate technology, a better option was to connect a record player to a tape player. One could make a clear recording on the tape. Individuals could record full albums from LP to cassette for portability to cars, ease of use, and to maintain the record in pristine condition. Quickly, individuals realized they could create their own compilations picking and choosing the songs and the order they wanted. By the late 1980s dual-deck tape recorders appeared on the market which made creating mixtapes even easier. The rewind and fast-forward function of a tape made it possible to set the master tape to the exact point where the recording should start. With dual-deck, one could press play on the master tape and record on the secondary tape which allowed for a seamless transfer of music. The recording function of a tape player also allowed for individuals to record their voices. Some mixtapes included commentary, introductions, and interludes woven into the songs. Whichever version used, each of these recording processes was manual and analog. It took time and patience. Drag-and-drop technology did not exist which is part of why people continue to consider their mixtapes precious. The time spent making them underscored their importance.

Good mixtapers had layers of nuance in what professionalized a recording. Most people knew to press pause at the end of a recording rather than stop. The stop button created an audible noise on the tape, the sure sign of a novice. For some people adding three to six seconds of silence between songs created a more polished sound resonant of commercial recordings. Most important was the length. As Angus Cargill describes, figuring out how to incorporate the songs was a mathematical process:

> Back in the day though, filling a C90 tape took hours of thought and preparation, as you shaped and ordered each forty-five-minute side. You had to be careful not to run over and cut a song short, while equally not leaving any kind of gap at either end.[7]

The attention to detail made the difference between a good and a great mixtape.

The technical know-how was key, but the artistry made the mixtape. Luc Sante described this nuance, "The mix tape can be transitive—a letter—or intransitive—a diary entry. [. . .] It is almost always fleeting—often more so than the songs it comprises—and endures best as a time capsule of a vibe gone by."[8] Would the mixtape have a theme? Would sides A and B have distinct subthemes? Were there rules about the choice of bands: no two songs by the same band back-to-back? Were there rules about the genres: no country and punk next to each other? Were there rules about the speed and tenor of songs: no short fast songs next to slow ballads? Or was the lack of coherence the rule: anything goes, keeps the listener on their toes? Chuck Klosterman tells a story about giving two different women the same mixtape, which he admits was underhanded. His description of his younger self thinking about how to compile the tape highlights the thought process,

> "The great thing about mix tapes was that you could anticipate the listener would have to listen to the entire thing at least once (and you could guarantee this by not giving them a track listing). Sequencing was very important. The strategy was to place specific "message" songs in-between semimeaningless "rocking" songs; this would transfix, compliment, and confuse the listener, which was always sort of the goal."[9]

For the recipient, the first listen to a new mixtape established tenor and impact. Thurston Moore describes the appeal of discovering an unknown mixtape. "Sometimes I go to yard sales to buy cassettes compiled by people who are complete strangers to me. You see something that has 'Marty's Mix' scrawled on it in a ballpoint pen. You take it home and you don't know if it's going to be US post-punk hardcore or Kenny Rogers. Whatever it is, though, I know I'm getting a slice of someone's life."[10] A good mixtaper could imbue a mixtape with a sense of personality and meaning.

For many, a mixtape was not complete without cover art, which balanced the artistry of the music and the production values. Every blank cassette

Figure 3.1   Two Self-made Mixtapes from the Early 1990s. Image Courtesy of the Author.

included J-Cards, most of them lined. For some, simply writing the song title and artist in legible pen was sufficient. For many people, the J-Card became a DIY creation, important in its own right. As John Komurki explains,

> At one extreme is the ornate, profuse look, doodles and elaborate typographical experimentation, sticks and collages. Here, the goal is to personalise the inlay as fully as possible, creating a Duchampian one-off. From a faceless commodity, the tape is transformed into a handmade object. At the other extreme are people for whom the tape and j-card are strictly functional items, with only the bare minimum or relevant information scrawled on them.[11]

The options were endless. Mixtapes could include liner notes and personalized commentary, inclusions familiar from vinyl albums. Jennifer Maerz describes the "mortifying" liner notes she had written on a mixtape for a then-boyfriend, "My liner notes, which take up the entire underside of the title card, make me cringe now. [. . .] Mortifying stuff to read. But like a journal, the mixtape is a snapshot of the mercurial emotions I had in high school."[12] These cases remain a quintessential aspect of mixtape memory. Seeing the physical artifact, even without hearing the music, recreates the mixtape for the recipient. Henry Rollins describes the importance of a mixtape made by a deceased friend, "This is his handwriting and he's gone but this is what he left behind. There's nothing digital about this, this was made in real time."[13] He holds the memory of his friend in the analog object that remains.

Not everyone finds cassettes compelling or nostalgia-inducing. Yet a dislike of cassette technology does not translate into a dislike of the mixtape. Journalist Stuart Heritage, questioning why anyone would want a tape resurgence because, "Tapes were terrible," nonetheless understands the mixtape's continued appeal. He declares,

> really, what was more romantic that a mixtape? The sheer effort that went into making one [. . .] was monumental. You had to get 20 different albums lined up in the right place, before manually starting and stopping the deck over and over again and writing the name of the song as legibly as you could in a genuinely minuscule space.[14]

Mixtapers poured their hearts into their mixtapes incorporating time, attention to detail, and artistry into a deeply personal gift. Mixtape recipients coveted their mixtapes because they were artistic, thoughtful, personally constructed tokens of communication, sharing, and connection.

MUSIC

The technology to create the personal self-made mixtape intersects with the rise of the hip hop mixtape, less individual, but no less personal. A hip hop mixtape history states, "In hip hop's early years, cassettes served as its docu-ment of record through bootleg recordings of old-school rap routines and DJ sets. The relative ease of re-recordings and low duplication cost opened new and extensive options for self-documentation to artists and listeners alike. [. . .] There was honesty in the live dubs; producers and rappers hadn't yet figured out how to replicate that feeling in a studio setting."[15] Around 1984 DJ David Anthony Love Jr, known as Kid Capri, began making tapes in his house, rather than recording live shows. He changed the game, creating a clear, profesionally-produced sound which lost the muddiness of a live show. Capri sold his tapes at local events like basketball tournaments for twenty dollars each.[16] His development shifted the mixtape from a purchased memory of a personal event to a consumable product to hear new music. The rise of MTV and a video generation underscored the rise of a golden age in hip hop from the mid-1980s to the late-1990s. The greater visibility for hip hop meant an expansion of the music into mainstream American culture which changed how the artists produced and released albums.[17] By 1991 DJ Clue began selling exclusive tapes with brand new songs that had not yet been released on vinyl and were not yet on the radio.[18] These mixtapes shifted into the realm of bootlegs undermining the eventual commercial release of a song; artists were not convinced these mixtapes would help their careers. A bootleg was viewed as the illegal release of song or album for profit while a mixtape became defined by its promotional use. Styles P, a mixtape artist in the 1990s described that era's mixtapes as "rapping over other artists' beats that's already out and known [. . .] And it's a free project. You don't charge for it and it's not original music."[19] Artists and local distributors released underground cassettes with unapproved samples. Although they were mar-keted as promotional material which could be given away without violating commercial agreements, they were often for sale. Mixtapes "became a tool for aspiring rappers to distribute their own work on the streets in the absence of a record deal, or for enterprising DJs to leverage their own personal con-nections and marketing savvy to act as cultural arbiters within the hip hop scene."[20] With label's growing interest in rap music, questions about legality, bootlegging, and sampling came to the forefront. Cummings argues,

> the artists themselves often pushed records that incorporated their own words and music with sounds borrowed from others, outside the normal conduits of the record business. In doing so, these listeners and artists showed how the industry might accommodate itself to a degree of copying, especially if it could profit from this unpaid promotion.[21]

With increased rap sales, producers created officially licensed compilations to amplify new rappers and released them as mixtapes.[22]

In 1995 Justo Faison, who saw value in formally acknowledging these promotional mixtapes, created The Mixtape Awards with financial assistance from Atlantic Records.[23] In 2005 he described the need for the awards, stating, "People didn't even want to give [mixtape DJs] records [in 1995]. Now they're the biggest stars DJing, period. They're as big as artists now. A lot of the new groups being found now are being found off mixtapes."[24] These awards "acknowledged the efforts of innovative underground hip hop, R&B and reggae DJs nationwide."[25] MTV and *Billboard* covered the awards, recognizing the winners as a fundamental part of the hip hop world.[26] A good mixtape DJ functioned as a musical artist. They "selected and juxtaposed parts of different recordings in the mix, creating a new kind of composition. They put a personal stamp on what they assembled, to a greater extent than the rock or jazz bootlegger who designed the packaging of a live recording."[27] Remembering Faison's role as an advocate for mixtape DJs, DJ EFN stated, "At a time when NYC reigned supreme over hip hop culture and industry, Justo reached out to mixtape DJs in other cities and tried to bring them into the national fold."[28] Faison's Annual Mixtape Awards in the decade from 1995 until his death in 2005 expanded the awareness and importance of the hip hop mixtape as a force in the industry, creating new stars and recognizing artists working outside of mainstream labels.

Meanwhile Brucie B and Kid Capri shifted their focus and initiated the next generation of mixtapes. They worked with distributors like Tapemasters Inc. and Tape Kingz to create commercial releases of live sets.[29] Access to these tapes created a subculture community, "there was always a subtext of exclusivity to the underground-rap-cassette experience. Copying or dubbing these tapes instilled the sensation of a certain special street-level awareness amongst consumers—you had to be in the know to some degree."[30] Stores sold the bootlegs, despite a growing discussion of their legality, and demand continued to grow. Distribution relied on word of mouth and sales in local stores and kiosks, primarily in New York City.[31] Mixtape collector Eric Johnson described his growing fascination with mixtapes when he was in the navy in the early 1990s.

> Traveling abroad, my taste in music evolved and I got heavy into dance hall reggae, but my true love was still New York Hip-Hop. This is when I discovered Tapekingz, in an advertisement in Hip-Hop magazine. They offered mixtapes via mail order. I started placing orders and really enjoyed mixtapes by Nick Bondz, Evil Dee, and Doo Wop, while being out to sea for long periods of time.[32]

Returning home, he continued to search out new mixtapes, traveling to New York stores like Harlem Music Hut, House of Nubian, and Fat Beats. For a time, an unspoken agreement existed between artists, the recording industry, and distributors. Labels knew they were victims of piracy but admitted that these mixtapes functioned as promotional material allowing fans to discover new artists.[33] Keeping their work independent, artists maintained sole control over their work. As DJ Drama said,

> The beauty of what a mixtape was is you didn't have to cross your Is and dot your Ts. So you didn't have to worry about clearances and splits and, you know, what the royalties were going to be and payouts. And it was just the wild, Wild West.[34]

The counterculture underground hip hop scene grew in the 1990s as a way to separate their music from the commercially sensationalized perspective of mainstream rap.[35] It allowed for a racial, regional, and social diversity independent of corporate releases.

Using Mixtapes As Inspiration

Musicians across genres who make mixtapes have a specific relationship to the sounds of music and often discuss the mixtapes in their past as a baseline for the genres of music they now perform. The stories transcend the songs and often remain tied to the relationship between the giver and the receiver of the tape. For a musician, a mixtape holds two layers of meaning. In interviews when musicians discuss the role of music, there is the logical discussion about its impact on their own craft: the sound of a song, the artist who created it, and the understanding of songcraft. When they specifically discuss mixtapes as their entry into music the discussion is more coherently tied to the relationship between the artifact and the conscious art of hearing it in that way, at that time. The person who made the mixtape, the order of the songs, and the cassette tape itself all factor into their relationship to the playlist.

In a 1986 interview for *The New York Times*, Paul Simon credited a "tape of 'township jive,' the street music of Soweto, South Africa" as the foundation of the *Graceland* album.[36] By 2016 *Graceland* had become famous and controversial in equal parts because of a discussion around apartheid, cultural appropriation, and how Simon benefitted. An article in *Rolling Stone* stated that Heidi Berg, a bandleader who had worked on *Saturday Night Live*, lent a cassette tape to Simon of "the bootleg 'Accordion Jive' tape" which he found "bewitching."[37] The literature described this as a "tape" or a "bootleg" tape. In the 2017 book *Vinyl Me, Please: 100 Albums You Need in Your Collection*, Ben Munson stated Simon created *Graceland* because he "heard a song he liked on a mixtape."[38] The slight shift in meaning from "a tape of township jive," to bootleg recording, to "mixtape" does not change the overall story, but the ideas behind those three different concepts are not identical. As a fan, Simon heard an inspirational sound to incorporate in *Graceland*. For the South African artists, their relationship to consumer culture shifted, depending on how one defines that cassette. They can credit Simon with introducing Western audiences to their sound through a bootleg tape and they can express frustration at the cultural cooptation of their music. For Munson "mixtape" simplified this loaded cultural debate about coopting music for commercial gain. The story has become *Graceland* lore and situates the discussion of musicians learning from and incorporating new musical styles based on hearing DIY cassette recordings.

For many artists, the influential mixtapes came from siblings and friends they trusted for their shared youth culture sensibility. The Mekons, a Welsh post-punk band, released an album in 1985 called *Fear and Whiskey*. Jon Langford, one of the founding members, had no use for country music. Discussing the link between punk rock and indie country, Langford said, "I thought country was rubbish, just right-wing crap that wouldn't possible be interesting. It was old man's music." Then he received a mixtape a friend made called *Honky Tonk Classics*. He became obsessed with the artists and sold the idea of the music to his bandmates because the subject matter of the blue-collar music was "so punk." The album they released, heavily influenced by a mixtape, became an early alt-country recording which solidified the band's sound moving forward.[39]

In an interview on the podcast *Song Craft*, Matthew Sweet talked about the impact mixtapes had on him as he developed his own musical taste and interest. While he argues mixtapes are a dead art form in the current world, he defined the importance mixtapes had in the 1990s as siblings and friends passed them along. He found hearing new music encouraged him to expand his horizons. He described his response to a tape he received from a friend whose older brother had originally put it together. "And it's got Toad the Wet Sprocket on it and you're like I think I'm supposed to like it. But I don't know if I do. [. . .] But I don't want to tell anybody because they'll think I'm dumb for not getting it."[40] For a young Sweet, the new music he heard from others gave him a broader musical education. As he grew into his musicianship, he became friends with Michael Stipe, lead singer of R.E.M. and received a mixtape from Peter Buck, the co-founder of the band with Stipe. He remembers the two bands Buck put on the tape for him: Graham Parsons and Sid Barrett. Two extremely influential musicians in the 1960s and 1970s, their style expanded Sweet's musical horizons.[41]

The appeal of the mixtape was often learning unfamiliar music from a friend with a wider or deeper knowledge about musical genres. Singer-songwriter Damien Jurado expresses this sentiment well in an interview on *Cassette: A Documentary Mixtape*.

You know if you said, "Do you remember the first time you heard the Violent Femmes?" Yeah, it was on a mixtape that a friend gave me. You know, do you remember the first time you heard the Butthole Surfers? Yeah, it was on a mix-tape a friend gave me. I can't tell you how many countless bands, Black Flag, Minor Threat, Fat Boys, Houdini, all on a mixtape, that was all on a mixtape.[42]

A Gen Xer who spent his teen years in Seattle, punk and new wave saturated Jurado's youth. In a short interview with the podcast *Snap Judgment* to share an "unlikely encounter with a stranger" which centers on mixtapes, Jurado narrates a story about a friend coming to school in 1986 with a cassette tape with Black Flag and other punk bands on it.[43] Intrigued by the music, he asked to meet the person who made the mixtape. "[T]his scrawny kid with like long blonde hair and a denim jacket" agreed to make Jurado and his friend a mix-tape a week for three to four months.[44] Over time Jurado lost track of "this scrawny kid" and eventually recorded over the mixtapes. In 1988 Jurado heard the song "Love Buzz" by Nirvana and decided to see the new band performing in Seattle. Jurado finishes his story, "I go to the show and out walks Nirvana, who opened up the show. And the lead singer, I remember just thinking to myself, he looks very—oh my God. That's the guy I was getting cassettes from. And that's how I met Kurt Cobain."[45] The story is fabulous because of the chance encounters and the different versions of a young Cobain before his fame. But it also highlights the key element of mixtape culture. It showcases how individuals shared music and increased their musical foundations. In a pre-streaming world, mixtapes produced unexpected relationships and diver-sified listening options which influenced a new generation of artists. Cobain's mixtape authority has become part of his legacy. A 2015 documentary about Cobain named *Montage of Heck* was based on a late 1980s mixtape he made. "What might just be the weirdest mixtape ever" included nature sounds, sound effects and songs from Black Sabbath, Cher, and Oscar the Grouch.[46]

Sub Pop Records, a label associated with punk and grunge music including Nirvana's albums, released Jurado's first four albums. The mixtapes Jurado discussed on *Cassette* could easily have been the mixtapes Cobain made for him. While Jurado does not sing like Minor Threat or any of the other bands he mentioned, he remains nostalgic for the style of music, the musicians, and the Seattle grunge community which brought him to his career. The Seattle grunge scene defined a music community in the 1990s which influenced the next generation of young musicians both through their sounds but also through sharing mixtapes and musical ideas.

Mixtapes in Song

In the mid-1990s, a handful of musicians used the word mixtape in their lyrics. For these songs, romantic appeals were not the theme. These were decidedly not nostalgic songs about mixtapes of the past. Instead, these young male musicians incorporated the mixtape in their daily lives, writing catchy songs to sell albums and get radio play. They told stories relevant to their lives and mixtapes were a part of their world.

The Beastie Boys, a punk rap group, had released their first album *Licensed to Ill* in 1986. By the early 1990s they were well-established bad boys of music. In a 2020 discussion with Rick Rubin, their first producer, Rubin reminisces about sitting in his college dorm and making mixtapes with members of the Beastie Boys as they worked on their first album.[47] This casual interaction reflected the friendship around shared musical identity. The band's lyrics run the gamut from goofy to profane but are rarely meaningful or romantic. The two songs which mention mixtapes, "Professor Booty" in 1992 and "Flute Loop" in 1994 reflect the party-rock attitude of guys who can rap and rhyme and want to have fun.[48] The lyrics, "Cause life ain't nothing but a good groove/A good mixtape to put you in the right mood"[49] and "A little wine with my dinner so I'm in my grape ape/I feel like a winner when I make a mix tape"[50] are not deep and profound. There is neither nostalgia nor romance in the songs. The lines rhyme and they fit into the rapping style of the band. The songs are not among the more well-known songs released by the band nor do they appear on well-known albums. The Beastie Boys lyrics are pure Gen X youth culture examples.

Another Gen Xer, Ben Folds wrote many of the songs for his group, Ben Folds Five. Their 1997 song, "Kate," is a more well-known song than the Beastie Boys inclusions, reaching 39 on the UK Charts in July of 1997. The song resonates with fans and Folds continues to play it as a solo artist. In this song, Kate is the epitome of the perfect person. The singer wants to be her "She plays wipeout on the drums," "She's everything I need, she's everything I'm not," and "Her mix tape's a masterpiece."[51] Like the Beastie Boys, this is not a song about romance. The humorous song uses fun pop culture references to describe the perfection of the song's titular character. These songs reflect an era when mixtapes were part of life. They were a normal object in these musicians' lives.

In 1996 the New Orleans band Better Than Ezra released the album *Friction, Baby*, a follow-up to their 1993 platinum album *Deluxe*. It included the song "Rewind" which is a direct reflection of love lost. This song shows a slight shift in how musicians incorporate the word mixtape moving forward. The mixtape is mentioned in every chorus of the song, underpinning the important role it plays in the story. It is a plot device to help tell a story. The song starts, "Cut a tape of my favorite songs/Said what I can't face to face."[52] This lyric begins the shift of musicians discussing mixtapes as a placeholder to express difficult emotions. However, the next lines clarify the tape did not work. Kevin Griffin sings, "Now there is nothing but a/Mix tape left behind" throughout the rest of the song.[53] This pop song moved the mixtape to the forefront of the story. A mixtape had become more than a background object; it became important enough to center a story.

The difference in tone between the Ben Folds song and the Better Than Ezra one reflects the shifting way creators used the mixtape through the 1990s. What started as a symbol of youth culture and music sharing began to reflect a larger emotional outpouring of personal connection, and particularly romantic interest. The same shift in music also appeared in the novels and films created during the 1990s. Some of the stories incorporated mixtapes to discuss a variety of music. By the end of the decade, they held a larger role in defining bonds between individuals, using an artifact as a representation of friendship or connection. The mixtape remained a tangible object, but its role increased beyond merely sharing music.

BOOKS

Stories written in the 1980s and 1990s discuss mixtapes from the vantage point of contemporary culture. These authors did not reminisce about a no-longer relevant analog object. Instead, they wrote about how music and cassettes connect characters and allow them to share emotion. They told stories about their worlds in which cassette tapes predominated. This generation of writers defined the newly emergent young adult fiction. Novels focused on the realistic lives of young people became a distinct genre for librarians and bookstores. With greater investment in the experiences of youth culture and music, *Less Than Zero, Morvern Callar,* and *Perks of Being a Wallflower* fit firmly into this young adult literature. *High Fidelity* is less a young adult novel with main characters in their late 1920s, but the centrality of its plot around cynical views of love defines it as a Gen X story. The authors of these books wrote about the mocking Gen X experience of the 1980s and 1990s and related to their characters through their emotional journeys. As music continually diversified and solidified identity and community building, literature reflected the role of music and friendship. Authors used music, the place of the cassette, and the mixtape to connect to their audience. Each of these novels reflects the relationship between the characters and the songs that united them.

Bret Easton Ellis was twenty-one when he published *Less Than Zero* in 1985. Ellis, labeled as a post-punk, brat pack writer, connected to readers who could relate to his elite urban experience.[54] Ellis named the book after an Elvis Costello song of the same name released on the 1977 album *My Name Is True.* This work is an example of anti-nostalgia as it underscores the sense of dislocation and disaffection of the extremely wealthy California youth at the time. Music is a touchstone for the characters. The story follows college student Clay, home for winter break, who parties, does drugs, and picks up individuals for one-night stands. Ellis is not making an appeal to the idealization of this time and place. He does not suggest anyone would desire to return there. He does not use music as a draw to the past. Instead, music represents a pervasive aspect of the world his characters inhabit. Music and mixtapes were a part of their daily lived experience, not something to highlight or dissect. They interacted with mixtapes passively. Ellis did not need to make the cassette tapes a conscious focus of the story.

Clay's crowd purchased the best portable technology in the late 1980s; they listened to music on cassette. Throughout the novel, Clay and his friends discuss contemporary groups like U2, Joan Jett, and the Human League. They attend multiple concerts, remaining unimpressed and uninvested in most of their experiences. Midway through the book Clay states,

> We get into Blair's car and she puts in a tape that she made the other night and Bananarama starts to sing and Trent asks her where the Beach-mix tape is and Blair tells him that she burned it because she heard it too many times. For some reason I believe this and unroll the window and we drive to After Hours.[55]

For these dislikeable, disenfranchised, exceedingly wealthy characters, physical items are worthless, items to trash or burn when they become boring. Mixtapes, like their lives, are inherently meaningless and expendable.

As Clay moves through the novel, he remains unimpressed with his life and is seemingly unable to respond genuinely to any of the unfolding events. While Clay has not achieved any sense of catharsis throughout the story, he sits by the pool watching his younger sisters play.

> I watch them and listen to the tape that's playing on the Walkman I'm wearing. The Go-Go's are singing, *"I wanna be worlds away/I know things will be okay when I get worlds away."* Whoever made the tape then let the record skip and I close my eyes and hear them start to sing "Vacation" and when I open my eyes, my sisters are floating face down in the pool, wondering who can look drowned the longest.[56]

As the reader, the lines from the Go-Gos represent Clay's entire social experience in the novel and express the emotional malaise he cannot state. Seemingly, things were better when he was not in Los Angeles. Yet this is not the point of the novel and not a topic Ellis dwells on. Instead, Ellis, as other authors and musicians do, allow the lyrics to speak on behalf of the character. Without engaging in self-reflection, they express the emotional toil Clay feels. For Ellis' characters, music is an emotive outlet. The tapes allow characters to express emotion without words. Mixtapes give authors the ability to string together disparate ideas and emotions. By pulling together songs from different artists and eras, cassette compilations allow Ellis to fortify his character's emotionality.

In *Less Than Zero* music is ubiquitous but impersonal. Clay seems unaware of who had made the tape to which he listens. There is not a personal connective story between the mixtape giver and receiver. Music and mixtapes are omnipresent in the world of 1980s upper-class Los Angeles. Instead, "Whoever made the tape," implies the irrelevance of a personal relationship.[57] While music pervades the novel, the self-aware interaction with the music or the material culture of the cassette as a sign of sentimentality does not exist. These rich elite youth have no appreciation for the tangible.

Two years later the film, staring Andrew McCarthy and Robert Downey Jr., took Ellis' edgy, dark story and brightened it for Hollywood audiences. While Rick Rubin, as music supervisor, created a star-studded soundtrack, the story no longer incorporated music as a discussion between characters. Anthropologist Kwame Harrison, reflecting on his outsized knowledge of hip hop as a rural high school student in the 1980s, described introducing a fellow basketball player to new hip hop songs released on the *Less Than Zero* soundtrack. "For our Saturday night project of filling a ninety-minute blank cassette with music, both songs ['Going back to Cali'" by LL Cool J and 'Bring the Noise' by Public Enemy] were 'must haves.'"[58] Harrison's reminiscence of mixtape creation incorporating newly released hip hop on a soundtrack about upper-class urban angst nicely blends the multiple stories of mixtapes. While Harrison's story was not intended as nostalgic, it combines an awareness of pop culture, musical genre knowledge, and technostalgia. As removed from nostalgia as the original novel was, Ellis' focus on music has achieved a nostalgic reflective quality among recent journalists. Websites have created playlists of the songs mentioned and discussed in Ellis' various novels. *NME,* a British music journalism magazine, interviewed Ellis in 2010 to discuss the role of music in his works. When asked why he named the book after an Elvis Costello song he replied,

> Who knows? I was working on this project starting when I was 16 and it was the "Less Than Zero" project. I was like most white, upper-class educated boys: I was obsessed with Elvis Costello. That was his main audience in the United States. That title seemed very evocative to me.[59]

Ellis' affinity for music in his works reflects an appreciation for the interplay between the written word and the song. However, unlike authors ten years later, Ellis did not use the cassette as a cultural point of reference.

Instead, he included them in his first novel because they were a pervasive, assumed part of elite, West Coast, youth culture.

Published nearly ten years after *Less Than Zero*, Scottish novelist Alan Warner's debut novel *Morvern Callar* won the Somerset Maugham award in 1996. Like *Less Than Zero*, this story reflects a nihilism and antipathy toward society. Music, for Morven, like it had been for Clay, is a balm and an escape. It is a way for the characters to express emotion without having to display or discuss it. The story revolves around protagonist Morvern who wakes up at Christmastime to discover the body of her boyfriend who had committed suicide. Leaving the body on the floor, she opens the presents he gave her to find "a dear-looking Walkman with batteries in."[60] This personal stereo and the accompanying cassette tapes surround the novel as Morvern listens to music while she navigates her life. Like *Less Than Zero*, personal stereos, cassette tapes, and mixtapes were standard. *Morvern Callar* represents an individual whose music reflects her disconnection from daily life.

Warner does not center the mixtape as a thematic organizing principle. Yet, he uses listening to music via headphones as Morvern's coping mechanism to separate herself from reality. Cassettes are typical technology, but Warner accentuates the mixtape as a critical component of the novel. The first time Morvern listens to her Walkman she states,

> I put the Walkman in the pocket and the plugs in my ears after fitting the long earrings on. I took some cassettes: new ambient, queer jazzish, darkside hard-core, and that C60 I'd made with Pablo Casals doing Nana on his cello again and again.[61]

Throughout the story, she mentions the music she hears which is often at odds with her physical reality. Analyzing the role of gender and authorship in *Morvern Callar*, Rachel Carroll highlights the privatization of Morvern's experience because she lives through her personal stereo. With a plot centered on the continual cover-up of her boyfriend's suicide and her exploitation of his work, the internal, personal perspective of the story is logical. Writing about the intrapersonal connection to personal stereos, Michael Bull stated, Walkmans create "an alternative soundscape which is more immediate and subject to greater control."[62] Morvern fits decisively into Bull's argument that Walkmans allow individuals to remove themselves from their own experiences and become passive observers in their own lives. Warner created a protagonist who mimics the sociological perspective outlined by Bull. When Morvern dismembers her boyfriend so she can get rid of his remains she had "recorded a suitable compilation," which included jazz pieces by Miles Davis.[63] The last three songs on the tape, "Taboo" and "Challenge to Manhood" by avant-garde jazz drummer

Ronald Shannon Jackson, and "Assassin" by Bill Laswell are mentioned in the compilation listing but not discussed. As with the lyrics Clay recounted in *Less Than Zero*, the titles of the songs intersect with the action Morvern is taking as she cuts up a body. She does not self-consciously discuss why or how she chose the songs, but Warner acknowledges her actions subtly. The music Morvern listens to on her compilation tapes creates a customized narrative for Warner's storyline.

In Carroll's analysis of *Morvern Callar*, she debates the musical choices Warner included, suggesting, "The tracks cited in Morvern's mixtapes are not popular generational standards; their very obscurity—for an uninitiated readership—confounds easy intertextual deductions. If they do suggest a community it is the select or exclusive kind of the connoisseur or collector."[64] Carroll asserts the music was likely selected for the mixtapes by her dead boyfriend, because they fit, as she sees it, more neatly into the pattern of "obsessive males, whose passion for collecting is often a substitute for 'real' social relationships, and who exhibit a 'train spotting' mentality towards music."[65] Morvern makes the compilation tapes, but it is unclear if she uses music previously owned by her boyfriend. She listens to obscure avant-garde jazz; Can, a West German Krautrock band; and occasional contemporary groups like This Mortal Coil and the Cocteau Twins. They function as an emotional and idiomatic soundtrack for Morvern's grief and guilt. When she decides to spend the weekend camping, she makes a tape with songs like "Up a Lazy River" by the Ink Spots and "Blue Bell Knoll" by The Cocteau Twins.[66] For this tape, Warner has used the song's titles to symbolize nature; the titles are the relevant factor for the story.

Like *Less Than Zero*, *Morvern Callar* became a feature film. Comparisons of the film and the novel highlighted the difference in the music selected. A *Guardian* article analyzing the best mixtapes in fiction discussed *Morvern Callar* stating,

> The official soundtrack to Lynne Ramsay's film adaptation consists of tracks from the mix tape—but completists, frustrated at the anomalies between the songs in the book and those in the film, have compiled Spotify playlists more faithful to the original novel.[67]

While many of the bands and songs are the same, there are notable exceptions. An article from 2014, nearly twenty years after the publication of the book and a dozen years after the release of the film, remained wedded to perfecting the track listing. In the film, the mixtape as the underlying focus of the story is significantly downplayed. During the first section of the film, Morvern opens a mixtape and wears headphones, lost in music. However, there is little discussion of the tapes or the role they play in distancing her from her lived experience. The audience senses the necessity of the music because it drowns out the background noise while she grieves and assesses her shifting world. Music is not fundamentally tied to songs chosen by her dead partner or for a particular adventure and placed on a mixtape. Nonetheless music remains a central theme in the movie.

Published one year before *Morvern Callar*, written with a vastly different tone, *High Fidelity* has become an ur-text in the pop culture world of mixtapes. Between the British novel and American film version starring John Cusack, *High Fidelity* and the description of how to make a perfect compilation tape has become canon. The story revolves around Rob Fleming, a record shop owner whose girlfriend has left him. Rob, trying to understand his failed relationship, contacts his former girlfriends and reexamines their relationships. Much of the story takes place in Rob's record store where he discusses music, mixtapes, and top-five lists with his coworkers. Rob's explanation of why a mixtape is a key to a relationship-has been quoted and modeled in a wide variety of publications since its original release. Geoffrey Sirc, writing about mixtapes as a functional model for teaching composition, described the novel as, "one of the most oft-quoted mix tape directives."[68] As narrator, Rob speaks to the reader and lets them know why the mixtape is key to his relationships,

> I said if she came next week I'd have a tape for her, and she looked really pleased.
>
> I spent hours putting that cassette together. To me, making a tape is like writing a letter—there's a lot of erasing and rethinking and starting again, and I wanted it to be a good one, because . . . to be honest, because I hadn't met anyone as promising as Laura since I'd started the DJ-ing, and meeting promising women was partly what the DJ-ing was supposed to be about. A good compilation tape, like breaking up, is hard to do.[69]

In this description, Rob stresses the necessity of crafting the perfect compilation tape for the moment; it requires thought and time. Rob represents an archetypical Gen X male who obsesses over music, wants connection, but does not always know how to express himself or understand his interactions with women. According to Hornby, these tapes

> Well, they are a kind of means of seduction. [. . .] he offers to make [Laura] a compilation tape of the music that she's been listening to and dancing to in this club. And so that becomes a very important thing, that he has introduced her to all sorts of things. And then there's an echo of that later on, where he meets somebody else and he finds himself making a tape for her, too, and Laura sees him and knows exactly what he's doing.[70]

For Hornby, the compilation tape in *High Fidelity* is a courtship token. It allows Rob to express himself through his musical choices and the order of the songs on the tape. However, Rob's emotional immaturity places him in difficult positions because he does not navigate real life as easily as he does music. When Laura catches Rob making a new tape he says, "I can't say it without blushing and staring intently at the cassette deck, and I know she doesn't really believe me. She of all people knows what compilation tapes represent."[71] Hornby clarifies that for a character like Rob, introducing a woman to music via a mixtape is a way of marking her and "turn[ing] the other person into a female version of yourself."[72] As suggested by Carroll in her analysis of *Morvern Callar*, the obsessive male music fan uses his knowledge as a substitute for genuine connections. Rob wholeheartedly represents this obsessive individual. This idea of wooing a new romantic partner, whether for selfish purposes as Hornby seems to suggest, becomes a predominant theme in much of the literature revolving around mixtapes.

High Fidelity is the story of cynical romance and an analysis of an obsessive music fan. As Hornby says, Rob "has very strict rules about compilation types, about what kind of music can go next to what kind of music. And he can't have black music and white music together, and you can't have fast stuff and slow stuff together; he has to build all these little bridges between tracks. So he's very finicky about the compilation tapes."[73] In an analysis of retromania and record collecting, Simon Reynolds highlights Hornby's male protagonists as men who find external obsessions as a safe outlet for their passions. They become emotionally attached to objects and collections to avoid the "too-real stuff."[74] This is a shift since the character of Clay ten years earlier in *Less Than Zero*. He was a character who found no attachment to objects. Through characters like Rob, "there's a critique—a partial self-critique on the part of the author—of masculinity in retreat from the mess and risks of adulthood into a more orderly world of obsessive fandom."[75] In this generation of novels, the role of nostalgia is not yet the preeminent tie to the music. Instead, there is a desire and a need to collect and control and understand music. Making a mixtape is in part about getting the girl. But it is equally about showcasing knowledge and power through collection.

Since the release of the book in 1995 and then the film in 2000, *High Fidelity* has become a central piece recognized by music fans and mixtape fans alike. In 2020 a new made-for-TV, episodic version of *High Fidelity* appeared for one season in which the main character was played by Zoë Kravitz. The new version, the twenty-fifth anniversary of the novel, and the twentieth anniversary of the film sparked a renewed interest in the text. What had been a normal part of daily life in the 1990s has taken on new meaning and become a nostalgic look at how people consumed and shared music in the past. Podcasts have revisited the original film to analyze how well it translates in the current day and the discussion continues to revolve around making mixtapes and the collector personality. In the podcast *Heat Rocks*, the two hosts Morgan Rhods and Oliver Wang interviewed film producer Drea Clark. They agreed Hornby's character influenced how they each made mixtapes and how they identify kinship by finding things they like in common.[76] While the hosts discuss consuming music differently in the past twenty years because of streaming, they also agree curating music has remained a fundamental aspect of music fandom and a way to share oneself. The legacy of *High Fidelity* and Rob's instructional narrative about music continues to play a role in current perspectives on the mixtape. However, unlike Rob, not all stories about music and mixtapes highlight social interaction.

Another story in which music is foundational and mixtapes permeate the plot is *Perks of Being a Wallflower*, but these relationships are not romantic. Published in 1999, Stephen Chbosky uses letters to tell the story of a suburban Pittsburgh high school student in 1991. Charlie, a freshman, is taken under the wings of two high school seniors, Patrick and Sam, who help him navigate school, dating, love, and life. As the story evolves, Charlie makes Patrick a mixtape as part of a secret Santa gift exchange. This epistolary novel shifts its tone relative to the mixtape. It bridges the gap to the newer generation of stories in which mixtapes are no longer background. They have become a representation through artifacts and music of emotion and connection. In 1991 a mixtape fit into the daily life of high school and therefore would not have been an unusual present, but here the tape does represent a coherent plot point in which Charlie employs a tangible artifact in an attempt to better connect to his peers. The songs chosen reflect Charlie's desire to share himself, because of his inability to speak directly.

Early in the novel, Charlie's sister receives a mixtape called "Autumn Leaves" from her boyfriend. Charlie describes the event saying, "he is always making mix tapes for my sister with very specific themes. [. . .] He included many songs by the Smiths. He even hand-colored the cover."[77] What Charlie views as a sweet caring gesture, his sister dismisses, giving the tape to Charlie. When this boy hits his sister Charlie is shocked because, "It was not like him at all to hit anybody. He was the boy that made mix tapes with themes and hand-colored covers."[78] This early interaction with mixtapes introduces a central theme with Charlie trying to understand personal relationships. He sees the care and attention taken with the mixtape as valuable and a sign of caring: a boy who made mixtapes would not hit someone. However, the tape is not cherished by his sister and the boyfriend is not in fact caring.

Three months later Charlie makes his own mixtape, which integrates aspects of the tape dismissed by his sister. He names the tape "One Winter," and includes "Asleep" by the Smiths, the song on the Autumn Leaves mixtape he had most appreciated. In replicating the ideas of the mixtape, Charlie attempts to create the thoughtful side of his sister's boyfriend, despite his later actions. Unlike the boyfriend, Charlie considers Patrick's interests and on side A includes, "a lot of songs by the Village People and Blondie because Patrick likes that type of music a lot."[79] Charlie's decision-making reflects common stories of how people choose songs for mixtapes; he balances Patrick's interests and his own. The tape's B-side includes "A Whiter Shade of Pale" by Procol Harum, "Gypsy" by Suzanne Vega and "Blackbird" by the Beatles.[80] It is a combination of current songs in 1991 and classics; music that reflects the winter theme and Charlie's personality. As the most self-reflective young character to think about a mixtape in the novels of the 1980s and 1990s, compared to Clay or Morvern, Charlie ponders the larger role of this mixtape and of the music he includes. He states,

> I spent all night working on it, and I hope Patrick likes it as much as I do. [. . .] I had an amazing feeling when I finally held the tape in my hand. I just thought to myself that in the palm of my hand, there was this one tape that had all of these memories and feelings and great joy and sadness. Right there in the palm of my hand. And I thought about how many people have loved those songs. And how many people enjoyed good times with those songs. And how much those songs really mean.[81]

Charlie uses the mixtape to connect individually to Patrick. But he also sees his link to the larger landscape of music fans. Charlie is overjoyed when Patrick likes the tape writing, "I think he knows that I'm his Secret Santa, though, because I think he knows that only I would do a tape like that."[82] Charlie is an introspective, emotional character and his willingness to pour his heart out in a personal gift like a mixtape showcases his personality and distinguishes him from his friends. Later, when Patrick is struggling with his own relationship Charlie notices Patrick is playing the Secret Santa mix tape.[83] A quick mention, it reinforces Patrick appreciated the tape in the way Charlie had hoped.

Since its publication, *Perks of Being a Wallflower* has become a well-regarded novel, loved by teens, and often read in high school classrooms. A dozen years after its initial release, Chbosky wrote and directed the screenplay. The popular film pushed the book's sales into the *New York Times* bestseller list. A key plot point in the novel revolves around hearing the song "Landslide" by Fleetwood Mac while Patrick speeds through a tunnel and across a bridge with his stepsister Sam standing and screaming. That song is the penultimate song Charlie includes on his holiday mixtape for Patrick. In the movie, the song playing is "Heroes" by David Bowie. For fans of the film and Bowie, this scene is paramount. The song matters despite Chbosky's different choice in the book. Both released in the mid-1970s, both having long-lasting appeal, the exact song is less important than the emotional, nostalgic feeling elucidated by the group sense of hearing and responding to something new, deep, and powerful. Charlie's self-reflective suburban experience is reflected in the musical choices Chbosky incorporated.

These books, turned films, exhibit the first generation of mixtape novelization. For each of them a mixtape was part of the contemporary lived reality. There was not a nostalgic goal in using this artifact of the recent past as a mnemonic to coalesce a storyline around friendship or romance. It remains one plot point to tie these, otherwise diverse, books together. For these novels, mixtapes were background normalness in an era of cassette tapes, personal stereos, and analog music. In her analysis of *The Perks of Being a Wallflower*, Gen Y writer Lenora Epstein writes, "Music and mixtapes are particularly essential to the plot, along with TV and movies, and these references were all dated by the time Millennials were reading."[84] She continued, "What stays with me now [is. . .] that his book bridged a generational gap, and that even though Charlie essentially went to Gen X High, we Gen Yers were able to innately relate."[85] For the young people who continued to read these stories and watch these films after their original publication, the mixtape began to symbolize an idea and a feeling. The reference, although defined by Gen X cultural references, started to shift into something new which millennials could also relate to and adapt. They unselfconsciously discussed a part of mainstream culture which was neither nostalgic nor unique. But these stories crafted an ideology of mixtapes which has not disappeared since. The role of the mixtape for the generation of creators who created, gifted, received, and took the mixtape for granted helps situate the place of mixtape nostalgia in the current era.

NOTES

1. Jude Rogers, "Total Rewind: 10 Key Moments in the Life of the Cassette," *The Observer*, August 30, 2013. https://www.theguardian.com/music/2013/aug/30/cassette-store-day-music-tapes

2. John Z. Komurki and Luca Bendandi, *Cassette Cultures: Past and Present of a Musical Icon*, English Edition 2019 Benteli ed. (Switzerland: Deutsche Nationalbibliothek; Braun Publishing AG, 2019), 51.

3. Damon Krukowski, *Ways of Hearing* (Cambridge: MIT Press, 2019), 92.

4. "Remember the Maxell 'Blown-Away Guy?'" Best Classic Brands website. https://bestclassicbands.com/maxell-blown-away-guy-2-3-18/ (Accessed September 11, 2020).

5. Ben Ratliff, "The Language I Learned from Cassettes," *NPR* (2019), https://www.npr.org/2019/07/24/744466017/the-language-i-learned-from-cassettes.

6. Jay Sweet, *Citizen Curious* 7, interview by Ryan Lee, 2020. https://citizen-curious.simplecast.com/episodes/episode-6-jay-sweet-part-1 (Accessed March 20, 2020).

7. Angus Cargill, "Compilation Tape Classics! Or So I Thought: Ten Songs Used on More Than One Occasion," in *Hang the DJ: An Alternative Book of Music Lists* (New York: Soft Skull Press, 2009), 187.

8. Luc Sante, "Disco Dreams," *New York Review* (2004). https://www.nybooks.com/articles/2004/05/13/disco-dreams/.

9. Chuck Klosterman, *Sex, Drugs, and Cocoa Puffs: A Low Culture Manifesto* (New York: Scribner, 2004), Chapter 11, Being Zack Morris 1:35.

10. Thurston Moore, 2009 as quoted in Komurki and Bendandi, 142.

11. Ibid., 131.

12. Jennifer Maerz, "Love's Mixtapes Lost: The High School Cassettes We Can't Throw Away," *KQED Arts* (August 17, 2015) http://ww2.kqed.org/arts/2015/08/17/loves-mixtapes-lost-the-high-school-cassettes-we-cant-throw-away/.

13. Taylor, "Cassette: A Documentary Mixtape" Documentary (Gravitas Ventures, 2018). DVD 88 mins.

14. Stuart Heritage, "Tapes Were Terrible So What's Behind the Great Cassette Tape Revival?", Entertainment, *Independent.ie* (January 2, 2020), https://www.independent.ie/entertainment/music/tapes-were-terrible-so-whats-behind-the-great-cassette-tape-revival-38827970.html (Accessed June 1, 2021).

15. Noz, "A (Not at All Definitive) History of Hip Hop Mixtapes," *Red Bull Music Academy* (June 12, 2013), https://daily.redbullmusicacademy.com/2013/06/history-of-mixtapes-feature (Accessed March 16, 2021).

16. Mr. Davey D., *Breakdown* FM, podcast audio, Interview with Justo Faison: The History of Mixtapes, 2005, https://soundcloud.com/mrdaveyd/breakdown-fm-intv-w-justo (Accessed May 12, 2021).

17. James Braxton Peterson, *Hip Hop Headphones: A Scholar's Critical Playlist* (New York: Bloomsbury Academic, 2016), http://search.ebscohost.com/login.aspx?direct=true&AuthType=sso&db=nlebk&AN=1331575&site=eds-live&scope=site&custid=s7614884&ebv=EB&ppid=pp_1. 5.

18. Mr. Davey D.

19. Dan Rys, "Mixtapes & Money: Inside the Mainstreaming of Hip-Hop's Shadow Economy," *Billboard* (January 26, 2017), https://www.billboard.com/articles/columns/hip-hop/7669109/mixtapes-money-hip-hop-shadow-economy-mainstream (Accessed March 19, 2021).

20. Alex Sayf Cummings, *Democracy of Sound: Music Piracy and the Remaking of American Copyright in the Twentieth Century* (New York: Oxford University Press, 2013), 169.

21. Ibid., 151–52.

22. Jack Denton, "A Generation of Hip-Hop Was Given Way for Free. Can It Be Archived?," *Pacific Standard* (June 25, 2019) https://psmag.com/social-justice/a-generation-of-hip-hop-was-given-away-for-free-can-it-be-archived (Accessed July 8, 2020).

23. Mr. Davey D.

24. Chris Harris, "Mixtape Awards to Honor P. Diddy as Top Executive," *MTV* (March 8, 2005), http://www.mtv.com/news/1497879/mixtape-awards-to-honor-p-diddy-as-top-executive/ (Accessed May 12, 2021).

25. "Justo Faison, Founder of Annual Mixtape Awards, Killed in Car Crash," *MTV* (May 16, 2005), http://www.mtv.com/news/1502356/justo-faison-founder-of-annual -mixtape-awards-killed-in-car-crash/ (Accessed May 12, 2021).

26. "7th Annual Justo's Mixtape Awards," *Billboard* (2002), https://www.billboar d.com/articles/news/73164/7th-annual-justos-mixtape-awards (Accessed May 12, 2021).

27. Cummings, 173.

28. DJ EFN, "EFN Remembers Mixtapes #1 Fan: Justo Faison," https://mixtape museum.org/2019/03/06/efm-remembers-mixtapes-1-fan-justo-faison/ (Accessed May 12, 2021).

29. DJ Semtex, "Street Dreams: How Hip-Hop Mixtapes Changed the Game," *Hip-Hop Raised Me* (Medium: Thames & Hudson, 2016), https://medium.com /cuepoint/street-dreams-how-hip-hop-mixtapes-changed-the-game-40af79e8d953 (Accessed July 15, 2020); Michael Kawaida, "Mixtapes: A Brief History of Hip-Hop's Ever Evolving Tool," *Hot New Hip Hop* (February 25, 2020), https://www .hotnewhiphop.com/mixtapes-a-brief-history-of-hip-hops-ever-evolving-tool-news. 103882.html (Accessed July 15, 2020); *The Day the Mixtape Died: DJ Drama*, pod-cast audio, Louder Than a Riot, 1 hr 5 mins 2020, https://www.npr.org/2020/10/27 /928307301/the-day-the-mixtape-died-dj-drama (Accessed October 29, 2020).

30. Noz.

31. *The History and Legality of Mix Tapes*, podcast audio, New & Notes, 2007, https://www.npr.org/2007/06/15/11114754/the-history-and-legality-of-mix-tapes (Accessed March 16, 2021).

32. Johnson's collection numbers in the thousands, with 7,500 cassette mixtapes and 10,000 CD mixtapes. Eric Johnson, interview by Mixtape Museum, 2017, website.

33. Kawaida. Semtex.

34. *The Day the Mixtape Died: DJ Drama.*

35. Anthony Kwame Harrison, *Hip Hop Underground: The Integrity and Ethics of Racial Identification* (Philadelphia: Temple University Press, 2009), 29.

36. The political controversy that surrounded this album because of South African embargoes and cultural cooptation are relevant but does not change the use of the mixtape as a form of inspiration for a musician. Stephen Holden, "Paul Simon Brings Home Music of Black South Africa," *The New York Times*, August 24, 1986.

37. Jordan Runtagh, "Paul Simon's 'Graceland': 10 Things You Didn't Know," *Rolling Stone* (August 25, 2016), https://www.rollingstone.com/music/music-feat ures/paul-simons-graceland-10-things-you-didnt-know-105220/.

38. Ben Munson, "Paul Simon: Graceland," in *Please, Vinyl Me*, ed. Emma Jacobs (New York: Abrams, 2016), 238.

39. Kyle Ryan, "Any Kind of Music but Country: A Decade of Indie Country, Punk Rock, and the Struggle for Country's Soul," in *Country Music Reader*, ed. Travis D. Stimeline (Oxford: Oxford University Press, 2014), 308–09.

40. Scott B. Bomar and Paul Ducan, *Matthew Sweet: Sick of Myself*, podcast audio, Songcraft: Spotlight on Songwriters, 59 mins 2019, https://www.songcrafts-how.com/ (Accessed July 23, 2020).

41. Ibid.

42. Taylor.

43. Damien Jurado, interview by Julia Dewitt, *Snap Judgement.* January 31, 2014, audio.

44. Ibid.

45. Ibid.

46. Kevin McFarland, "What's on Kurt Cobain's Lost 'Montage of Heck' Mixtape," *Wired* (May 1, 2015), https://www.wired.com/2015/05/kurt-cobain-mon tage-of-heck/ (Accessed September 22, 2020).

47. Rick Rubin and Malcolm Gladwell, *Beastie Boys and Spike Jonze*, podcast audio, Broken Record, 1hr 7 mins, 2020, https://brokenrecordpodcast.com/#/episode -51-beastie-boys-and-spike-jonze/ (Accessed June 23, 2020).

48. "Professor Booty," Beastie Boys, on *Check Your Head*, Capitol Records, 1992. And "Flute Loop," Beastie Boys, on *Ill Communication*, Capitol Records, 1994.

49. "Professor Booty," Beastie Boys.

50. "Flute Loop," Beastie Boys.

51. "Kate," Ben Folds Five on *Whatever and Ever, Amen,* 550 Music, 1997.

52. "Rewind," Better Than Ezra on *Friction, Baby*, Electra, 1996.

53. "Rewind," Better Than Ezra.

54. Generation X Goes Global: Tales of Accelerated Cultures Christine Henseler in Christine Henseler, ed. *Generation X Goes Global: Mapping a Youth Culture in Motion* (New York: Taylor & Francis, 2012), 9.

55. Bret Easton Ellis, *Less Than Zero* (United States: Vintage Contemporaries, 2010), 118.

56. Ibid., 198.

57. Ibid.

58. Harrison, 55–56.

59. NME, "Bret Easton Ellis—Pieces of Me" (August 5, 2010) https://www.nme .com/blogs/nme-blogs/bret-easton-ellis-pieces-of-me-773471#Go1JwfJBsOGVlIDK .99 (Accessed July 9, 2020).

60. Alan Warner, *Morvern Callar* (New York: Random House, 1997), 3.

61. "From "Morvern Callar," *Grand Street* 57, no. Summer (1996), https://www .jstor.org/stable/25008049.

62. Michael Bull, *Sounding out the City: Personal Stereos and the Management of Everyday Life* (Oxford/New York: Berg Publishing, 2000), 78–79.

63. Warner, *Morvern Callar*, 85.

64. Rachel Carroll, "'[S]He Loved Him Madly': Music, Mixtapes and Gendered Authorship in Alan Warner's Morvern Callar," in *Litpop: Writing and Popular Music*, ed. Rachel Carroll, et al. (New York: Taylor & Francis, 2016), 193.

65. "Beyond the "high fidelity" Stereotype: Defining the (Contemporary) Record Collector *Popular Music* 2004 quoted in Carroll, 194.

66. Warner, *Morvern Callar*, 92.

67. Mark Hooper, "The Best Mixtapes in Fiction," *The Guardian*, September 5, 2014.

68. Geoffrey Sirc, "Serial Composition," in *Rhetorics and Technologies: New Directions in Writing and Communication*, ed. Stuart A. Selber, Studies in Rhetoric/Communication (Columbia: University of South Carolina Press, 2010), 66.

69. Nick Hornby, *High Fidelity* (New York: The Berkley Publishing Group, 1995), 88–89.

70. Nick Hornby, "Writer Nick Hornby on 'High Fidelity' and Pop Culture Obsession." By Terri Gross. *Fresh Air* (1995).

71. *High Fidelity*, 314.

72. "Writer Nick Hornby on 'High Fidelity' and Pop Culture Obsession."

73. Ibid.

74. Simon Reynolds, *Retromania: Pop Culture's Addiction to Its Own Past* (New York: Faber and Faber, Inc, 2011), 100.

75. Ibid.

76. Morgan Rhods and Oliver Wang, *Heat Rocks*, podcast audio, Music and Popcorn #5: Drea Clark on the "High Fidelity" soundtrack (2000), 53 mins, (Accessed March 5, 2020.)

77. Stephen Chbosky, *Perks of Being a Wallflower* (New York: Gallery Books, 1999), 10.

78. Ibid., 11.

79. Ibid., 61.

80. Ibid., 62.

81. Ibid.

82. Ibid., 63.

83. Ibid., 156.

84. Eve Epstein and Lenora Epstein, *X vs. Y: A Culture War, a Love Story* (New York: Abrams Books, 2014), 183.

85. Ibid., 185.

Chapter 4

Analog Nostalgia

NOSTALGIA AND COLLECTIVE MEMORY

To see mixtapes as a point of "nostalgia," it is worth analyzing the academic meaning of the term. The memoir by Rob Sheffield and edited stories by Jason Bittner and Thurston Moore solidified this nostalgic, suburban, male, Gen X perspective of the mixtape and shaped how the concept would come to be viewed over the next decade. Nostalgia became the predominant perspective of the mixtape in the early twenty-first century. Physicians had coined the term "nostalgia" in the seventeenth century as an affliction akin to homesickness among military men. "*Nostos*" meaning return home, and "*algia*" meaning longing, allowed for a scientific way to think about desire to return to an unrealizable place. Alain Corbin has argued that village bells in nineteenth-century France invoked strong auditory nostalgic memories for village life.[1] He suggested the sound of the bells represented an idea of home, which people longed for. Over time, the definition changed from longing for a different location to a longing across time, searching "for unrealized possibilities, unpredictable turns and crossroads."[2] In the nineteenth century, Charles Baudelaire and Friedrich Nietzsche both grappled with happiness and modernity which revealed nostalgic concerns.[3] Nostalgia could not have existed in a pre-modern era; the change of pace and the unpredictability of the present and the future created a longing for the simpler past. In the modernizing nineteenth century, Europeans began to feel a collective longing for a simpler, bygone era.[4] Many individuals increasingly had the freedom of time to sit and analyze their feelings and sense of dislocation from lived reality. In addition, individuals began to view themselves subjectively as part of history: as those whose personal views and experiences deserved remembrance.[5] For

Baudelaire and Nietzsche, nostalgia implied estrangement from the concerns of modernity and the reality of the present. It became possible, based on their analyses, to become nostalgic for tradition and for an unattainable idea. For Nietzsche, the concern rested in the "unrepeatability of experience."[6] Nostalgia overlaps with melancholy and "a feeling of disconnection with the past, a growing dread of the future, and uncertainty over the capacity to act or reform."[7] This argument about the sociocultural concerns about "now" and the desire to move back to a cherished past remains prescient in contemporary culture. In Walter Benjamin's early twentieth-century study of media, modernity revolved around collecting memorabilia as an attempt to create a future nostalgia.[8] He began to think about how mechanical reproduction impacted meanings, associations, and contradictions of artistic and political statements.[9] Benjamin's analysis of nostalgia, the use of the term and its relation to music and specifically artifacts which store music, start to coalesce.

In the twenty-first century discussions about nostalgia have expanded and become a concept frequently cited not only in academia but also in pop culture. Removed from academic analysis, it indicates an audience's desire to engage with post–World War II products. Nostalgia has become privatized; rather than a collective longing for "home," individuals began to long for their own childhoods.[10] In interviews, articles, and mainstream media, authors use nostalgia as an appeal to the past. Paul Grainge states, "In the last three decades of the twentieth century, nostalgia was commodified and aestheticized in American culture as perhaps never before."[11] As the concept of nostalgia moved out of the academy and into the mainstream, consumer experience around nostalgia is mediated by corporate commodification. Collectively, the public can become nostalgic for an undefinable past in eras of uncertainty and social unease. In her book *The Future of Nostalgia*, Svetlana Boym argues that "restorative nostalgia" creates a collective mythmaking in which cultural groups create an idealized past to which individuals hope to return.

While different senses can trigger nostalgia, auditory and visual are key for this study; mixtapes engage both senses independently. Nostalgia allows individuals to sanitize the past and see it in an idealized way, removed from the possible negative realities. It can function as an escape and music helps to engage in nostalgic idealization. Neuroscience has established that music generates emotional arousal which becomes part of encoded memory. When individuals hear music, they construct memories which cognitively connect them to the past. In his essay "Recorded Music and Practices of Remembering," Ben Anderson shows how music allows for "intentional remembering."[12] Hearing a song can transport an individual to the time and place in which they first heard specific music. Listening to familiar songs helps people remember the moments and emotions from the past, often editing out the negative aspects. When people choose to listen to specific songs, they are using music to self-consciously create a mood. Auditory nostalgia allows an individual to remember not only a moment in the past, but the feeling imbued in that memory. Music becomes an expression of nostalgia and the mixtape becomes a physical artifact to allow for the restorative nostalgia of an idealized past. Through the collection and curation of the cultural artifact those songs become auditory memories. Hearing familiar music allows people to engage the emotions from previous listening experiences. This reflective desire to remember the past highlights a key facet of the mixtape.[13]

UNDERSTANDING EMOTIONALITY AND MUSIC

As the understanding of nostalgia and collective memory highlight, emotion plays a central role in how people relate to the past. As George Simmel wrote in 1882 "music is emotionally charged speech."[14] Neuro-cognitive studies have demonstrated that individuals relate specific music to concrete emotions and those emotional memories are often associated with particular individuals. In her study on the Lou Reed mixtape recently discovered in the Andy Warhol archives, Judith Peraino questions, "If the mixtape—this specific one, and countless others—materializes an affective relationship between audio fidelity and love (or other complex emotions), then we might also ask, what is the relationship of the mixtape to subjectivity and embodiment?"[15] While the Reed/Warhol mixtape demonstrates a specific queer relationship between two infamous individuals, Peraino's question accesses the detailed understanding of how mixtapes, and music, allow individuals to express themselves emotionally without stating those complex feelings verbally. Emotionality underlies the relationship between the mixtape recipient and the mixtape creator.

Musicians combine lyrics, instrumentation, and form to construct a sonic resonance imbued with meaning. From classical to death metal, musicians use tempo, rhythm, and sound design to construct an aural soundscape to make their listeners feel.[16] Artists use emotion to connect to their audience directly and indirectly. Nolan Gasser asserts, "Music operates vibrantly on an emotional level within us, but there cannot be true preference if there is not also a practical, technical, and intellectual dimension that registers favorably to our ears and brain - whether or not a listener could articulate or define it."[17] Through his research he analyzes how various styles of music use sound to create meaning and emotion. Auditory memory plays into how people remember and relate to music. Through time, different genres of music echo different generations and their appreciation of sound. Pierre Bourdieu defined taste in music as "a sort of road map for what is socially acceptable for one's class."[18] Extending his definition, social acceptability delineates generational divides as well as race, sex, and class ones. The music a baby boomer found likeable was not the same music appreciated by Gen X.

Theodor Adorno's seminal work on the sociology of music studied popular song hits, which he described as staged and lacking in uniqueness. However, he believed, "The hits not only appeal to a 'lonely crowd' of the atomized; they reckon with the immature, with those who cannot express their emotions and experiences, who either never had the power of expression or were crippled by cultural taboos."[19] Adorno's statement supports the concept of music as a vector through which individuals can understand and express their emotions without having to speak them directly. Audience interpretation does not always align with the intended connotation of the artist, but the ability for people to construct a personal relationship to make music popular. The construction of a mixtape imbues songs with new meanings based on the creator and their expectations for the tape. The choice of songs becomes its own new musical story which allows individuals to share their feelings indirectly without having to state them.

In the past twenty-five years, scholars have reexamined questions of masculinity and men's ability to display emotions publicly. Traditionally men were depicted in pop culture and mass media as intellectual, while women were portrayed as emotional.[20] Depictions in television and film affirmed power and anger as the only appropriate display of male emotionality. Over time, scholars argue, this led men to have trouble expressing positive emotions like love and affection which has led to concerns about intimacy and commitment.[21] In a society which discourages men from displaying their affection audibly, music has become a tool in which they can place their feelings. Billy Idol, whose band helped coin the term "Generation X," wrote songs about competing emotions from anger and love to rejection and affirmation.[22] Punk, hip hop, and grunge (and all their derivations from metal to EDM) music allowed for expressions of anger, depression, and negativity about society, less common in earlier lyrical music. Riot grrrl allowed women to express negative emotion and female empowerment, less common features in prior popular music sung by women. Emerging in the late Gen X/early millennial generation, emo music incorporated a sadness and a discontent, again shifting the accepted sonic emotionality in pop music. The study of masculine repression of emotion emerged in the late-1990s as Gen X youth reached adulthood and confronted their place in the world. The perception of Gen X as cynical and sarcastic correlates to the musical tones of these genres but also exhibits a shift in the perception of men as publicly emotional and not merely dispassionate.

Music, and mixtapes specifically, allow men to assert traditionally viewed-as feminine emotions in a way society deems appropriate. Books, like *Old Records Never Die: One Man's Quest for His Vinyl and His Past* and *Vinyl Freak: Love Letters to a Dying Medium* show men absorbed in collecting music because of their emotional ties to it.[23] Musicians write songs which assert a variety of feelings which fans and audience members can then interpret. Individuals take these songs, compile them into a unique new product and share them with others. Whether a mixtape functions as an expression of love or friendship, this object has become a marker of emotional representation. From Rob Sheffield's autobiography *Love is a Mixtape*, to the character Baby in *Baby Driver*, mixtapes are a physical representation of socially coded female emotions. Since the 1980s men have used mixtapes as a tool to express companionship, desire, and sadness. While many of these expressions of musical emotionality exhibit authenticity, there are pop culture models which have taken nostalgia and turned it into a commercial commodity.

In his book *Analog Revolution*, David Sax argues contemporary cultures fetishize the hands-on appeal of the past.[24] He claims individuals today are turning their backs on an exclusively digital world in the hopes of reclaiming the simplicity and ease of earlier eras. Peter Fritzsche, analyzing nostalgia and modernity suggests,

> It is worth considering the shape of nostalgia in the present, when fragments of the past are energetically manufactured and avidly consumed but do not necessarily correspond to the evidence of experience. The interiorized voice and vernacular location of nostalgia have been made more obsolescent by the ability of the mass media to package and repackage the past in a way that facilitates its omnipresence and sensuousness [. . .] but diminishes its pertinence to particular lives.[25]

While his article focuses on the understanding of nostalgia as a modern phenomenon in the nineteenth century, this statement highlights the experience of the recent past and the way in which individuals consume, package, and redefine nostalgia. Pop culture discussions incorporate talking points about nostalgia extensively. Marketing campaigns use retro items and introduce kitsch to appeal to nostalgic impulses. The mixtape signifies a cultural artifact around which one can understand the phenomenon of nostalgia imbued in a technologically and musically defined item. Creating a personal, artistic, tangible finished product holds an appeal for an American consumer culture which feels inundated by the hurry of twenty-first-century life and the digital focus of connectivity. The rise of vinyl and the resurgence of a population who prefers to locate, analyze, and buy an artifact over the ease of downloading a digital playlist codifies the appeal of the tangible merchandise. In her description of Gen X, Eve Epstein writes, "In our childhood and adolescence, medium and message reinforced each other [. . .] until it wasn't just the song itself we loved but the thing it was recorded on, the cover for that thing, the shelf we stored it on, and the room where that shelf was."[26] This often white, male subculture fetishizes vinyl and cassettes. They use nostalgia and collective memory to encapsulate an ideology of an idealized, simplified past. Interviewers and critics discuss nostalgia and kitsch as assumed markers of contemporary culture. Artists use mixtapes to tell stories.

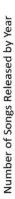

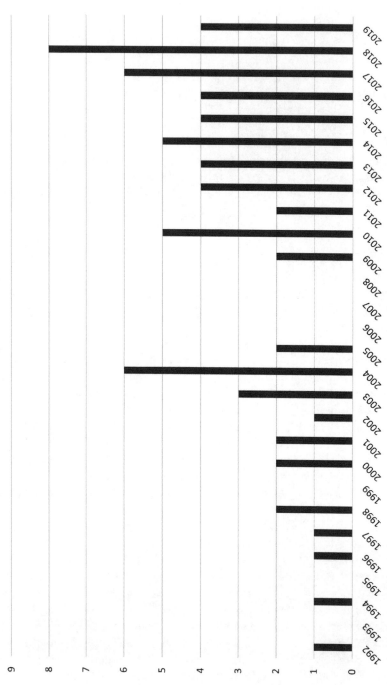

Figure 4.1   Songs Released by Year Which Included "Mixtape" in Their Lyrics This Chart Does Not Include Hip Hop Songs Nor Songs in Languages Besides English. Chart created by the author. (Data collected from genius.com 2020 and discogs.com 2020)

MIXTAPE LYRICS

At the turn of the millennium, cassette sales fell, streaming replaced analog listening, and mixtapes stopped being a normal part of young adult life. However, while the physical artifact no longer permeated youth culture, the idea of the mixtape resonated with individuals who came of age with them. Between 1998 and 2019 more than seventy musicians released songs in English about mixtapes.[27] Of those nearly six dozen songs, ten were titled "Mixtape." The songs range from emo hardcore to pop to country and include artists from Florida Georgia Line to Björk. Artists, who engaged with mixtapes in their adolescence, wrote many of them. These songs represent a cross section of lyrics which incorporates the word "mixtape" as a signifier and reflection of a nostalgic past. The hip hop definition of a freestyle or remix album, which remains a contemporary cultural concept, appears occasionally in these non-hip hop contemporary songs. Some songs reflect a simple idea young artists took for granted. The inclusion of mixtape ideas in rock and country songs at the turn of the millennium represents a link to an artifact because of the symbolism rather than the artifact itself.

Semisonic's 1998 alt-rock, pop song, "Singing in My Sleep," focused on the mixtape in a way artists in previous years had not, building on the themes of Better than Ezra's "Rewind." One review described it as "A melodic ode to the art of making mix tapes."[28] Another reviewer wrote, "'Singing in My Sleep' is the perfect song for anyone who's ever made or received a mix tape for/from that possible new someone. Mix tapes were the great seducer of a generation—the thought that went into the selection of each song, even the creation of the tape case itself, was a secret message sent and hopefully received."[29] Music critic Jim Walsh described the song as "a musical tribute to the compilation tape as courting device."[30] Dan Wilson, leader singer and songwriter, understood the place of a mixtape in romantic life. The catchy pop song, which gave young people a sense of romantic intrigue without the overly emotional focus of a slower romantic song, hit number eleven on the Billboard Alternative song list. In the song, Wilson sings, "Got your tape and it changed my mind/Heard your voice in between the lines"[31] Mixtape imagery allowed for sharing unstated feelings. He follows up singing, "Now I'm falling in love too fast/With you or the songs you chose." His nuance underscores a truism for a mixtape: the connection to the songs may supersede feelings for the mixtape creator. While mixtapes represent emotional links, they also represent introductions to new music. Wilson has highlighted the role of the mixtape to attract a potential romantic partner by picking songs to appeal to that person. The idea of hearing a person's voice "in between the lines" aptly demonstrates how the personal choice of songs and order represents more than the original intent by the songwriter. They are a way of sharing feelings and ideas without stating them out loud. The recipient of the tape can listen repeatedly and fall in love based on the ideas in the music. Wilson sings about the all-encompassing interaction with the experience, comparing the mixtape to Romeo and Juliet when he sings, "I've been living in your cassette/[. . .]/Singing up to a Capulet."[32]

Heartbreak songs can follow a similar trajectory. Paul Kelly's 1998, "I'd Rather Go Blind (Than See You With Another Guy)" is an attempt to manage his persistent unhappiness. While the title has a humorous tone, the lyrics solidify his heartbreak. He sings, "You made a special tape for me/With songs from all your favourite cd's," reflecting on a happier moment. He finds listening to the music, "From Junior Brown to Dr Dre" causes too much pain.[33] Kelly highlights he and his ex-partner's diverse shared interests, from classic country to hip hop. For the listener, the artists are significant because hearing Dr. Dre, a rap artist, in conjunction with Junior Brown, a Texas Country singer, is unexpected. Written before the surge in hip hop mixtapes as a mainstream discussion, those artists only make sense for the creator and the recipient of that specific mixtape. His line offers an insider's view into the specificity of the relationship for which diametrically different music had an impact for those two people. The 2004 rock song, "I've Got Five" by New Jersey band, Madison, is a public lament of loneliness and a lack of understanding when the band sings, "What is it that you really wanted?" They continue "Taking pictures by your house, hearing music from your room/But it's not me, my mixtape must mean nothing to you."[34] The sense of longing while driving by after a breakup is familiar. For the narrator, it hurts to recognize the mixtape they shared no longer holds the same meaning. The lyric highlights the frustration at no longer being together as codified in the removal of the mixtape as a sign of togetherness.

For some artists, the mixtape was a token that defined their songwriting rather than a personal artifact of emotional connection. Select musicians enhanced their musical knowledge and developed their sounds listening to mixtapes given by older members of their generation, highlighting the shared openness to cultural sounds. Courtney Barnett, an Australian rock musician credited her early interest in rock music to the mixtapes her older neighbors made during her childhood. Barnett's childhood bridged the gap between tape and CD. In an interview. Barnett corrected host Bob Boilen asserting her mixtapes were cassettes and not CDs, an important distinction. Growing up in Sydney, she described her parent's music as jazz and classical. Aside from ABBA, her parents did not listen to popular music. The radio played "very commercial" music. As an older millennial with Gen X siblings, Barnett found greater appeal in the music of her peers than she did in what she heard from her parents or commercially. Her neighbors' mixtapes led her to musicians like, "Nirvana and Hendricks and Red Hot Chili Peppers and Guns 'n'

Roses,"[35] a less commercial side of music imported from the United States. Her introduction to guitar-based rock developed out of an affinity for the tapes she and her brother received. Those tapes sparked Barnett's interest in playing the guitar. She stated, "Probably the mixtapes, ya know, just hearing music that someone who I know hands to you and says, I reckon you'll enjoy this. That's got so much more power than like everything else."[36] Its distinction from mainstream music appealed to Barnett. Emulating adolescents she admired, the first album she purchased herself was Nirvana's *Nevermind*. Barnett also discussed her relationship to Australian bands. You Am I's 1998 song, "Heavy Heart" remains "one of [Barnett's] favorite songs," which she first heard on a compilation tape as a teenager. It has become a standard cover in her shows.

Not all musicians received their mixtapes from others. Some made their own mixtapes, pulling together found music from the radio, albums, and streaming services. Amythyst Kiah, a vocalist, guitarist, and banjo player, known for her work with the band *Our Native Daughters* also reflects on the role mixtapes played in giving her the foundation as a musician. Kiah enjoyed making mix CDs she listened to alone. As a budding guitarist, Kiah sought out music and fan forums, using file-sharing programs like Kazaa and Limewire. Those mixes she made influenced her musicianship and introduced her to a variety of music in a pre-streaming era. She enjoyed the challenge of hunting out music and admitted in a 2020 podcast interview, "There was something about finding songs and putting together a mix CD that I loved. It was fun. That way of consuming it, you had to be more a lot more deliberate and think about what you were doing. [. . .] That hunt of going in and finding it had its own catharsis that was just as important as listening to the music."[37] For Kiah a mix was a self-created artifact which helped her hone her interests and her skills as a guitarist but also a cultural experience and pastime in its own right.

Bonny Light Horseman have incorporated music from an earlier era into their current sound. This group, which includes Anais Mitchell, well-known for her creation of the Broadway musical Hadestown, and Eric D. Johnson, lead singer of the Fruit Bats, perform updated versions of old folk songs. In an interview with the *Newport Folk Fest podcast*, Johnson explains their choice to play Tim Buckley's "Buzzin' Fly" came directly from a mixtape he received from a girlfriend's older brother in 1997. In the interview, guitarist Josh Kaufman interjects, "I feel like it's good to have a girlfriend whose older brother is musically eloquent. I feel like a lot of people are introduced that way to music." Johnson replies, "Yeah, it was an iconic mixtape [. . .] It was a mixtape that truly changed my life. And this song was on there."[38] Like many musicians, the members of Bonny Light Horseman can trace their knowledge of and curiosity about previous eras of music to a mixtape gifted by a fellow youth culture elder. The role of the mixtape is self-evident for musicians. Hearing, sharing, and writing music about music connects the artist to the artistry and the artifact.

BOOKS

Memoir

Thurston Moore's 2004 collected essays and art book *Mix Tape: The Art of Cassette Culture* and Jason Bitner's 2009 collected essays, *Cassette from My Ex: Stories and Soundtracks of Lost Loves* moved the narrative storytelling in which mixtapes played a role from lyrics to prose. Both Moore and Bitner are musicians with multiple ties to the world of music and music writing. Moore, most well-known as the frontman of Sonic Youth, has contributed to many groups and run a record label. Bitner is a drummer who has played with Shadow Kills, Overkill, and other thrash metal bands. They both took their collective interest and incorporated friends and colleagues who each wrote an essay about an important mixtape from their past. According to Moore in the introduction to *Mix Tape*, "When preparing this book, almost every person I solicited had a tale to tell about the mix tapes they had made for themselves or others, and ones they received in return. And almost every person bemoaned the fact that their beloved tapes had vanished."[39] Moore and Bitner's edited books encapsulate how much mixtapes represent emotions and time more than actual music. In his introduction, Bitner wrote, "Mixtapes are like personal time capsules. Not only do you get the physical tape and homemade artwork, but you've got memories attached to each of the handpicked songs."[40] These books pay homage to the cassette and the art as important facets of mixtape creation, while situating the mixtape in the realm of emotional connective artifact. Photographs and drawings of the cassettes centralize the artistry and physicality of the tapes. Not love stories, but in many cases, love lost, or the birth of friendship stories, the authors in Moore's and Bitner's books focus on personal bonds and the memories those relationships create. The two books work together to assert the idea of the mixtape as a site of cultural collective memory tied to musicianship, friendship, and emotional connection at the end of the twentieth century.

The cover of *Mix Tape* is a black 1970s style "compact cassette" with a white sticker label. The title "mix tape" is a faded, typed font with uneven lettering. The back cover shows the B-Side of the tape with the names of the contributors in typewriter font, reminiscent of a track listing on a tape.[41] Everything about the cover expresses kitsch cassette nostalgia. The cover of Bitner's book is two hand-drawn cassette tapes. The A-Side incorporates "cassette from my ex" in hand-drawn red script. The B-Side has "stories and soundtracks of lost loves" in handwritten blue ink. The background resembles lined notebook paper.[42] Both books have photographs to accompany each of the stories. They vary from a black Maxell XLII cassette with stickers of cute baby animals[43] to a simple TDK D90 clear cassette tape with a sticker and the handwritten word, "Reggae."[44] Each book incorporates the J-Cards and cover art for the mixtapes. They range from hand-written lists of songs and artists to DIY magazine cut-out art. The key factor is not the artistry, the professionalism, or the memorability of the J-Cards. The significant feature is the personalization. These mixtapes tell a deeply personal story about who recorded songs onto these cassettes and why those stories deserve remembrance. David Nadelberg, an author in Bitner's book, placed hope into receiving the perfect mixtape from the perfect person, "We shared an appreciation for the artistry involved in coming up with mixtape titles, artwork, and of course, the perfect set list. To me, mixtapes were more than mere compilations. They were expressions—portraits of personalities, feelings, or relationships."[45] The mixtape as a "portrait of [. . .] feelings" sums up their uniqueness in the canon of musical playlists. The songs may represent ideal music the listener loves, but many mixtape stories reflect the affinity for the tape, the place, and the time. It is less about the actual sound. Writer Katie Krentz maintains that the songs are almost inconsequential, "The songs on this tape don't remind me much of Luke. And I'm pretty sure these songs don't remind him of me, either. These songs reminded us of our respective friends we so desperately missed, because at that age finding people who get you is everything."[46] Her statement reflects the community identity music solidified for teenagers.

For Moore, the mixtapes allowed him to find people who understood him because of the music they shared. He describes mixtapes his neighbor, artist Dan Graham, made for him of new punk and new wave records. Wanting to absorb this music on his own terms, he began making his own mixtapes.

I also felt I needed to hear these records in a more time-fluid way, and it hit me that I could make a killer mix tape of all the best songs from these records - and since they were all so short and they all had the same kind of sound and energy, the mix tape would be a monolithic hardcore rush. As we had access to Dan's apartment, I went up there and did just that. I made what I thought was the most killer hardcore tape ever. I wrote 'H' on one side, and 'C' on the other. That night [. . .] I put the cassette on our stereo cassette player, dragged one of the little speakers over to the bed, and listened to the tape at ultra-low thrash volume. I was in a state of humming bliss.[47]

Moore cemented his love affair with mixtapes and the cassette. He became both a mixtape creator and a recipient making mixtapes for his then wife Kim Gordon and for the band and collecting hip hop mixtapes in New York City in the mid-1980s. Having still more to say, Moore wrote his 2014 song *Tape* about a mixtape cassette.

Among Moore's collaborators was Dean Wareham, founder of the bands Galaxie 500 and Luna. The tape he describes mirrors the black cassette from the cover of the book. The title on the photographed J-Card reads "The Tape that Dean made one night." Wareham states, "Looking over the track listing on this tape is like reading an old diary entry, and I was taken back to my life in 1987." Fellow band member Naomi Yang affirms, "[this tape is] like a little time capsule of musical influences at a particular moment." Third band member, Damon Krukowski, adds, "If you cut random bits of this tape together, you'd probably come up with an alternate version of the first Galaxie 500 album." Like the interviews of musicians from The Mekons to Amythyst Kiah, musicians use other songs to influence the music they then create. As Moore's book accentuates, the artifact on which they put this music together is as relevant as the sound of the music on the tape. A mixtape is a moment in time. It is a nostalgic reflection of musical relationships and feelings. Wareham reflects on the idea of the mixtape saying, "It takes time and effort to put a mix tape together. The time spent implies an emotional connection with the recipient. [. . .] Like all gifts, the mix tape comes with strings attached." For these musicians, the mixtape signaled a solidification of their friendship and it prefaced the music they would write. Fifteen years later, one of them still had the mixtape allowing them to reminisce and share their ideas anew.[48]

Mac McCaughan owes some of his musical styling to mixtapes made for him by friends. McCaughan, a founding member of the band Superchunk and the owner of the independent record label Merge Records described an album made for him by a friend in the 1980s. He writes,

> *Don't Take My Word For It* is the name of one of many elaborate mix tapes made for me back in college (oh the '80s—the decade of the mix tape!) by Jonathan Marx (founding member of the band Lampchop) [. . .] My band, Superchunk, ended up covering a Flys song on our first single, a song I first heard on one of Johnathan's tapes.[49]

McCaughan's example reinforces the appeal of bands recreating music first heard on a beloved mixtape. The mixtape includes "seemingly incongruous" music from Pere Ubu and the Mekons to Bob Willis and Patsy Cline.[50] After leaving Superchunk, McCaughan remained well-versed in the music world, founding a well-respected record label representing groups like Arcade Fire. A theme permeating mixtape discussions is the lack of genre structure. Among the most memorable tapes are those that pair unexpected music which catches the listener off-guard and can work to introduce them to new bands and songs they would not have heard otherwise. McCaughan's description and tape enlighten his later identity as the founder of a record label, exploring and appreciating a wide diversity of musical styles.

McCaughan, like other musicians, took his love of music and moved into the record label business. Slim Moon created and owned the Kill Rock Stars label in Washington. Among the first to release albums by riot grrrl bands like Bikini Kill, Bratmobile and Sleater-Kinney, he credits those women with introducing him to their genre of music.

> It was embarrassing, back in the '80s, when I was a teen, to admit that the person who most greatly schooled me in rock (and personal/social politics) was younger than me, but that's how it was. [. . .] I've learned by far more from [Tobi Vail and Jean Smith] than anyone else in life, they are my mentors for how to live, what is important, and what matters most, and these tapes were my schoolbooks.[51]

Describing his mixtapes as schoolbooks, Moon highlights the place of self-crafted tapes in educating individuals like himself. He defines these female musicians as mentors underscoring how important sharing musical knowledge was for young people. Moon cites mixtapes and the friendship surrounding them as his entry into membership of a distinct musical genre community. These tapes gave him the foundation to work in that world.

Building community through music extended from co-musicians to friends to loved ones. Moore reached out to Leah Singer, the wife of Lee Renaldo, a fellow co-founder of Sonic Youth. Singer described the tape Renaldo gave her before they married, "This is one of the first tapes Lee gave me. We were just getting to know each other, a good time to exchange mixed tapes because it's such a powerful way to reveal who you are. The tape exemplifies who Lee Renaldo is. [. . .] Listening to it again after all these years it remains an accurate portrait of him."[52] The mixtape, which played a fundamental role for musicians to learn about music and how to craft albums, also functioned as romantic overtures. Renaldo educated his future wife about himself via a tape with songs by Nick Cave and Buddy Holly, alongside soundtrack dialogue from Jack Kerouac and Jean-Luc Godard. He also included an interview of his band from 1989, which Singer described as a bit of rock star superficiality. Renaldo's unique mixtape solidified his relationship with Singer, and it showcased his understanding of the rise and fall of albums. The finished product worked as an emotional impression, a study in crafting albums, and, for Moore's book, as a nostalgic reminiscence of courtship.

Rather than the uplifting tales in Moore's book, many of the stories in Bitner's book, *Cassettes from My Ex*, end unhappily or unexpectedly as the title suggests. These are not the love affairs of Semisonic, but the heartbreak of Paul Kelly. But they are no less poignant for the lessons learned. Ben Greenman, author of *Superbad* and collaborator with Questlove on *Mo' Meta Blues* and *Mixtape Potluck*, tells a story about loving a woman who "punished [him] for it." He writes, "We made each other tapes because we believed that music articulated what we could not otherwise express. We may have been right about this . . . ."[53] Although the relationship ended badly with his girl-friend moving, Greenman considers the experience fondly. He understands the role of music in allowing them to express themselves more deeply than they could have with words. The collaborators include memorable lines throughout the book like, "These were the moments of being young when everything in life seemed to be changing, you know, hurtling forward into some unknown realm of adulthood, and maybe that's why these were all such good songs, because they were all peculiar and memorable at such an impor-tant moment."[54] and "He designed this mixtape for me for that long drive to Dakota. Listening to it now after many years, it's a perfect snapshot of that goofy, gleeful era and our quirky, novel love."[55] The reflections in *Cassettes From My Ex* highlight the emotionally tinged reminiscences of the mixtapes. While the stories do not end in romantic bliss, the authors rhapsodize about young love and heartache. The book reinforces the importance of music as an emotional outlet. The mixtapes from those days have become the nostalgic artifacts around which individuals hold onto the memories and the innocence of youth.

These books highlight the way mixtapes encourage contemplation. They bring back feelings and reminiscences of being a different person in a differ-ent time. For many of the individuals writing these stories, "I've still got the tape in a box somewhere, and although I'll never listen to it again it reminds me of a time when I was really crazy about someone."[56] In this era the tape became the memory, not the songs and their order. Their materiality is what distinguishes mixtapes from other types of playlists. The emotion with which they are imbued creates a nostalgic emotive tie which overlays the sounds coming from the machine playing the songs.

Two authors without as direct a connection to music as Moore and Bitner wrote memoirs using the memory of music and mixtapes to tell their sto-ries. In 2003 Nick Hornby, author of *High Fidelity*, penned a collection of essays titled *Songbook* using a song title for each of his chapters.[57] For Rob Sheffield's memoir, *Love is a Mixtape: Life and Loss, One Song at a Time*, he titled each chapter after a mixtape he or his wife had made. Both authors, immersed in a world of music and pop culture, felt the best way to share stories was using music as a through line to organize their ideas and reach their audiences.

Hornby published *Songbook* eight years after *High Fidelity*. Through these essays, the reader learns the personal rapport Hornby has to music and realizes Rob in *High Fidelity* was not entirely fictional. Hornby's musical interests range from Santana and the Beatles to Teenage Fanclub and Ben Folds Five. Not content to stop at the thirty-one songs his chapter list outlines, he briefly discusses fifteen albums and includes an additional dozen tracks like "What to Do" by OK Go and "The Seed (2.0)" by The Roots in his discography.[58] Hornby declares, "very occasionally songs and books and films and pictures express who you are perfectly,"[59] a concept he incorporates in many of his novels, including *High Fidelity*. In his discussion of Nelly Furtado's "I'm Like a Bird," Hornby analyzes pop music, who its target audience is, and whether it is worthwhile. He concludes that not all music has to stand the test of time; temporary appeal is relevant too. For him music in the moment is as relevant as music that lasts generations. As a then forty-six-year-old man, writing at the end of the analog era, Hornby states, "A couple of times a year I make myself a tape to play in the car, a tape full of all the new songs I've loved over the previous few months, and every time I finish one I can't believe that there'll be another. Yet there always is, and I can't wait for the next one; you need only a few hundred more things like that, and you've got a life worth living."[60] The strong association he has for music permeates his essays. Creating a compilation of titles, Hornby told one version of his story via a musical montage: a mixtape.

The concept of using mixtapes to analyze love, and particularly love lost, must include Rob Sheffield's touching and humorous 2007 memoir. The story encapsulates his personal recollections of mixtapes, music, and romance. Sheffield, a *Rolling Stone* journalist, author, and music critic, arranged his first memoir about his relationship with his late wife Renee around the mixtape. Throughout the book, he connects important moments in their life to music. Each chapter starts with a date, cover of a mixtape, and a playlist. The music ranges from Sir-Mix-a-Lot to Pavement to Prince. In each chapter, Sheffield highlights individual songs from the opening list and uses them to tell stories about his life with Renee. Chapter One opens, "The playback: late night, Brooklyn, a pot of coffee, and a chair by the window. I'm listening to a mixtape from 1993. Nobody can hear it but me. [. . .] This mix tape is just another piece of useless junk that Renee left behind. A category that I guess tonight includes me."[61] *Rumblefish,* the mixtape made by Renee, encapsulates the memoir's theme: the despair of love lost and finding meaning anew. The narratives and the music are an homage to Sheffield's love affair, marriage, and grief at the loss of his wife. As Sheffield writes, he attempts to find meaning in his own life and ultimately the meaning in the mixtapes he kept. The tales in the music allow Sheffield to reflect on how music tells the story of a life, both his and his wife's. By the end, Sheffield no longer views his mixtapes as junk. He admits many of his friends no longer listen to cassettes but for him, "the rhythm of a mix tape is the rhythm of romance, the analog hum of a physical connection between two sloppy, human bodies. The cassette is full of tape hiss and room tone; it's full of wasted space, unnecessary noise."[62] Sheffield's work shifts discussions of the mixtape from purely a way to share music to an analogy for romance and shared interactions. After analyzing the highs and lows of sharing music, of creating a life, and of using music to grieve over the loss of that love and life, Sheffield asks, "What is love?" The final line and the conclusion to his book is, "Love is a mix tape."[63] This work establishes the next generation of mixtape literature because it grounds the ideas in the music and the cassette technology but contextualizes the artifacts into a larger sense of communal identity and meaning.

Sheffield's book is not only about his love affair with his wife, but also about his love affair with music, and specifically with analog music, pop culture, and mixtapes. Sheffield has written many books since the publication of *Love is a Mix Tape* and yet that book holds a place in many people's hearts. One reader described first seeing the book when she was fifteen. "I've grown to accumulate four or five copies over the last ten years, and I had no idea the illustrated cassette tapes on the cover would become one of the central images in my life."[64] She admits she, "just wanted to read about someone who lived his life obsessed with making mix tapes on ACTUAL cassettes!"[65] Sheffield's book appears on the top ten lists of music books to read, including lists by *Pitchfork* and *Billboard*, well-known and respected music sites. The *Pitchfork* description of *Love is a Mix Tape* starts, "the mixtape has maintained an improbably prominent place in popular culture, from Nick Hornby's *High Fidelity* and its movie adaptation to Thurston Moore's *Mix Tape: The Art of Cassette Culture*, [and] Jason Bitner's *Cassette From My Ex.*"[66] It concedes what could have been "affected" because of its structure instead is a moving story.[67] Inclusion in this triumvirate of quintessential mixtape reading showcases the important role Sheffield's book has in understanding the place of the mixtape in pop culture. In a popular 2018 tweet, Harry Styles, singer of One Direction fame, posted an image of himself reading *Love is a Mix Tape* and mentioned it as one of his favorite books.[68] Published more than ten years earlier, the book remains relevant to a younger generation who did not grow up with cassette technology.

Sheffield's memoir, like *High Fidelity*, has become a foundational work in the continuing discussion of mixtapes. Rather than an idiosyncratic memoir relevant only to a generation of music lovers who crafted their own mixtapes, Sheffield's story has transcended generations and continues to inspire both writers and music lovers. The model of using a mixtape as an organizational guideline for his life solidified with Hornby and Sheffield but has been modeled by other authors since. Sheffield's love affair with cassettes has also formalized him in the world of analog music fans. He has continued to write about and be interviewed about analog music. As a ubiquitous music fan who writes about the latest, biggest pop culture stars, Sheffield bridges the gap between generations because he both praises Taylor Swift and Ariana Grande and unselfconsciously praises the quirky, dirty, messiness of a mixtape.[69] Sheffield introduces young fans who appreciate his current musical knowledge into the deeper history of musical, and particularly analog, appreciation.

In 2010, Mark Hogan wrote an article in *Pitchfork* magazine called "This Is Not a Mixtape" to assess the resurgence of cassette culture among small indie noise bands. Revisiting the legacy of the cassette, he highlighted Sheffield and Nick Hornby's memoirs writing, "A few years ago, during the most recent outpourings of nostalgia for cassettes, writers focused on the mixtape: [. . .] In an age of total customizability, the new cassette culture looks to tapes for their lack of it."[70] This line encapsulates the key shift in understanding the mixtape. Holding a tangible item allows people to cherish and collect music rather than store the largest number of songs on a computer. Starting in the 2000s mixtapes represented nostalgia. Streaming music shifted user's perspective to nostalgia for the cassette, as well as nostalgia for the physical artifact and the time and attention devoted to creating a mixtape. Hogan stated, "Many children of the 1980s first owned their music on cassette, so for them the format represents a nostalgia for simpler times; younger kids probably never owned cassettes in the first place, so for them tapes don't have any negative associations."[71] The books written for this generation demonstrate this move from ordinary technology to nostalgic identity. For the adults who had lived with cassettes, mixtapes became a site of nostalgia and memories of their experiences. Mixtapes signified positive feelings as the cassette lost tangibility and became an object of technostalgia.

Fictional Representations

Published in 2004, Joe Meno's semi-autobiographical *Hairstyles of the Damned* incorporates cassettes, romance, the validity of a punk ethos and "the way a mix-tape can change a person's life."[72] Like nonfiction authors, Meno plays on the nostalgia of his past. Mixtapes introduced Meno to politically and socially aware bands like Black Flag and Minor Threat which "just had a huge effect on the way that I looked at the world and also what I thought music could actually mean to people."[73] Similar to Stephen Chbosky, Meno builds a fictional story using music and mixtapes as the emotional through line. He situates the novel in a Chicago southside Catholic high school which chooses to have a segregated prom because the White and Black students cannot agree on what kind of music to play: an experience he lived through in 1991.[74]

Like Meno, the main character, Brian, finds meaning in the punk music his friends introduce him to on mixtapes. Brian falls for his best friend, Gretchen, because of her incredible musical taste and remorseless attitude.

> Gretchen's mix-tapes, her music choices, were like these songs that seemed to be all about our lives, but in small random ways that made sense on almost any occasion. [. . .] To me, the tapes were what made me like her, then love her so much: the fact that in between the Misfits and the Specials, she would have a song from the Mamas and the Papas, "Dream a Little Dream of Me" or something like that. Those mix-tapes were the secret soundtrack to how I was feeling or what I thought about almost everything.[75]

Gretchen exemplifies teenage angst and frustration through the songs on her mixtapes, from The Smiths and Social Distortion to Mötley Crüe. Brian hopes the perfect mixtape will have the same power over her as her mixtapes have for him. In a Cyrano de Bergerac moment, he asks his friend Rod "who was black and maybe even a homosexual [. . . and] had the largest record collection of anyone I knew" to help him pick out songs for Gretchen from his collection of classic jazz and blues.[76] Rod resists, stating, "That would be like writing somebody else's love letter. [. . .] I'm not helping you out. If you like this girl, you should be able to pick the songs out you want her to hear yourself."[77] Meno created an authentic teenaged boy who has honest desires paired with a lack of confidence in his own feelings. Brian, with his shallow observations, obsession with sex, and appreciation for the physical, finds music a compelling outlet of expression.

The rage and growing political awareness of urban youth overflow in Meno's novel. The music he incorporates showcases a 1990s subculture of punk youth angry at the wider world's lack of understanding. The characters, the story, and the music in *Hairstyles of the Damned* coalesce into a frank look at a disenchanted population. Like *Less Than Zero* published nearly 20 years earlier, Meno's novel remains a story of mixtape normalcy for unhappy adolescents, but he was writing about a moment in the past, not the present. Music signals emotions, bonds, and a way of being seen and understood.

Like novelists, playwrights have used the mixtape to help tell a story of uneven, covetous romance. In the originally produced off-Broadway play, *Avenue Q,* the mixtape is a sign of eccentric kitsch in which puppets think about friendship and relationships through song. *Avenue Q* opened in 2003 at the Vineyard Theatre, an off-Broadway venue. The show played on the nostalgia of Sesame Street and the Muppets but took the themes and pitched them for an adult audience. It moved onto Broadway and won three Tony Awards.[78] The quirky musical addresses inequality, sexuality, and schadenfreude. Despite the puppet players, the show incorporates profanity, nudity, and adult themes. The Broadway cast recording of *Avenue Q*, the first cast recording with a Parental Advisory label, remained a *Billboard* Top Cast Album for over three years.[79] Among the songs in the show is the aptly named "Mix Tape" sung by Kate Monster about the mixtape Princeton, the lead character, has given her. Although not the most (in)famous song on the album, it typifies the ideas and the cultural world embodied by the characters in *Avenue Q*.

Princeton sings, "Listen, I was going through my CDs yesterday/And I kept coming across songs I thought you'd like."[80] In good Gen X style, Princeton has made a tape for a friend. The cassette represents different ideas to the creator and the mixtape recipient. The songs on the tape confuse Kate, causing her to question what message Princeton intends. She sings "They'll make you a mix tape/To give you a clue."[81] However, the first group of songs have a decidedly unromantic feel. Kate Monster lists a song from a Disney movie and the theme from the Friends TV show, suggesting there is no romantic interest. The next group of songs includes "Kiss the Girl," another Disney song, and Stevie Wonder's "My Cherie Amour" encouraging her sense of Princeton's affection. As she continues singing, listing the songs on the tape, she moves from Queen's "Fat-Bottomed Girls" to Titanic's "My Heart Will Go On." While Kate Monster vacillates between faith in Princeton's feelings and confusion, Princeton states, "Aww, well, I'm glad you like it but I have to go now/I'm gonna make one for Brian and Christmas eve, and Gary,"[82] which only adds to her uncertainty. Near the end of the song, Princeton asks Kate on a date and she concludes singing, "He likes me!"[83]

Songwriters Robert Lopez and Jeff Marx capture the idea of the mixtape and the era in their pithy well-worded song. By including songs from the Beatles and the theme-song from Cheers they have grounded their song and their show in the 1980s and 1990s. The audience who will best understand the variety grew up with animated Disney films and television sitcoms. Without being explicit, the songwriters solidify their nostalgic musical knowledge in the lyrics. "Mix Tape" blends the role of the mixtape from the generation who grew up with cassette tapes and can appreciate emotional turmoil trying to decode the song choices in a gift and a younger generation who chose the show because it addressed contemporary twenty-first-century issues using puppets as a vector for analysis. The audience can engage on multiple levels, which defines the best of Broadway, and the best of Sesame Street. Audience members walk away with diverse feelings, and the mixtape has become multi-generational without being overtly nostalgic.

In song lyrics, nonfiction, and imaginary stories the mixtape, codified largely still as cassettes, became a less relevant icon of youth culture. Creators used a familiar object to make a larger statement about connection. As cassettes gave way to CDs and streaming became a new way of engaging with music, the mixtape moved from grounded in the lived experience, to a dated item, out of step with the current era. However, for individuals who had come of age and made names for themselves during the 1990s and early 2000s, the mixtape was a part of their teenage experience, having lived through the creation of and stories about mixtapes. By 2007 *Love is a Mixtape* became the nonfiction equivalent to *High Fidelity*. This memoir of music, love, and grief has resonated with music fans since its publication.

Mixtapes are memories. They are the stories of love and friendship and defining oneself through music. In this generation of mixtape stories, the mixtape changed from typical technology to nostalgic artifacts. This generation of stories solidify the role of the mixtape. Moore and Bitner's books reflect the desire of musicians to codify their appreciation for the mixtape and share their emotive stories using the cassettes. Only older cars had cassette players as the main source of music. Even CDs had waned in sales by the end of the decade and streaming became the predominant way many people in the United States listened to music. The mixtape no longer held a central place and as a result stories about mixtapes shifted. These works led to the upcoming perception of the cassette mixtape as an artifact of collective analog nostalgia.

NOTES

1. Alain Corbin *Village Bells* 80 quoted in Michael Bull, "The Auditory Nostalgia of iPod Culture," in *Sound Souvenirs: Audio Technologies, Memory and Cultural Practices*, ed. Karin Bijsterveld and José van Dijck (Amsterdam: Amsterdam University Press, 2009), 86.

2. Svetlana Boym, *The Future of Nostalgia* (New York: Basic Books, 2008), eBook, Introduction.

3. Ibid., Chapter 2.

4. Peter Fritzsche, "Specters of History: On Nostalgia, Exile, and Modernity," *The American Historical Review* 106, no. 5 (2001): 1591.

5. Ibid., 1589.

6. Boym, Chapter 2.

7. Fritzsche, 1592.

8. Boym, Chapter 2.

9. Ibid., Chapter 2. and Ryan Moore, *Sells Like Teen Spirit: Music, Youth Culture, and Social Crisis* (New York: New York University Press, 2010), 201.

10. Michael Roth "Returning to Nostalgia" in *Home and Its Dislocation in Nineteenth-Century France* (Albany: SUNY 1993), 25–45, quoted in Boym, Chapter 5.

11. Paul Grainge, "Nostalgia and Style in Retro America: Moods, Modes, and Media Recycling," *Journal of American & Comparative Cultures* 23, no. 1 (2004): 27.

12. Ben Anderson, "Recorded Music and Practices of Remembering," *Social & Cultural Geography* 5, no. 1 (2004): 17.

13. Leon Botstein, "Memory and Nostalgia as Music-Historical Categories," *The Musical Quarterly* 84, no. 4 (2000): 535 and Kay Kaufman Shelemay, "Music, Memory and History: In Memory of Stuart Feder," *Ethnomusicology Forum* 15, no. 1 (2006): 30.

14. Georg Simmel. [1882] 1968. "Psychological and Ethnological Studies on Music," 98–140 in *The Conflict in Modern Culture and Other Essays*, translated by K. Peter Etzkorn. New York: Teachers College, Columbia University. As quoted in Timothy Dowd, "The Sociology of Music," in *21st Century Sociology: A Reference Handbook* ed. Clifton D. Bryant and Dennis L. Peck (Thousand Oaks, CA: Sage, 2007), 2.

15. Judith A. Peraino, "I'll Be Your Mixtape: Lou Reed, Andy Warhol, and the Queer Intimacies of Cassettes," *The Journal of Musicology* 36, no. 4 (2019): 432.

16. Nate Sloan and Charlie Harding, *Switched on Pop: How Popular Music Works and Why It Matters* (New York: Oxford University Press, 2020). and Ben Yagoda, *The B Side: The Death of Tin Pan Alley and the Rebirth of the Great American Song* (New York: Riverhead Books, 2015), Chapters 3 & 5.

17. Nolan Gasser, *Why You Like It: The Science & Culture of Musical Taste* (New York: Flatiron Books, 2019), 8.

18. Ibid., 489.

19. Theodor W. Adorno, *Introduction to the Sociology of Music*, trans. E. B. Ashton (New York: The Seabury Press, 1976), 26–27.

20. Fred J. Fejes. "Masculinity as Fact: A Review of Empirical Mass Communication Research on Masculinity" in Steve Craig, ed. *Men, Masculinity and the Media* (California: Sage Publications, 1992), 11.

21. Tim Edwards, *Cultures of Masculinity* (New York: Routledge, 2006), http://ebookcentral.proquest.com/lib/pointpark-ebooks/detail.action?docID=201200. Chapter 1.

22. Christine Henseler, ed. *Generation X Goes Global: Mapping a Youth Culture in Motion* (Taylor & Francis, 2012), 9.

23. John Corbett, *Vinyl Freak: Love Letters to a Dying Medium* (North Carolina: Duke University Press, 2017). and Eric Spitznagel, *Old Records Never Die: One Man's Quest for His Vinyl and His Past* (New York: Plume, 2016).

24. David Sax, *The Revenge of Analog: Real Things and Why They Matter* (New York: United States: Public Affairs, 2016), Introduction.

25. Fritzsche, 1618.

26. Eve Epstein and Lenora Epstein, *X vs. Y: A Culture War, a Love Story* (New York: Abrams Books, 2014), 147.

27. This number would be exponentially larger if it included the hip hop and foreign language songs that reference mixtapes.

28. Michael Frey, "Semisonic 'Singing in My Sleep'," All Music Review (no date) https://www.allmusic.com/album/singing-in-my-sleep-us-mw0000048356. (Accessed July 15, 2020).

29. Cindy Speer, "Semisonic: Feeling Strangely Fine," Pop Matters, https://www.popmatters.com/semisonic-feeling-2496084000.html. (Accessed March 23, 2020).

30. Jim Walsh, *Bar Yarns and Manic-Depressive Mixtapes: Jim Walsh on Music from Minneapolis to the Outer Limits* (Minneapolis: University of Minnesota Press, 2016), 62.

31. "Singing in My Sleep," Semisonic, on *Feeling Strangely Fine,* MCA Records, 1998.

32. "Singing in My Sleep," Semisonic.

33. "I'd Rather Go Blind (Than See You With Another Guy)," Paul Kelly on *Words and Music*, Vanguard Records, 1998.

34. "I've Got Fives," Madison on *For the First Time In Years . . . I'm Leaving You,* Fidelity Records, 2004.

35. Courtney Barnett. "Guest DJ Week: Courtney Barnett." interview by Bob Boilen. *All Songs Considered* (August 17, 2017).

36. Ibid.

37. Amythyst Kiah, interview by Cindy Howes, *Basic Folk* January 23, 2020, interview 54, audio.

38. Newport Folk Festival, *Bonny Light Horseman// Tim Buckley*, podcast audio, Newport Folk Podcast, 21 mins 2020.

39. Thurston Moore, ed. *Mix Tape: The Art of Cassette Culture* (New York: Universe Publisher, 2004), 12.

40. Jason Bitner, ed. *Cassette from My Ex: Stories and Soundtracks of Lost Loves* (New York: St. Martin's Press, 2009), 1.

41. Moore.

42. Bitner.

43. Ibid., 44–45.

44. Ibid., 156.

45. Nadelberg in Bitner., 29.

46. Krentz in Bitner., 186.

47. Moore, 10.

48. Ibid., 28–31.

49. Ibid., 37.

50. Ibid.

51. Tobi Vail is co-founder of Bikini Kill. Jean Smith is a fine artist. Ibid., 56.

52. Ibid., 45.

53. Bitner, 76.

54. Ibid., 99.

55. Ibid., 46.

56. Ibid., 167.

57. In the United Kingdom the book was released as *31 Songs*. Nick Hornby, *Songbook (New York: Riverhead Books, 2003)*.

58. Ibid., 207.

59. Ibid., 9.

60. Ibid., 18.

61. Rob Sheffield, *Love Is a Mix Tape: Life and Loss, One Song at a Time* (New York: Crown Publishers, 2007), 1–2.

62. Ibid., 218.

63. Ibid., 219.

64. Taylor Hodgkins, *Sides One and Two: Rob Sheffield's Love Is a Mix Tape and Me* (March 28, 2019), https://medium.com/@taylor.m.hodgkins/sides-one-and-two -rob-sheffields-love-is-a-mix-tape-and-me-7409dedbae89. (Accessed July 10, 2020).

65. Ibid.

66. Ibid.

67. "Words and Music: Out 60 Favorite Music Books," Features, *Pitchfork* (July 11, 2011), https://pitchfork.com/features/lists-and-guides/words-and-music-our-60 -favorite-music-books. (Accessed July 10, 2020).

68. Harry Styles, "Twitter Update" (Twitter: @hsdaily, 2018).

69. Zack Taylor, "Cassette: A Documentary Mixtape" Documentary (Gravitas Ventures, 2018). DVD 88 mins.

70. Marc Hogan, "This Is Not a Mixtape," *Pitchfork* (February 22, 2010), https:// pitchfork.com/features/article/7764-this-is-not-a-mixtape/ (Accessed July 10, 2020).

71. Ibid.

72. Joe Meno, *Hairstyles of the Damned* (New York: Akashic Books, 2004), back cover.

73. Joe Meno. "'Hairstyles of the Damned' Puts Punk on the Page." Scott Simon. *Weekend Edition Saturday* (January 22, 2005).

74. Ibid.

75. *Hairstyles of the Damned*, 4–5.

76. Ibid., 48.

77. Ibid., 51.

78. Karla Hartley, "Cast and Creators Recall the Birth of 'Avenue Q'," (November 22, 2017), https://stageworkstheatre.org/cast-and-creators-recall-the-birth-of-avenue- q/ (Accessed July 10, 2020).

79. Billboard, "Year-End Charts: Cast Albums," 2006 https://www.billboard .com/charts/year-end/2006/cast-albums (Accessed July 10, 2020). Ernio Hernandez, "Fantasies Come True: Broadway's *Avenue Q* Cast Recording Released Oct. 7," *Playbill* (2003), https://www.playbill.com/news/article/fantasies-come-true-broadwa ys-avenue-q-cast-recording-released-oct.-7-115590 (Accessed July 10, 2020).

80. "Mix Tape," Robert Lopez and Jeff Marx, on *Avenue Q, The Musical Soundtrack*, RCA Victor, 2003.

81. Ibid.

82. Ibid.

83. Robert Lopez and Jeff Marx, "Mix Tape," in *Avenue Q Soundtrack* (Masterworks Broadway, 2003).

Chapter 5

Retromania

By the turn of twenty-first century, the cassette no longer held sway as a predominant musical technology. The mixtape, whether a discussion of listening to a playlist on a cassette, or the visual representation of a cassette labeled a mixtape, has become imbued with nostalgic meaning. Even the CD would wane in this decade as streaming and digital music grew. The shift to digital led to a new relationship to mixtapes. No longer part of everyday life, they became a point of nostalgia. The people writing and thinking about mixtapes in this decade spoke of them with reverence as a part of the rose-colored past. The role of nostalgia and collective memory is fundamental to see how the mixtape moved from a tangible reality to an idealized concept.

In this era musicians and authors continued to engage with the mixtape, but they now framed it as an item from the past which explained emotional connection between young people. Musicians wrote songs lamenting past mistakes, remembering friends, and desiring a return to the good old days, couched in memories of the mixtape. Novelists wrote stories about earlier periods in which the mixtape was important for how it connected people together. These objects became sites of emotive connection. They stand outside of the everyday experience as something worthy of notice and discussion.

The hip hop mixtape transformed, losing its definition as a DJ-curated compilation. With this shift to digital and streaming, the music industry cracked down on illegal bootlegging and piracy which brought an end to the generation of hip hop mixtape cassette and CDs sales. What emerged out of this musical cessation was an entirely new concept of the mixtape defined by its digital identity. Mixtape in rap became a non-commercial, solo artist release intended to exist outside the label mainstream. The artists who restructured around self-released artist mixtapes jump-started the careers of a new generation of musicians and reinvigorated the concept of a mixtape, but one which hardly interacted with the emotive Gen X mixtape at that time. The two different meanings existed largely independently in this decade. The Gen X mixtape and its growing resurgence in pop culture intersects contemporary investment in remembering, recreating, and analogizing the past: imbuing a cassette tape with nostalgic meaning.

CULTURAL MEMORY

Unlike the mainstream understanding of nostalgia, collective memory remains a more coherently academic term which has a formalized definition on how representations of the past are used to create shared cultural knowledge by future generations.[1] Much of the literature on commemoration as a focus for collective memory resides in shared symbols and imagery.[2] Mixtapes and pop music are contemporary mass media examples of this concept. Only recently have scholars begun to think in terms of auditory collective memory as equally relevant to the physical representations. The shared collective memory of groups like The Beatles or The Rolling Stones has constructed an iconography around classic rock and its fan base. Cultural history allows scholars to acknowledge, "culture shapes, as much as it is shaped by, the social structure."[3] Personal memory, as a result, changes over time as collective memory influences personal recollection. Sales of live or remastered albums, reanalysis of festivals like Woodstock, and even retro music tours by aging bands have modified how individuals relate to and remember their youthful interactions. Memory remains imprecise and can change as larger events supersede personal stories.

Groups of individuals can utilize music and other media to share common experiences and solidify their importance as memorable. This type of collective memory overlaps with the studies of collective auditory nostalgia. An early analysis of American phonograph listeners from 1921 suggested that listening to records transported Americans, often of immigrant background, back to absent homes and families. The music they heard triggered an auditory response which they felt as nostalgia for a distant place. The actual song was less important than shared musical style.[4] Histories of the radio have demonstrated that the curated format of radio stations allows listeners to self-select a musical genre which holds a personal appeal. Although the listener does not have power over the songs they hear, they have chosen a station which plays the style of music they desire. An "oldies station" allows listeners to share a collective, albeit imaginary in many cases, experience with other listeners.[5] The music has created a "mood" or a cultural familiarity with a relatable past.

Not all experiences of collective auditory nostalgia or collective memory indicate a dislocation of time and place. For many individuals, the mere experience of youth created an indelible auditory memory. The rise of counterculture and individualization of music listening, codified in the technology which allowed for taping, organizing, and sharing artifacts with one another, reflects a coherent subculture in the late twentieth century. While not all individuals listened to the same types of music, music as a youth culture phenomenon became a quintessential identity market. The diversification of musical styles from the 1950s forward not only helped to define youth cultures but also allowed for a nostalgia tied to both music and technology. Those individuals who find meaning in the visual representation or literary reinterpretation of the mixtape as a definitive cultural artifact of their youth share a common history and memory. In her study "Music, Memory and History" author Kay Shelemay proves musical experiences shift over time as collective experience impacts personal memory. Key to her analysis is understanding how music "is valued as an experience that joins individuals with a group."[6] Over time one's personal memory can become reflective of a generational collective memory of the past. The nostalgic emotional appeal of the past becomes codified in the music of a generation, or the physical representation of it via a mixtape.

With technological advancement in music production and listening, collective memory and auditory nostalgia have shifted. The creation of the Walkman and eventually digital streaming devices allowed music listening to become a predominantly private experience. Rather than sharing music as a group experience, individuals can curate compilations of individually relevant songs. Professor of Sound Studies, Michael Bull argued, "The coupling of the personal to the commodity is a hallmark of iPod culture with users in potentially constant touch with their narrative past."[7] This idea predates the iPod; the mixtape, a technological product, allowed users to connect to their narrative pasts. As Bull states, "Sound is a powerful aphrodisiac when it comes to evoking memory."[8] The mixtape functions as a shared personal memory. While many mixtape stories include a romantic connection, they frequently evoke emotional ties between creator and recipient. The order of the songs and the physical item on which they had been recorded are of equal importance for a mixtape. The mood of a mixtape could shift from song to song, but the order of the songs alongside the choice of song title or artist created a unique artifact in which individuals could store emotional nostalgia. Listening to the mixtape allowed for the auditory nostalgic response. Over time, the nostalgia became imbued in the physical item, regardless of the ability to listen to the songs.

In an analysis of mixtape discussions since 2000, nostalgia is the most often evoked model. While individuals listen to or remember mixtapes with nostalgia, they have become vectors of the emotion itself. Interviewers have gifted mixtapes with the weight of nostalgia. Writers harken back to the "good old days" and deliberately use the term "nostalgia" to describe their reflections. The pop-culture definitions of nostalgia often assume a white, middle-class experience that simplifies and can distort reality.[9] An idealization of the past in which mythmakers see the golden age as a perfect moment that ignores cultural disparity and disregards tension undermines the nuance of any historical period. The further one moves away from the mixtape as a staple of youth culture life, the less the auditory nostalgia becomes a point of reference. The mixtape becomes a visual representation of a technology and an idealized past. The mixtape has become a cultural icon of Gen X in particular: a paradigmatic youth culture experience that, like all cultural memory, oversimplifies historical reality.

Once we understand the meaning of nostalgia as a longing for a simplified past and the fascination with retro as an investment in the past and a semi-rejection of the present, the next step is to understand how marketing and consumer identity used the ideas of nostalgia and retro-ness. The term "retro" first emerged in the 1960s as an abbreviation of the French term *rétrograde*. The original term in French implied those who opposed progress or wanted a return to an earlier state. By the 1970s a return to a style, idea, or fashion from the recent past became the accepted definition. Retro rarely implies a return to anything older than the twentieth century. In *Retromania*, Simon Reynolds clarifies the definition stating,

> The word "retro" has a quite specific meaning: it refers to a self-conscious fetish for period stylisation (in music, clothes, design) expressed creatively through pastiche and citation. Retro in its strict sense tends to be the preserve of aesthetes, connoisseurs and collectors, people who possess a near-scholarly depth of knowledge combined with a sharp sense of irony. But the word has come to be used in a much more vague way to describe pretty much anything that relates to the relatively recent past of popular culture.[10]

The immediacy of a retro culture often still resides in living memory. A retro model suggests pop culture artifacts found in flea markets rather than in auction halls. It implies an amusement and at times an ironic affiliation rather than a serious academic analysis of the past. Retro rarely indicates a specific, narrowly defined era. Instead, "a pseudohistorical imitation of fashion and commodities from a 'dead past,'" combine multiple periods into an amalgamated prior era.[11] A criticism of current realities, this idea suggests the forgotten past is preferable to today. Retro evokes the past because what *was* has a greater appeal than what *is*. Like nostalgia, retro often refers to an appeal for the past but through tangible, visible artifacts.

With the current appeal of "retro" in pop culture and mass media, the term has at times developed a negative connotation to imply a campiness and an appeal to trendiness without any appreciation of an artifact's original meaning.

Reynolds asks, "Is nostalgia stopping our culture's ability to surge forward, or are we nostalgic precisely because our culture has stopped moving forward and so we inevitably look back to more momentous and dynamic times?"[12] Likewise, Bull questioned if consumer culture has commodified the past to simulate and sell nostalgia.[13] Yet both authors, while acknowledging the consumptive appeal of nostalgia, argue that consumers choose to re-appropriate the past because technology allows them to access the past with ease. Paul Grainge on the other hand claims, "the commodification of nostalgia perhaps more accurately demonstrates the contingencies of niche marketing than any particular index of cultural longing."[14] Nostalgia is a marketing strategy to incorporate niche audiences in an expanding consumer market. Music lovers have long had the ability to access music from any past period because of the continued sale of music from all generations. Nostalgia in the music industry has allowed for reissuing back catalogs of old recordings for profits. This type of nostalgic accumulation allows for profit from old products.[15] Music is a realm in which the audience can participate in micro-scale product creation because of the ability to create compilations, whether through a cassette mixtape or through a digital playlist.

Nonetheless, the continued role of creativity and individual ways of rethinking the past has allowed for new consumer products to not merely recreate the past but create new products to interact with the past. Sampling music, as is common in hip hop, is one example of using old sounds in new material; it is not merely borrowing from the past. "New old music," which plays on the styles of the past but allows for the creation of new bands, new songs, and new artistic endeavors incorporate nostalgia by merging the old and the new.[16] Psychedelic rock musician Damon Krukowski writes, "Surface noise and tape hiss are not flaws in analog media but artifacts of their use."[17] Hip hop and genres like lo-fi also revel in the whine and hiss of tape technology, using both digital and analog means to insert audio noise to music which sounds too pure.[18] In writing about the future of nostalgia Boym clarifies, "Nostalgia is about the virtual reality of human consciousness that cannot be captured even by the most advanced technological gadgets.[. . .] Creative nostalgia reveals the fantasies of the age, and it is in those fantasies and potentialities that the future is born."[19] For Boym, nostalgia is about the present and the future, as much as it is about recreating and redefining the past; it can be continually created and modified.

The Mixtape as Nostalgia

The mixtape has become an icon of a concrete "souvenirization of the past."[20] For some individuals, the discovery of the physical object from a personal past allows for the "reflective nostalgia" of personal recollection. In a 2005 discussion of Thurston Moore's book *Mix Tape*, author Sara Bir claimed cassettes were becoming irrelevant, but mixtapes remained relevant. "I still have all of my old mix tapes; disposing of a mix tape is like throwing away a handwritten letter. [. . .] in the wow and flutter of thinning magnetic tape, as beautiful in its hiss as medieval manuscripts are in their decay."[21] Her description of the tangible distortion emphasizes the technostalgic appeal for the tape's imperfection.

In her article which analyzes how pop music signifies memory, Comparative Media Studies professor José van Dijck states, "Audio artifacts and technologies apparently invoke a cultural nostalgia typical for a specific time and age."[22] She asserts music creates a living memory, in which hearing a song elicits a reflective emotional response to the original moment of hearing the song. With a mixtape, it is more than the individual song, it is the series and order of the entire tape that elicits a collective memory. The imperfections in the cassette personalize and solidify the specific mixtape version of a given song. This memory includes events around listening to the song, the mixtape creator, and the recipient of the tape. Mixtapes represent private auditory narratives of youth culture related to friendship, shared cultural exchange, or romantic encounters. Listening to music as a young person in the late 20th century exemplified social and cultural exchange.

How individuals remember music is shaped through individual emotion but also reflective of the social and cultural milieu of hearing music. This idealized past is not necessarily a political moment in time, but instead an examination of material culture and an analysis of emotional memory tied to a physical object and the music on that object. The actual songs on a mixtape have less relevance than the idea of someone self-consciously choosing songs and a playlist order for those songs. The song that triggers an emotional, nostalgic response is personal. Bull argues for a "mediated nostalgia": self-consciously created using mechanical reproduction—whether a gramophone, an iPod, or a mixtape.[23] In this way, the nostalgia inherent in a mixtape is quantifiable because of the physical artifact. The tangible item is as important as the music recorded on it, if not more important. The concept of nostalgia suggests a longing for the past associated with happy memories; a past "golden age" of stability and authenticity.[24] Moreover, it signifies a modern middle-class population which self-consciously names emotion. Songs often evoke memories of general times and places. Mixtapes, and the music on them, emphasizes a sense of emotionality at remembering the past and reflecting on those moments.

MUSICIANS MAKING MIXTAPES

By the twenty-first century, rap and hip hop had become predominant genres in American music. No longer sidelined as independent music outside the mainstream label system, rap had become a powerful industry player. Attention focused on the legality of sampling and the marketing of popular artists shifted the relationship musicians had to mixtapes. In the 1980s hip-hop mixtapes had appeared as independent compilations released by DJs on cassette. By the 1990s more mixtapes appeared in the commercial industry, but they remained independent compilations, released on cassette or CD. The move to label an album a mixtape shifted in the 2000s and the number of albums released grew tenfold. From the 530 listed mixtape albums in Discogs released in the United States for the entire 1990s, the number jumped to 4,300 in the 2000s.[25] By 2005 music had moved into digital sales. The RIAA estimated that mixtapes generated as much as $150 million each year in the first years of the twenty-first century.[26] In retaliation they filed lawsuits against the illegal bootlegging and raided local record stores, confiscating hip hop mixtapes and attempting to shut down the extra-legal creation and sale of artist-made mixtapes.[27] Between 2005 and 2007 the RIAA worked with local law enforcement to shut down the illegal mixtape game. In January 2007 DJ Drama and DJ Don Cannon, co-founders of Generation Now who had created a prominent mixtape series called *Gangsta Grillz*, were arrested on bootlegging and federal racketeering charges tied to their sales of mixtapes.[28] The RIAA confiscated more than 80,000 CDs and recording equipment from the teams' Atlanta studio.[29] *Gangsta Grillz'*, which had unauthorized remixes of commercial releases, shut down almost immediately. Mixtape DJs became obsolete as the industry attempted to criminalize the mixtape and co-opt it for a new generation.[30] In a retrospective on the closing of *Gangsta Grillz'*, a *Billboard* journalist claimed,

> By the time of the raid, mixtapes had grown from homemade mix cassettes sold on street corners and barbershops to an underground, semi-legal marketplace where album-quality releases from high-profile rappers generated between 30 million and 50 million sales each year, according to the RIAA, working out to a conservative estimate of $150 million to $250 million annually by the end of 2006.[31]

With the end of the DJ-created analog mixtapes, a new generation redefined what a hip hop mixtape was. In the first decade of the 2000s mixtapes "became a tool for aspiring rappers to distribute their own work on the streets in the absence of a record deal, or for enterprising DJs to leverage their own personal connections and marketing savvy to act as cultural arbiters within the hip-hop scene."[32] In 2002, after Columbia Records had dropped him, 50 Cent released the album *50 Cent Is the Future*.[33] The prophetic title ushered in a new era of album, rapping over and transforming other artist's songs. This album "demolished the unspoken division between street rapper and pop artist, uniting hardcore and pop while embracing sing-song hooks with sardonic glee."[34] 50 Cent's mixtape, the first created solely by a single artist, shifted the idea of how mixtapes could function and earned him a record label contract. He won "Best Artist on a Mixtape" Award at the 2002 7th Annual Justo's Mixtape Awards.[35] Jay Z released *The S-Carter Collection* in 2003, which also included him rapping over other people's music to showcase his skills.[36] Between 2007 and 2009 Nicki Minaj, a female rapper from Queens, released three mixtapes, *Playtime Is Over, Sucka Free*, and *Beam Me Up Scotty*.[37] She used her overt sexuality, visually and musically, to promote herself and gain the attention of the recording industry.[38] These artists skyrocketed into the mainstream through their independent mixtapes. Their ability to engage fans on their own terms showed the industry the fanbase and hype they could create autonomously. Maintaining independent power, the digital generation of hip hop artists propelled the genre to new heights. The hip hop mixtape had again shifted definitions, but it remained a staple of an ever-expanding musical genre. Young people, the world over, have heard, accessed, and interacted with hip hop in no small part because of the artists' ability to modify and utilize the mixtape to reach their audience. [39]

Existing largely independently from the hip hop mixtape, most mentions of mixtapes in rock songs represent nostalgic youth culture. While mixtapes reflect a certain generation of music listeners, they cross demographics of musical genre ranging from emo to boy band to "Indietronica."[40] The genre with the largest number of mixtape-themed songs outside of hip hop is country music. Across genres, the most interesting aspect of the songs is how the songwriters use the word mixtape to represent a simpler era in the past. More than once, musicians mention specific ages and dates, like, "Well I can't believe we were seventeen"[41] or "Do you remember me, we were only fifteen."[42] In both songs, by The Night Game and JP Cooper respectively, the songs nostalgically harken back to high school and the innocence of those years. The Night Game song further establishes its timeline singing, "It was the summer before our senior year."[43] For the artists, the mixtape is a way to situate a moment in which music set the tone for their high school adventures and romances.

Throughout their songs, musicians reference one another. This reference demonstrates a band's credentials by acknowledging their musical forbearers or highlighting other musical influences. Country singers Brett Kissel and Jake Owen both describe a "George Strait mixtape."[44] As musicians releasing music since 2015, they establish their roots by referencing a well-known male country

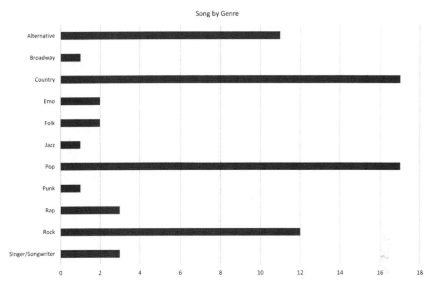

Figure 5.1 Songs Released by Genre Which Included "Mixtape" in Their Lyrics. This Chart Does Not Include the Wide Number of Hip Hop Songs Which Use "Mixtape" as the Context for an Independent EP. Those Songs Number in the Hundreds. (Data collected from genius.com 2020 and discogs.com 2020) Chart Created by the Author.

singer. In their 2012 song, "This is How We Roll," country band Florida Georgia Line shows they are not only country fans, nor do they expect their fans to only listen to country. They sing, "The mixtape's got a little Hank, little Drake,"[45] referencing king of country music Hank Williams and popular hip-hop artist Drake in the same breath. Twangy Texas musician Adam Fears sings a similar line "Mix up the boom or the bang. Dre or the Hank/Anything just to get us singin'" alluding to Dr. Dre, another quintessential rapper and Hank Williams again.[46] The strong sales of hip hop across demographic lines in the past ten years is a logical reason for bands to mention rap artists; it speaks to the young generation they want to buy their music and it reflects the popularity of the hip hop mixtape. Two years later in their 2014 song "That's What's Up," Florida Georgia Line again references a variety of musical influences singing, "A little bit of Skynyrd on the box" and later in the song "It's even better than Alabama's Greatest Hits."[47] Rather than speak to a young audience aware of current releases, this song mentions two popular bands in the 1980s. In 2013 Luke Bryan sang, "Put in my country rock hip hop mixtape/Little Conway, a little T-Pain, might just make it rain."[48] Like Florida Georgia Line, this contrast between country and hip hop stands out for its diversity. It not only showcases a greater depth of musical knowledge by bands, it also connects them to main-stream record sales. For audiences it allows them to feel connected to a variety of seemingly disparate genres when the bands themselves respect these artists. Young country artist Ashley McBryde likewise highlights her models when she sings, "Mama kept Police playin' in the kitchen turned up just a little too loud/Daddy was a rockstar ridin' on a tractor, listenin' to Townes Van Zandt."[49] Her tune "Radioland," an homage to the role the radio played in her musical education growing up, later references "Jack and Diane," the infamous 1980s song by John Mellencamp.

Country songs are not alone in situating their music within the realm of other bands and musicians. The 2000 hardcore emo song "Make Me a Mixed Tape" by the Promise Ring requests, "Make me a mixtape, don't leave out Husker Du/Put something on that The Cars did in 1982."[50] This choice of bands showcases an awareness and an appreciation of earlier generations of punk and new wave music, whose sounds are echoed in the Promise Ring's music. Like others, Why Don't We's 2018 pop song "Trust Fund Baby" grounds their lyrics in both old and new bands. They mention Missy Elliot and 50 Cent, two artists whose influence emerges in how the musicians sing talk their songs, similar to rapping. British Jazz artist Jamie Cullum's 2010 "Mixtape" claims, "I'll make you mixtape that's a blueprint of my soul." As proof of his claim, throughout the song he mentions Morrisey, John Coltrane, Cinematic Orchestra, De La Soul, the Shangri-La's, Nine Inch Nails, Louis Armstrong, and Thelonious [Monk]. This list of musicians "details everything that's running 'round my head."[51] Cullum uses his lyrics to boast about the depth of his musical knowledge. Like other musicians, Cullum's description of mixtapes highlights the appeal of the physical artifact when he describes it as, "a sparkling jewel of manual labor."[52]

Listing bands can also anchor a song in a certain era. In his 2015 melancholic electronic song "Perfect Life," Steven Wilson included the line, "We'd listen to her mix tapes; Dead Can Dance, Felt, This Mortal Coil."[53] This trio of indie British and Australian bands all released music in the mid-1980s which situates the song. Like the mention of hip hop and country artists above, this also defines the world in which the music lives, mentioning bands listeners may know. Not all songs use mixtapes as literally. Mixtapes are incorporated into lyrics to create an image. The playlist is less important than the artifact.

Musicians sing about the mixtape as an analogy for emotional attachment both overtly and subtly. Swedish musician Jen's 2018 "Mixtape" overtly states that the mixtape he intends to make is to "let the songs on it explain/ The way I feel about you."[54] Throughout the song he clarifies his feelings, asking for reconsideration. He admits including "romantic songs" is "kinda old-school" but he hopes it will refresh memories of time together.[55] JP Cooper's "September Song" also mourns lost innocence. Reminiscing about the past, and putting it in contemporary terms, he admits he "feel[s] like my heart couldn't take it/'cause if we met [now] we'd be strangers."[56] Yet he repeatedly listens to their mixtape from the past. The noise pop band Scarling released "City Noise" in a 2005 lament which touches on abusive relationships. They discuss depression, learning to fight, and "the final kiss from a lover's fist."[57] For this band "the mixtape in your heart" represents the internal repression of the emotions they cannot express outwardly.[58] Not all sentimental songs are about people. Brooke White's "Phoenix" manifests nostalgia in its truest form, singing about home. She reminisces about "making mixtapes in the backyard by the pool," and remembering her time there. She follows up "Oh let the light shine down on Phoenix when it rains/Cause I can't leave here knowing all of my favorite things have changed."[59] There is a hint in her lyrics that one of the things to have changed was a person she wanted to hold onto. These diverse songs all utilize the mixtape as a representation of emotional outpouring, whether the feelings are upbeat, wistful, or overwhelmed. Mixtape becomes metaphorically relevant as a placeholder for emotionality.

Tift Merritt opened her 2010 album *See You on the Moon* with the song titled "Mixtape." Merritt uses a mixtape as an allusion to romance and love. She sings, "I'm just making you mixtapes with homemade covers/Analog to show we're lovers," not only mentioning the artifact she is creating, but the throwback technology of using analog over digital.[60] In an NPR interview, Afton Lorraine Woodward described the song, stating it "faithfully captures the nostalgia attached to the mostly bygone plastic representation of young and uncertain love."[61] This interview reflects the way mainstream media discusses mixtapes through the lens of nostalgia and retro appeal. Merritt sings, "And here under the jacket folds inside/I've taped my heart for you to find," referencing the J-Card album art. With lyrics like "I la love you/With this plastic cassette"[62] Merritt demonstrates the way a small physical object can represent a much larger idea. Releasing this song in 2010 places her in a generation that relates to how people invested in the mixtape. But it also suggests, as does the NPR discussion, the continued recognition of what these objects represented. Woodward not only describes the "earnestness and dedication that goes into a mixtape" but also the nostalgia of reflecting on a time in the past, which underscores the continued impact of memory tied to these objects.[63]

Not all singers who reference mixtapes rely on personal memory. Young Australian singer Cody Simpson was born after their demise. Yet, he sings about them in his 2013 wooing song "If You Left Him For Me." In the first verse, Simpson asks, "Does he make you laugh, When he's texting you in class, girl?" which situates the song in the smartphone era.[64] In the second verse, Simpson asks, "Does he make you mixtapes/When you've had a bad day," asserting he/Simpson would.[65] The line stands out in contrast to the contemporary reference to texting. As a sixteen-year-old who never lived in the cassette era, Simpson references mixtapes and roses as recognizable romantic gestures which do not need explanation. The assumption of understanding a defunct artifact highlights the continued appeal for this object among a new youth generation.

Desire replaces wooing for some musicians. Cullum sings, "I'll make you a mixtape that will charm you into bed," in his 2010 piano-driven "Mixtape."[66] Björk's 2017 "Arisen My Senses" alludes to sex with lines like "Every cell in my body/lined up for you."[67] She describes the things she wants to do as "weaving a mix-tape/with every crossfade," which is a figurative imagery representative of her eclectic songwriting. All Time Low sing about a "Pretty little time bomb" who is "sex in stereo," in their 2009 song "Lost In Stereo."[68] The band imagines her with a "mixtape of her favorite bands/tearin' up the radio."[69] The visuals they incorporate create an image of an unattainable object of lust. Less nostalgic than the wistful songs, these descriptions of physicality and ardor also use a stylistic imagery in which the mixtape creates desire.

The break-up songs are an important flip side to the romantic wooing tape. In 2010, the same year as Tift Merritt's song, the band Jimmy Eat World released another song called "Mixtape" on their album *Invented*. Unlike the hopefulness in Merritt's song, fellow Gen Xer, Jim Adkins' voice and lyrics represent the epitome of the breakup mixtape, "Maybe we could put your tape back on/Rewind until the moment we went wrong." His lyrics illustrate his attempt to understand what went wrong, singing, "I was always just a little bit lost."[70] Adkins can express his confusion and despondency through nostalgic, emotion-driven lyrics. In this song, the nostalgia reflects not only the lost era of the mixtape and the means of sharing ideas, but also the nostalgia for a love gone wrong. Both Merritt and Adkins came of age when the mixtape encapsulated emotions and love and connections. The mixtape no longer existed in its cassette form by 2010, but the idea of an object to analyze meanings of love and reminisce about happier times remained.

Continuing the emotional journey, emo band Brand New moved from sadness to resentment in their mention of a mixtape. When they released their first studio album, *Your Favorite Weapon*, in 2001, an online review highlighted the song "Mixtape" as one of the two worthy songs. The angry, emo song points fingers at an ex-lover for their foibles. The lyrics outline all the ways the ex- is fallible including, "And the way you always criticize the Smiths, /And Morrissey."[71] Once again, other bands are referenced in a song, but in this case to condemn someone. Jesse Lacey, the lead singer, harps, "I really mean I wish that you'd grow up. /This is the first song for your mix tape."[72] For this band, the lyric suggests they intend to make and deliver a break-up mixtape which allows them to pour out their sadness and irritation through music. Using music to express anger remains more socially palatable than expressing it physically.

In his review of Brand New, Adam Dlugacz wrote they, "exhibit a heart-on-the-sleeves style that works," which he describes as "immature brilliance."[73] The song chastises an ex-girlfriend with lines like, "I got a twenty-eight dollar bill/That says no one's ever seen you without make-up" The sense of anger at a love gone wrong is exhibited in the lyrics and the guitar riffs. The break-up tape, the songs one listens to in anger or depression, is a well-known mixtape trope. It is a way of expressing frustration and sadness, again without having to state it. The lyrics echo the type of music. Although Dlugacz describes the guitar riffs as generic, the guitar-based rock song accentuates the line, "And I know that you're a sucker for anything acoustic." The final emotive outburst comes with the line, "And the way you don't appreciate Brand New, /Or me."[74] This song is not merely about love lost, but passionate pride over someone not understanding their music.

Woven into many of the songs is the overarching association with music and memory. The term "mixtape" references a simpler era in which an analog creation defined a personal relationship. In addition to the pervasive romantic themes are the friendship, fun, and partying songs. They include lines about being a teenager like, "Do you remember me, we were only fifteen,"[75] and "Nothing will ever be/Like when were seventeen,"[76] or "It was the summer before our senior year,"[77] and "That runaround freedom summer eighty-nine."[78] Another song laments, "Need a teenage time machine [. . .] Too cool to care, too young to know."[79] Mixtapes factor into all of these memories with lines like, "Found one of your old mixtapes"[80] and "Mixtape blew out the speakers on that old ragtop"[81] which again illustrate the position of a mixtape to represent nostalgia. All five of these tunes, ranging from country pop to hard rock, were released between 2016 and 2018. They illustrate the link between a simpler time and the mixtape as its manifestation. The artist's age is inconsequential which demonstrates the ubiquity of the mixtape as a placeholder for the past regardless of the musicians' concrete interaction with cassettes.

BOOKS

Memoir

In 2011, possibly in response to books like Thurston Moore's and Jason Bitner's, Courtney Smith published her series of essays called *Record Collecting for Girls: Unleashing Your Inner Music Nerd, One Album at a Time*, in which she shared, "I wondered, what would a female music nerd have to say? Because girls get their hearts broken and make mix tapes about it, too."[82] Smith contends male voices tend to dominate the discussion about music fandom and obsession and she aimed to revise that narrative. Playing directly on *High Fidelity*, she has a chapter entitled, "Top Five Lists" in which she expresses her frustration with how often women were dismissed from top-five lists of artists. As a result, she walks readers through her own rules to making Top Five artists' lists.[83] Her book is part memoir, and part an explanatory analysis of how and why people share, collect, and engage with music. Smith, who worked for MTV, describes her deep engagement with music from a young age, remembering lyrics, and details from various bands. To underscore her youthful devotion she admits, "I was listening to the radio and making mix tapes or playing records on my sweet Fisher-Price turntable," outlining how young she would have been.[84] With chapter titles like "Are We Breaking Up?" and "Our Song, Your Song, My Song," much of Smith's analysis evaluates music as a shared social bond. She analyzes mixtapes to understand the different personal relationships she has had over time. She writes,

> I spent a lot of time thinking about what it means to share your music with someone when you're in a relationship, [. . .] When guys make us mix tapes and play us songs, they aren't just showing off. They're trying to tell us some truth about themselves through the sounds and words of an intermediary. The realization has made me appreciate all the mix tapes I've ever received all the more.[85]

This statement reinforces how "guys" use music to speak feelings they cannot state openly. While Smith incorporates personal stories, her book is not a nostalgic memory of her past. Instead, the specific examples allow her to write about how people use music as a connective framework. The focus on romance and the title of the book made at least one interviewer ask if she wrote her book exclusively for "girls" as the title suggests. Smith explained she wrote it for anyone who "talks about music more than is socially acceptable," but with a female perspective.[86] Smith's title acknowledges women, but her statement aligns with a Gen X narrative which is not outwardly feminist. While Smith is not the only woman who wrote about mixtapes in this generation, she remains in the minority. As books about music and record collecting are often written from a male perspective, she defends her deep knowledge of music as "socially acceptable," regardless of her gender. Smith's book highlights a continued fascination with the mixtape. She incorporates writing tropes borrowed from her music-influenced forefathers. Like musicians and novelists' post-2010 she imbues the term "mixtape" with nostalgic connection tied to retro artifacts.

Fiction

In 2009 two novels were published which used mixtapes to unify characters. These authors wrote in an era in which they chose to use a technology which was no longer relevant and slowly becoming nostalgic. The role of the cassettes shifts from esoteric to ideological. No longer are cassettes a part of the mainstream lived experience. Instead, they become passé, out of touch, and then nostalgic. The authors navigate their created worlds; they shift their discussions and use of the cassette and the mixtape to propel their stories.

David Nicholls wrote about the recent past in which mixtapes permeated young people's lives. His novel *One Day* follows the life of two British college friends, Emma and Dexter, on the same date every year for twenty years. The episodic interaction, beginning in 1989, offers Nicholls the opportunity to play with shifting technology. The mixtape from the beginning of the book, becomes a mix CD eleven years later. Eventually Dexter decries the ridiculousness of spending time making a compilation tape. While the story centers on unrequited love, Nicholls' novel showcases this early twenty-first-century transition away from analog technology.

In 1989–1990 Emma and Dexter live on opposite sides of the world. Emma, who pines for Dexter, sends him a mixtape. The narrator clarifies, "Letters, like compilation tapes, were really vehicles for unexpressed emotions and she was clearly putting far too much time and energy into them."[87] The next year, a drunk Dexter replies to Emma writing, "It's CHUCKING IT DOWN, Em, so loud that I barely hear the compilation tape you made me which I like a lot incidentally except for that jangly indie stuff because after all I'm not some GIRL."[88] Dexter sees emotionality as feminine and ignores the message Emma intended with her tape. Through the novel Dexter is unable to recognize how important Emma is; he often derides the centrality of their friendship and only realizes her significance in retrospect. This uneven relationship permeates the first half of the novel.

Emma remakes the same compilation as a CD and gives it to Dexter on the anniversary of their friendship. Time, maturity, and shifting life experiences allow Dexter to understand the importance of both Emma and the music she had shared eleven years earlier. She included a birthday card with the CD, clarifying, "Here it is—a homemade present. Keep telling yourself—it's the thought that counts it's the thought that counts. This is a loving CD reproduction of a cassette compilation I made for you ages ago. None of your chill-out rubbish; proper songs. Hope you enjoy this."[89] Emma's feelings have changed. No longer pining for Dexter, her gift acknowledges their long friendship. This compilation CD flips the tables and Dexter becomes the reflective partner considering the music and Emma's importance. He listens to songs by groups like Massive Attack and Public Enemy and reminisces dancing to the Smiths, a band he never particularly liked. Seeing Emma's handwriting and hearing the music, Dexter has a wave of desire to talk to her. Emma's friendship is central, but the representation of her in the mixtape

reflects a nostalgia for their past selves. Maturity and time have shifted a
compilation mix from irrelevant to nostalgic.

Eventually Emma and Dexter marry. Reflecting on their connection
through the years, Dexter ponders romance as a married man nearing forty.
He suggests stability supersedes emotional uncertainty:

> Falling in love like that? Writing poetry, crying at pop songs? Dragging
> people into photo-booths, taking a whole day to make a compilation tape, [. . .]
> Ridiculous at thirty-eight, to expect a song or book or film to change your life.
> No, everything had evened out and settled down and life was lived against a
> general background hum of comfort, satisfaction and familiarity. There would
> be no more of those nerve-jangling highs and lows.[90]

Dexter believes compilation tapes and overt emotionality are only relevant
for younger people. Nicholls' episodic novel shows how technology shifted
at the end of the twentieth century. Early in their relationship Dexter rebuffs
Emma's emotionally laden mixtape. Ten years later, the recreated mix CD
allows Dexter to rethink his connection to Emma. By the novel's end, mixtapes are no longer relevant, nor are the emotions tied to them. For Dexter,
and Nicholls, the mixtape represents a past to put aside.

Unlike David Nicholls who wanted to show how relationships shift over
a long period, Yvonne Prinz wrote a book mired in teenage interaction
and the immediacy of strong feelings. In *Vinyl Princess*, sixteen-year-old
"music geek" Allie loves music, bemoans the lack of interest in the physical album, and falls into an unexpected relationship. However, the lamen-
tation over the death of LPs and the rise of the digital medium highlights
a specific "present," because the resurgence of vinyl had not yet occurred
when her book was published. Yvonne Prinz, co-owner of Amoeba Music
of Berkeley, the largest independent record store in the country in 2009,
released *Vinyl Princess* that year.[91] Amoeba Music had a policy of buying music directly from the artist which made it popular with independent
musicians and hip hop artists in particular.[92] Prinz's familiarity with the
anti-commercial music scene authenticates her book and understanding of
music culture. The story takes place after cassette sales waned, in the surge
of streaming and downloading music, and before the nostalgia for vinyl
had kicked in. Prinz stated, "I did want to ride that nostalgia train in a big
way with a dollop of new indie thrown in, all the while trying not to stray
too far from the mainstream. I had to keep my reader in mind and I didn't
want too many young readers saying, 'Huh?'"[93] In this way, Prinz bridges
the gap between her desires to write about a poignant concept yet maintain
relevance for a young audience. Much YA literature that engages with mixtapes attempts this balance.

Prinz's knowledge and love of music permeates the story; "[She] wanted to write a *High Fidelity* for kids," and succeeded.[94] Allie, a music junkie, works in a Telegraph Avenue music store, has created a blog about her love of vinyl, and knows everything there is to know about music released in the vinyl era. She mixes classic rock like Bob Dylan and Pink Floyd with contemporary musicians like Gogol Bordello and Dropkick Murphys. While at work Zach, an incoming Berkeley freshman who she has shared musical jabs with, stops by. For Allie, cassettes are passé. When he brings Allie a mix CD, she considers it "the mating call of the romantically challenged."[95] He included "a giant moth on the cover. It looks like he cut it out of a *National Geographic* magazine," which to Allie is embarrassing and too earnest.[96] Allie dismisses both the idea of a physical mix CD as underwhelming and potentially embarrassing. The idea of a DIY cover further horrifies her sensibilities. She asserts no good will come of his terribly underwhelming attempt. Prinz gives Allie agency to reject a boy's courtship attempt through music. The relationship evolves through shared interest and not a heart-on-the-sleeve physical token. When Prinz wrote *Vinyl Princess*, a mix "tape" seemed anachronistic because the novel appeared prior to cassette tape nostalgia. As a vinyl lover who disliked the digital medium, a mix CD would have been the only logical medium on which to create and give a mix. The creation of a mix CD codifies the characters of Zach and Allie as post-mixtape, anti-digital playlist, pre-nostalgia vinyl/cassette throwback.

The relationship between Zach and Allies grows and she changes her impression of him. A shared love of music, specifically vinyl, connected Zach and Allie while the mix creation underlined what Allie missed at first, "Zach's mix brings me to my knees."[97] He had reached out in the hopes of connecting and she eventually recognized him as a soulmate. After listening to the entire mix, full of artists like Ella Fitzgerald, Crowded House, the Kinks, and Iggy Pop, Allie realizes:

> Just for the record, I'm a girl who considers herself the all-time reigning queen of the mix. My mixes are legendary but, I have to admit, not one of them even comes close to the CD Zach made for me. If I'd never met Zach before and I was handed the mix and told to listen to it, I would probably propose marriage, sight unseen, or I'd at least offer to be his girlfriend. I abandon the blog and listen to the CD over again with my eyes closed.[98]

Her perception of Zach shifted because of his mixing ability. Prinz lists every song and artist on the mix to underline the concrete importance of the music. For these characters, the music is the connection.

Musical taste, the ability to create a good track list, or the appeal to emotional heartstrings can change the way a mixtape creator is viewed. Allie views Zach differently because of the amazing compilation he created for her. She describes his mix in a blog entry entitled "The Art of the Mix," a title directly reminiscent of *High Fidelity*. She writes, "An unexpected mix like this can take you somewhere; it can make you feel nostalgic and renewed or it can completely undo you."[99] Zach and Allie bond over understanding a mix is "so much more than throwing a bunch of songs on a CD."[100] The novel is not only a coming-of-age romance story, it is also a love affair with physical music. Although the record store closes as vinyl sales decline, the story ends, "That night I finally finished Zach's mix CD, and I was right: It blew his mind."[101] Allie will continue to engage with analog music on her terms.

Prinz specifically uses nostalgia to discuss her book. She grounded her YA novel in the world of music and mixtapes she understands from her adolescence. Nicholls' book also uses mixtapes to connect characters and to express difficult emotions, similar to the way artists sang about mixtapes as a placeholder for emotionality. The fiction in this time period illustrates the shifting depiction of the mixtape from the normalness of the 1980s and 1990s to the emerging nostalgic appeal of physical artifacts in the twenty-first century.

PERFORMANCE

In the realm of performance, one show took the nostalgia of the mixtape and the retro appeal of the 1980s and turned it up to the maximum. In 2010 the new musical called *miXtape—the Greatest Hits of the 80s* premiered in San Diego. Created by local members of the theatre, Jon Lorenz, Colleen Kollar Smith, and Kerry Meads play into the camp of 1980s retro pop culture. They staged the show 760 times in 3 years.[102] The simple premise involves seven individuals walking on stage with their cell phones and being magically transported back to the 1980s to relive their young adulthood. The show is a medley of over 100 songs from the 1980s including cartoon and TV theme songs. It holds a record as "the longest-running homegrown musical in San Diego history."[103] When the show announced its closing date in 2013 public interest allowed a short extension. Playing for four years in its first run, the show reopened in 2019 for a second, updated run.

In a 2011 interview Leonard Patton, one of the show's actors, discusses the musical's appeal and the place of mixtapes in the 1980s. "You sat by the radio and you would record for hours [. . .] Everybody had mixtapes for every single occasion, their boyfriend, girlfriend, for their friends going on road trips."[104] For fans, the nostalgia brings them in; the actors use the excesses of camp to invest the audience in a ridiculous, yet appealing, over-the-top idea. Audiences attend in costume including neon, bangle bracelets and side ponytails. They often sing along to familiar songs by groups from Depeche Mode to Donna Summer.[105] An online review of the show encouraged people to go stating, "It is a nostalgic look back to a time when a tremendous range of musical styles came onto the scene. [. . .] you will find yourself singing along, dancing in your seats and for many, reflecting on a simpler time when computers and cell phones did not dominate our every waking moment."[106]

The campy, light-hearted musical plays on material culture nostalgia. Incorporating as many pop culture elements as possible into the show, using exaggerated fashion and quintessentially campy behavior, the creators and actors have recreated what the review describes as a simpler time. Mixtape, for this play, symbolizes the mishmash of songs to create something brand new; it personifies nostalgia using retro motifs and kitsch costumes.

Memories of mixtapes, whether the physical cassette tape received in high school or the story in which a mixtape solidified the link between two characters, permeate American youth cultures. The mixtape, like the vinyl revolution, signifies a reflective nostalgia for a moment in the recent past. The auditory aspect of the cassette tape grounded the mixtape in culture originally. The incorporation of outdated technology has led to a resurgence in the mixtape's appeal. The retro appeal of imagery that incorporates neon tones and outmoded cultural artifacts dovetails easily with the cassette culture. When explaining the contemporary nostalgia, the Epstein sisters write, "The reason we have all that nostalgia is that *we lost those things* for a while. There was no Internet to constantly catalog and reference yesterday's episode of *Mister Rogers* or mem-ify *The Little Mermaid*. So when those things came back via digital media, we got the chance to rediscover them."[107] Interviews in which the mixtape is a point of conversation often incorporate nostalgia. The mixtape is a coherent point of remembering and recreating the late-20th century because of the diverse ways it has been incorporated into a variety of different artistic endeavors in the twenty-first century.

In popular culture, creators, from authors to playwrights to musicians have used the mixtape as a basis for a story. Over time the idea of a mixtape shifted from a tangible technological norm to a nostalgic idea of a simpler analog past. This revision of how a community understands and uses a term implies an "armchair nostalgia," in which there is no coherent collective memory or lived experience.[108] Instead there is an accepted social understanding of an idea; creators reconcile the role of pop music and new technology in their work but continue to integrate mixtapes. Literature written since the 2010s has shifted from the mixtape as technologically relevant to the mixtape as nostalgically appealing. The idea of looking back fondly on a moment defines the memoirs and novels. These stories have allowed the term "mixtape" to become a recognizable "pop culture" term again as a technostalgic appeal for cassette culture. While auditory nostalgia remains relevant for many purveyors of the mixtape, it becomes less crucial over time. "Mixtape" becomes a term with a broader meaning than merely a personally crafted cassette tape with a series of songs. The mixtape often signifies a desire to slow down and create a durable item signaling care and emotion. It represents a creative endeavor that unites individuals through the curated music placed on a cassette tape.

NOTES

1. Alon Confino, "Collective Memory and Cultural History: Problems of Method," *The American Historical Review* 102, no. 5 (1997): 1386.

2. Ibid., 1389–90.

3. Ibid., 1395.

4. William H. Kenney, *Recorded Music in American Life: The Phonograph and Popular Memory 1890–1945* (Oxford: Oxford University Press, 1999), 8–10 quoted in Karin Bijsterveld and José van Dijck, eds., *Sound Souvenirs: Audio Technologies, Memory and Cultural Practices* (Amsterdam: Amsterdam University Press, 2009), 85.

5. Susan J. Douglas, *Listening in: Radio and the American Imagination from Amos 'n' Andy and Edward R. Morrow to Wolfman Jack and Howard Stern* (New York: Times Books, 1999), 348 quoted in ibid., 85–86.

6. Kay Kaufman Shelemay, "Music, Memory and History: In Memory of Stuart Feder," *Ethnomusicology Forum* 15, no. 1 (2006): 17–37.

7. Michael Bull, "The Auditory Nostalgia of iPod Culture," in *Sound Souvenirs: Audio Technologies, Memory and Cultural Practices*, ed. Karin Bijsterveld and José van Dijck (Amsterdam: Amsterdam University Press, 2009), 89.

8. Ibid.

9. Stephanie Coontz, *The Way We Never Were: American Families and the Nostalgia Trap* (New York: Basic Books, 1993), 6.

10. Simon Reynolds, *Retromania: Pop Culture's Addiction to Its Own Past* (New York: Faber and Faber, Inc, 2011), xii–xiii.

11. Ryan Moore, *Sells Like Teen Spirit: Music, Youth Culture, and Social Crisis* (New York: New York University Press, 2010), 166.

12. Reynolds, xiv.

13. Bull, 91.

14. Grainge's focus on television examines an audience with a passive relationship to the art they consume; actively searching out old television shows and movies in the pre-digital era was more difficult than finding old music. Moreover, his TV audiences are not involved in recreating commercialized products. Paul Grainge, "Nostalgia and Style in Retro America: Moods, Modes, and Media Recycling," *Journal of American & Comparative Cultures* 23, no. 1 (2004): 32.

15. Ibid.

16. Reynolds, xii.

17. Damon Krukowski, *The New Analog* (2017), 171 as quoted in John Z. Komurki and Luca Bendandi, *Cassette Cultures: Past and Present of a Musical Icon*, English Edition 2019 Benteli ed. (Switzerland: Deutsche Nationalbibliothek; Braun Publishing AG, 2019), 89.

18. Anthony Kwame Harrison, "'Cheaper Than a CD, Plus We Really Mean It': Bay Area Underground Hip Hop Tapes as Subcultural Artefacts," *Popular Music* 25, no. 2 (2006), https://www.jstor.org/stable/3877563.

19. Svetlana Boym, *The Future of Nostalgia* (New York: Basic Books, 2008), eBook, Conclusion.

20. Ibid., chapter 3.

21. Sara Bir, "Mix Emotions: The Mix Tap, Cultural Touchstone of the Analogue Generation," Metro Publishing Inc. (June 22, 2005) http://www.metroactive.com/pap ers/sonoma/06.22.05/mixtapes-0525.html (Accessed June 28, 2020).

22. "Audio Technologies, Memory and Cultural Practices" José van Dijck Bijsterveld and van Dijck, 113.

23. Bull, 85.

24. Grainge, 28.

25. "Exploring Mixtape and Hip Hop," Discogs, https://www.discogs.com/search /?q=mixtape&type=all&page=2&genre_exact=Hip+Hop (Accessed May 12, 2021).

26. Michael Kawaida, "Mixtapes: A Brief History of Hip-Hop's Ever Evolving Tool," *Hot New Hip Hop* (February 25, 2020), https://www.hotnewhiphop.com/m ixtapes-a-brief-history-of-hip-hops-ever-evolving-tool-news.103882.html.

27. *The Day the Mixtape Died: DJ Drama*, podcast audio, Louder Than a Riot, 1 hr 5 mins 2020, https://www.npr.org/2020/10/27/928307301/the-day-the-mixtape-died-dj-drama.

28. Dan Rys, "Mixtapes & Money: Inside the Mainstreaming of Hip-Hop's Shadow Economy," *Billboard* (2017), https://www.billboard.com/articles/columns/ hip-hop/7669109/mixtapes-money-hip-hop-shadow-economy-mainstream.

29. Ibid.

30. *The Day the Mixtape Died: DJ Drama*.

31. Rys, "Mixtapes & Money: Inside the Mainstreaming of Hip-Hop's Shadow Economy."

32. Alex Sayf Cummings, *Democracy of Sound: Music Piracy and the Remaking of American Copyright in the Twentieth Century* (New York: Oxford University Press, 2013), 169.

33. DJ Semtex, "Street Dreams: How Hip-Hop Mixtapes Changed the Game," *Hip-Hop Raised Me* (Medium: Thames & Hudson, 2016), https://medium.com/c uepoint/street-dreams-how-hip-hop-mixtapes-changed-the-game-40af79e8d953.

34. "The 50 Best Rap Mixtapes of the Millennium: From Lil Wayne to Max B to Nicki Minaj, a Look at the Best Free Downloads, Tapes, and CD-Rs Released since 2000," *Pitchfork* (2016), https://pitchfork.com/features/lists-and-guides/9908-the-50-best-rap-mixtapes-of-the-millennium/ (Accessed March 19, 2021).

35. "7th Annual Justo's Mixtape Awards," *Billboard* (2002), https://www.bil lboard.com/articles/news/73164/7th-annual-justos-mixtape-awards (Accessed May 12, 2021).

36. "The 50 Best Rap Mixtapes of the Millennium: From Lil Wayne to Max B to Nicki Minaj, a Look at the Best Free Downloads, Tapes, and CD-Rs Released since 2000."

37. Ibid.

38. James Braxton Peterson, *Hip Hop Headphones: A Scholar's Critical Playlist*, (New York: Bloomsbury Academic, 2016), http://search.ebscohost.com/login.aspx?direct=true&AuthType=sso&db=nlebk&AN=1331575&site=eds-live&scope=site&custid=s7614884&ebv=EB&ppid=pp_1. 53.

39. Anthony Kwame Harrison, *Hip Hop Underground: The Integrity and Ethics of Racial Identification* (Philadelphia: Temple University Press, 2009), 99.

40. Hip hop and rap mixtapes were not included in the data. The pervasiveness of the term would significantly shift the statistical data.

41. "Coffee and Cigarettes," The Night Game, on *The Night Game*, Universal Music Group, 2018.

42. "September Song," JP Cooper, on *Raised Under Grey Skies*, Island Records, 2017.

43. "Coffee and Cigarettes."

44. "Cool With That," Brett Kissel, on *Pick Me Up*, Warner Music Canada, 2015 and "Homemade," Jake Owen on *Greetings From . . . Jake*, Big Loud Records, 2019.

45. "This is How We Roll," Florida Georgia Line on *Here's To The Good Times*, Big Machine Records, 2012.

46. Although the song title references the classic 1991 film Boyz n the Hood, there is no obvious overlap between the song and the film. "Boyz On the Hood," Adam Fears on *Golden Gravel Radio*, Landstar Entertainment, 2013.

47. "That's What's Up," Florida Georgia Line on *Anything Goes*, Big Loud Mountain, 2014.

48. "That's My Kind of Night," Luke Bryan on *Crash My Party*, Capitol Records, 2013.

49. "Radioland," Ashley McBryde on *Girl Going Nowhere*, Warner Music Nashville, 2018.

50. "Make Me a Mixed Tape," The Promise Ring on *Electric Pink,* Jade Tree, 2000.

51. "Mixtape," Jamie Cullum on *The Pursuit*, Universal Music, 2010.

52. Ibid.

53. "Perfect Life," Steven Wilson on *Hand. Cannot. Erase.*, Kscope, 2015.

54. "Mixtape," Jens Leckman (Single Release), Universal Music, 2018.

55. Ibid.

56. "September Song," JP Cooper, on *Raised Under Grey Skies*, Island Records, 2017.

57. "City Noise," Scarling on *So Long, Scarecrow,* Sympathy For the Record Industry, 2005.

58. Ibid.

59. "Phoenix," Brooke White on *High Hopes & Heartbreak* June Baby Records, 2009.

60. "Mixtape," Tift Merritt on *See You On the Moon*, Fantasy, 2010.

61. Afton Lorraine Woodward, "Tift Merritt: A Song for Every 'Mixtape,'" Review, *NPR Music* (2010), https://www.npr.org/templates/story/story.php?storyId=127089755.

62. "Mixtape," Tift Merritt.

63. Woodward.

64. "If You Left Him for Me," Cody Simpson on *Surfer's Paradise*, Atlantic, 2013.

65. Ibid.

66. "Mixtape," Jamie Cullum on *The Pursuit*, Universal Music, 2010.

67. "Arisen My Senses," Björk on *Utopia*, One Little Indian, 2017.

68. "Lost in Stereo," All Time Low on *Nothing Personal*, Hopeless Records, 2009.

69. Ibid.

70. "Mixtape," Jimmy Eat World on *Invented,* DGC Records, 2010.

71. "Mixtape," Brand New on *Your + Favorite + Weapon*, Triple Crown Records, 2001.

72. Ibid.

73. Adam Dlugacz, "Brand New: Your Favorite Weapon," *Pop Matters* (July 7, 2003), https://www.popmatters.com/brandnew-yourfavorite-2495835944.html (Accessed July 13, 2020).

74. "Mixtape," Brand New."

75. "September Song," JP Cooper on *Raised Under Grey Skies*, Island Records, 2016.

76. "The Silence," Halestorm on *Vicious*, Atlantic Records, 2018.

77. "Coffee and Cigarettes," The Night Game.

78. "Can't Be Replaced," Dierks Bentley on *Black*, Capitol Records, 2016.

79. "Too Young to Know," Jessie James Decker on *Gold*, Epic Records, 2017.

80. "The Silence," Halestorm.

81. "Too Young To Know."

82. Courtney E. Smith, *Record Collecting for Girls: Unleashing Your Inner Music Nerd, One Album at a Time* (New York: Houghton Mifflin Harcourt Publishing Company, 2011), 3.

83. Ibid., 5–6.

84. Ibid., 73.

85. Ibid., 151–52.

86. Smith, Courtney E. "Amazon Exclusive: A Q&A with Author Courtney Smith." interview by Amazon Editorial Reviews (2011).

87. David Nicholls, *One Day*, Vintage Contemporaries ed. (United States: Vintage Books, 2010), 22.

88. Ibid., 38.

89. Ibid. 319.

90. Ibid., 382.

91. Joel Selvin, "Music Store a Castle to 'Vinyl Princess,'" *SF Gate* (December 26, 2009), https://www.sfgate.com/entertainment/article/Music-store-a-castle-to-Vinyl-Princess-3277548.php#item-85307-tbla-1 (Accessed July 10, 2020).

92. Harrison, *Hip Hop Underground: The Integrity and Ethics of Racial Identification*, 61.

93. Amoebite, "Vinyl Princess: Interview with Author Yvonne Prinz" (February 13, 2010), https://www.amoeba.com/blog/2010/02/amoeba-music/vinyl-princess-interview-with-author-yvonne-prinz.html (Accessed June 19, 2020).

94. Selvin.

95. Yvonne Prinz, *The Vinyl Princess* (United States: Harper Collins, 2009), 200.

96. Ibid., 200–01.

97. Ibid., 246.

98. Ibid., 246–47.

99. Ibid., 248.

100. Ibid., 274.

101. Ibid., 313.

102. BWW News Desk, "Lamb's Players' Mixtape Extends into Fourth Year, Now Thru 2/17," *Broadway World* (2013), https://www.broadwayworld.com/san-diego/article/Lambs-Players-MIXTAPE-to-Extend-Into-Fourth-Year-110-217-20130109 (Accessed July 10, 2020).

103. James Hebert, "The '80s Live! And So Does 'Mixtape,' Returning to Lamb's Players Theatre Nearly a Decade after Its Debut," *The San Diego Union-Tribune* (June 11, 2019), https://www.sandiegouniontribune.com/entertainment/theater/story/2019-06-11/the-80s-live-and-so-does-mixtape-returning-to-lambs-players-theatre-nearly-a-decade-after-its-debut (Accessed July 10, 2020).

104. KPBS, *Journey Back into the 80s with 'Mixtape'* (San Diego 2011), YouTube video. https://youtu.be/fLMVJ5G6JZc (Accessed July 12, 2020).

105. TR Robertson, "'Mixtape—the Best of the 80's' Returns in Lamb's Players Theatre," *The Vista Press* (July 1, 2019), http://www.thevistapress.com/mixtape-the-best-of-the-80s-returns-in-lambs-players-theatre/ (Accessed July 10, 2020).

106. Ibid.

107. Eve Epstein and Lenora Epstein, *X vs. Y: A Culture War, a Love Story* (New York: Abrams Books, 2014), 187.

108. Boym, Chapter 3.

Chapter 6

Kitsch Commodification

By 2010 the 1970s and 1980s became retro-cool. What had been passé a decade earlier now reemerged in youth and pop culture as aspirational and interesting. The mixtape moved from nostalgic to kitschy. Instead of a reflection of a shared past era, these items now became defined as a curiosity about the analog past. Novelists wrote stories situated in their own youth. They incorporated cassette tapes and Walkman but had to explain them and describe them as worthy of attention because of their tangibility, artistry, and emotionality. Memoirists wrote about mixtapes, but they became less concrete and more conceptual. Borrowing on the legacy of Rob Sheffield, these individuals used the mixtape as organizational structures for their writing but did not write about actual physical cassette tapes.

Since 2013, cassettes have made an unexpected resurgence. A medium declared dead by 2010 has since reappeared. Like the reappearance and reinvestment in vinyl, music and technology fans have rediscovered the cassette tape and are describing it in nostalgic ways. Local bands are releasing and selling their work on cassette and vinyl. Journalists are writing articles about the return of the cassette. Fans of cassettes share statistics about the huge jump in sales. According to *Time* on the fiftieth anniversary of the cassette, "200,000 albums sold on tape in the U.S. in 2012."[1] This tiny blip in the sales has created a renewed interest in cassette culture. *Billboard* indicated cassette sales spiked 76 percent in 2016.[2] A British tech review announced in the first half of 2019 more cassettes had sold than since 2004, a 115 percent growth over the first six months of 2018.[3] Billie Eilish's debut album, *When We All Fall Asleep, Where Do We Go*, accounted for 4,000 of the cassettes sold in that time.[4] They concluded, "That probably tells you all you need to know about the type of people flocking to cassette releases, right?"[5] The excitement for cassettes remains tied to specific subgenres of music and subcultures of listeners.

Cassette resurgence overlapped with two franchises which launched the mixtape back into the mainstream. They reinvigorated the fascination both with curated musical playlists and with cassettes. *Guardians of the Galaxy* used the mixtape as a feature of retromania and to emotively connect a character to his past. Between the first and second films, the mixtape became a kitschy product placement which became a representation of the film and the fascination with the music from earlier eras. Where *Guardians of the Galaxy* tied retro and kitsch to the mixtape, *Hamilton* tied the personal mixtape and the hip hop mixtape back together for the first time since the 1980s. Originally calling his concept the *Hamilton Mixtape*, Lin-Manuel Miranda brought the word mixtape into the Broadway realm and used celebrities in the world of rap and DJing to tell his story. These two stories took the mixtape from its limited scope, still largely among music afficionados, and brought it into the commercial mainstream.

KITSCH AND CAMP

The mixtape has shifted context from a means of listening to music to a visual cultural artifact saturated with meaning removed from playing music. The mixtape is not only an item imbued with auditory nostalgia; it has become a kitsch artifact. In his introduction to *The Social Life of Things*, Arjun Appadurai states, "Commodities [objects of economic value], like persons, have social lives."[6] The original meaning of mixtape implied an object exchanged freely outside of the capitalist market. However, the mixtape has transformed into a commodity and become a consumer object imbued with a history and an identity that far outweighs its usefulness as a way to listen to music. Mixtape imagery has expanded a personal noncommercial product into a visual representation of an object which can be sold or used as a marketing tool for other merchandise. The preservation of a no longer relevant item in today's technological world gives it power and meaning. It is the emotional bond to the physicality of the object and the desire to reintroduce an outdated object into contemporary culture which creates a story worth telling. The ability to commodify the idea of the mixtape, as the image on a t-shirt or the marketing for a concert, despite its lack of continued usefulness and consumability allows for a transfer of meaning from tangible to emotional. The emotional tie individuals have to the visual representation of a mixtape connects this object to the realm of camp and kitsch culture.

The terms "kitsch" and "camp" overlap in pop-cultural usage but they have slightly different meanings. Each of these terms has a melodrama, a tongue-in-cheek quality to underscore the self-referential humor in the performance pieces of the artists who employ these characteristics.[7] Current culture's reinvestment in analog technology, specifically codified in the mixtape, absolutely indicates a kitsch fetishization of music and cultural artifacts.

"Kitsch," borrowed from German, first appeared in the late-nineteenth century, as a term to describe cheap marketable items with an exaggerated sentimentality. Walter Benjamin studied this idea and described it as art with "instantaneous availability for consumption."[8] Kitsch products are those creations consumers enjoy, sometimes ironically, aware of their ugliness or sentimental humorousness. The term remained mostly German-defined until the 1970s. For Americans, a velvet Elvis painting typifies kitsch art, highlighting the word's pejorative overtones. Kitsch can also function as a signal of personal memory of friends and places left behind. In the nineteenth century, Western family life began to invest new meanings in heirlooms and family souvenirs. With an increase in literacy and free time, people began to commemorate their own family histories.[9] Memory, imbued in personal cultural artifacts, became a foundational norm. The display of mass-produced souvenirs allows for a display of collective shared memory, even for an item that might not individually hold sentimental appeal.[10] A collection of mixtapes exemplifies the desire to preserve memories, regardless of aesthetic appeal. The mixtape as a cultural artifact, which people recognize by sight, has overtaken the functional use of a cassette tape on which to play music. The memory exists in the item itself. One can purchase mass-produced stickers and pins with mixtape imagery as souvenirs of locations and events.

The self-aware desire to collect art without aesthetic value creates an ironic appeal which indicates how kitsch is often used in pop culture today. The contemporary use of mixtape is visual and rhetorical, but not playable cassette tapes. This commodification of the term and the image reflects the past without assuming a coherent nostalgic desire for the past. Individuals who never owned a playable cassette tape may still desire products with cassette imagery prominently displayed.

While kitsch and camp are often used in pop culture synonymously, the formal distinction is that an object can be kitsch, while a performance can be camp: the physical artifact versus the performance. "Camp," first used at the beginning of the 1900s as a term discussing fashion, implied a self-consciously exaggerated theatrical style or behavior. Camp originally described an effeminization of mannerisms and was used almost exclusively to illustrate homosexual men's aesthetic choices. It appeared most often as a descriptor for drag performances. In 1964 Susan Sontag defined camp as frivolous and excessive, but again, like kitsch, self-aware.[11] By the late 1970s camp had come to mean any ironic music, art, literature, or object that appealed because of its extremes and "bad taste." From that period on, performers have used "camp" as a reaction to the excesses of consumer culture and frustration with mainstream dominant norms. Liberace and RuPaul are familiar representatives of an ironic self-aware campiness.

Both camp and kitsch have played a decisive role in music of the past forty years. A musician can use camp as a performative model which highlights an exaggeration of performance aspects. Like RuPaul, singers like Cher and Megan Thee Stallion have challenged political norms by over-exaggerating their performative selves to create icons who critique social realities. Since the 1970s certain artists have worked against mainstream capitalist consumer culture. Musicians have used camp in their performances to over-exaggerate and highlight constructed social and political norms with a growing awareness among minority groups of the appeal of camp as a mode of critique. New wave in the 1980s used excessive camp to highlight a discomfort with mainstream consumer culture. The B-52s, described as "trash chic" exemplify this campiness.[12] While the mixtape was not originally created as a mode of kitsch art, there is a decided overlap in the anti-consumer capitalist culture and the creation of a product to circumvent corporate norms. Moving from the original creation of mixtapes in the 1970s–1990s to the current era of mixtape nostalgia, there is a growth of campiness and kitsch in the products that represent a mixtape as a cultural artifact, but no longer have a concrete association with musical sound. The representation of the mixtape as a visual demarcation of the past has allowed it to symbolize the collective memory of the analog recent past.

DIGITAL MIXTAPES

Although cassette culture has reappeared amongst those who anxiously await Cassette Store Day, few people use cassettes daily. However, the incorporation of retromania into new kitschy artifacts has encouraged entrepreneurs to rethink the mixtape. Technologically savvy individuals have considered how to combine the appeal of the mixtape with the ease of digital online technology, selling new products to recreate the best aspects of the mixtape.

The internet changed how people listened to music. From Napster to iTunes, music became a downloadable product no longer requiring album sales in a physical format. Platforms like MySpace and Soundcloud allowed musicians to upload music directly for their fans, circumventing the need for recording labels. By 2008 iTunes, which began working with the recording industry, had become the United States leading music retailer.[13] This shift moved music from an analog platform to digital. YouTube became the go-to site for videos, allowing users to pick the music they heard rather than relying on DJs and VJs to dictate airplay. Streaming platforms like Spotify and

Pandora created a digital way to stream music through the internet which reduced sound quality but expanded access to music. Internet streaming services have taken the concept of a playlist and removed the individual user from its creation.

Thinking about the differences between mixtapes and playlists, Mike Glennon stated, "The mixtape has been touted by corporations such as Spotify and Apple as an antecedent to the curated playlists which have become an increasingly prominent factor within the contemporary music industry. [. . .] This contemporary manifestation of the mixtape is located somewhere between sound art and the DJ mix."[14] While users can create playlists, picking and organizing songs (drag and drop), many apps can also digitally curate a list based on genre, mood, or musical group. Apps like Spotify have begun creating curated playlists for listeners using algorithms. The science behind this involves comparing what one listener has added to a playlist with the music listeners with similar tastes have added. Then they use "collaborative filtering," to fine-tune options.[15] Despite requests from artists and labels, Spotify claims they never intentionally add specific songs to playlists. Nonetheless, *Rolling Stone* magazine stated in 2017, "For artists, getting placed on a prominent playlist has become nearly as important as radio play."[16] The commercial nature of the Pandora, Apple, or Spotify playlist mimics the hand-curated mixtape, but it replaces the nostalgic sentimental attachment with a commercial sales aspect. The time it takes to create a mixtape also adds to the emotional experience in contrast to the speed of dragging and dropping songs.

These avenues introduce fans to new bands, new music, new sounds they might not otherwise have heard. The streaming apps can "learn" a user's listening taste and can effectively create an enjoyable list. Personalized listening experiences on these services became a crucial aspect of the music industry which sanctions the recordings available, formalizing access distinct from the analog mixtape.[17] While digital platforms continue to improve how they function, a streamed playlist does not have the personality of a hand-curated mixtape. Not only is there less physical connection to a tangible object—users can edit or delete a playlist—Spotify's weekly digital playlists are actively deleted at the end of each week unless a listener saves them externally. A mixtape on the other hand, cannot be edited and remixed. In her analysis of playlists as synonymous with mixtapes, Musicologist Joanna Demers contends recording labels have co-opted the vocabulary of mixtapes by "touting platforms that supposedly curate personalized listening experiences." She further states, "playlists are resurrecting mixtape aesthetics selectively, deploying DIY rhetoric to repackage material that lacks the intimacy and personal contingency of the mixtape."[18] While they mirror mixtapes in theory, they fail in the personal interconnectedness which keeps the mixtape potent. By claiming a digital playlist as a mixtape, companies can use the visual imagery of a colorful cassette tape which again solidifies the notion of a playlist as something tangible and real. It eschews the concept of the computerized version as mere ephemera.

Between 2004 and 2012 iTunes included iMix; replicating a mixtape "iTunes promises the 'instant fame' that comes with 'shar[ing] your good taste with the rest of the world.'"[19] While this feature allowed a user to create a compilation of songs, it relied exclusively on the music then available on iTunes (e.g., which had no Beatles), and on digital rights management which restricted copying and transferring of songs. Moreover, while one could share an iMix with a friend digitally, the friend not only had to have iTunes themselves, but they also had to pay to download the playlist. As one critique clarified, "when you give your friends a homemade mix you don't usually ask them to pay for it."[20] This interim mixtape platform relied on user familiarity with the idea of a mix, which Apple knew existed. But this digital format removed the interpersonal, non-corporate aspect of the mixtape and commodified it for marketing and promotional purposes.

In 2015, Apple again attempted to rethink and recreate the mixtape. They submitted a patent application for a "Digital mixed Tape" which would allow a user to create a personal playlist and gift it online. Unlike iMix, the creator paid for the music rather than the recipient—a worthwhile upgrade. The Apple product could include movies, digital media, and images expanding beyond audio-only cassettes. To encourage the feeling of a cassette, users could restrict skipping songs. While Apple submitted a patent for the idea, the final product as described in tech websites never appeared.[21] In time for the 2019 holidays they did release a modified version. *Fast Company* described the concept: "Your last-minute gift plan: Make a free retro mixtape thanks to Apple."[22] It states,

> *It's just like 1995*, but with less cursing and re-spooling. Instead, you can simply record a 90-second voice introduction telling your besties/crushes/partners how dreamy they are, and then pick the songs that express your soul along with cover art that features, say, you.[23]

As the author highlights, this free app solves the problem of not having purchased a present in time for Christmas; it is the antithesis of the time and energy spent on crafting a physical mixtape. Undermining their own argument about the digital product, the author concludes with a "Pro Tip" suggesting an actual cassette tape mixtape as a better gift.[24] Apple's continued reinvention of the mixtape shows the sustained appeal of the artifact. But as the owner of iTunes and the purveyors of playlists, they want a digital update with a technostalgic touch.

Popular streaming platforms have incorporated celebrities to personalize their conceptual musical ideas. In 2015 musician Annie Clark, known as St. Vincent, posted on her Facebook page, "Sometimes, the best remedy for what ails us is the perfect mixtape. So, St. Vincent would like to create a personalized 'mixtape' just for YOU. [. . .] what in your life would benefit from a St. Vincent curated playlist."[25] Placing "mixtape" in quotation marks and using "playlist" in the same sentence emphasizes the mixtape is not a tangible item. According to *Pitchfork* she crafted these mixtapes for her Beats 1 Apple Music show. While she incorporates individuals' stories to create the playlist, the endgame has become a semi-regular series entitled St. Vincent's Mixtape Delivery Service.[26] Numbered in the 90s, each episode has a unique icon to describe the theme. There is a cassette tape image for every episode.[27] This series has merged music, emotional stories, and images of cassettes into a digital product. By calling the show a "mixtape," Apple is appealing to the past: a consumable, commodified past.

MUSIC

By 2007 hip hop mixtapes had also shifted from physical technology to digital releases. Companies like Datpiff.com and LiveMixtapes took over the distribution and digital library of mixtapes.[28] The mixtape morphed into a noncommercial release by an individual artist, often relying on samples and pre-recorded music, to showcase a sound that did not have industry backing. These artists use underground hip hop to re-legitimate and reassert their voice, independent of commercial labels. The internet gave hip hop artists direct access to their audience and the digital hip hop mixtape became an artist's key marketing strategy to garner fan feedback before a commercial release.[29] It ensured the audience had opportunities to hear and respond to the music which confirmed an artist's street credibility. These digital releases created major label–bidding wars for the next generation of multi-platinum recording artists. Rappers Wiz Khalifa, Mac Miller, and Meek Mill all rose to fame via these independent, fan-based digital mixtapes.[30] The professionalism of the hip hop mixtape shifted in this decade as "mix tapes became far more polished, essentially functioning as ersatz albums, with high production values, sharp lyrics, and considerable listenership."[31] New artists could now use mixtapes to gain renown while established artists used them to generate discussion before a major label release.[32] DJ Semtex states, "The mixtape is a powerful, cost-effective way of introducing new music to potential new fans. People listen to them with the intent and expectation of discovering new music and artists."[33] By 2014 the top three mixtape sites had more than seven million visitors per month. Soundcloud emerged, leading artists like Chance the Rapper and Migos to host their projects because they appreciate the open platform system.[34] At this point, labels began to release mixtapes digitally as retail mixtapes or EPs. As *Billboard* stated, "That had the effect of turning the promotional product back into the retail product—and permanently blurring the line between a promotional street mixtape and an official retail album."[35] In the United States, the concept of an independently curated mixtape, created by a DJ curating a set list or a mixtape or a rapper rapping over samples, had largely disappeared. While the "underground hip hop mixtape" remains, the term has become subsumed in hip hop culture and now has morphed with traditional album releases. With increased rap sales, producers created officially licensed compilations to amplify new rappers and released them as mixtapes.[36] As hip hop grew internationally, hip hop culture has become a global force to share the voice of the dispossessed.[37]

In 2017 Essential Library released a series of books called *Hip-Hop Insider* aimed at young adults providing, "a comprehensive look at hip hop: the music, the dance, the culture, and its stars."[38] Alongside a discussion of sampling, the book included a definition of mixtape which states, "Mixtapes help artists break into the music industry. Aspiring stars sample songs from other artists and blend them into a new interpretation. They compile a collection of these creations on a cassette tape or CD, the mixtape. Artists who are not represented by a record label can distribute their mixtapes cheaply to build a fan base."[39] This simplified definition of a forty-year history confirms the culturally recognized description of a hip hop mixtape tied to the artist releasing music independently. For the larger fan culture, this continuing shift and negotiating of the "hip hop mixtape" has kept the term in the popular imagination. By the mid-2010s the intangible mixtape had a resurgence as a result of the continued nostalgia of the Gen X personally curated mixtape and the publicly discussed and released hip hop EP album.

A keyword search for mixtape in Discogs results in over 14,000 releases categorized as hip hop, with additional rap songs referencing "mixtape" in the lyrics.[40] Unlike the Gen X personal mixtape, it has become a staple of rap artists and signifies a specific type of release, distinct from an album. Musical artist, Skinny Friedman describes the current hip hop mixtape as having

> come a long way from DJ-mixed compilations of hot tracks that complement radio and club play, over the years mutating into all-star line-ups of emcees spitting hot bars over familiar beats, then to a single crew spitting bars over familiar beats, then eventually to a single crew (or artist) spitting bars over unfamiliar beats. At that point, they became "street albums," basically just full-length projects that didn't go through standard record label vetting and distribution.[41]

In hip hop, a mixtape is a career enhancement; it gives artists an opportunity to try something different from what they would produce for a label. In a world of digital releases and streaming music, album sales have declined, and the hip hop mixtape has allowed musicians to adapt to the current industry norms. The popularity of the hip hop mixtape has helped to keep the word mixtape in pop culture.

A far cry from the world of hip hop, Country singer Lee Brice is no stranger to romantic songs. Two of his chart-topping songs include the 2009 "Love Like Crazy" and the 2011"A Woman Like You" which both evoke romantic gestures geared at objects of affection.[42] Yet, in the summer of 2015, he shifted gears and released an EP crafted in the style of a hip hop mixtape, titled *Mixtape: 'Til Summer's Gone*. The EP, different in lyrical style and length relative to the albums for his label, situates Brice's work within the style of hip hop mixtape releases, although Brice and his reviewers do not discuss it as such. The song "Mixtape" allowed Brice to craft a more risqué, guitar-heavy song than the country crooner normally performs. With lyrics like, "We're a mixtape/Every song has sex in the title," Brice playfully incorporates sex rather than romance. Later he sings, "they know I'm taping more than just my feet to the music" and they "might just have to play the extended version."[43] Sex in lyrics is nothing new in the world of music but according to the website *Nashvillegab* Brice's song is an "extreme departure from the sensitive crooner."[44] Using the metaphor of a tape, he has found a way to use double entendre to sing about sex. Using the hip hop model, Brice could work around the expectation of him within the industry to craft a different persona. The album title, *Mixtape* references hip hop ideas while the song title "Mixtape" alludes to the cassette tape concept.

Singing about Merchandise

As the mixtape has moved from personal object to kitsch nostalgia, the overlap of product placement became an aspect of song lyrics. Cassette technology intertwined mixtapes and cars. Many people associate their mixtapes with driving around listening with friends or on road trips. Musicians have taken this link and used it to write songs about both. Thirteen mixtape songs mention cars. Seven country songs highlight trucks with lines like, "The truck's jacked up"[45] and name brands like, "I'll fire up my step-side Chevy."[46] These phrases create a visual image and a link between driving and listening to music. In their pop music book, Nate Sloan and Charlie Harding declare, "Chevys and Fords are almost compulsory in a country song [. . .] There's a poignant nostalgia in [country songs] yearning for a golden age."[47] This nostalgia for a golden age dovetails with the nostalgic appeal of the mixtape. Lady A sings about the Chevy van and the classic Coke which go hand-in-hand with the "summer jam mixtape" in "Freestyle."[48] In his 2016 song, "Can't Be Replaced," country singer Dierks Bentley sings about his "Levi jacket broken in just right" and his Chevy Cavalier along with his "Memorex mixtape" and the freedom of the summer of 1981. For fans, the mention of nostalgic artifacts from the recent past cement the story these artists tell with their song. The 2016 Dirty Heads song, "That's All I Need," is a more direct reflection of the past and the nostalgia of a better time. Like other musicians, Duddy B Bushnell situates his song in the first stanza by singing about "where [his] Catalina idled,"[49] He describes the Pontiac, last made in 1981, as his first love. Singing about partying with his friends in the past he clarifies, "I'm feeling like old school, mixtape/That's all I need."[50] The specificity of his car and the description of "Rolling through [his] neighborhood," situates the song in a visualizable time and place. Singer-songwriter Clara Charron uses cars as a critique rather than a balm. She critiques a mate who asserts, "This afternoon is bright and sunny/Perfect for a drive in our Ferrari."[51] The use of a luxury car shows the inconsistency in their relationship She sings about their problems as reflected in "raggedy mix-tapes" confirming, "Maybe if we push a little harder/This old car might roll again," an allusion to their incongruent perceptions.[52]

Like Lady A and Dierks Bentley who mention specific cars and specific brands, other artists include pop culture paraphernalia in their songs alongside the cars to situate the song. Twelve mixtape songs discuss drinking and five of those specify beer, Miller Lite in particular, or Bourbon.[53] In 2016 Lonely Island recorded the song "Things in My Jeep" for the mockumentary *Popstar: Never Stop Never Stopping*. As the song delineates everything character Connor Friel has in his jeep, he mentions iconic items like a Rubik's cube, a Tic-tac, and "A mixtape, push play on it."[54] While this song has an obvious tongue-in-cheek quality, many other songs include brand-name items in a similar way, signifying time, place, and listener recognition. Summer Fever's "Little Big Town" also tells a story about a Jeep, "With that old school mixtape playing," dancing in the sand, "Got the wind in my hair, Ray-Ban glare."[55] The iconic brand of sunglasses had a surge of popularity in the mid-1980s. The James Barker Band's 2017 song "Throwback," oozes a twangy nostalgia. Barker references multiple pop culture artifacts including Polaroid cameras, boomboxes, and Casio watches. He also sings about Reeboks' and how he is "Gonna take the Trans Am down off the blocks."[56] Barker's song exudes retro kitsch alongside a passionate plea. When he sings, "Dust off that 70's vinyl, 80's 8-track, 90's mixtape, rewind playback" he intends seduction. He wants to, "park it at the drive-in" and make out, without modern distractions.[57] Ashley McBryde's nostalgia is an homage to her childhood radio. She specifies the era when she sings, "Casey Kasem in an old Panasonic countin' down my Saturday."[58] The Gym Class Heroes song

"Stereo Hearts" also reflects an auditory nostalgia tied to music technology. They ask, "If I was an old-school, fifty pound boom box/Would you hold me on your shoulder, wherever you walk" and follow up, "And all I ask is that you don't get mad at me/When you have to purchase mad D batteries."[59] They solidify the iconic weight and power-draining nature of an old-school boombox, speaking to the technostalgia of their listeners and telling them to "Appreciate every mix tape your friends make."[60] Also playing on nostalgia, Jim's Big Ego's glib rock song "Mix-Tape" self-consciously tells the story of a cassette tape. Jim Infantino sings, "Your cassette player's gone the way of the Dodo/you only keep it now to listen to your mixtapes."[61] Released in 2003, the song predates the cassette culture revival but alludes to the kitsch nostalgia of those consumers, "'cause all of your CDs sound too sterile and clean/all those squeaky little ones and zeros."[62] They describe the mixtape as "future retro" because it is "like a time machine."[63] What Jim's Big Ego does explicitly, many of these musicians have done more obliquely. By naming merchandise from their lives, they have not only connected to their fans who remember the same products, they have situated their songs and their memories in the mixtape era.

Whether writing a song to describe the perfect person, to lament a loss of connection and love, or to reminisce about the fun of youth, musicians have found the imagery of a personally crafted cassette tape useful in their songwriting. The word mixtape has come to represent an idea more than it does an object. Hearing that word, many individuals picture an unplayable artifact stored in a box in the closet. They have a story of who made the tape, when they last played it, or why they kept it. Young songwriters continue to find appeal in the concept of a mixtape, even though they have likely never owned a personally crafted cassette tape nor played one on a Walkman or boombox. The kitsch appeal of the concept merged with the continued release in hip-hop has kept the object in the collective memory of today's youth.

BOOKS

Memoir

Through this era mixtapes speak to the authors who incorporated them. These are individuals who grew up with cassettes and those cassettes defined their young lives. The audiences for their books likely also remembered cassettes which make the mixtape a logical touchpoint. By the mid-2010s though, the link to the music and the mixtape as a specific physical artifact became less tangible. A shift began in which mixtapes become less about the object and more about the idea.

Bree Housley's, *We Hope You Like This Song: An Overly Honest Story about Friendship, Death, and Mixtapes* is ostensibly about mixtapes, but not about record collecting or musical fandom. Housley's 2012 memoir memorializes the life of her best friend Shelly from their meeting as teens until Shelly's death from preeclampsia at the age of 25. This is a story less about mixtapes, and more a narrative about the goofiness of growing up a teenager in a small town in America. After Shelly's death, Housley "found a way to keep Shelly's memory alive—by spending a year doing crazy things Shelly would have done, like giving Valentines to strangers, singing at a karaoke bar, and letting her boyfriend pick out her outfits for a week."[64] While mixtapes have a role, they are a small part of a much larger story. In her quest to attend live music shows for a week, Housley reminisces,

> I hunt down the mix tape Shelly made for me when I left for Florida. Like any good significant other, she came to the airport with me that day. And like any good significant other, [. . .] When it was time for me to head through the gate, she handed me a CD titled *A Musical Tribute to Our Friendship*. If that isn't romantic, I don't know what is.

> Music speaks to us in ways people can't, takes us back to places we can no longer go, and brings out emotions we can't control.[65]

This gift is the sole mention of a mixtape in a book that lists mixtape in its subtitle. The overriding love and friendship housed in the physical artifact strengthens the place of mixtape in the book's title, despite its rare inclusion in the text. Housley does not address the title in published interviews, leaving the choice unclear. The book highlights Housley's relationship with Shelly and how music allowed her to honor and recognize the friendship. As a mixtape recipient, Housley vested symbolic importance in a single moment to reflect on her long-standing friendship. Housley's use of mixtape and music dovetail the emotive representation of music. The single mixtape moment encompasses the love, friendship, and sadness of the entire memoir, giving credence to the final word in the title.

Brendan Leonard self-published *The New American Road Trip Mix Tape* in 2013. Leonard a contributing editor at *Adventure Journal* and a columnist at *Outside*, has since published a variety of humorous and adventure books. In his first book, Leonard recounts his initial experience living out of his car, driving around the West, staying with friends, and climbing any set of rocks he could convince friends to join him on. He mentions music a handful of times and discusses the necessity for a good playlist for the car. Leonard had not intended to recommend music to his readers despite the thirty-three different songs he mentions in the text; he discussed music because it was important to him. Leonard made dozens of mixtapes in the 90s for friends, for his car, and for potential partners.[66] For him the cassette and the mixtapes are nostalgic. He admits he loves the convenience of every song at his fingertips, but he misses having all the time in the world to sit on the floor and make mixtapes. Love of music tied Leonard to his readers; a fan turned the songs Leonard mentioned into a Spotify playlist.[67]

Leonard's narrative focus is his time spent in the outdoors, exploring the West and discovering himself while traveling solo. He owes allegiance to travel writers like Jack Kerouac who's *On The Road* tells the story of adventure and travel, grounded in the world of mid-century American Jazz. Like Kerouac, Leonard's story integrates his musical soundscape. The book cover shows Leonard standing in the middle distance, mountains stretching behind him and the dashboard of a car in the foreground. It represented, "a point where [he]'d been living out of a vehicle on the road for almost two years, and [his] life was still one big road trip."[68] Multiple cassette tapes are strewn across the dashboard, including one labeled "ROAD TRIP" which, according to Leonard, was a thrift store tape he and a friend covered with tape and renamed.[69]

Josh Harmon, poet, professor, and author published his memoir *Annotated Mixtape*, in 2014. Harmon reflects on his life as a collector and a music obsessive. Like Nick Hornby, Harmon uses songs as chapter titles for a mixtape-style organization with added liner notes. The 400-page book covers everything from Reaganomics to working in a vintage clothing store. He quotes Theodor Adorno describing records as reflections of their owners, giving weight to his ideas and the intersection between collecting and identity. Harmon defines his life around the music he listened to. In the first essay "C-90" Harmon describes his mixtape making as a teenager:

> While burning a CD or uploading a playlist takes no more than a moment, making tapes devoured more than real time. A ninety-minute cassette involved hours of effort: gather the chosen records, determining a sequence, dubbing each song to tape, re-recording mistakes, erasing a few songs when the order seemed wrong, writing out the tracklist, and drawing or collaging cover art. "*Making* tapes," we called this activity, to emphasize the personally constructed, labor-intensive process: [. . .] our attention and care transformed each one into something singular —and, of course, we found pleasure in the production as much as in giving each other the tapes.[70]

Harmon, a self-defined Gen Xer, heralds the mixtape era as thoughtful and pleasurable. There is nostalgia in the youth he describes. His story coalesces with retromania, lamenting the loss of innocence and time. In his chapter "Love Will Tear Us Apart" about the well-known Joy Division song, Harmon writes about a pen pal he had in his middle teen years. They wrote letters back and forth; she drew cartoon sketches of herself while he sent her mixtapes. When he emphasizes how the time between letters allowed him to write more eloquently, Harmon reinforces the appeal of a simpler era.

The cover of Harmon's book is a swirl of black cassette tape spooling from the bottom of a cassette with the title interwoven in yellow text. Like the chaos of the cover, Harmon's self-indulgent essays reflect a mixtape without a coherent theme. The idea looks relevant on paper; the inclusion of bands like Bauhaus, New Order, and Big Star suggests a logic. Yet, the stories never coalesce. It reads like disparate songs without a logic to the order.

Housley, Leonard, and Harmon chose to use mixtape as the final word in their titles, but the foundation of the stories is not music. Leonard considered his book a mixtape because he references other stories of road trips. It "was sort of a mixtape in which I drew from some of my favorite works to build something new."[71] These memoirs introduce a new perspective in how authors incorporate mixtapes differently than Sheffield, Bitner, and Moore. For Housley and Leonard, a mixtape speaks to them as a concept. There is little direct association to a specific physical artifact around which they have coalesced their thoughts. Instead, mixtape has become a notion: neither a playlist, nor a physical object. These two books highlight what will become the way authors and artists define mixtape by the end of the 2010s.

Fiction

Written as a YA novel in 2012, *Supergirl Mixtapes* reads more like Bret Easton Ellis and Alan Warner's teen novels of the 1990s. Bridging the cassette-era generation and the post-cassette era, in Brothers' story mixtapes are not nostalgic. The novel takes place in a grungy 1990s New York City with cassettes, CBGBs, and the dynamic punk scene. Maria flees rural South Carolina to spend time with her estranged artist mother. She brings the mixtapes her friend Dory made of empowered female musicians. Music is a through line of the story, paying homage to musicians like Sonic Youth, Patti Smith, and Nirvana. Looking for self-empowerment and escape from the leering male gaze, Maria parallels the Gen X world of the riot grrrl. Throughout the story she learns her mother is not the ideal parent she had envisioned and debates whether to stay. As she grapples with the difficulties of life in New York, Maria takes the new music she has heard to make a mixtape:

> I wanted to make the perfect tape for Dory. I wanted it to rise and fall, to put the perfect songs in the perfect order, the way she did. But mostly I wanted to paint this picture for her. This picture of New York, of everything I'd heard since I moved here. Mom's music, Travis's and Gram's, and mine, now. The songs I'd

taken as my own, that looped in my head as I walked the streets and rode the subways. [. . .] the voices we knew as well as our own. I wanted to paint this picture for Dory to let her know I was okay, that I was over it now, that I had gotten better and I wasn't alone anymore.[72]

The book title originates in the female-centered mixtapes Dory sent Maria. The mixtape Maria constructs demonstrates her personal growth. Brothers uses music and the New York music scene to tell a coming-of-age story in which life is difficult and not everyone is redeemable. There is a nostalgia in the writing of the book because Brothers conveyed an earlier New York. Although it is not kitschy in its irreverence, she imbued the story with the artistry of the era. Her story of the artists is reverential, introducing readers to greats from the past.

Like Brothers, Rainbow Rowell uses mixtapes to connect characters in her YA novel *Eleanor & Park*. Rowell has highlighted the role of music in her writing. She creates playlists to write to which she shares with her fans.[73] Published in 2012 and set in 1986, *Eleanor & Park* opens with a discussion of XTC, Skinny Puppy or the Misfits as the right listening choice on the bus. Rowell's story manifests the male/female interaction inherent in Gen X music expectations. Park is the musical intellect who shares his knowledge with Eleanor. As the two main characters get acquainted, Park introduces Eleanor to his world of music, "That night, while he did his homework, Park made a tape with all his favorite songs, plus a few songs by Echo & the Bunnymen and Joy Division."[74] He broke through Eleanor's barriers by playing music for her and giving her an outlet for her fraught emotions.

> She had Park's songs in her head—and in her chest, somehow. There was something about the music on that tape. It felt different. Like, it set her lungs and her stomach on edge. There was something exciting about it, and some-thing nervous. It made Eleanor feel like everything, like the *world*, wasn't what she'd thought it was. And that was a good thing. That was the greatest thing.[75]

Her less than coherent analysis emphasizes the depth of feelings she did not know how to express. In her dysfunctional world, Park's music is an escape and a baseline to ground their friendship.

> Later she'd listen to music. She'd saved the last two batteries Park had given her so that she could listen to her tape player today when she missed him most. She had five tapes from him now—which meant, if her batteries lasted, she had 450 minutes to spend with Park in her head, holding her hand.[76]

Rowell focuses on the specificity of listening to the cassette on a personal stereo and how important it became to ground Eleanor.

Rowell acknowledged the conscious incorporation of a mixtape,

> People my age have really deep, deep memories [getting mixes on] cassette tapes, and I think younger people have a nostalgia for that time because mixtapes represent something they will never experience. [. . .] When [Park] gives [Eleanor] a mixtape, that's a real gift.[77]

Eleanor & Park requires analog technology; using a Walkman, thinking about how batteries last, and creating and sharing a mixtape define her story. The physicality of the cassette tape and the time and energy Park spent lets Eleanor know she is important and worthy of attention. Rowell's story needed the tangibility of cassette technology to ground the interaction between these two characters. Telling a story outside the lived experience of many of her readers, Rowell believes correctly they will still relate to the intentionality of music connecting people.

Novels are not the only fictional form to consider the mixtape. The comic book and graphic novel have grown in popularity in the twenty-first century. Free-form, adult-focused stories have emerged covering all genres from stereotypical superheroes to nonfiction narratives. Among comic books, a few include mixtapes as a plot element while adding the visual imagery of cassettes. In 2016 graphic memoirist Lucy Knisley released her book *Something New* about marriage as a modern American institution and her expectations as she navigated her engagement and wedding. Knisley focuses on how to DIY her wedding to save money and reject commercial pressure. In the chapter titled, "It's Electric," she and her fiancé make a playlist for the wedding, much to her mother's despair, rather than pay for a band. The opening page is a background color photograph of mixtapes and a superimposed hand-drawn cassette with the title.[78] Considering how to whittle down the list to a manageable and appropriate size, Knisley depicts her father making mixtapes, recording music from records onto tapes. Above a cassette situated in an open jewel case entitled 'Lucy's traveling tape," Knisley writes, "Growing up, my dad's mixes (which he would make from actual records) were legendary. It gave me a deep appreciation for the personal stake you can have in an arrangement of songs you dig."[79] She concludes the chapter with a drawing of mixtapes titled "Rock the Barn" and "Tie the Knot."[80] Playing into nostalgia, collaboration, and childhood reminiscences, Knisley employs the mixtapes to validate distancing herself from the overwhelming capitalist impulse of the wedding industry and creating a unique personal outcome.

Written the same year, author Dan Watters and Artist Caspar Wijngaard released their first stand-alone, limited comic series *Limbo*. Slated as a multi-part series "where '50s noir and '80s neon are smashed together to produce one truly surreal comic," the cover art for the first issue of the series showed a bandaged hand holding a cassette tape.[81] The spooling tape wrote out the title, *Limbo*.[82] The protagonist, a detective with no memory, interacts with multiple characters to figure out his world, including "a voodoo queen with a penchant for mixtapes and hi-tops."[83] The story, saturated with 1980s nostalgia, leans into the love of analog with objects to create a unique visual world. Comics blog *Broken Frontier* claims, "Limbo is also liberally peppered with 1980s pop-culture kitsch, as if Wijngaard went to a John Hughes garage sale for inspiration. He deftly enhances the nostalgic vibe of the series with mix-tapes, Walkmans, vinyl LPs, garish TV talk shows, VCRs and a kooky action figure."[84] Watters furthers this idea, describing mixtape ideology as the premise of the whole series. When asked about the disparate characters in the *Limbo* world, Watters stated, "the whole concept for the book was sort of cut up and mashed up the idea of splicing tapes together."[85] Relishing the 1980s and 1990s imagery they had grown up with, Watters and Wijngaard effectively incorporated kitsch 1980s nostalgia throughout their series.

One of the main characters, Sandy, a young, green, bald woman, consistently wears old-school headphones and listens to a personal stereo. More than the simple background, her mixtapes are crucial to the plot. She listens to music to summon and speak with voodoo spirits. Sandy uses the rare vinyl she purchases to create mixtapes. She offers them up as a sacrifice to the Loa, Haitian voodoo gods, rather than the more traditionally imagined food or animal sacrifice. Papa Legba, the intermediary between Loa and humanity, appears to Sandy as the outline of a man in a top hat, which is a familiar image of this character. However, Wijngaard drew his outline from the spooling tape emerging from the cassette. Discussing the power of their story Wijngaard states,

> To me there is something very charming and personal in the analogue technology, mix tapes and home videos.
>
> There is a soullessness in digital culture, not a lot of effort goes into making a digital playlist with mp3s downloaded from iTunes and simply hitting a button to skip tracks.[86]

Using the visual medium, Wijngaard pays homage to the 1980s. He incorporates the mixtape as a key plot element with magical power so a character can interact with the beyond. The plot would feel inconsistent if structured with any other musical artifact because of its grounding in 1980s visual imagery. These graphic novels have effectively used the mixtape as a reference to the specificity of the 1980s and 1990s. The drawings are both kitsch and direct nostalgia.

As authors write in an era in which the mixtape has become a sight of nostalgia, mixtape can become less a plot point and more a sales pitch. More authors have published books with mixtape in the title since 2015 than in the previous thirty years.[87] A search of books available on the Amazon Kindle page includes *The Devil's Mixtape, Made Marian Mixtape: A Made Marian Collection*, and *Full Moon Mixtape (Tales of Urban Horror Book 2)*. These books run the gamut from books of poetry and play to memoirs and novels. Nestled within this era of mixtape books are poetry compilations including *The Mixtape: Side A, Love Songs on a Mix Tape*, and *Mixtape: A Bipolar Anthology: Poems Written before, during, and after Some Gnarly Psychosis*. With an overlap between lyrics to songs and poems, the interplay of these two ideas is not unexpected.[88]

Across the genres, these books vary in quality and reflection on the mixtape as a coherent ideology. The large rise in the number of books written with mixtape in the title reflects the growth of self-publishing and sales of eBooks as much as it correlates to the mixtape resurgence. For these authors, attempting to draw in a reader and convince them to try their book, the "mixtape" has become a familiar artifact and idea which evokes recognizable imagery. Authors have seized on this term as an evocative way to attach meaning to a story before reading page one. For many of the authors, the mixtape represents one of two concepts: a song per chapter/poem/theme as an organizing principle or a story in which individual music plays a role and therefore it seems logical to take those songs and set them up as a newly minted "mixtape."

One example of this commercially driven, self-published rubbish is the 2019 *Mixtape: A Love Song Anthology*.[89] The marketing line reads, "What's more romantic than a love song? A mixtape full of them. Twelve bestselling and award-winning authors have curated an anthology of brand-new, standalone stories inspired by love songs."[90] The cover shows a well-toned, bare-chested, bronzed man. Although the clothing style screams romance novel, the allusion to the Lloyd Dobbler image from *Say Anything* is obvious. In both instances the men hold a silver and black boombox outstretched over their heads. They both peer out at the audience with piercing, pleading looks. There is a similarity in the hairstyles: dark, slightly mussed. This edited book of contemporary romance short stories exemplifies mixtape's diverse meanings.

Each story opens with a picture of a mixtape and the name of a song and artist which inspired the story. However, the link is tenuous, at best. In many of the stories the inspiration is only that. Music is not a theme in the story, nor is the song even necessarily referenced. This anthology typifies one current usage of mixtape: a loosely defined idea which does not have to reflect any concrete examination. There is no reference to cassettes, but the boombox on the cover is key. Unrequited love, sex, and reconnection are the focus. Some of the stories emphasize nostalgia and the desire to rekindle feelings which forefront the mixtape theme.

The diverse genres of fiction which have utilized the "mixtape" in the 2010s demonstrate how much the term has grown. No longer do all authors use mixtapes as a physical item tied directly to a cassette tape. "Nostalgia" predominates the work, but it has also become a marketable term to pull in a mainstream audience. While interpersonal bonds, sometimes romantic, remain a predominant model for mixtape fiction, the imagery of a personalized cassette tape has begun to lose coherent meaning. Many of the authors remain wedded to the kitsch nostalgia of the Gen X past in which people prefer analog bonds over the intangibility of the digital present. However, as the Kindle books show, mixtape has become a campy catch-all concept to draw readers' attention. The growing appeal did not appear by happenstance. Two specific franchises solidified the mixtape in the popular imagination.

PERFORMANCE

The Broadway world underwent a seismic shift with the opening of the musical *Hamilton*. The show took the world by storm winning eleven Tony's in 2016 including Best Musical and receiving the Pulitzer Prize for Drama. It has sold out shows since it premiered on Broadway and launched careers for the principal actors. Lin-Manuel Miranda has become a household name, not only for individuals who have an investment in Broadway theatre. Miranda created the foundation of his show in 2009. On May 12, a nervous 29-year-old Miranda rapped a song from a new project called *The Hamilton Mixtape* at the White House's "Evening of Poetry, Music, and the Spoken Word."[91] On July 27, 2013, Miranda and eight other singers performed the *Hamilton Mixtape* at the Vassar Reading Festival in Poughkeepsie, New York.[92] Two years later, in February 2015 *Hamilton*, having dropped *Mixtape* from its title, debuted off-Broadway. On August 6, 2015, the musical *Hamilton* transferred to the Richard Rodgers Theatre on Broadway and became a world-famous smash.[93] Reflecting on the show's success in *Fresh Air* interview, Miranda credited mixtape creation as a steppingstone to writing Broadway scores. He said,

> mixtapes were an important part of the friendship and mating rituals of New York adolescents. If you were a girl and I wanted to show you I liked you, I would make you a 90 minute cassette, [. . .] subliminally telling you how much

I like you with all of these songs. You're learning about rise and fall and energy and tempo shifts. You're showing off your tastes and your references. You're trying to be witty through placement of music you didn't write. And so it's no accident the name for my show was the Hamilton Mixtape. [. . .] And the reason I make the distinction cassette before CD, is you have to listen to it in the order I curated it for you.[94]

Miranda's background in musical theatre, combined with his knowledge of and investment in hip hop, allowed him to merge the idea of the hip hop mixtape and the nostalgic 1980s mixtape in a way few other individuals have achieved.

During 2016 the producers for the cast album, Miranda, Ahmir Thompson (Questlove), and Tariq Trotter (Black Thought) worked together. Miranda's songwriting skills and his awareness of cultural touchstones blended into a chart-topping, recording-breaking phenomenon. He merged multiple genres to create a new way of perceiving American history and a new style of musical that incorporated hip hop music and actors from more diverse ethnic backgrounds who reflect the founders of hip hop. Miranda originally thought of *Hamilton* as "a hip hop concept album in which celebrated rappers would give voice to different historical characters."[95] Questlove and Black Thought, the co-founders of The Roots, have a deep understanding of the history of music, and rap in particular. The combined intellect of this trio defines the idea of the *Hamilton Mixtape*. In an analysis of *Hamilton*, Questlove describes the correlation between rap and the Broadway show, explaining how both borrow from multiple musical genres. This defines the association between the Gen X personally curated mixtape and the rap sampled, freestyle mixtape. Speaking about Miranda's work he said, "When I talk to Lin, or when I sit in the presence of the thing he has made, I feel the spirit of hip hop. [. . .] Hip hop and Broadway have met now, and shaken hands, and both have walked away elevated."[96] Miranda's original work reflects his awareness and knowledge of the hip hop culture and their genre-specific definition of the mixtape.

In December 2016, Miranda, Thompson, and Trotter produced an additional album called *The Hamilton Mixtape*. On this new album pop musicians sang covers of the Broadway songs, adding their own personality and charm to the now-familiar tunes. The album also included previously unreleased tracks cut from the musical. It debuted at number one on the Billboard charts, making it the first Broadway-related album to top the charts since Hair in 1969.[97] *The Hamilton Mixtape* allowed Miranda to work with respected rappers like Busta Rhymes, Chance the Rapper and Nas as well as pop musicians like Kelly Clarkson and Regina Spektor. Trotter described the process, "It was magical after hearing it all come together and hearing what my DJ, J

Period, did to actually give it a more mixtape feel. So hearing it in its entirety as an actual 'mixtape,' that was a bit of a moment for me."[98] Trotter suggests J Period's DJ experience with samples and allowing rappers to freestyle came to the fore because the team used the *Hamilton* backbone as the samples and allowed the artists to create their own vision over the familiar tracks.

Scholar Justin Williams defended the *Hamilton Mixtape* as a hip hop mixtape.[99] This album merges the two ideas of mixtape more coherently than most any other work of art. Through the choice of artists on the tracks and the sounds of the remixed songs on the *Hamilton Mixtape*, Miranda showcased the idea of an independently released rap album—a hip hop mixtape. By using multiple artists from a variety of genres, creating a track list of already-existing songs, Miranda crafted his own emotional, nostalgic mixtape, reminiscent of the type he described on Fresh Air. The tracks do not mirror the track listing on the Broadway album. By calling the album *The Hamilton Mixtape*, Miranda engaged in remix culture, a staple in the music industry.[100] This album created a novel product which pulls together disparate traditions from Broadway and rap in a consumable, commercial product. Miranda blended different audiences: the fan of the hip hop mixtape who appreciate the artists on the album, the Broadway fan who appreciated the show, and the fan of the Gen X mixtape who revel in the nostalgia of a crafted playlist created for idealized listening.

Hamilton introduced new audiences to both Broadway and hip hop because of the cross-cultural investment the creators incorporated into their work. Miranda's acknowledgment of the role mixtapes played in his musical creations is even more direct in the *Hamilton Mixtape*. This show and this album define the place of the mixtape in current pop culture. Creatives who recognize the appeal of the cassette mixtape, working with individuals who understand the contemporary role of the hip hop mixtape, have fashioned mixtapes for a new youth culture that is not directly connected to cassette tapes or the kitsch of nostalgia. This show has factored into the reintroduction of a mixtape to another generation.

Like *Hamilton, Guardians of the Galaxy* created a mixtape that also defines multiple generations. A 2014, Marvel Universe, action-adventure comic book film, this blockbuster had a distinct impact on pop culture. Taking little-known characters from the comic book universe, James Gunn directed a movie that caught the audience's imagination. The film begins in 1988 when Peter Quill is abducted from earth by aliens. One of the only items he has with him is a Sony Walkman with a mixtape full of songs from the 1960s and 1970s. For Gunn, the Walkman and the songs it plays are fundamental to the script and to the character, "It's very dear to [Quill]. It's the umbilical cord that connects him to earth and the home and family he lost."[101] Gunn insisted the music on the soundtrack reflect the songs Quill would have had on his only cassette.[102]

The Walkman ties Quill to Earth, connects him to the audience as a human outside of his time and place, and solidifies his emotional tie to his mother.[103] The music and the cassette tape are nostalgic memories of the earth he left behind. Released within a year of *Eleanor & Park* and Leonard's memoir, one sees the shift from the mixtape as a coherent part of the lived experience to a meaningful concept. Because of the campy supernatural comic book aspect of the movie, the mixtape is a grounding force humanizing Quill and reflecting a time when his mother would have made a mixtape.

Equally important for marketing the film was the appearance of the soundtrack, aptly named *Awesome Mix Vol. 1*. The cover art signifies a retro moment full of kitsch identifiers. The cassette tape emblazoned cover includes a slightly worn red and white striped sticker with the title hand-written in blue ink. The cassette rests in a generic silver tape deck with familiar triangular symbols for play, stop, fast forward, and rewind. This imagery relaunched the mixtape for a new young, comic-book-loving generation into the mainstream. The younger fan base of *Guardians of the Galaxy* did not live in a world of mixtapes and cassettes (although the parents who accompanied them likely had). Yet this film spurred a resurgence in mixtapes in popular culture. Like *High Fidelity* had done nearly twenty years earlier, *Guardians of the Galaxy* reintroduced the word mixtape to a wide audience. This new audience had little tie to the cassette tape or the original meaning of the artifact.

The songs Gunn included solidified the nostalgic appeal of the mixtape. "Hooked on a Feeling," hit number five on the Billboard Top 100 in 1969.[104] It would not have been defined as a classic song until after the *Guardians of the Galaxy* trailer. With the ability to download the song digitally, it jumped more than 700 percent in sales in the winter of 2014.[105] The album topped the *Billboard* charts in August 2014 and became, "the first time a soundtrack consisting entirely of previously released songs has topped the chart."[106] When asked about his decision to include all previously rereleased tracks, Gunn said, "All those days as a child I spent locked in a room listening to AM radio were not wasted! Somewhere in a boardroom right now a movie executive is trying to give a film that's not testing well the 'Guardians soundtrack treatment but with a new twist.'"[107] Gunn's suggested new twist has done more than inspire other films, it has helped create a resurgence in the entire concept and appeal of the mixtape.

Marketing enhanced the role of the cassette. Marvel Music/Hollywood Records, a division of Disney Music Group released a limited-edition cassette of the soundtrack, with an accompanying digital download, exclusively for Record Store Day in 2014.[108] The first cassette released by Disney since 2003 emerged the same year cassette sales dropped to less than one percent of total music sales.[109] The 2014 cassette release had the same red and white striped sticker on the tape as had been photographed for the CD and vinyl release.

Expanding the concept, the marketing team included cover art reminiscent of the most quintessential personal mixtape. The J-Card has a standard black-lined space for the creator to handwrite the track listing. Side A and Side B are filled out in blue pen with a slash between songs.[110] This album accentuated the kitsch memorabilia of a mixtape and reintroduced a new generation to a familiar sight for a Gen Xer. The excitement around the cassette release of the soundtrack inspired articles in music forums like *Billboard* and *Consequence of Sound*. After its original exclusive release, the cassette remained popular enough to sell for a minimal price on major online shopping forums.

Guardians of the Galaxy represents a shift in the pop culture use of the mixtape. It functions both as a tangible artifact for Quill to remember his mother. The Walkman and the mixtape delineate his humanity and the actual cassette ties him back to himself. But for the marketing team hyping the film, the idea of the mixtape becomes larger than life. The music launched old songs onto the charts and created a blockbuster album to complement a blockbuster film. However, for many of the movie's fans, the soundtrack and the idea of the awesome mix remained intangible concepts. Only diehard fans bought the cassette. Few audiences would listen to a cassette tape of the soundtrack on a Walkman or a boombox. And for those who did, the appeal was campiness as much as authenticity. The incredible success of this film returned the word mixtape to the popular imagination, separating it from the perception of an object and turning it into an idealization of the past. The visual artistic representations of mixtape recipients varied in style, but each connected audiences to the appeal of a kitsch artifact and brought the idea to the pop-culture forefront.

Three years after its initial release Quill returned in the *Guardians of the Galaxy* sequel. The film grossed more than half a billion dollars cementing the series' popularity in the mainstream. Once again, the mixtape grounded the movie's marketing when Quill discovered *Awesome Mix Vol. 2* at the end of the first film.[111] For Gunn, even more explicitly in the second soundtrack, the songs had to reflect Quill's mother Meredith. He picked songs reflective of her.[112] A larger budget and the success of the first soundtrack also scored Gunn a bigger budget to include a handful of songs by superstars like George Harrison and Fleetwood Mac.[113] Like the first soundtrack, the sequel also scored a cassette release in the summer of 2017.[114] In 2014 the release of a cassette for the *Guardians of the Galaxy* soundtrack was a novelty. In 2017 journalists heralded the release of the cassette for the sequel as nostalgia revolution for the cassette, writ large. Although sales remain paltry compared to other music technology, they did jump 35 percent between 2016 and 2017.[115] *Guardians of the Galaxy* albums represented the top three cassette sales according to Nielsen Music's sales, the third being a cassette of songs from a *Guardians of the Galaxy* animated series.[116]

One of the more unique marketing tie-ins for *Guardians of the Galaxy 2* was the limited release bag of Doritos complete with a faux-cassette player on the bag, headphones, and a rechargeable micro-USB with songs from the film.[117] The bags, described as "a bizarre, yet weirdly delightful marketing mess," by *engadget*, retailed for thirty dollars. They sold out immediately. On *eBay* the bags fetched prices of $120–500.[118] This consumable item created an "armchair nostalgia," a marketing strategy to trick consumers into missing something they had not lost.[119] The push-button interface completed the sensory appeal of an analog product and highlighted a campy marketing focus.[120] While the bag had an inexpensive circuit board, the button feature was functional.[121] Fans collected this kitschy item which pulled together different generations of technology to create a mock-up cassette mixtape using modern digital technology. While one could play music on the chip bag, it was unlikely people bought the Doritos for that purpose.

This film displays a new generation of fans who relate the mixtape to a particular character and a particular idea. The cassette is removed from the marketing for all but the dedicated cassette culture fans. In mainstream pop culture *Guardians of the Galaxy* introduced new consumers to the idea of a mixtape, but without the artifact and the DIY aesthetic of the original items. *Hamilton* solidified the hip hop mixtape as a novel compilation. These depictions shifted the mixtape from a tangible artifact to a marketable idea.

A new generation had come of age in a world of streaming services and music at their fingertips. Services like Spotify, Pandora, and YouTube changed the way young people engaged with music. The smartphone became ubiquitous in the hands of millennials. As a result, the mixtape should have no longer had a coherent meaning. Cassettes were dead technology. And yet, the retromania generation felt a lack in their totally accessible 24/7 world. Certain people craved the ability to slow down, shop for the unique vinyl releases, and hear the cracks and hisses analog technology could create. If the cassette has become a valuable commodity again in the 21st century, it is in part because of the mixtape. A Discogs blog looking at the rise of cassette sales asserted,

> There are some pretty obvious reasons why cassettes are popular again. They have a certain charm about them, especially the packaging. Then there's the quaint nostalgia for a long dead epoch in which we could touch and feel everything we loved, including our music. Back then, if we loved a person enough, we could even make them a cassette mixtape of our favourite songs (probably recorded on the fly off the radio).[122]

For a Gen Xer a mixtape remains a point of nostalgia; for younger generations mixtapes represent either the analog past or a shared sentimental rapport. For pop-culture advertising, mixtapes represent a kitsch commodity with marketability. The combination of these various ideas, alongside a growing mainstream appeal of hip hop music, the power of comic book heroes, and the Gen X authors who continued to write from their own lived experiences, allows mixtapes to have resurged in the popular imagination.

In contemporary society, defined by the digital experience and a perceived lack of personal bonds, the mixtape has come to encapsulate a more personally connected, idealized simpler past. These creators incorporated familiar tropes of music and cassette tapes to showcase bonds and nostalgia. Memoirists Bree Housley and Brendan Leonard indicated the changing relationship between a physical mixtape and the music individuals shared versus the idea of using a mixtape as a guiding principle to organize ideas and plots. But it existed at a remove from the daily lives of their audiences until the release of *Guardians of the Galaxy*. Because of the incredible success of the film and the soundtrack, the idea of a mixtape became a mainstream phenomenon. The hype surrounding *Hamilton* helped to reintegrate the various subcultural uses of "mixtapes," creating a more unified twenty-first-century definition of the term. The mixtape, no longer a personal, shared, individually crafted piece of art, had become a commodified idea marketed through imagery and words. Mixtape has become a metaphor, often distinct from tangible, quantifiable objects.

NOTES

1. Although fans love to share statistics to highlight this growth, these numbers are somewhat misleading. The number is, "a fraction of a percent of the 316 million total albums sold but a 645% increase over 2011 cassette sales." Lily Rothman, "Rewound: On Its 50th Birthday, the Cassette Tape Is Still Rolling," *Time*, August 12, 2013.

2. Peter Hartlaub, "The Case for Cassettes: Still Bumping in 2017," *San Francisco Chronicle*, July 28, 2017.

3. Chris Smith, "Forget Vinyl, Cassette Tapes Are the Musical Comeback Story of 2019," *Trusted Reviews* (2019), https://www.trustedreviews.com/news/cassette-tape-comeback-3927671 (Accessed June 1, 2021).

4. Ibid.

5. Ibid.

6. Arjun Appadurai, ed. *The Social Life of Things: Commodities in Cultural Perspective*, Cambridge Studies in Social and Cultural Anthropology (Cambridge: Cambridge University Press, 1986), 3.

7. Ryan Moore, *Sells Like Teen Spirit: Music, Youth Culture, and Social Crisis* (New York: New York University Press, 2010), 165.

8. [APk3a, 1 Benjamin Arcades Project] quoted in Winfried Menninghaus, "On the 'Vital Significance' of Kitsch: Walter Benjamin's Politics of 'Bad Taste,'"

in *Walter Benjamin and the Architecture of Modernity*, ed. Andrew Benjamin and Charles Rice (Melbourne: re.press, 2009), 41.

9. Peter Fritzsche, "Specters of History: On Nostalgia, Exile, and Modernity," *The American Historical Review* 106, no. 5 (2001): 1616.

10. Svetlana Boym, *The Future of Nostalgia* (New York: Basic Books, 2008), eBook, Chapter 16.

11. Susan Sontag "Notes on Camp (1964) as quoted in Moritz Basler, "'New Stands of Beauty and Style and Taste.' Expanding the Concept of Camp," ed. Paul Ferstle and Keyvan Sarkhosh, *Quote, Double Quote: Aesthetics between High and Popular Culture* (New York: Rodopi, 2014), https://ebookcentral.proquest.com/lib/pointpark-ebooks/detail.action?docID=1686923. 24.

12. Theo Cateforis, *Are We Not New Wave? Modern Pop at the Turn of the 1980s* (Ann Arbor: University of Michigan Press, 2011), Chapter 4, 98.

13. Greg Kot, *Ripped: How the Wired Generation Revolutionized Music* (New York: Simon & Schuster, Inc., 2009).

14. Glennon, Mike. "Mixtapes V. Playlists: Medium, Message, Materiality." In *Sounding Out*. 2018. https://soundstudiesblog.com/2018/06/25/mixtapes-v-playlists-medium-message-materiality/ (Accessed July 17, 2020).

15. Collaborative filtering is comparable to the Amazon "customers also bought . . ." feature. Adam Passick, "The Magic That Makes Spotify's Discover Weekly Playlists So Damn Good," *Quartz* (December 21, 2015), https://qz.com/571007/the-magic-that-makes-spotifys-discover-weekly-playlists-so-damn-good/ (Accessed July 14, 2020).

16. Steve Knopper, "How Spotify Playlists Create Hits," *Rolling Stone* (August 15, 2017), https://www.rollingstone.com/pro/news/how-spotify-playlists-create-hits-200277/ (Accessed July 14, 2020).

17. Glennon.

18. Joanna Demers, "Cassette Tape Revival as Creative Anachronism," *Twentieth-Century Music* 14, no. 1 (2017): 112–13.

19. Rob Drew, "Mixed Blessings: The Commercial Mix and the Future of Music Aggregation," *Popular Music & Society* 28, no. 4 (2005): 542.

20. Ibid., 543.

21. Mikey Campbell, "Apple Invention Looks to Revive the Mixtape, with a Digital Twist," *Apple Insider* (August 6, 2015), https://appleinsider.com/articles/15/08/06/apple-invention-looks-to-revive-the-mixtape-with-a-digital-twist?curator=MusicREDEF. Lucy England, "Apple Has Filed a Patent That Could Completely Reinvent the Idea of a Mixtape," *Business Insider* (2015) (Accessed July 14, 2020).

22. Arianne Cohen, "Your Last-Minute Gift Plan: Make a Free Retromixtape Thanks to Apple," *Fast Company* (December 12, 2019), https://www.fastcompany.com/90446645/your-last-minute-gift-plan-make-a-free-retro-mixtape-thanks-to-apple (Accessed July 14, 2020).

23. Ibid.

24. The review linked to a *Medium* article: Timothy S. Boucher, "Make Spotify Mix Tapes," *Medium* (September 2, 2017), https://medium.com/@timboucher/make-spotify-mix-tapes-15f473ef584b (Accessed July 14, 2020).

25. Molly Beauchemin, "St. Vincent Will Make You a Mixtape," *Pitchfork* (June 12, 2015), https://pitchfork.com/news/59936-st-vincent-will-make-you-a-mixtape/ (Accessed July 14, 2020).

26. Ben Kaye, "St. Vincent Pays Tribute to Prince on Her Beats 1 Radio Show - Listen," *Consequence of Sound* (February 15, 2017), https://consequenceofsoun d.net/2017/02/st-vincent-pays-tribute-to-prince-on-her-beats-1-radio-show-listen/ (Accessed July 14, 2020); Beauchemin.

27. Apple Music, "St. Vincent's Mixtape Delivery Service," https://music.apple. com/us/curator/st-vincents-mixtape-delivery-service/1002618148 (Accessed July 14, 2020).

28. Jack Denton, "A Generation of Hip-Hop Was Given Way for Free. Can It Be Archived?". Pacific Standard, https://psmag.com/social-justice/a-generation-of -hip-hop-was-given-away-for-free-can-it-be-archived (Accessed July 8, 2020); Dan Rys, "The Evolution of the Mixtape: An Oral History with DJ Drama," Billboard, https://www.billboard.com/articles/columns/hip-hop/7669073/history-dj-drama-mixt ape-evolution (Accessed January 26, 2021); Dan Rys "Mixtapes & Money: Inside the Mainstreaming of Hip-Hop's Shadow Economy," *Billboard* (2017), https://www .billboard.com/articles/columns/hip-hop/7669109/mixtapes-money-hip-hop-shadow -economy-mainstream (March 19, 2021).

29. Michael Kawaida, "Mixtapes: A Brief History of Hip-Hop's Ever Evolving Tool," *Hot New Hip Hop* (2020), https://www.hotnewhiphop.com/mixtapes-a-brief -history-of-hip-hops-ever-evolving-tool-news.103882.html; Rys, "The Evolution of the Mixtape: An Oral History with DJ Drama."

30. Rys, "Mixtapes & Money: Inside the Mainstreaming of Hip-Hop's Shadow Economy."

31. Adam Bradley and Andrew DuBois, eds., *The Anthology of Rap* (New Haven: Yale University Press, 2010), 566.

32. DJ Semtex, "Street Dreams: How Hip-Hop Mixtapes Changed the Game," *Hip-Hop Raised Me* (Medium: Thames & Hudson, 2016), https://medium.com /cuepoint/street-dreams-how-hip-hop-mixtapes-changed-the-game-40af79e8d953 (Accessed July 15, 2020).

33. Ibid.

34. The three companies were Datpiff, LiveMixtapes and AudioMack. Rys, "Mixtapes & Money: Inside the Mainstreaming of Hip-Hop's Shadow Economy."

35. Ibid.

36. Denton.

37. Marcyliena Morgan and Dionne Bennett, "Hip-Hop & the Global Imprint of a Black Cultural Form," *Daedalus* 140, no. 2 (2011), https://www.jstor.org/stable /23047460.

38. Judy Dodge Cummings, *Hip-Hop Culture* (Minneapolis: Abdo Publishing, 2017), http://search.ebscohost.com/login.aspx?direct=true&AuthType=sso&db=nle bk&AN=1491310&site=eds-live&scope=site.

39. Ibid., 20.

40. Discogs is a user-built database of music with more than twelve million recordings. This search includes song lyrics, album titles, and descriptors of a

certain non-commercial release. Discogs. www.discogs.com (2020). Accessed July 17, 2020.

41. Skinny Friedman, "The Real Difference between a Mixtape and an Album," *Vice* (December 10, 2013), https://www.vice.com/en_ca/article/rmx446/the-real-diff erence-between-a-mixtape-and-an-album (Accessed July 17, 2020).

42. Lee Brice, "Music," https://www.leebrice.com/#!/releases (Accessed August 5, 2020).

43. "Mixtape," Lee Brice on *Mixtape: 'Til Summer's Gone*, Curb Records, 2016.

44. Jen Swirsky, "Review: Lee Brice's "Mixtape: 'Til Summer's Gone" EP," *Nashville Gab* (2015), https://nashvillegab.com/2015/07/lee-brice-mixtape-til-summers-gone-ep.html (Accessed July 13, 2020).

45. "This is How We Roll," Florida Georgia Line on *Here's To The Good Times*, Big Machine Records, 2012.

46. Cool With That," Brett Kissel, on *Pick Me Up*, Warner Music Canada, 2015.

47. Nate Sloan and Charlie Harding, *Switched on Pop: How Popular Music Works and Why It Matters* (New York: Oxford University Press, 2020), 157.

48. In a 2020 response to the Black Lives Matter protests, Lady Antebellum changed their name to Lady A. "Freestyle," Lady Antebellum on *747*, Capitol Records, 2014.

49. "That's All I Need," Dirty Heads on *Dirty Heads*, Five Seven Music, 2016.

50. Ibid.

51. "Sisyphus," Clara Charron on *Chai Tea Lattes*, Pop of Color Records, 2017.

52. Ibid.

53. "Homemade" Jake Owen on *Greetings From . . . Jake*, Big Loud Records, 2019. And "Perfect Storm" Brad Paisley on *Moonshine In the Trunk*, Arista Nashville, 2014.

54. "Things in My Jeep," Linkin Park, The Lonely Island on *Popstar: Never Stop Never Stopping*, Republic Records, 2016.

55. "Summer Fever," Little Big Town single, Capital Records Nashville, 2018.

56. "Throwback," James Barker Band on *Game On*, Universal Music Canada, 2017.

57. Ibid.

58. "Radioland," Ashley McBryde on *Girl Going Nowhere*, Warner Music Nashville, 2018.

59. "Stereo Hearts" Gym Class Heroes featuring Adam Levine on *The Papercut Chronicles Part II*, Fueled by Ramen, 2011.

60. Ibid.

61. "Mix Tape" Jim's Big Ego on *They're Everywhere*, self-released, 2003.

62. Ibid.

63. Ibid.

64. David Dean, "Bree Housley: 'We Hope You Like This Song,'" *Serial Optimist* (December 27, 2012), https://www.serialoptimist.com/conversations/bree-housley-we-hope-you-like-this-song-12104.html (Accessed July 10, 2020).

65. Bree Housley, *We Hope You Like This Song" an Overly Honest Story About Friendship, Death, and Mix Tapes* (Berkeley, CA: Perseus Books Group, 2012), 111.

66. Brendan Leonard, interview by Jehnie Burns, May 20, 2020, Email.

67. Ibid.

68. Ibid.

69. *The New American Road Trip Mixtape* (USA: Semi-Rad, 2013).

70. Joshua Harmon, *The Annotated Mixtape* (Ann Arbor: Dzane Books, 2014), 6.

71. Leonard, "The New American Road Trip Mixtape."

72. Meagan Brothers, *Supergirl Mixtapes* (New York: Henry Holt and Company, 2012), 171–72.

73. Erica Futterman, "Literature's John Hughes: Rainbow Rowell on Her Love Affair with Music and Writing" (July 15, 2014), http://www.buzzfeed.com/ericaf utterman/music-and-writing-sitting-in-a-tree#.byvE9NXEE (Accessed November 10, 2016).

74. Rainbow Rowell, *Eleanor & Park* (New York: St. Martin's Press, 2013), Novel, 45–46.

75. Ibid., 57–58.

76. Ibid., 75–76.

77. Futterman.

78. Lucy Knisley, *Something New* (New York: First Second, 2016), Graphic Novel, 154.

79. Ibid., 158.

80. Ibid., 162.

81. Dan Watters and Caspar Wijngaard, interview by Laura Sneddon, February 10, "Get Stuck into 'Limbo with Caspar Wijngaard and Dan Watters," 2016. Image Comics, "Limbo #1," Image Comics, https://imagecomics.com/comics/releases/ limbo-1 (Accessed July 12, 2020).

82. Ibid.

83. "Limbo TP," Image Comics, https://imagecomics.com/comics/releases/limbo -tp (Accessed July 10, 2020).

84. Matthew Box, "Through the Magnavox Looking Glass: We Enter the Weird World of 'Limbo' with Writer Dan Watters," *Broken Frontier* (April 15, 2016), http:// www.brokenfrontier.com/limbo-image-comics-dan-watters-caspar-wijngaard-intervi ew-review/ (Accessed July 10, 2020).

85. Dan Watters and Caspar Wijngaard, interview by Chris Hayden, June 29, "Interview: Dan Watters & Caspar Wijngaard Talk about the Musical Voodoo of Limbo," 2016.

86. "Get Stuck into 'Limbo with Caspar Wijngaard and Dan Watters [Interview]."

87. This statement is based on Google and Amazon keyword searches. Amazon Kindle often comprises self-published titles not released through major publishing houses,

88. The books in this section are all from searches of the Amazon Kindle Store Database in the summer of 2020. Kindle Store Amazon, "'Mixtape' Search," https:// smile.amazon.com/s?k=mixtape&i=digital-text&ref=nb_sb_noss.

89. Nikki Sloane, ed. *Mixtape: A Love Song Anthology* (USA: Shady Creek Publishing 2019).

90. "Nikki Sloane," Squarespace, https://www.nikkisloane.com/shop/mixtape-a -love-song-anthology (Accessed July 10, 2020).

91. The Obama White House, *Lin-Manuel Miranda Performs at the White House Poetry Jam, An Evening of Poetry & Music: The Spoken Word* (YouTube 2009). https://youtu.be/WNFf7nMIGnE (Accessed August 1, 2020).

92. Nicole Scholet, "Hamilton Mixtape Unveiled at Vassar Reading Festival," *The Alexander Hamilton Awareness Society* (August 27, 2013), https://the-aha-soci ety.com/index.php/publications/articles/87-aha-society-articles/145-hamilton-mix tape-reading (Accessed July 10, 2020).

93. Eric King, "Everything We Know About 'the Hamilton Mixtape,'" *Billboard* (August 12, 2016), https://www.billboard.com/articles/news/features/7469389/eve rything-we-know-about-hamilton-mixtape (Accessed July 10, 2020).

94. Lin-Manuel Miranda. "Lin-Manuel Miranda on Disney, Mixtapes and Why He Won't Try to Top 'Hamilton.'" By Terri Gross. *Fresh Air* (January 3, 2017).

95. Ayun Halliday, "Watch Lin-Manuel Miranda Perform the Earliest Version of *Hamilton* at the White House, Six Years before the Play Hit the Broadway Stage (2009)," *Open Culture* (March 4, 2019), http://www.openculture.com/2019/03/watch -lin-manuel-miranda-perform-the-earliest-version-of-hamilton-at-the-white-house. html (Accessed July 10, 2020).

96. Ahmir "Questlove" Thomspon, "Questlove on 'Hamilton' and Hip-Hop: It Takes One," *Rolling Stone* (September 28, 2015), https://www.rollingstone. com/culture/culture-news/questlove-on-hamilton-and-hip-hop-it-takes-one-34370/ (Accessed July 10, 2020).

97. Chris Molanphy, *Hit Parade*, podcast audio, The Lullaby of Broadway Edition, 1hr 18 mins 2019.

98. Dan Rys, "The Roots' Black Thought on Lin-Manuel Miranda, Perseverance & 'the Hamilton Mixtape,'" *Billboard* (November 30, 2016), https://www.billboar d.com/articles/columns/hip-hop/7595776/hamilton-mixtape-the-roots-black-thought -on-lin-manuel-miranda (Accessed July 15, 2020).

99. Justin A. Williams, "'We Get the Job Done': Immigrant Discourse and Mixtape Authenticity in *the Hamilton Mixtape*," *American Music* 36, no. 4 (2018). 489-90.

100. Remix reflects the early days of rap which sampled familiar genres of music and incorporated new iconic musicians.

101. Sam Ashurst, "Guardians of the Galaxy: James Gunn's Trailer Breakdown," *Total Film* (February 19, 2014), http://www.totalfilm.com/features/guardians-of-the -galaxy-james-gunn-s-trailer-breakdown/star-lord-s-walkman (Accessed May 28, 2020).

102. Brian Hiatt, "Inside the 'Guardians of the Galaxy Vol. 2' Soundtrack," *Rolling Stone* (April 19, 2017), https://www.rollingstone.com/music/music-features/ inside-the-guardians-of-the-galaxy-vol-2-soundtrack-123648/ (Accessed May 28, 2020).

103. Marion Kirkpatrick, "Why a '70s Mixtape Propels the Plot of 'Guardians of the Galaxy,'" *Billboard* (August 1, 2014), https://www.billboard.com/articles/news/ 6204544/guardians-of-the-galaxy-soundtrack-james-gunn (Accessed May 28, 2020).

104. First released in 1968 by B. J. Thomas, Blue Swede re-recorded and released "Hooked on a Feeling" in 1974. This version included the familiar "Ooga-Chaka" intro and became the number twenty song on the Billboard 100.

105. Keith Caulfield, "Blue Swede's 'Hooked on a Feelin' Sales Soar Thanks to "Guardians of the Galaxy' Trailer," *Billboard* (February 2, 2014), https://www.bil lboard.com/articles/news/5915510/blue-swedes-hooked-on-a-feeling-sales-soar-than ks-to-guardians-of-the-galaxy (Accessed May 28, 2020).

106. Greg Gilman, "'Guardians of the Galaxy' Becomes First Soundtrack in History without New Songs to Land No. 1 Spot," *The Wrap* (August 13, 2014), https ://www.thewrap.com/guardians-of-the-galaxy-soundtrack-soars-to-no-1-on-billboard -200/ (Accessed May 28, 2020).

107. Facebook post as quoted in ibid.

108. Keith Caulfield, "Exclusive: "Guardians' Soundtrack to Be Released on Cassette Tape," *Billboard* (October 20, 2014), https://www.billboard.com/articles/ news/6289124/guardians-of-the-galaxy-soundtrack-cassette-tape (Accessed May 28, 2020).

109. Ibid. RIAA, "U. S. Sales Database," https://www.riaa.com/u-s-sales-data base/?fbclid=IwAR2-IuPU0w989pz0nuGsZflTrF3BFdK1C9FhpD3PfHg1CJTt4b s86UzPOvY (Accessed July 8, 2020).

110. Alex Young, "Guardians of the Galaxy's Awesome Mix Vol. 1 Is Finally Being Released on Cassette Tape," *Consequence of Sound* (October 20, 2014), https:/ /consequenceofsound.net/2014/10/guardians-of-the-galaxys-awesome-mix-vol-1-is-finally-being-released-on-cassette-tape/ (Accessed May 28, 2020).

111. Hiatt.

112. Ibid.

113. Ibid.

114. Ben Kaye, "Guardians of the Galaxy Vol. 2 Soundtrack Coming to Vinyl and Cassette," *Consequence of Sound* (June 6, 2017), https://consequenceofsoun d.net/2017/06/guardians-of-the-galaxy-vol-2-soundtrack-coming-to-vinyl-and-casse tte/ (Accessed July 10, 2020).

115. Julie Muncy, "*Guardians of the Galaxy* Is Leading the Unlikely Cassette Tape Revival" (January 6, 2018), https://io9.gizmodo.com/guardians-of-the-galaxy -is-leading-the-unlikely-cassett-1821838451 (Accessed July 10, 2020).

116. The fourth album was the *Stranger Things* soundtrack, also a bid for 1980s nostalgia. Ibid.

117. Mike Sorrentino, "This Doritos Bag Plays 'Guardians of the Galaxy' Music," *c|net* (May 5, 2017), https://www.cnet.com/news/guardians-of-the-galaxy-vol-2-dori tos-bag-soundtrack/ (Accessed July 10, 2020).

118. Sean Buckley, "We Destroyed a Collectible Doritos Bag to Get at Its Hidden Mp3 Player," *engadget* (April 28, 2017), https://www.engadget.com/2017-04-28-we -destroyed-a-collectible-doritos-mp3-player.html.and Sorrentino (Accessed July 10, 2020).

119. Boym, Chapter 3.

120. Andrea F. Bohlman and Peter McMurray, "Tape: Or, Rewinding the Phonographic Regime," *Twentieth-Century Music* 14, no. 1 (2017): 15.

121. Buckley.

122. Discogs, "The Cassette Comeback, by the Numbers," Discogs, https://blog.di scogs.com/en/the-cassette-comeback-by-the-numbers/ (Accessed July 8, 2020).

Chapter 7

Technostalgia

The success of *Hamilton* and *Guardians of the Galaxy*, combined with a renewed fascination with analog technology brought the mixtape back into mainstream culture. While young people likely did not own cassette players, they now became familiar with mixtapes. The film *Baby Driver* represents a new era of film in which mixtapes are fundamental to the story, overlap with hip hop creations, and still tie characters together emotionally. However, it has become a grounded site of cultural memory which continues to reflect on the tangibility and emotional connectiveness of the nostalgic past. Streaming technology began to use the word "mixtape" as a synonym for playlist which solidified it as a renewed twenty-first-century concept, but shifted the meaning from a physical, tangible product to a metaphor. Mixtape is proxy for disparate lists that have broad thematic connections. Academics have used mixtape as a teaching tool to explain difficult concepts or modes of writing to students, connecting familiar (enough) terminology to larger ideas. Podcasters have also attached themselves to mixtape as a thematic idea that ties them to their listeners. Different audiences can relate to the term through music, lists, pop culture, or as a metaphor. "Mixtape" has become a ubiquitous term which reflects varied social, cultural, and demographic definitions.

Within the larger scope of analysis about nostalgia, one can assess different specific facets of nostalgic appeal. As with the specificity of kitsch, technostalgia allows for the sense of an exaggerated sensibility and association with an item. Technostalgia is "the bittersweet longing for past technologies."[1] "Technostalgia" is a specifically modern aspect in the discussion of nostalgia, acknowledging an awareness of the digital landscape in which young people live. Trevor Pinch and Frank Trocco who helped coin the term in their discussion of synthesizers stated, "[Artists and engineers] sense a missed opportunity, a technology that slipped through their fingers without being exploited to the full."[2] In his analysis of memory and memorialization Andreas Huyssen states, "The ever-increasing speed of technical, scientific, and cultural innovation produces even larger quantities of the soon-to-be-obsolete, and it objectively shrinks the chronological expansion of what can be considered the (cutting-edge) present at any given time."[3] What had once taken generations to become outdated has moved closer to the present as a result of increasing technological advances. There has been a growing appeal for the vintage technologies of records and cassettes. Vinyl and cassette cultures have grown and created a renewed interest in contemporary sales of old technology. The mixtape, like the resurgence of vinyl, highlights a disconnect with the present and indicates a "desired return to an ideal past in response to a troubled present."[4] In his analysis of the resurgence of cassette culture, Craig Eley argues that the process of relating to technologies as "both ongoing and multiple" is a social construction much the same way Arjun Appadurai discussed commodities as having social lives.[5] In exploring the resurgence of cassette culture in the 2010s, Eley states, "Today's cassette culture, by eschewing contemporary media forms for more esoteric ones, is building on the older cassette culture tradition of rejecting dominant industry formats. However, contemporary cassette distributors aim not so much to make music cheap and widely available as much as they do to make it physical, and ultimately, collectible."[6]

Technological shifts to less expensive record players and digital tape players have created a niche market for once outdated products. Technostalgia creates a marketable appeal for those items. For David Sax, the need to slow down the pace of life has created a desire for the past. When vinyl surged and sales skyrocketed worldwide in the early 2000s, the tech and music industries tried to understand what had happened. Sax declared, "Commonly cited marketing buzzwords, such as *authenticity, nostalgia,* and *millennial,* were deployed in various combinations. Others just pinned it on the dreaded *hipster,* that ill-defined species of early aughts youth culture, which remains the preferred scapegoat for any urban gripe from gentrification to the tightness of jeans."[7] The vocabulary used in reviews and discussions of the renewed appeal of analog technology created a self-perpetuating cycle in which the technostalgia led to the desire for the analog which created a market for the newly crafted analog products. For Sax, the inefficiency and lack of perfection created the appeal of the analog. What had been a liability has become an advantage. Sax contends that consumers desire nostalgia, yet mixtape imagery shows artists have commodified technostalgia.

In 2019 Discogs concluded cassettes are back. On their blog they asserted cassette mixtapes have played into the marketing of renewed cassette sales. In addition, they believe non-mainstream genres, from ambient to metal core, use cassettes to put music in front of an audience. For fans, it shows an artist's commitment to their music. For the artists, they are the cheapest analog media to produce, especially in small numbers.[8] Cassette enthusiasts would argue there is a practical reason for the return of the cassette. Alongside the modest expense, they are more portable and durable than vinyl.[9] They are easier to transport from show to show. Moreover, there are those in the music world who argue the tape hiss and the imperfection of a cassette are more genuine and "nakedly honest" than any other medium. A *Medium* think piece outlining why cassettes have resurfaced, stated, "Even distortion on tape is valuable, adding textural qualities that cannot be emulated on digital tech. For an artist looking for inspiration and something different amongst the never-ending options of digital recording, analogue is certainly appealing."[10] This argument highlights the desire for both authenticity and uniqueness. Musicians need a way to distinguish themselves from the competition and a cassette tape signifies a specific community

The significant expansion of the vinyl industry has pushed for the resurgence of the cassette. Years ago, vinyl was inexpensive, and fans could find good records in one- and two-dollar bins. However, consumer culture has become invested in vinyl fandom and has reinvested in the industry creating new, exclusive special releases. The price has skyrocketed, with unique pressings sold yearly on Record Store Day for $50–100. While looking for vinyl, it remains possible to find cheap classic cassettes selling for significantly less than vinyl or digitally. A record store owner in Oakland, California said,

> It's getting harder to walk away from a vinyl rack with 10 good records for $20. But the dollar bin for cassette tapes can yield a weekend's worth of music for the price of one pristine LP. And unlike with vinyl, cassettes allow you to blast your favorite local artist on the way home.[11]

While record player technology has improved in the past twenty years, Americans still own cars with cassette players to immediately listen to their purchases.

The collectability of the analog plays into the discussion about technostalgia and cassette culture. As with kitsch, those invested in cassette culture are looking for a tie to the past. Music scholar Timothy Taylor claims the physicality of retro instruments creates a pleasurable tactical experience for musicians they cannot replicate digitally.[12] For the fans, collecting is part of the experience, which highlights the need for the tangibility of an artifact, and the excitement over a find when there is a scarcity to the object.[13] "Much of this music and the cover art are appreciated for its kitschiness. But it is still an affectionate appreciation."[14] Kitschiness then becomes codified in the technological artifact of the cassette. The anti-consumer desire of contemporary fans to eschew the mainstream music industry plays out in the search for the music of earlier generations.

Authors thinking about their own link to artifacts and nostalgia have attempted to quantify how their perception of analog technology differs. In her analysis, self-touted Gen Xer, Eve Epstein waxes poetic about the *"there-ness"* of earlier technology which she does not see as "blind nostalgia."[15] She states, "We attached our love to actual things, things which had a distinct and differentiated purpose."[16] For her the digital is too amorphous, and therefore not authentic. For Simon Reynolds, who both understands and despises the culture of retro, the cassette tape represents a moment of inscrutability. He understands why certain artists find them aesthetically appealing and cost-efficient. But as he states,

> The cult of the cassette has spread beyond the no-fi undergrad to become a retro fad, with young hipsters wearing T-shirts adorned with cassettes or belt buckles actually made out of old cassette shells. During the writing of this book, our twenty-four-year-old babysitter turned up with a chic tote bag decorated with the image of a blank cassette; the plastic was writeable, allowing you to person-alise the cassette with the name of a band or the title of an imaginary mix-tape. There is a massive cult among the young for dead media and outmoded appli-ances, although it rarely extends beyond displaying the image to actually *using* the bygone format or device.[17]

The *retromania* Reynolds describes above solidifies how the mixtape has resurfaced in mainstream culture. The technostalgia combined with the kitsch appeal has created a nostalgic desire simply for the imagery. The current DIY model of creating cassette tapes, which are inefficient and lower audio qual-ity, has commodified the mixtape as a marketable product.

Like Reynold's argument, Rob Drew analyzed the vocabulary of mixtape, whether as a physical product or a digital recreation, as a commodification in commercial marketing. For him, the commercial mix, the compilation album sold as a promotional product by a corporation, exploited the nostalgic appeal of the mixtape. When a company like Starbucks or Victoria's Secret branded a mix to "complement the 'lifestyle' defined by the companies' products," they capitalized on the term "mixtape," yet diminished its role as a personal, emotive object.[18] Drew's argument emerged in the lull of mixtape popularity with the rise of digital platforms like iTunes. He feared commercial defini-tions would undermine and destroy the inherent "interpersonal context" of the mixtape, devaluing the meaning of the artifact.[19] As the continuation of mix-tape imagery after 2005 shows, Drew's argument has merit, but did not herald an end of the mixtape. Retromania and technostalgia, for the idea and the image as much as the product, remained key factors in the continued presence of the mixtape in pop culture. The physical representation of mixtapes on commercial merchandise highlights the trendiness of the visual representation of cassettes. The passion artists display in their discussions of mixtapes indicates mixtape culture is not merely simulated for greater profitability.

BOOKS

Fiction

By the mid-2010s mixtapes had become a somewhat familiar trope in pop culture again. Firmly immersed in the generation in which digital streaming predominates music sharing, a subculture invested in the nostalgia of analog had surfaced. Authors who connect to their younger identity with mixtapes or mix CDs, inserted mixtapes into stories to solidify bonds between characters. The authors of these books remained individuals who had lived with mixtapes in their own youth and saw the role of the cassette tape as a logical link. For their readers who had not grown up with cassettes or CDs, authors had to present them in a coherent way.

Libby Cudmore, author of the 2016 *The Big Rewind*, tackles the debate between generations of music lovers head on. A *Book Page* interview with Cudmore opens:

> Digging into an old box of mixed tapes leads one direction—toward nostalgia, and most likely into the tricky land of exes. Libby Cudmore's debut, *The Big Rewind*, is much like that box of mixtapes, with its mystery buried beneath affairs of the heart, wry jokes about hipster Brooklyn and a steady stream of The Smiths, Warren Zevon and Talking Heads.[20]

As the interview progresses, Cudmore deems herself the "queen of the mix CD" as she walks through the art of making the ideal compilation. This interview typifies Cudmore's debut novel. The cover of *The Big Rewind* places the cassette at the center of the story. A black cassette with a pink and purple striped sticker covers the bottom third of the image. A bundle of black twisted spooling tape winds across the top two-thirds, with the title in white. The cover blurb states, "Like Nick Hornby's *High Fidelity* for women . . . ."[21] Hornby remains the reference point for books about cassettes.

In the story Jett Bennett receives a mixtape for her friend KitKat who has just been murdered. Jett solves the mystery by analyzing the songs and tracking down the mixtape creator. Add in romance, and the story is a fun light romp. The mixtape, which is anachronistic in the contemporary story, situates the plot. On page one Jett states,

I've got a smartphone, but I'm not too young to remember the exact weight and
feel of a Maxell mix tape. They're just slightly heavier than a regular cassette,
weighed down with love and angst, track lists thick with rubber cement and
collage.[22]

By 2016 when Cudmore published *The Big Rewind,* cassettes and mixtapes
had reemerged in pop culture dialogue. Cudmore helps to quantify the mixtape, grounding it in emotion and DIY art.

Cudmore consciously compares the cassette tapes to the current culture of
smartphones and playlists. Understanding her audience, she recognizes the
need to explain the appeal of an artifact from an earlier generation. Finding
a friend with a tape deck so they could listen to KitKat's tape, the characters
muse about the past. "Finding that tape in your locker, playing it over and
over, trying to figure out what he was trying to say. Tapping a playlist off
some guy's iPhone just isn't the same you know. How the hell else are we
supposed to know what love is, from a Facebook update? Give me a Sony any
day."[23] As Jett navigates mystery solving and her relationships, she repeatedly returns to her "boyfriend box" full of memorabilia including mixtapes
and CDs. Like Rob in *High Fidelity,* she rehashes what had destroyed relationships and the role music had played in navigating those feelings. Near
the end of the novel, Jett exclaims, "Fuck nostalgia. Fuck all of it. Cassie
murdered KitKat because she couldn't let go of the past. I pulled out love
letters, mix tapes, and burned CDs with decoupaged liner notes, stuffed animals, college T-shirts, broken necklaces, guitar picks . . . ."[24] The past, which
haunted the characters, turned nostalgia into a negative association which
hindered Jett. However, her love for the mixtape does not disappear completely. Jett receives a smartphone case that looks like a cassette and a playlist
downloaded onto her phone from her new partner. She mixes the present and
the past as she negotiates a new relationship.

Despite the digital conclusion of her novel, Cudmore is not her characters.
She concedes, "Spotify playlists just won't do the job." The physicality of
an artifact distinguishes it from the playlist, "it's the cover art, the physical
arrival of the object, whether you pull it from a purse or a jacket pocket or
they come home from work and find it in the mail. Nothing is ever going to
replace that thrill."[25] For the author, the DIY artistry remains at the forefront
of a good mixtape

The 1980s and 1990s created a legacy for DIY art. Cassettes prevailed
in the punk music scene because of their ease and expense. The riot-grrrl
generation, raised on Bikini Kill and third-wave feminism encapsulated a
subculture in this larger punk world. Authors who grew up in that world have
incorporated riot-grrrl ideology and used mixtapes and female empowerment

to write stories for young readers. In these stories young women consume older, non-pop culture music as a sign of individuality and pride. The sharing of mixtapes is not a sign of courtship but a sign of bequeathing a legacy of gendered strength. *The First Rule of Punk* tells the story of Malu, a seventh grade, Chuck Taylor-wearing girl trying to maintain a connection to her father during her parents' divorce and a move from Florida to Chicago. As Malu and her mother pack to leave, her father gives her a gift,

> The other item in the shoe box was Dad's old Walkman cassette player and a cassette in its plastic case.
> "Cool! You made me a mix?"
> "I put some new stuff and some old stuff on there," Dad said. "I hope you like it."
> "Is the Walkman a gift too?" I asked hopefully.
> "How about I let you borrow it?" Dad said. "Return it when you're back home again."
> I threw my arms around Dad and kissed his cheek.
> "You may be far from home, kid, but you can take the music anywhere," Dad said. "It's always with you."[26]

The personal stereo and the cassettes create a link between generations as a middle school girl who would have no personal tie to this technology sees the meaning in this gift from her dad. The music and the Walkman connect Malu and her father while giving her the skills to navigate the challenges of middle school.

Celia Pérez's book uses loud, brash punk music as a means of expression. *The First Rule of Punk* is geared towards an upper-elementary student, the youngest audience addressed in a book with mixtapes. Rather than the romantic feel of Rainbow Rowell's book, this story acknowledges emotions like anger and frustration, feelings not always viewed as appropriate for young women. Struggling with her new life Malu calls her dad, "After I hung up, I grabbed Dad's Walkman and hit play on his mix. As the bouncy, poppy-punk song filled my head, my insides relaxed and expanded. I couldn't deal with the even-numbered problems that awaited me on pages nine and ten of my algebra book, so I pulled out my zine supplies instead."[27] Making a zine connects Malu to the Bikini Kill generation and their fans who made and sold zines at shows in the 1990s. Later, an older friend introduces Malu to the East Los Angeles punk band, The Brat, to familiarize Malu with Hispanic history. Learning history through punk personalizes Malu's background and she cultivates an appreciation of her heritage.[28] DIY publications and punk music, like the mixtape, reflect an anti-consumer edge which incorporated women into the independent music scene and allowed them to see themselves reflected in creative works. Pérez writes an empowering novel introducing Gen X attitudes to a new generation of girls who can apply it to their worlds.

Chelsey Johnson's 2018 novel *Stray City* also reflects the 1990s fascination with mixtapes, zines, and Gen Xers relating to the next generation. Carrie Brownstein, actor, first-generation riot-grrrl, and lead singer of Sleater-Kinney, wrote one of the praise-filled blurbs for the novel. *Stray City* tells the story of Andrea Morales' life from a Gen X adolescent in the late 1990s to a mom of her own tween. She flees her Midwestern upbringing and settles in Portland where she can embrace her new queer identity. Centered on the Portland DIY art world, Johnson's plot promotes riot-grrrl culture. Near the end of the novel, Andrea searches out a trinket to unite her daughter with the father she never knew.

> And here were the cassettes: a few mixtapes from Ryan [. . .]. They had lived such analog lives then. Letters, photocopied zines, videocassettes, mixtapes in a Walkman. It used to take her hours to make a mixtape. That was the art of it—you had to measure your time so carefully, rationing those forty-five minutes per side, and sequence with precise intent since the order of the songs was fixed forever. Time then was more like space—you traveled it like land, minute by minute, mile by mile.[29]

While mixtapes are not fundamental to the plot, the mention of them, and the reflection on making them accentuates a parent's nostalgia of a past they want to introduce to their children. Setting the story in the 1990s Pacific Northwest solidifies its connection to the grunge scene out of which riot grrrl emerged. For these two authors the mixtapes, like the zines and the mention of riot-grrrls, situate their stories in a time and place.

For both Pérez and Johnson music and mixtapes help tell their stories. They both reference songs throughout their novels and use the mixtapes as links between generations. Andrea, wanting to connect to her daughter, contemplates the importance of the DIY culture and the difference in how she lived in the past. The nostalgia for the analog overlaps with the present storyline. Both authors have website pages with Spotify playlists corresponding to their stories.[30] The playlist has become the twenty-first-century version of the mixtape, and these authors use the newest technology to create another layer of outreach to their audience. They have incorporated the mixtape as an aspect of Gen X collective memory, tying the emotionality to the artifact.

Creating and incorporating a Spotify playlist is a marketing tool which Jane Sanderson also used for her 2020 novel, *Mix Tape*.[31] The American cover includes a drawing of an orange cassette tape with black tape spooling out. The mess of tape turns into the silhouette of a man and a woman and intertwines to become the book title. The end sheets replicate the cover with two hand-drawn black cassette tapes on opposite edges. The pages are filled with intertwining spooled black tape subtly depicting the same silhouettes as the cover. Without reading a word, the basic romantic plot joined through music is clear. The back cover encapsulates the role of music, "Daniel was the first boy to make Alison a mix tape. But that was years ago. And Ali hasn't thought about him in a very long time. Until Dan's name pops up on her phone, with a song from their past. Ali can't help but respond in kind. And so begins a new mix tape . . . ."[32] Sanderson explained that seeing people sharing music via social media inspired her to write a story in which two people connected entirely through music.[33]

In the book, teenage Daniel gave Alison a mixtape called *The Best Last Two*, sets of two songs by the same band because she preferred listening to songs in order. Sanderson's novel uses the stereotype of a musically knowledgeable boy sharing both his heart and his wisdom as a sign of courtship. For young Daniel, making mixtapes began his life-long appreciation for music, "by then he had the mix-tape habit and he carried it on, making real mixes, properly mixed up, just for himself, or for friends, or for girls he fancied, speaking to people through music."[34] Giving Alison the mixtape embodied teen courting in the 1970s and 1980s. For grown-up Ali, memories of the mixtape helped to solidify her renewed relationship with Dan,

> She recalled a lingering kiss against the wall of his house, the feel of the cassette in her coat pocket, and the very first time she heard the playlist, alone in her bedroom, in an empty house [. . .] she'd listened to this tape in her cold bedroom, and loved it, and loved Daniel for thinking of it.[35]

When Ali receives a song on Twitter from Dan it reminds her of their teenage relationship.

> She'd remembered the cassette yesterday evening, [. . .] she'd found it in a cardboard box of sundry items, safe and sound in its plastic case. There was no track list, he hadn't written one, so Ali had to dig out an old cassette player to remind herself what he'd chosen all those years ago. She'd listened to the songs in the permanent twilight of the loft, feeling melancholy, nostalgic, and entirely lost for a while in Daniel's musical obsessions of 1979.[36]

The nostalgia of the moment and the music, connected to the thirty-year-old physical item, solidified the reemerging relationship between Dan and Ali. Dan considers sending Ali the song as, "An intimate dialogue in music, an eloquence beyond the written word. It was genius."[37] While Sanderson's novel revolves around digitally sharing songs via social media, the physical

mixtape merges the past and the present. The music underscores the relationship. The songs reflect nostalgic and romance.

Asked what she remembers about mixtapes in her own life Sanderson
starts,

> I only ever received mix tapes from one boyfriend, who shall be known hence-
> forth as Mix Tape Man. [. . .] Mix Tape Man presented me with a curated
> compilation very early on in our relationship, and he immediately had my full
> attention. He named the cassette Sloppy Bugger Music, and that first tape was
> followed by more; laboriously-compiled recordings of his favourite songs,
> which made me overlook, for twelve months, all the many reasons why he
> wasn't right for me.[38]

She concludes, "I've always been grateful for that musical legacy, and it
was often in my mind when I wrote *Mix Tape*, and trawled through playlists
and memories, my own and those of my friends, searching for the songs that
would draw Ali Connor and Dan Lawrence back together."[39] Sanderson's
personal nostalgic reminiscence fashioned a world in which mixtapes define
the bond between people across a lifetime. This romance novel contributes to
the collective memory of the 1980s personally crafted cassette mixtapes and
the renewed appeal of this retro technology to tell a story.

Memoir

As with fictional work, nonfiction authors have engaged with the technostalgia of the mixtape as a point of confluence. Jim Walsh's memoir *Bar Yarns
and Manic Depressive Mixtapes: On Music from Minneapolis to the Outer
Limits* presents his experience as a music writer working in the Minneapolis
music industry. Organized loosely around song titles, he moves from childhood to parenting, with listening to, loving, and interviewing Prince scat-
tered throughout. By the mid-2010s the mixtape had become an identifier
interlaced with vinyl culture. Music writers often identify their level of
insiderness by their mention of these two tangible artifacts. Walsh writes,
"For anyone who was raised on vinyl [. . .] the ritual of older sisters or
brothers handing down records to their younger siblings is as time-honored
a custom in rock fandom as first beers, first concerts, first crushes."[40] This
description ties together Walsh's age, his affinity for the tangible artifact,
the association music creates among people, and the role of music in making memories.

Five of Walsh's twelve chapters are mixes he creates to facilitate his
story. He includes an array of artists like Roseanne Cash, Son Volt, U2, and
Nick Lowe, showing his props as a writer immersed in music. As with other

mixtape memoirs, Walsh glorifies the cassette tape. In a long description of the tapes he has made and received he defines the best in his collection:

> All have one thing in common: they are fiercely antiformat, very DIY, and decidedly free-form. Cabaret Voltaire segues naturally into Leonard Cohen into Nick Lowe and Tupac Shakur into the Undertones into Rose Royce into Boss Hog into a klezmer band into a Hawaiian slack-key guitar master into "'Til There Was You" (from *The Music Man*) into Mark Eitzel into Black Flag into "Somewhere over the Rainbow" into Chet Baker into the Hudson Brothers into GG Allin into live bootlegs into cruddily recorded songs or spoken words from the tape-makers themselves.
>
> On paper, it looks scattershot. But the beauty of the mixtape is that no matter how eclectic the mix, in the end it all makes perfect sense—to the listener, perhaps, but mostly to the maker.[41]

Walsh highlights, the tangible purposefulness in a creator's unique and specific mixtape. There are no layers of analysis to assess whether it is good or artistic or appealing. The mixtape represents the reflective nostalgia of personal appeal over artistic perfection.[42] His memoir combines concrete mixtape memories with the metaphorically designed mixtape playlist to construct a twenty-first-century story. Analog technology, love of music, and personal stories establish a collective memory of the Minneapolis music scene as told by one man.

Another author who describes the power of music to define a life is one of the few mixtape memoirs written by a female. Cristela Alonzo published *Music to my Years: A Mixtape Memoir of Growing Up and Standing Up* in 2019. Alonzo, a comedian, actor, and writer briefly appeared on *The View* as a guest host. Her memoir charts her life as a first-generation Mexican-American born and raised in Texas. She describes her memoir writing, "Each significant moment of the book relates to a song, and the resulting playlist is deeply moving, resonant, and unforgettable. *Music to My Years* will make you laugh, cry, and even inspire you to make a playlist of your own."[43] Alonzo graces the book's cover, casually dressed, Vans displayed proudly, a cassette tape in her left hand. Alonzo's fashion and accessories assert her credibility as a woman grounded in 1990s pop culture. Like other memoirists, she uses music as an organizational idea, but the actual cassette is less important than the concept. In an interview Alonzo stated, "I wanted to come up with a way that could connect everybody. And I started thinking about it and you know, everybody has a song. Songs for some reason are so moving that they can always take you to a place in your life."[44] Alonzo built a track list as the table of contents for her book. Alonzo has mirrored her memoir on Nick Hornby's *Songbook* and Joshua Harmon's *Annotated Mixtape* which both use the same chapter naming structure. She emphasizes specific songs to tell different moments of her life. The artists range from Eminem to Selena to the theme song from *The Golden Girls*. As Alonzo states in her introduction these songs are "the mixtape of [her] life" because,

> My love of music and television became not only my best friend but my teacher as well. It taught me to love art. It taught me to speak English (Spanish was my first language). It taught me how to "be American." [. . .] Music taught me a more abstract lesson: it taught me how to feel. A good song entertains you. A great song takes you on a journey you'll never forget. When I look back and think of some of the purest moments of joy I had with my family, music was usually involved.[45]

Music, then, is the predominant theme for Alonzo. But the tangible cassette tape is not part of the story. This is the mixtape as an organizing principle and not an object. She talks about vinyl, cassettes, and CDs. She describes the book as "a mixtape or playlist" she has curated, suggesting the tangibility is irrelevant.[46] Her use of mixtape highlights its shifting definition in the previous twenty years. As with novels written by Gen Xers, it reflects a way of connecting to her audience. Alonzo frequently explains life pre-internet, as though her audience would have little concept of that world. She uses mixtape as a familiar and understandable concept, but she also defines the term early on. A "mixtape memoir" is not about cassette culture; it is about ideas and organization using music.

One of the more unique additions to the realm of mixtape stories is Questlove's *Mixtape Potluck*. While this is genuinely a cookbook, and not a memoir, it fits into the personal non-fiction storytelling aspect of a memoir. Questlove, extremely well-versed in music history and hip hop culture in particular, has written multiple books about music, food, and creativity.[47] His cookbook combines his various interests into a unique product with music, stories, and recipes. He approached friends, both from the music and the cooking world, selected a song for them and asked them to use the song as inspiration for a recipe. He wanted the songs to function as introductions to the contributors.[48] The overarching mixtape is as much about the people in Questlove's life. Music is always important, but it is secondary to this story. In the margins of each recipe Questlove explains the logic of the song he chose; it varies from lyrics to sounds to titles depending on the person. As is often the case for the musical savant, the choices of artists range from classics like Cab Calloway and Jelly Roll Morton to contemporaries from Daft Punk to Mos Def. The contributors for recipes are equally eclectic. They range from celebrities Martha Stewart, Fred Armisen, and Q-Tip to well-known chefs like Frenchman Éric Ripert and Padma Lakshmi.

Immersed in a world of hip hop, Questlove's book allows for the sampling, freestyle aspect of the hip hop mixtape. But it also functions in the sense of a mixtape as a collective story pulling disparate ideas together to make something new and comprehensive. Each recipe pulls together a song, a chef, and a recipe. The collection of recipes, organized like a party from arrival foods to small plates to soups and stews, tells a story. And Questlove, through his music, his writing, and now his cookbook, thinks of stories like mixtapes: they are compilations of a variety of ideas and sound pulled together to make something new and unique to share.

PERFORMANCE

Combining celebrity and music remains standard in Hollywood. In 2017 director Edgar Wright released the film *Baby Driver* which also interacted with the idea of technology, mixtapes, and nostalgia. The protagonist, Baby, listens to mixtapes throughout the film on a variety of vintage iPods. Like Quill in *Guardians of the Galaxy*, for Baby the music is a poignant tie to the past and the death of his parents. It also allows the character to dull his constant tinnitus. Baby has songs he relates to particular people and times in his life including a version of the Commodores "Easy" sung by his mother.[49] A review suggested iPods were a necessary choice because if the director "had used smart phones instead of iPods the movie would have been outdated before it even hit the editing room. So Edgar Wright chose to use an already vintage but iconic music player."[50] A *New York Times* article claims *Baby Driver* spurred a nostalgic desire for the iPod.[51] While the owners of Sony Walkmans and cassette tapes might not view the iPod as an analog retro throwback, for a younger generation, it may hold the same tangible appeal because of the time and place in which they owned one. The iPod is an example of "archaeology of the present" and the need to collect memorabilia to tie the present to the past.[52] *Baby Driver* exists in a digital world with playlists, but the songs Baby listens to and the need for a specific analog technology on which to hear them connects this film to the larger wealth of mixtape iconography. When putting together the sound for the film, Wright approached DJ Eric San, known as Kid Koala, a performer and visual artist with a background in hip hop, classic rock, blues, and jazz. San felt a kinship with the title character, "[Wright] said 'Imagine if you will . . . an awkward kid who really lives in his headphones, and just likes to stay at home and make weird homemade mixtapes and stuff.' And I said, 'Uh, I think I can imagine that. You're pretty much describing my entire life in high school.'"[53] San created convincing, but not professional-sounding remixes for Baby based on his own love of the mixtape.

Described in the *Los Angeles Times* as a "vehicular-action-thriller-jukebox-musical-romance" the music defines the action in the film.[54] The soundtrack includes three original songs and twenty-seven re-releases spanning three decades. In *Consequence of Sound*, Michael Roffman described the film as, "the closest approximation to an action movie musical the silver screen has ever seen, and part of its genuine appeal is the unpredictable soundtrack."[55] A review heralding *Baby Driver* as "the best mixtape on screen this year," states, "[Director Edgar] Wright is back to redefine the '"soundtrack as mixtape"' trope."[56] In the first twenty minutes of the film there is almost no dialogue, but the music is not merely a cover for a montage. Instead, it establishes the film, the character, and the narrative arc. The beat, sound, and pacing of the music seamlessly mesh with the images on the screen. The action in the film is choreographed to the beat of the music, much as dancers' movements in a musical. As the story develops, this alignment shifts to a more traditional pairing of music functioning as a score in a film. San's musical craft has taken the concept of a hip hop mixtape to the next level by using sampling and remixing as choreography for a car chase. For the more traditional moviegoer and music fan, they can experience the film's music as Baby's link to his past and his continued existence. Baby's iPod, like Quill's Walkman, ties the young men to their past. Combining music from various generations, these mixtapes, which become film soundtracks, are both nostalgic entities in the film and marketing products for the film.

MIXING ANALOG AND DIGITAL TECHNOLOGY

Focusing on the cassette itself, rather than on the visual imagery of a mixtape, a handful of products have attempted to recreate cassette culture, allowing individuals a way to listen to cassette tapes using updated technology. These digital products replicate analog technology, finding the appeal in the old merged with the new. They epitomize technostalgia. Among the products marketed in the past few years are Sharetapes, marketing cards shaped like a cassette, Wavesfactory's "Cassette" audio plug-in; Elbow, an updated medium to play cassette tapes; and Mixxtape, an mp3 player built to look like a cassette tape.

Perfecting playlists has remained the goal of multiple entrepreneurs. Sharetapes, created in 2013 by Tactify, are cards designed to look like cassette tapes with a link to a digital playlist. The cofounders, who described themselves as "big mixtape guys growing up," launched their product based on their shared interests.[57] In Sharetape's first iteration, a company could purchase packs of "retro-styled cards" designed to look like cassette tapes, on which users could upload a playlist: a modern, physical, digital mixtape.[58]

Sharetapes have become a marketing tool for companies. Examples on the Tactify website include large group events, like a Bud Light Promo for a 2017 SXSW showcase.[59] Despite *Daily Dot's* defense that "Tactify wants to bridge this gap [between a tangible product and the ease of digital] by bringing back the mixtape—but with an added flair of modernity so you won't have to run out to the nearest Goodwill and find a cassette deck," Sharetapes are not personal modern mixtapes.[60] They are a disposable marketing gimmick aimed at the retronostalgic cassette tape. Similarly, the already defunct website, Retrojam, used Spotify data to create playlists of seventeen to twenty-four popular songs based on year. Websites like MTV and *Daily Dot* heralded the nostalgic aspect of Retrojam's curated mixtape of the past.[61] But users do not need an independent website to create those playlists and there is no sense music lovers' memories reflect Billboard-charting songs.

Wavesfactory, a company which creates audio tools for musicians and engineers, took the idea of cassette culture in a different direction, thinking about the audio sound of a cassette rather than the physical artifact of the tape. They created "Cassette" an audio-editing plug-in which "emulates the sound of vintage cassette tapes and decks."[62] This plug-in replicates an analog process used by underground tape producers who aspire to a lo-fi analog sound. In this subculture the "cruder" sound suggests an authenticity to "legitimate hip hop artists."[63] Some underground hip hop producers in the early 2000s sent their music through four-track cassette recorders to "dirty them up."[64] With Wavesfactory another analog process has moved digital. The creators have incorporated detailed features which allow for sonics like compression, dynamic noise, and hiss. Intended for professionals, the goal is to take a modern digital recording and imbue it with analog sounds. Described as "A love letter to simple things," the plug-in description states, "Magnetic tape is not a sterile media. [. . .] Cassette imprints instant nostalgia, movement and analog feel all around in its path."[65] While audiophiles in the past have complained about the low-quality sound of cassette tapes, it has become a commodified ideal among certain genres of music.

In 2017 a Lithuanian company called BrainMonk designed a prototype for a product named Elbow. Elbow was a simplified clip-on cassette player with a single wheel pulley attached to one spool of a cassette which used an optical sensor to play tapes. It had a headphone jack, reminiscent of the Walkman, and a micro-USB charging cable. Briefly, fans of cassettes heralded the Elbow as a viable means to bring back cassettes. The Elbow press release stated,

> The rise of cheap and convenient digital formats has made all physical media "outdated," if not altogether extinct. Still, there remains a niche audience willing

to appreciate the tape medium, with all it's [sic] intricacies and flaws. The tactile intimacy of physical formats is dearly missed.[66]

The designers accentuated the desire for analog physicality, hoping to bring it into the modern era. The release continued, "Despite being such an ordinary everyday object, the audio cassette is not just a medium—it's a cultural icon."[67] This sentence stresses the nostalgic appeal of cassettes. Elbow enticed design and technology specialists. One product design website described it as "innovative, geeky, kitschy, revivalist, and incredibly cool . . . all together!" while another declared it logical "in an industry obsessed with nostalgia."[68] An audio blog introduced Elbow with a personal reminiscence, "Somewhere in my basement, I have a box of old cassette tapes. Most of them aren't store-bought ones, but custom-made mixtapes that I created for myself, back in the days long before CD players, MP3s, and streaming media."[69] The author hoped it would reinforce the cassette resurgence. Despite enthusiasm, Elbow admitted defeat on their Facebook page in the spring of 2019.[70] A failed contest submission and a lack of financial backing brought the concept to a close. Cassette afficionados had to continue using traditional tape recorders.

Mixxtape advances the concept of a cassette tape differently. Rather than a product to play old cassettes, it is an mp3 player which resembles a cassette. Begun as a Kickstarter campaign in 2016, Mixxtape had over 1,700 backers and received pledges of more than $100,000.[71] Since 2018 it has successfully transitioned to a finished product available through their website for $100.[72] On the Kickstarter campaign creator Paul Burns, known as "Mixxim," declared, "We didn't want to build a music player that simply looked like a cassette. We wanted a genuine cassette experience complete with reels that spin and analog playback."[73] Connecting the latest technology with the retro technostalgia of the tactile product, Mixxtape plays directly into Bluetooth-connected headphones or speakers. Certain tape players will play Mixxtape as an analog cassette tape as well.[74] Mixxim described his motivation,

As a teenager, my mixtapes were mostly love letters to girls. A streaming playlist could never be quite as romantic—or half as embarrassing.

The mixtape was the purest product of the cassette age, a lovingly prepared journey through someone's musical taste. The maker controlled the rise and fall, the moods and the motion. It was a democratised concept album with a very particular, personal story.[75]

He returns to the appreciation for the tactile, analog experience of the past. Understanding his audience, he does not reject digital streaming but recognizes the limitations of the playlist. More importantly, he argues music fans do not listen to music on a single format. Mixxtape functions as both an analog and a digital musical experience.

Mixxtape, like Elbow, captivated audio and tech blogs. A review of the Kickstarter campaign asserted that high school students have possibly never heard music played on CD, much less cassette. It then declares, "Mixxtape is pretty versatile: Use it as a music player, or upload a playlist of ten grunge songs and go analog, toting a boombox outside your crush's bedroom window."[76] Emphasizing pop culture nostalgia, its reference to the iconic *Say Anything* boombox scene appeals to readers. Another review focused on the updated technology of a digital music player which is also "dripping in retro chic, styled, as it is, like a 1980s cassette."[77] The kitsch appeal is equally as important as the functionality of the product.

Mixxim's successful product launch acknowledged the renewed interest in the personally created analog mixtape. He included a section of his Kickstarter to appeal to the technostalgic consumers:

Originally it was a combination of many little pieces that made cassettes what they were: the sound, the physical object, the customization, the personalization, the accessibility, the secrecy, the community. [Music] was tangible. It was meaningful. It was personal.

Today, cassettes trigger responses in people of all ages. For some it's autobiographical nostalgia and reminds them of the good old days. A world that was simpler and perhaps happier. For others, they may also feel nostalgia for time periods when they weren't alive; perhaps their parents played old cassettes around them when they were young, and now, they associate those sensory details with positive memories.[78]

Mixxim has discovered a successful way to blend the retro analog technology and the modern digital world. The product ships with a USB-C charging cable and a jewel case. A product launch review confirmed, "MIXXTAPE is a magical blend of nostalgia and modern technology."[79] From the name "Mixxtape" to the cassette tape visual, this product successfully combines the nostalgia for the tangible and the continued desire for the new.

The resurgence of cassettes has encouraged designers to create updated portable audio cassette players. Among the options in 2019 and 2020 were The Mystik, the "It's Ok" and the "We Are Rewind."[80] Each of these products launched Kickstarter campaigns. These artistically designed upgrades to the 1980s Sony Walkman technology highlight the continued and renewed interest in cassette players. In 2021 R.E.M. a quintessential Gen X band reissued their debut single "Radio Free Europe" complete with a 45-rpm single, a cassette tape, and a limited-edition portable cassette player.[81] The website describes the cassette player as "a limited, custom-branded cassette player commemorating the first ever reissue of Cassette Set, [. . .] The player features iconography from the Cassette Set artwork." It confirms the machine includes "play, stop, fast fwd, rewind + record push buttons."[82] The clarification plays into the technostalgia appeal of the analog. Multiple generations see the technostalgia of the Walkman and appreciate merging analog and digital technology.

A technology once declared passé has resurfaced as relevant and modern, yet appropriately nostalgic and retro. Not only are there updated digital mixtapes, mirroring earlier mixtape creation, fans of old-school analog cassette culture also remain. YouTube videos on how to make a mixtape exist for the current youth generation. The YouTube page VinylEyezz created a 2017 how-to-make-a-mixtape video. The creator views digital options as "cheating." Instead, they suggest purchasing a cassette player on eBay and explain various methods of both analog and digital recording.[83] Undoubtedly a niche corner of the internet, with 150 thousand views, nearly 700 comments and 171,000 followers, the VinylEyezz channel confirms a continued interest in analog music and a population curious to learn about an old technology.

For those who prefer the step-by-step text format, the onehowto website includes "How to Make a Mixtape for Someone" in their Arts & Crafts section. Mary Smith, the author, seems to have little nostalgic patience for the cassette. For her, the cassette,

> has its limitations, namely the inability to skip tracks. If there is a particular song you want to get to, you have to go to the right part of the tape reel on the right side of the cassette. To do this, you have to hold down fast forward or rewind (some real old school cassette players only have fast forward buttons). It can produce loud squeals and is perhaps frustrating for a generation who are used to having all their content on demand.[84]

Her detailed description of a known reality for cassette users reveals her work as written for the digital generation. However, despite the cassette's limitations, Smith concludes that digital mixtapes on Spotify or YouTube, "often feel disposable and impersonal," which is why a cassette mixtape remains desirable.[85] The debate showcases why the desire for a combination of analog and digital persists: personalized yet convenient.

The appeal for the tangible artifact has remained at the root of the digital/analog combination mixtapes. A *Medium* article entitled, "Quick guide to recording digital music to cassette tapes" declares, "Have been getting back into cassette tapes. I grew up with them, so there's a nostalgia for sure. [. . .] You can listen to them without the internet. They're a physical thing,"[86] as though a "physical thing" is a novelty. For the author, the audio playback on his personal stereo "is pretty weird (e.g., bad), but I've grown to kind of love it, not in spite of, but because of it's [sic] flaws"[87] The charm of technostalgia signals a rejection of current technology. The author rejects the normalness of digital perfection and differentiates himself because he appreciates the flaws. For many of these writers and creators, cassette culture is appealing because it continues to distinguish itself from mainstream culture. Some individuals have managed to weave together the analog and the digital into new products. Other individuals have embraced the analog because of its quirkiness. They all share an appreciation for the mixtape which keeps it in the pop-culture imagination.

ORGANIZATIONAL STRUCTURE

Scholarly

The mixtape has also made forays into academic outlets. Scholars across disciplines invariably encounter JSTOR, an educational database that houses millions of sources across the academic spectrum.[88] The JSTOR homepage incorporates articles from their archives to analyze current events. In 2016 and 2017 the Arts & Culture page created "A Very JSTOR Daily Mixtape."[89] An orange background with a grey cassette tape titled "JSTOR Mixtape" in a hand-written black font dominated the page. A short article connects six musicians who have published work in JSTOR. It includes a Spotify playlist of their songs, a link to the articles they have each written, and a short annotation connecting the artist and the article. The second JSTOR mixtape, now a blue-backgrounded, clear mixtape called "JSTOR Mixtape 2" states, "From the vintage shades of Leonard Cohen (R.I.P.) to the feminist punk of the riot grrrl movement, our latest JSTOR playlist showcases the complex, energetic artistry of several radical scenes. These greats were no slouches when it came to scholarship and poetry, either."[90] The annotations include poetry, interviews, and articles by diverse musicians from Kathleen Hanna of Bikini Kill to Milo Aukerman of the Descendents.

The eye-catching imagery translated well to social media where digital media staff shared them, bringing attention to the articles and the website. Academics retweeted and liked both mixtape offerings. In each instance, the articles reflected a group of musicians and songs the authors wanted to share. The lack of logical link between the different artists or topics they had written about meant the author needed a connecting idea. This disparate, tangentially linked construction has become a way of using mixtape. It allows someone to think about a topic without having to have a coherent through line aside from music or musician. On their own, these two lists have little to connect them.

By starting with the phrase mixtape, they become their own new compilation which makes sense in its diversity.

Taking scholarly ideas to a more mainstream audience, two academics debated the future of higher education in *The Atlantic*. A January 2015 article presents the idea of the mixtape as disparate and unconnected as the foundation for an argument about the current state of higher education. The title "Higher Education Is Not a Mixtape: Economists predict that colleges will soon become 'unbundled' by the Internet. But that won't—and shouldn't happen,"[91] highlights this idea of a mixtape as unrelated and, in this case, lesser for that lack of synthesis. In the article author Derek Newton argues against a 2014 *Atlantic* article titled, "What universities have in common with record labels."[92] The 2014 article by Martin Smith began, "If you spent the 1990s plucking songs from a stack of cassettes to make the perfect mixtape, you probably welcomed innovations of the next decade that served your favorite albums up as individual songs, often for free."[93] He continued to make parallels between the recording industry and higher education suggesting the consumers, that is students, are the winners of unbundling because they have greater choice and lower cost for album, that is tuition, for class. However, the musicians, read professors, lose out because the increasing operating costs will lead to job insecurity and shrinking incomes. For Smith, this unbundling allows for great freedom of choice, much like the 1970s argument about creating a personal mixtape instead of buying the album.[94]

In his refutation Newton argues universities are not record labels because, "Consumers are buying the music and artist, not the companies behind them:" Princeton is not Sony.[95] Newton cites economic and reform factors, arguing against the consumerization of education. Newton does not return to the mixtape concept his title starts with; the attention-grabbing title has made its point. For Newton, this is an argument about the sanctity of higher education. A mixtape is only an idea he crafted to suggest a disparate product created by an individual consumer, pulled together in a nonlinear way. The mixtape is not a nostalgic idea heralded as romantic or emotional. Instead, he uses mixtape as shorthand for a compiled mishmash without necessary coherence. The kitschiness and technostalgia of the mixtape have solidified its familiarity in mainstream media, allowing scholars to reference it knowing readers will understand its meaning.

Podcasts

Podcasting, a mainstream audio format since 2014, has generated a new forum for listeners to engage with thousands of topics. In 2019 *Forbes* confirmed with over 8,000,000 active podcasts over 60 million Americans listened each week.[96] Finding a niche to draw listeners in starts with a name, and seventy-five podcasts chose to incorporate mixtape. While this is a minute percentage of the total number of podcasts, the incorporation of mixtape imagery speaks to the continued appeal of the artifact in contemporary society.

The definition of mixtape varies depending on the podcast. Occasionally podcasts connect their theme to a physical cassette or to music, while some of the programs use "mixtape" to represent a curated list. The number of episodes ranges from a single episode, an unsuccessful idea, to the three 150-plus episode podcasts. A New Zealand–based music label and marketing agency published seventy-eight episodes of *Mixtapes* between 2005 and 2016 to showcase the label's music. Six other pre-2016 podcasts focus on music, whether music to run to, video game music or music mixes. This first generation of podcasts links mixtapes with music listening.

Since 2016 the number of podcasts about mixtapes has expanded; the majority cover music in a broad fashion. They range from a BBC Radio show, *Introducing Mixtape*, in which a DJ handpicks new music for listeners to *The New LoFi Mixtape*, an hour-long mix corresponding to music discussed in the creator's blog. DJs and hip hop artists have podcasts, like *Electro Mixtape* produced by Huge Carter in 2018, to showcase and share their music. *Cross Fire Mixtape*, started in 2017, explores "Faith-based music."[97] *Uncle Eddy's Mixtape*, made by host Ed Purcell, is the partner podcast to the "video mixtape" that appears on *The Farsighted Blog*.[98] Some of the episodes are digital compilations of physical mixtapes; others are based on memories of childhood in the 1980s.[99] Compiling music into new playlists and sharing those songs grounds the idea of the mixtape in these podcasts. The aptly named *Nostalgia Mixtape* merges music sharing and nostalgia. Described as "A story-telling series rooted in the music that soundtracks our memories," this show incorporates storytelling and music. The host Sama'an Ashrawi is interested in how a particular song manifests a specific memory. The song is the premise, but it is not the focus of the episode. In this podcast, music is the foundation, but it is not the feature.[100] These podcasts reinforce that "mixtape" has expanded beyond its meaning as a physical artifact or even as a visual image of a cassette tape.

Music playlists only describe a handful of the seventy-five podcasts. Many others use mixtape even more broadly. In each episode of *Mixtapes and Mixology* an artist names a song for a bartender to make a drink based on how the song made them feel. *Motivation Mixtape* interviewed British athletes about which songs inspired them for the Rio Olympic Games. These podcasts incorporated music to expand their theme and engage their hosts. *Movie Mixtape*, *Comedian's Mixtape*, and *Indie Mixtape* analyze films, comedians, and independent video games, respectively, in short episodic doses. The creators curate a list of "best ofs" in the same way a traditional mixtaper would craft a tape of the best songs.

There are mixtape podcasts which signal longing for the 1980s and 1990s but do not focus on music, underlining the perception of the mixtape as a site of nostalgia. The *Midlife Mixtape* began as a blog in 2011 and became a podcast in 2017. Author Nancy Davis Kho states, "the Midlife Mixtape blog has been where I share my writing about the track list of life as a Gen Xer here at the midpoint: a blending of the demands of parenting, marriage, work, nostalgia, and the things for which we're still passionate, [. . .] hearing live music and reading books."[101] The podcast extension "interviews Gen Xers and icons of Generation X about how they're thriving in the years between being hip and breaking one."[102] With a lighthearted attitude, Kho combines her love of music and her age with a nostalgic focus. Music is not the foundation of the podcast and the blog, but it remains an underlying theme, dovetailing with her age and her interests. Music may attract an audience, but it is not the focus of her work. Slightly younger, but still nostalgic, the tagline for 2019's *Mixtapes and Rollerblades* states, "Zach and Erica can't get enough of the 1990's. Join them [. . .] as they discuss all of their favorite things about the best decade ever!"[103] Topics include The Spice Girls, Happy Meals, and a single episode on mixtapes. For this podcast, the preeminent theme is nostalgia. Another series, *The Nostalgia Mixtape*, hosted by Tai and Christina, states it, "is an eclectic compilation of pop culture memories from the 1980s through the early 2000s that gives us all the feels."[104] Some episodes cover music, such as their favorite R&B artists and music videos of the 1990s. Other episodes discuss TV shows and cereal.[105] *The BS Mixtapes* tagline describes the show as "Two nerds navigating politics, pop culture and getting through this thing called life."[106] Music appears in nearly all the shows, yet nostalgia is the more predominant theme.

By the late 2010s mixtape no longer only signified technostalgia and the cassette tape. For some it is interchangeable with playlist. For many it communicates nostalgia and personal ties to the past. Yet it has also become a marketing tool which divorces its original meaning from its current usage. *Marketing Mixtape* "interviews successful marketers to help you start a business, lead a team, understand consumer behavior, deliver and communicate benefits to your customers, and market new products."[107] Among the more unique mixtape-themed podcasts is 2018's *Cemetery Mixtape*: "Like unboxing videos, but for graves! Author Adam Selzer digs into the stories behind interesting graves around the country, with musical guests adding original songs."[108] Selzer incorporated music into his stories about cemeteries possibly to justify the show's name. In the 2018 *Minimalist Mixtape* "Joy and Michael discuss their adventures in minimalism."[109] *The Village Mixtape* is "a community podcast about the implementation of regenerative culture, holistic sustainability, and community living."[110] Laura Pasquini, originator of the 2019 *Learn/Perform Mixtape* describes her show as "a podcast of my student notes as I prepare for the Certified Professional in Learning and Performance (CPLP)."[111] *The Mixtape Marriage* podcast "covers all the topics we talk about around our big table: marriage, family, parenting, hospitality, ministry, adoption, adventure, and life. [. . .] we dive into conversations, share laughs, and invite you to think about what God is doing in your daily experiences."[112] These podcasts confirm how far from music and cassette tapes the word mixtape has strayed.

Thumbnail images are equally important marketing tools for podcasters to engage listeners. Of the seventy-five mixtape podcasts, thirty-three of them include a cassette tape in their cover art. One includes a Walkman with headphones, one includes a boombox, and one includes a reel-to-reel tape machine: technostalgic musical iconography of the 1970s and 1980s. Whether a show incorporates a cassette tape is unconnected to the role of music. *The Comedian's Mixtape* and the *Learn/Perform Mixtape*, neither of which are about music, both have a black cassette tape as the predominant image. The two marketing podcasts for *The Side Hustle Show* both include a small cassette tape image in the top right corner as does *the Marketing Mixtape* with its large yellow mixtape. The Tai and Christina *Nostalgia Mixtape* integrates a white cassette tape with Day-Glo lightning bolts and squiggles to signal the 1990s theme of their show. The simple, line-drawn, monochromatic cassette tape images are attention grabbing. The fonts, the styling of the cassette tape, and the colors personalize the podcasts. In the twenty-first century few people own tape players. Very few people make tangible mixtapes. Podcasts, by their nature, are a streaming experience. Yet, the term "mixtape" and the visual of a cassette tape remain cogent to listeners. Whether the shows cover music or have nothing to do with nostalgia and cassette tapes, the word mixtape and the image of a cassette tape with handwritten words across the front speak to this audience. As the era of the mixtape recedes further into the past, the need to tie the mixtape to tangible items on which someone built a compilation playlist becomes unnecessary. The idea of mixtape as a list has superseded the original meaning of the word.[113]

In the world of visual culture, the mixtape has become a codified image of a cassette tape with some type of hand-written tag distinguishing it from a commercially released cassette album. This post-2010 visual culture expanded the idea of mixtape as a trendy two-dimensional representation of a physical artifact. There is a campiness tied to the imagery of an analog representation of the past. This fetishization of the physical representation of a mixtape cassette has created a newly engaged consumer audience who can now purchase products emblazoned with the representation of a mixtape as a self-referential awareness of the kitsch and nostalgia of a simpler, slower bygone era. Music is no longer foregrounded in the current generation of mixtape memorabilia. The collective understanding of the mixtape as a site of memory and a way to think about organization has allowed it to become a ubiquitous ideology. The visual of a cassette with a handwritten label has shifted into a representative idea rather than a tangible musical artifact.

NOTES

1. Ties van de Werff, "Technostalgia," Next Nature, https://nextnature.net/2010 /07/technostalgia (Accessed July 26, 2020).
2. Trevor Pinch and Frank Trocco, *Analog Days: The Invention and Impact of the Moog Synthesizer* (Cambridge: Harvard University Press, 2002), 318.
3. Andreas Huyssen, *Present Pasts: Urban Palimpsests and the Politics of Memory*, Cultural Memory in the Present (California: Stanford University press, 2003), 22.
4. Karin Bijsterveld and José van Dijck, eds., *Sound Souvenirs: Audio Technologies, Memory and Cultural Practices* (Amsterdam: Amsterdam University Press, 2009), 20.
5. Craig Eley, "Technostalgia and the Resurgence of Cassette Culture," in *The Politics of Post-9/11 Music: Sound, Trauma, and the Music Industry in the Time of Terror*, ed. Joseph P. Fisher and Brian Flota, Ashgate Popular and Folk Music (New York: Routledge, 2011), 45.
6. Ibid., 47–48.
7. David Sax, *The Revenge of Analog: Real Things and Why They Matter* (New York: Public Affairs, 2016), xii.
8. Discogs, "The Cassette Comeback, by the Numbers," Discogs, https://blog.di scogs.com/en/the-cassette-comeback-by-the-numbers/.
9. Peter Hartlaub, "The Case for Cassettes: Still Bumping in 2017," *San Francisco Chronicle*, July 28, 2017.
10. Aubrey Norwood, "Why 2019 Will Be the Year of the Cassette (Again)," *Medium* (Decembe 30, 2018), https://medium.com/@aubreynorwood/why-2019-will-be-the-year-of-the-cassette-7f9fb91859a3 (Accessed July 9, 2020).
11. Hartlaub.
12. Timothy D. Taylor, *Strange Sounds: Music, Technology & Culture* (New York: Routledge Press, 2001), 110–11.
13. Eley, 52. and Taylor, 99.
14. Taylor, 100.
15. Eve Epstein and Lenora Epstein, *X vs. Y: A Culture War, a Love Story* (New York: Abrams Books, 2014), 146–47.
16. Ibid.
17. Simon Reynolds, *Retromania: Pop Culture's Addiction to Its Own Past* (New York: Faber and Faber, Inc, 2011), 250–51.
18. Rob Drew, "Mixed Blessings: The Commercial Mix and the Future of Music Aggregation," *Popular Music & Society* 28, no. 4 (2005): 539.
19. Ibid., 545.

20. Libby Cudmore. "Debut Mystery from the 'Queen of the Mix CD.'" Interview by Cat Acree. *Book Page* (February 2, 2016).

21. Libby Cudmore. *The Big Rewind* (New York: William Morrow Paperbacks, 2016).

22. Ibid., 1.

23. Ibid., 65.

24. Ibid., 235.

25. "Debut Mystery from the 'Queen of the Mix CD.'"

26. Celia C. Pérez, *The First Rule of Punk* (New York: Viking, 2017), 21.

27. Ibid., 71–72.

28. Celia Pérez. "Celia Perez's New Novel 'the First Rule of Punk' Comes with Advice for Adolescents." Interview by Kelly McEvers. *All Things Considered* (September 1, 2017).

29. Chelsey Johnson, *Stray City* (New York: Custom House, 2018), 362.

30. "Chelsey Johnson," http://www.chelseyjohnson.com/stray-city. and Celia Pérez, "Celia C. Pérez Playlist," http://celiacperez.com/playlist (Accessed May 28, 2020).

31. Jane Sanderson, "Mix Tape: Introduction," Square Space, https://janesanderson.com/books/mix-tape/ (Accessed May 28, 2020).

32. Jane Sanderson *Mix Tape* (London: Transworld Publishers, 2020), Back Cover.

33. The Book Trail, "Travel across the World with a Mix Tape and Jane Sanderson," https://www.thebooktrail.com/authorsonlocation/travel-with-a-mix-tape-and-jane-sanderson/ (Accessed May 28, 2020).

34. Sanderson, *Mix Tape*, 49.

35. Ibid., 94.

36. Ibid., 95.

37. Ibid., 157.

38. The Book Trail.

39. Ibid.

40. Jim Walsh, *Bar Yarns and Manic-Depressive Mixtapes: Jim Walsh on Music from Minneapolis to the Outer Limits* (Minneapolis: University of Minnesota Press, 2016), 2.

41. Ibid., 61–62.

42. Svetlana Boym, *The Future of Nostalgia* (New York: Basic Books, 2008), eBook, Chapter 5.

43. Cristela Alonzo, "Cristela Alonzo," http://cristelaalonzo.com/ (Accessed July 10, 2020).

44. Cristela Alonzo. "A Mixtape Memoir: Cristela Alonzo and the Songs That Shaped Her Life." Interview by Kristen Carbrera. *KUT: Austin's NPR Station* (October 9, 2019).

45. *Music to My Years: A Mixtape Memoir of Growing up and Standing Up* (New York: Atria Books, 2019), 3–4, 7.

46. Ibid., 6.

47. He published this work with his familiar co-author Ben Greenman and Lauren Schaefer in 2019. Greenman also co-wrote *Mo-Meta Blues: The World According to*

Questlove and *Something to Food About: Exploring Creativity with Innovative Chefs with Questlove.*

48. Ahmir "Questlove" Thompson, Ben Greenman, and Lauren Schaefer, *Mixtape Potluck: A Cookbook: A Dinner Party for Friends, Their Recipes, and the Songs They Inspire* (New York: Harry N. Abrams Book, 2019), 16.

49. Actress and singer Sky Ferreira. Olivia Truffaut-Wong, "Sky Ferreira Switches It up in 'Baby Driver,'" *Bustle* (July 11, 2017), https://www.bustle.com/p/who-plays-babys-mom-in-baby-driver-the-singer-took-off-her-pop-persona-for-the-r ole-69511 (Accessed July 10, 2020).

50. Skip Owens, "The iPods of 'Baby Driver,'" *Geek Dad* (February 12, 2018), https://geekdad.com/2018/02/ipods-baby-driver/ (Accessed July 10, 2020).

51. Sridhar Pappu, "'Baby Driver' Stirs Nostalgia for iPods," *The New York Times*, July 13, 2017.

52. Boym, Chapter 2.

53. Scott Meslow, "The Real DJ Behind the *Baby Driver* Jam You'll Be Humming All Summer," *GQ* (June 30, 2017), https://www.gq.com/story/kid-koala-baby-driver. (Accessed June 14, 2020).

54. Justin Chang, "Review: Edgar Wright's Exuberant 'Baby Driver' Is an Automotive Musical Like No Other," *Los Angeles Times*, June 27, 2017.

55. Michael Roffman, "Soundtrack to Baby Drivers Spans 30 Tracks and Multiple Decades," *Consequence of Sound* (June 2, 2017), https://www.latimes.com/entertainment/movies/la-et-mn-baby-driver-review-20170627-story.html?_ga=2.2 41958082.1551556259.1591026382-1270204586.1590782768 (July 10, 2020).

56. David Molloy, "Baby Driver Is the Best Mixtape on Screen This Year," *The Brag* (July 10, 2017), https://thebrag.com/baby-driver-best-mixtape-screen-year/ (Accessed July 10, 2020).

57. A. J. Dellinger, "The Art of the Mixtape Gets a Digital Makeover," *Daily Dot* (March 1, 2020), https://www.dailydot.com/debug/sharetapes-mixtapes/ (Accessed July 14, 2020).

58. The product uses a unique code on the card. "Sharetape Puts a Modern Twist on the Physical Mixtape," *New Atlas* (February 12, 2013), https://newatlas.com/shar etapes-nfc-qr-mixtape/26202/ (Accessed July 14, 2020).

59. Tactify, https://www.tactify.com/ (Accessed July 14, 2020).

60. Dellinger.

61. Deepa Lakshmin, "Retrojam's Playlists Will Make You Nostalgic for Your Play-Doh Eating Days," *MTV* (February 2, 2015), http://www.mtv.com/news/2 066209/retrojams-playlists/ (Accessed July 14, 2020). Selena Larson, "Retrojam Makes a Mixtape of All the Songs You Listened to as a Kid," *Daily Dot* (March 1, 2020), https://www.dailydot.com/upstream/retrojam-song-flashback/ (Accessed July 14, 2020).

62. Wavesfactory, "Cassette," https://www.wavesfactory.com/cassette (Accessed September 1, 2020).

63. Anthony Kwame Harrison, "'Cheaper Than a CD, Plus We Really Mean It': Bay Area Underground Hip Hop Tapes as Subcultural Artefacts," *Popular Music* 25, no. 2 (2006), https://www.jstor.org/stable/3877563.

64. Ibid., 294.

65. Wavesfactory.

66. Brainmonk, "Elbow Cassette Player," news release, 2017, http:/elbow.co.nf/ img/ELBOW_PRESS.pdf (Accessed August 15, 2020).

67. Ibid.

68. Beatrice Murray-Nag, "The Elbow Clip-on Cassette Player Is a Turntable Tonearm for Tapes," https://www.designboom.com/technology/elbow-casette-pla yer-brain-monk-05-03-2017/ (Accessed July 14, 2020). and Sarang Sheth, "Hello Cassette My Old Friend," *Yanko Design* (May 4, 2017), https://www.yankodesign.c om/2017/05/04/hello-cassette-my-old-friend/ (Accessed July 14, 2020).

69. Paul Strauss, "The Elbow Reinvents the Portable Cassette Player," *Technabob* (August 9, 2017), https://technabob.com/blog/2017/08/09/elbow-minimal-cassette -player/#ixzz6OWA8u9kf (Accessed July 14, 2020).

70. Elbow Cassette Player. "Hello everyone. The dust has settled." May 8, 2019. https://www.facebook.com/ElbowCP (Accessed July 14, 2020).

71. Mixxim, "Mixxtape," Kickstarter, https://www.kickstarter.com/projects/mix xtape/mixxtape-the-cassette-reinvented (Accessed July 14, 2020).

72. "Mixxtape," https://mixtapeboss.com/products/mixxtape-1 (Accessed July 14, 2020).

73. Ibid.

74. The small print clarifies that a tape deck must have has "tape movement sen- sors" for Mixxtape to work. Ibid.

75. "Mixxtape."

76. Nick Hastings, "Get Your '80s on with Mixxtape, the Portable Music Player That Works Like a Cassette," *Digital Trends* (June 15, 2017), https://www.digitalt rends.com/home-theater/mixxtape-music-player-bluetooth-cassette-tape/ (Accessed July 14, 2020).

77. Joe Svetlik, "Dust Off Your Boombox, Mixxtape Is a Digital Music Player That Doubles as an Old School Cassette," *Trusted Reviews* (June 8, 2017), https:/ /www.trustedreviews.com/news/mixxtape-is-a-cassette-shaped-music-player-that-p lays-in-a-tape-deck-2950650 (Accessed July 14, 2020).

78. Mixxim, "Mixxtape."

79. PR Newswire, "Mixxtape Reinvents the Cassette," PR Newswire, https://ww w.prnewswire.com/news-releases/mixxtape-reinvents-the-cassette-300053848.html (Accessed July 14, 2020).

80. The "It's OK" and "We are Rewind" were successfully backed. Boudruche, Romain "We Are Rewind," Kickstarter https://www.kickstarter.com/projects/wea rerewind/we-are-rewind/description; NINM Lab, "IT's OK – Bluetooth 5.0 Cassette Player," Kickstarter, https://www.kickstarter.com/projects/ninmlab/its-ok-the-worl ds-first-bluetooth-50-cassette-player Recording the Masters, "Mystik: A next-gen- eration portable cassette player," Kickstarter, https://www.kickstarter.com/project s/rtm2020/mystik-a-next-generation-portable-cassette-player (Accessed July 14, 2020).

81. Nick Reilly, "R.E.M. Announce 40th Anniversary Reissue of Debut Single 'Radio Free Europe,'" *NME* (May 18, 2021), https://www.nme.com/news/music/r

-e-m-announce-40th-anniversary-reissue-of-debut-single-radio-free-europe-2943191 (Accessed May 19, 2021).

82. R.E.M. Headquarters UK Store https://ukstore.remhq.com/collections/radio-f ree-europe/products/ultimate-radio-free-europe-bundle?fbclid=IwAR2NHW18knEQ UWligbX5YEVgM9hGGJOeCXGCsxmM6em8LRrnZ4lNEIz7HT0 (Accessed May 19, 2021).

83. "Make a Mixtape!" YouTube video, 5:38, posted by "Vinyl Eyezz" May 22, 2017, https://www.youtube.com/watch?v=POzBPM5YRJc&ab_channel=VinylEyezz

84. Mary Smith, "How to Make a Mixtape for Someone," (June 3, 2018), https://arts.onehowto.com/article/how-to-make-a-mixtape-for-someone-12635.html (Accessed July 14, 2020).

85. Ibid.

86. Timothy S. Boucher, "Make Spotify Mix Tapes," *Medium* (September 2, 2017), https://medium.com/@timboucher/make-spotify-mix-tapes-15f473ef584b (Accessed July 14, 2020).

87. Ibid.

88. The database is described on the JSTOR Daily website as "a digital library of academic journals, books, and other material. We publish articles grounded in peer-reviewed research and provide free access to that research for all of our readers." JSTOR Daily, "JSTOR: Where New Meets Its Scholarly Match," Ithaka, https://daily .jstor.org/ (Accessed July 1, 2021).

89. L. Herfenberger, "A Very JSTOR Daily Mixtape," https://daily.jstor.org/a -very-jstor-daily-mixtape/ (Accessed December 10, 2020).

90. Elliott Vanskike, "A Very JSTOR Daily Mixtape: Volume 2," JSTOR, https ://daily.jstor.org/jstor-playlist-mixtape-2/ (Accessed December 10, 2020).

91. Derek Newton, "Higher Education Is Not a Mixtape," *The Atlantic* (January 27, 2015), https://www.theatlantic.com/education/archive/2015/01/higher-education -is-not-a-mixtape/384845/ (Accessed July 9, 2020).

92. Martin Smith, "Are Universitisities Going the Way of Record Labels?," (July 7, 2014), https://www.theatlantic.com/education/archive/2014/07/how-universities -are-like-record-labels/374012/ (Accessed July 9, 2020).

93. Ibid.

94. Ibid.

95. Newton.

96. Brad Adgate, "Podcasting Is Going Mainstream," *Forbes* (November 18, 2019), https://www.forbes.com/sites/bradadgate/2019/11/18/podcasting-is-going -mainstream/#bbf1a9a1699d (Accessed July 14, 2020).

97. Cross Fire Mixtape presents *Cross Fire Mixtape* (podcast), 2017, https://play .google.com/music/listen#/ps/Idehytggtadugam6q5brg75mmxy (Accessed July 2020).

98. The Farsighted Blog to Uncle Eddy's Mixtapes, July 15, 2020, https://farsigh tedblog.com/series/uncle-eddys-mixtapes/ (Accessed July 2020).

99. "Debut Mixtape: Reliving Classic Christmas . . . 80s Style" on ibid.

100. Sama'an Ashrawi presents *Nostalgia Mixtape* (podcast), 2018, http://thenos-talgiamixtape.com/ (Accessed June 2020).

101. Nancy Davis Kho presents *Midlife Mixtape* (podcast), 2017, https://midlife-mixtape.com/about (Accessed June 2020).

102. Nancy Davis Kho, "Midlife Mixtape," https://midlifemixtape.com/ (Accessed June 2020).

103. Erica Tourville presents *Mixtapes and Rollerblades* (podcast), 2019, https://www.stitcher.com/podcast/anchor-podcasts/mixtapes-rollerblades (Accessed June 2020).

104. Tai and Christina present *The Nostalgia Mixtape* (podcast), 2017, https://play.google.com/music/listen#/ps/Imlonolpftp4kuha46s2uyez3cm (Accessed June 2020).

105. Ibid.

106. Jasmine & Ceej present *The BS Mixtapes* (podcast), 2016, https://play.google.com/music/listen#/ps/I3rpxdbudfnzj3npzrq3hqc5apa (Accessed June 2020).

107. Scott Davis presents *Marketing Mixtape* (podcast), 2017, https://play.google.com/music/listen#/ps/Inoks5utgfgby47rt6fved3ms3u (Accessed June 2020).

108. Cemetery Mixtape presents *Cemetery Mixtape* (podcast), 2018, https://play.google.com/music/listen#/ps/Ivrvnqnmgegh2ty3pkjcx6zneyi (Accessed June 2020).

109. Joy springer and Michael Springer present *Minimalist Mixtape* (podcast), 2018, https://play.google.com/music/listen#/ps/Ile2z5k2srhm4aciir5xa23zqma (Accessed June 2020).

110. Well 'n Green presents *The Village Mixtape* (podcast), 2018, https://play.google.com/music/listen#/ps/Ihyytbwdoelwvldacoiekv53fzm (Accessed June 2020).

111. Pasquini, Laura presents *Learn/Perform Mixtape* (podcast), 2019, https://play.google.com/music/listen#/ps/Ikbdpwm6tsfcfza5ona5pc6fc2y (Accessed June 2020).

112. Lancaster, Camille presents *The Mixtape Marriage* (podcast), 2019, https://play.google.com/music/listen#/ps/Ic6hhhsa2ktw4weo63hb3cfbcli (Accessed June 2020).

113. For a complete list of mixtape podcasts, see Appendix C. All podcasts were found on either Google Play, Google LLC, 2020. https://play.google.com or Pocket Casts V.7.11.0 John W. Gibbons CEO, 2020. pocketcasts.com.

Chapter 8

Metaphor and Merchandising

Sometime between 2000, with the Hollywood release of *High Fidelity*, and the 2014 release of *Guardian of the Galaxy*, the perception of a mixtape shifted. Where it once spoke directly to an audio creation attached to specific songs, it has become kitsch: a reflection of an analog technology and emotional attachment. It has moved from a concrete tangible artifact to a conceptual idea centered around both organizational structure and expressive connection. Since 2010 the imagery of a cassette tape has expanded onto merchandise as diverse as yoga leggings, high ball glasses, and vinyl stickers of all shapes and sizes. The items range from the inexpensive mass-produced sticker to one-of-a-kind, hand-crafted products. Artists have fashioned merchandise around mixtapes which signal their feelings about music through visual artistic pieces. Some consumers appreciate the colorful, personalized, mixtape imagery as a nostalgic reminder of their youth. Others because they enjoy the kitsch of an analog retro idea. Mixtape representations have removed the auditory musical quality, except as marketing tools. The emotive tie to the mixtape image has become imbued with a visual kitsch nostalgia reflective of a simpler time.

AS A TEACHING TOOL

For an academic, creating a framework to understand a concept helps readers relate to the material. A handful of scholars, who have their own history grounded in the world of analog technology and who recognize the power of music for youth cultures, have used the mixtape as the foundation for their theoretical work. These scholars have taken "mixtape" as an assumed familiar concept and woven it into their writing. Academics have written sociology textbooks framing the Walkman as a founding idea, chapters in composition textbooks employing the mixtape to think about writing and rhetoric, and cultural studies textbooks applying the mixtape to think about organizing secondary source material. In these new conceptual ideas, music may lay at the foundation of the discussion, but it is not the sole purpose for the author or the reader. Instead "mixtape" becomes a catchphrase to pull in a reader's attention and a way to think about organization.

Professors endeavor to engage students by employing themes students find intriguing, unintimidating, and comfortable. Music can allow teachers to use a medium familiar to students to teach academic, analytical argument writing. Assignments which use music proliferate in contemporary theory and culture studies: hip hop as cultural identity, songs as current events, or critical analysis through music reviews.[1] A handful of academics have integrated pedagogy using music with mixtapes because it allows for a discussion of music, but also incorporates larger processes like rhetorical awareness, transitions, and critical analysis.

Composition Professor Geoffrey Sirc wrote a chapter in the 2010 textbook *Rhetorics and Technologies: New Directions in Writing and Communication* called "Serial Composition" asserting new models to rehabilitate college writing in contemporary practices. Among his ideas is to use the mixtape as a foundational element around which to organize writing. Like musicians who have discussed learning the art of albums or scores, Sirc believes the theme and linear logic of a mixtape is a useful model for students. He quotes *High Fidelity* as a way to consider transitions. He thinks about the length of a cassette as a useful limiting factor in organizing writing. He quotes bloggers' and journalists' discussions of mixtapes to help ground the argument he makes. While music is at the root of his discussion, the art of the mixtape—the organizing, the choice of style and theme, the artistry of transitioning—is the real appeal. The analog mixtape has a greater appeal in this discussion than the electronic version because the ease of drag and drop, like the appeal to cut and paste for a student, undermines the art of the creation.[2] Sirc's concept of introducing college writing using familiar tropes like a mixtape offers a novel way for teachers to engage with students that appeals to their sensibilities but remains academically grounded.

On their website, W. F. Hsu, a scholar of Critical and Comparative Studies in Music, outlines a Mixtape Project assignment they have used in Cultural Studies courses at various institutions.[3] Hsu starts, "With analog nostalgia hip in our digitally enabled environment, the mixtape as an object and a metaphor now carries some fun resonance."[4] In the assignment, Hsu never defines a mixtape nor asserts a connection to cassettes; the term "mixtape" stands on its own without the need for a definition of explanation. Hsu outlines the assignment prompt which includes building a compilation of songs, writing a "liner notes" essay, and presenting the project orally. The detail of Hsu's assignment encouraged students to think broadly, creating thematic playlists from K-pop to Arabic Hip Hop. Students built YouTube playlists, PowerPoint presentations, and blogs to showcase their final products. While Hsu begins the description mentioning analog nostalgia, the students' projects existed in a purely digital world. The assignment reflects critical analysis, not technostalgic physical recreation.

Professor Olivia Hernández used the ideas present by Hsu and found in a *New York Times* article from 2018 called "Nine Teaching Ideas for Using Music to Inspire Student Writing,"[5] to create an English 101 assignment around the mixtape. She presented her teaching pedagogy at the Museum of Pop Culture Virtual Conference in September 2020.[6] As a professor at a community college with a large Hispanic/Latinx and first-generation population, her goal is to create a pedagogy that is culturally responsive to her students' needs, which the mixtape allows. She references Rob Sheffield's memoir *Love is a Mix Tape* to describe how mixtapes tell stories and share feelings: useful tools in a composition course. When defining a mixtape, Hernández confirmed she had never made a mix "tape," but she had burned mix CDs and she viewed any list of songs as a valid mixtape.[7] This introductory assignment in Hernández's class encouraged student participation because music is a medium they felt comfortable discussing and they could make it personal.

Like Sirc and others, Cultural Studies scholars sought a conceptual framework to help students understand their field of study. In 2013 several scholars created a Cultural Studies textbook offering a novel way to think about their interdisciplinary field. Considering various models, they chose the Walkman as the organizing principle in their work because "The Walkman, by contrast, had the advantage of being a very discrete entity, on subject to much popular discussion and debate (and moralizing), but little academic analysis."[8] Students are familiar enough with the artifact to understand what its role was, but old enough it existed outside of their lived experience. While not concretely about the mixtape, like Sirc's article, this book focused on the portability of music and the role of cassette culture to engage students in academic analysis. As they state in the first chapter, personal stereos, "overall effect has been to maximize personal choice in listening. You can not only put together a selection from many musical genres and thus construct a medley of different moods and impressions, emotions and fantasies, a personal ensemble to suit your own tastes."[9] Alluding to the mixtape, this textbook helps students to think through the "Interplay between practices of regulation, consumption, production, identity-work and representation in the assembling or putting together of contemporary material cultural artefacts."[10] In the second edition they admit not anticipating the book becoming a referenced text on the history of music technology. The interest people showed demonstrated a dearth of scholarship on the topic. The idea of using a short-lived technology based on private music listening via cassette highlights again the idea of the mixtape—and in this case the ability to listen to cassettes via Walkman—as an organizational principle to appeal to both the authors and their academic audience. Music started the discussion, but it became an argument about the idea of personal music listening, not an argument about musical choice.

In the same way, the co-authored critical analysis, *American Studies: A User's Guide*, published in 2017 took the mixtape as the organizational idea for their work. Two American Studies scholars, Philip J. Deloria and Alexander I. Olson, used the mixtape as a way for graduate students to think about how they could make sense of the broad interdisciplinary subject of American Studies. They wanted to offer students frameworks for creating comprehensive exam lists. Exhaustive lists in an interdisciplinary field are impossible; finding a way to justify and narrow a list to a manageable size is a useful task for a graduate student. The mixtape became an effective metaphor because it forced a limitation to the number of "songs"—or in this context, books—one could include in a single list. Anyone who has made a mixtape knows they have an infinite choice in what to include. As any number of authors have discussed, the editorial choice of what artists, what songs, and what order makes a mixtape special. Deloria and Olson used the narrowing and choice of items to ground their argument about organizing the field of American Studies.

The mixtape allowed the authors to acknowledge they had made editorial choices in these lists, limiting the texts to not become overwhelmed. Deloria and Olson create four American Studies mixtapes, pulling together four sets of ten books each. In explaining their process, they state,

> Curating a mixtape is not just about finding songs that work well together, but also about setting up contrasts and juxtapositions to keep the listener engaged. A mixtape samples freely and fearlessly, since it's not intended to be a commercial release. And not every mixtape has the same structure. Some might have a steady progression of songs based on a single artist, place, or feeling, whereas others are all about tensions and dissonance, with the listener getting exposed to a variety of tempos, keys, and even genres that play off one another. But either way, the mixtape can't go on forever; you need to make choices about what to include and what to cut.[11]

For Olson, the limited length of a mixtape legitimized the choices they had made; each mixtape included ten books that covered a variety of time periods and topics. After discussing the mixtapes they had created, they acknowledged they could remix and reorder each of those tapes. One list is not superior to another; the ability to defend one's choice is the key to a good mixtape.

As with Cultural Studies, the interdisciplinarity played into the use of the mixtape to understand the field. Students can relate to a compilation of songs from various time periods and diverse genres. This text took that concept and applied it to the wealth of scholarship which might feel overwhelming without this framework.

In a conversation about his book, Olson conceded mixtape and playlist are relatively synonymous in his mind, but the analog structure of a mixtape remains cogent because it does have a limitation and cannot go on endlessly.[12] Using the mixtape metaphor from the book offered readers a formula to critically analyze and create their own comprehensive, but limited, exam lists. The power of a mixtape is to create a unique list and defend the choice. Near the end of the book, Deloria and Olson participate in the discussion of analog versus digital music technology as a way of thinking about older, possibly dated, texts in the field. "[They] pulled out old 78s and 45s in order to share with you some classic vinyl from the early years of the field. [They] walked through the historiographical equivalent of eight-tracks and cassettes, compact discs and digital streaming services."[13] For a younger reader, this imagery of outdated technology next to contemporary ideas helps to ground the relevance of seemingly irrelevant texts because of their age and unfamiliarity. Old does not necessarily mean bad. The metaphor of mixtape creation, remixing, and justifying choice became an ideal format to help graduate students in American Studies think about how to understand their field. Olson's "endless tinkering with mixtapes,"[14] took a theoretical approach to the historiography of an interdisciplinary field and made it easier to understand. The mixtape as an idea grounded what could have felt overwhelming and indeterminate.

These metaphorical, academic uses of "mixtape" differ from the wider pop culture uses of the term as a sign of emotional attachment. The scholarly imagery succeeds because of pop culture's continued investment in and continued reintroduction of the mixtape in commercial media. Scholars have chosen the term "mixtape" as a metaphor on which to ground their theories because it has become a recognizable term for readers without being deeply grounded in a concrete, specific format. These studies showcase the continued relevance and popularity of the term.

Today the hip hop mixtape holds a place both as a viable method for artists to break into the industry, continuing the tradition of a promotional track released outside the corporate mainstream. But the hip hop mixtape also functions as a nostalgic artifact tied to the fifty-year history of the genre. Collectors, archivists, historians, and fans collect these mixtapes and share their stories. Scholar Kevin Holt describes the importance of the hip hop mixtape when he says, "Mixtapes are the distribution of the grassroots and they were central to hip-hop's growth. To historicize this is to call attention to the subversive way people have been able to create music and gain a bit of agency that they wouldn't be afforded through the traditional route."[15] For scholars like Holt, memorializing the hip hop mixtape gives greater recognition to the work of artists who did not have major label recognition, but had a significant impact on the music industry. Like Holt, The Mixtape Museum (MXM) is a digital archive project, "established to collect, preserve, and share knowledge related to mixtape history."[16] Through social media, exhibitions, and presentations, Mixtape Museum discusses cassette culture, hip hop culture, and shares stories of mixtape collectors to help measure the influence they have had.[17] On their Soundcloud page, they explain,

> MXM is an archive project dedicated to rescuing, preserving and sharing vintage DJ-mixes, particularly those originally distributed on analog mediums, i.e., compact cassette. These analog recordings, some of which are over two decades old are deteriorating and in danger of being lost forever. Our belief is that these analog recordings are records of time and should be handled as artifacts. We're talking about mixes from DJ icons like, DJ Hollywood, Brucie B, Kid Capri, and more. Many of the mixtapes featured are ripped from compact cassette and will include a Side A and Side B, additionally the sound quality is not digital, and may include that cassette tape hiss similar to that of the vinyl pop and crackle. Embrace the hiss![18]

This description highlights the technostalgia of the current moment: appreciate the analog sound but maintain access through a digital medium. Here the mixtape has become a scholarly artifact, important for preserving a cultural legacy. The increased awareness of the history of hip hop and the role of the hip hop mixtape has allowed for a collective memory of a field that has been ignored in academic scholarship for too long.

VISUAL REPRESENTATION

Merchandise

The 2010s have seen a resurgence in retro illustrations. Along with the rise in vinyl sales, fashion from the 1980s and 1990s has returned, bands from every era have engaged in reunion tours, and TV shows have rebooted classic popular sitcoms for new audiences. Mixtape culture has played into the consumer desire for retro merchandise by labeling, marketing, and crafting new products. Gen X creatives have taken ideas from their past and produced new, unique, marketable items. While sales are paramount for many of these artistic endeavors, these creations are also labors of love, made by individuals who imbue their goods with meaningful imagery. They have used visual representations that encapsulate cassette culture to build marketing campaigns around board games, bars, and commercial goods to appeal to twenty-first-century consumers. From how-to-write-a-memoir books to craft coffee beans, the idea and image of a mixtape has become an engaging, marketable, fun concept. More than merely marketing campaigns, it is a nostalgic tie to an aspect of their lives which continues to speak to them, long after they made and shared mixtapes.

The catalog *Uncommon Goods* often sells reflectively nostalgic designs: an experience and an idea as much as a knickknack. Mixtape merchandise blurs the line between mixtape culture and cassette culture, at times replicating the musical representation of a mix and at others emphasizing the technological details of a dead audio technology. Their 2017 objects included a doormat, a pillow, a cassette "tape" dispenser, a felt cassette pouch, and a set of highball glasses which all incorporated the terms "retro" "kitsch" or "nostalgia" in their product descriptions.[19] Among the more unique wares was the "cassette player future fossil," a matte-grey hand-cast sculpture made to look like fossilized rock or a work sculpted out of stone.[20] The artist, Jeff Klarin, who also crafted a "fossil" ViewMaster, joystick, and Polaroid camera, described his art as a "handmade sculpture of a Walkman in fossil form [which] is a nod to nostalgia and age-related humor."[21] The catalog description begins, "What's A Cassette Player? Actual quote from one of our interns: [. . .]The beloved cassette player is a fossil."[22] The marketing allusion to the nostalgia of listening to a cassette and "remember[ing] the good times" reinforces Klarin's idea. To own a recreation of an outdated pop culture item suggests a sentimentality for the past. The playful nature of a "future fossil" mirrors many kitsch products.

The *Uncommon Goods* doormat, throw pillow, and highball glasses concretely display mixtapes. The marketing text tells stories to engage customers. The doormat copy says, "In its heyday, the mixtape was a musical love letter, specially planned to covertly express hidden crushes, power ballad-worthy connections, and good old-fashioned friendship. Welcome guests to your home using the same nostalgic expression. [. . .] they can't be furtively slipped through the slots in your cute lab partner's locker"[23] While the doormat emphasizes sharing a mixtape, the pillow highlights receiving a mixtape. The marketing description states, "Back in the big-haired heyday of cassettes, there was nothing quite like finding a mixtape in your locker, rushing home to your Walkman, and listening to a musically coded love letter. Curl up with a bit of nostalgia (and maybe dust off your classic road trip mix from your freshman year)."[24] These descriptions incorporate nostalgia, love, and ways to speak to individuals who made and received mixtapes.

The artistry of the baubles tangibly engages with mixtape impressions. Each item has an artistic cassette tape as the central feature; a black accurately detailed cassette tape with a white and red label ornaments the doormat and throw pillow. Personalization, as titles on the tape, use a loopy script, reminiscent of an adolescent, complete with circles to dot the i's. The models include phrases like "Mike's House Mix" and "The Smiths." Clearly a play on words, The Smiths represent either a family surname or a well-loved English band. The marketing image of the doormat includes a pair of black Converse low-top sneakers. On a surface level, the shoes mirror the doormat, but the choice of brand recalls familiar punk fashion. The visual imagery, the design layout, and the catalog's marketing-speak have emphasized the nostalgic focus of their merchandise.

The set of six highball glasses have a screen-printed cassette tape with a different colored label on each. The whimsical description states, "Take all-occasion glassware on a retro rewind with these colorful mixtape glasses. The blank tape allows partygoers to write their names or favorite power ballad on the cassette."[25] While the glass has a kitsch cassette tape stamped on it, the description pulls in music. Using the phrase "retro rewind," they connect to the music and the appeal of the glassware. The catalog examples have handwritten labels like "Sarah Mixalot" and "DJ Jazzy 'Jess'" combining personalization and retro symbolism.

The cassette tape visual became part of a larger retro nostalgic experience. In the fall of 2013, the catalog marketing team included cocktail recipes and mixtapes on their blog *The Uncommon Life*. Images of the glasses are lined up with links for mixed drinks and phrases like "Weather any storm with a mellow music mix."[26] The many ways *Uncommon Goods* markets products through retro descriptions and contemporary appeals to cocktails showcase how mixtape culture imagery has crossed generations. One customer review lauded the retro mixtape theme for her musician son, even though he was too young to remember cassettes.[27] Her response hit on a key factor in the 2010s mixtape. These items no longer connect exclusively to the generation who created, listened to, and remember mixtapes. Cassette likenesses on merchandise have reintroduced mixtapes to a new generation who incorporate a new nostalgic identity with analog music culture and kitsch mixtape paraphernalia.

One of the items sold through *Uncommon Goods* is the board game, Mixtape, conceived by Kansas City graphic designer, Joel Johnson. To found and market the game Johnson launched a Kickstarter campaign which raised over $15,000. In May 2019, the game made an appearance in *Rolling Stone* magazine on the "Summer: Hottest Must-Haves" page.[28] In October 2019, Johnson updated the Kickstarter page stating, "Most of you know this, but last year we licensed Mixtape to Breaking Games. Then they sold 49,997 Mixtape decks to Target. So, yeah we did it."[29] What started out as an idea based on his childhood love of sharing music on road trips, had become a successful marketable game with a presence in mainstream stores and quirky catalogs. To continue to build on his success, Johnson added a mobile app to play on streaming music services.

Johnson had originally called the game *Soundtrack* but changed it because as someone who used to make mixtapes, the name "just seemed logical."[30] The description on the Breaking Games website mirrors his statement, "*Star Wars* and *Saturday Night Fever, Titanic* and *The Graduate*—a distinctive soundtrack can make a movie unforgettable. This game invites you to tell the story of your life through the soundtrack that backs it."[31] In changing the name, Johnson felt Gen Xers would absolutely recognize the term "mixtape" which would pique their curiosity. For young people, Johnson dubbed the mixtape "more popular than a rotary phone" and an item which has continued pop cultural awareness.[32]

Mixtape is a cross-generational family card game. Johnson said, "[the game] challenges players to find the 'best' companion song to specific life scenarios, such as a date or road trip."[33] He described the game's foundation in an online presentation:

> Music has a profound effect on culture and life. We at MIXTAPE feel that everyone has a story to tell and a song to play. A favorite love song or sing-in-the-shower song. [. . .] Call it soundtrack syndrome or montage mania, this was just something we did to kill time. MIXTAPE provided the outlet for the "best song to do blank to . . ." challenge we were constantly pitching to each other. MIXTAPE gives you an opportunity to play your friends the soundtrack to your life. Music tied to memories, memories tied to emotions, emotions tied to life.[34]

To play Mixtape, players draw a card with a scenario and pick a song to communicate the theme. The themes vary from, "What is the song that goes with your most memorable childhood music video?" to "You are a 150 year old Saguaro cactus. You've watched the sunrise over a beautiful mountain vista your entire life. Tomorrow you've learned you will see your last sunrise. What song do you play?" The deck includes additional cards with broad themes like "Request & Dedication: Play a song for that special someone in the room." and "Picture This. The player that pulls this card needs to show the group an image/video. Everyone then plays a song to #MIXTAPE that moment." Johnson intended the game to "share ourselves with people."[35]

Players have told Johnson the songs they chose established a personal context for the game. Johnson himself has learned stories from his dad and gotten to know complete strangers while playing Mixtape. The universal appreciation of music, regardless of the style or genre individuals pick, characterizes the game. He imagined a scenario in which a composer could play all classical music, a music nerd could pull obscure Bob Dylan songs and another player could choose Top 40 songs. But the songs work together because of the nature of the cards and the game play. In an interview about the success of the game, Johnson declared, "People are always curious—especially if you blow their mind with a song that's completely unexpected. People generally will open up and tell that story where they were on a road trip or they climbed a mountain, or they got their heart stomped on."[36] As with a good traditional mixtape, the genre or the song is less important than the collective whole. The game functions as a representation of collective memory through artifacts and music.

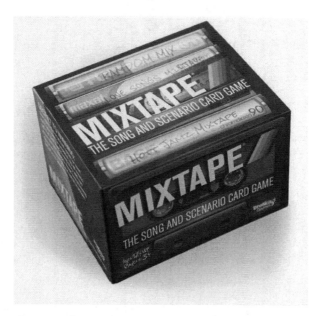

Figure 8.1   Mixtape Card Game, Breaking Games. (Joel Johnson/AdMagic Games, 2020. https.//www.mixtapethegame.com) Image courtesy of AdMagic Games and Joel Johnson, Game Creator.

The box for the game's second edition resembles a six-pack of tapes. Johnson worked with a design team who produced the new box style, aiming for a nostalgic visual that "really said cassette tape by looking at it."[37] The label reads "Mixtape the song and scenario card game" in a font and colors reminiscent of a blank Maxell tape from the 1980s. Across the top is an image of cassette tapes named "Random Mix" "Love Songs Mixtape" and "Hott Jamz Mixtape." Breaking Games marketing pitch for the game ends with the phrase, "Rather than knowledge or skill, the game plays on emotions, memories, and life experiences."[38] Each game is the creation of a mixtape.

Applying a different medium of art, Jeff Skierka made a mixtape out of reclaimed wood. In 2012 Skierka fashioned a one-of-a-kind, twelve-to-one scale wooden mixtape coffee table. The original prototype garnered enough attention to launch him to local fame in Seattle and allow him to mass-produce the coffee table. Skierka insisted on a finished, reverse B-side of the table as a key feature. Tech podcasts like Gizmodo and CNet wrote articles describing the "Retro-rific" coffee table.[39] Next Nature Network declared the piece a "good example of technostalgia, wherein we idolize old-fashion technologies in response to what feels like an overwhelming rate of technological change."[40] One design website opined: Skierka had created merely a cassette table, nothing distinguished it as a mixtape.[41] Yet the appeal of the word mixtape underscores the success of Skierka's work. On his design website, with multiple wooden objects for sale, the mixtape table sells for $6450 and remains the foundation of his work.[42]

Other creative individuals have also considered how to engage in mixtape nostalgia while generating artistic material. Memoirs and journaling are popular outlets in today's ruminative culture. Robert K. Elder, the author of a dozen books on a wide variety of topics, chose mixtapes as an ideal entrée into personal storytelling. Elder photographed musicians from Marilyn Manson to Ben Harper and recently donated his collection of negatives, prints, and fan club memorabilia to the Rock and Roll Hall of Fame.[43] His long-standing investment with music translated into his 2018 venture as the designer of *The Mixtape of My Life: A Do-It-Yourself Memoir*. The marketing description states, "Everyone has those songs that take them back—to their first love, their favorite concert, or a memorable Saturday morning cartoon."[44] In an interview, Elder said, "I wanted to know what memories songs and artists brought up. I was really focused on cultivating memories."[45] For him, sharing stories through music, "brings people together through commiseration and empathy. 'All these stories create a bond'."[46]

In the Introduction, Elder explains why he chose music as the organizing principle for a journaling memoir, "It's said that smell is the sense that most strongly evokes memory. For me, that's never been true. It's always been hearing music. Music is the key to the time machine in my brain. To this day, a song I haven't heard in years can unlock a memory or a sensation I'd long forgotten."[47] He reminisces about three memories tied to three specific songs and concludes, "It's not about creating lists of songs, but rather cataloging stories from the soundtrack of your life."[48] Although Elder does not use the word nostalgia in his description, his work signifies a desire to remember the past fondly and to use audio experiences as the touchstone to refresh those stories.

The journal's cover sets the tone with various gray-tone cassette tapes. Within the book, the same tape design in a blue-tone constitutes the background art. The illustrator, Rob Marvin, sprinkled drawings throughout the book which display familiar icons of cassette culture: someone winding a cassette tape with a pencil eraser, a couple sitting close, sharing earbuds, and an iPod—not cassette culture, but personal music culture. The open-ended questions intended to spur stories are similar to questions in Mixtape the Game: "What's the best bit of philosophy offered by a song? How did it affect your life?" and "Which album are you most likely to give as a gift?" It also includes drawing prompts like, "Draw your favorite concert t-shirt" followed by "Where did you wear it? Did it help you make new friends? And Where is it now?" Questions like, "Make up album names for: your teen years, your college years, and the last few years" create a self-reflective opportunity to tie music and identity together.[49] Elder uses music as a touchstone for identity. A Virginia newspaper picked Elder's book as one of their five best Father's Day Gift ideas for 2018 stating, "If your dad couldn't live without music, 'The Mixtape of My Life: A Do-it-Yourself Music Memoir' [. . .] is the gift he never knew he needed."[50] Recommending this book for a parent underscores the idea of collective memory: a way to share ideas across generations with family. Mixtapes give music the emotional touchstone to ground the philosophy of the journal.

Using an emotional pull in a vastly different arena, two entrepreneurs crafted a location centered on the mixtape. Elaina Holko and Katie Molchan co-owned the Pittsburgh, Pennsylvania cocktail bar, Mixtape. Molchan stated "Mix tapes were a labor of love, and so is our bar."[51] The bar opened in late 2015 where they, "combine[d] the best of traditional music venues, community spaces and cafes."[52] The owners described the name in social media:

> We grew up creating one of the 80s-90s most time-consuming labors of love . . . mixtapes. You'd sit by the radio for hours, ready to hit those "play" and "record" buttons at just the right moment, piecing together your audible masterpiece to share with friends (or your latest crush). Once it was done, we'd come together to laugh and sing our way through both sides of that Maxell 60-minute tape.
>
> We strive to bring back that feeling of togetherness . . . but this time over great drinks.[53]

Their description exhibits a nostalgic craving for community and mixtape artifacts. They used the concept of a mixtape to generate the community feeling they wanted to build. A review declared, "I'll go right out and say it: if you don't like over abundant music references and pop culture clichés, odds are good the theme at Mixtape is not for you."[54] Not intended as a critique, the statement expresses what the bar did with flourish and detail. They curated playlists to meet the vibe of the moment, stating playfully on their Facebook page, "After all . . . we have to keep the 'Mix' in 'Mixtape.'"[55]

Catchy signature cocktails promoted the playfulness of the bar. The "Classic Cocktails" page included cassette tape iconography entitled "Classics mix" connecting the style of drink, the name of the bar, and the cassette tape. "Side

A" of the menu includes "Chart Toppers" like Moscow mules and whiskey sours. "Side B" of the Classic Cocktails Menu had "$8 Tracks," another fun spin on classic audio culture. The playfulness of the bar oozed through the catchy signature cocktails on their menu. In the winter of 2020, they had drinks named "Cranmaster Flash" and "Posh Spice" which underscored their spirit, musical knowledge, and desire to keep the bar fresh and fun. An earlier version of the menu described the aptly named, "Livin' La Vida Mocha" smoothie with "Once you've had a taste, you'll never be the same." Playing on kitschy jokes, they had a salad on the menu called "Spring Mix-a-Lot" which they described as, "If we're lucky maybe Nicki Minaj will sample it."[56] The visuals and the references incorporate a hip hop vibe into the venue as well. For the bar, a mixtape reflected different subculture identities, overlapping the personal Gen X nostalgic mixtape and the contemporary hip hop mixtape.

The venue had active social media accounts where they expanded their exploration between music and drinks. They interspersed 1980s and 1990s music culture impressions between images of cocktails and bottles of alcohol they served. In one post, they uploaded an image of a multicolor boombox called the "Lasonic TRC-975 Double Cassette" player with the accompanying text, "We all bopped around with our ghettoblasters and Sony Walkmans (Walkmen?) in 1991, but did you know that the cassette tape was introduced in the early 1960s? We have a flare for the 80s and up, [. . .] No, Mixtape isn't a 90s bar. It's a vibe."[57] That year they posted an artistic off-center image with a handful of cassette tapes stacked in a martini glass. A recognizable Memorex cassette tape is placed visibly in the glass which sits next to two bottles of liquor. The caption reads, "#memorex90 // we put the same love into our mixed drinks that we used to put into our mixtapes."[58] Mixtape's social media outreach displayed a balance between music, nostalgia, and mixtapes. These posts allow the bar owners to distinguish themselves in the competitive world of bar culture and relish in their name and their love of music.

The artistic details in the bar itself played on the direct link to cassettes. The awning of their building was a black canvas with a large, angled white cassette tape and the name "Mixtape Caffeine & Cocktails." The same image appeared on their gift certificates and hand-crafted wooden coasters. Their decor included mixtapes, musicians, and cassette culture imagery. An art piece from an upcycled dictionary page had a hand-painted Memorex cassette tape. The bright blue, yellow, and fuchsia accents of that recognizable tape are iconic for Gen Xers. Holko and Molchan embraced the nostalgia of Gen X youth and designed a lively coffee and spirits bar to draw in their audience. Using strong marketing tools, they incorporated mixtape metaphors at every level of their venture, underlining their commitment to mixtape culture.[59]

Another city also designed a venue to celebrate the mixtape. An artist collective in Oklahoma City established Factory Obscura in 2017 "to support, create, and awaken our community and our world."[60] They built interactive art exhibits bringing community members together in a fun unique, modern way. In February 2020, one of the collective's musicians recorded a physical mixtape of the Oklahoma City music scene. She reached out to local bands who wrote songs inspired by a physical space inside Factory Obscura reflecting "joy, angst, love, melancholy, hope, and wonder." They worked with a local studio to produce, mix, master, and release a cassette tape with the six songs they had written, titled appropriately *Mix-Tape Volume 1*.[61] The cassette includes a digital download, highlighting the reality of the analog to digital crossover in the contemporary music world. They performed their songs and sold their cassette to a sold-out crowd at a 2020 Valentine's Day event. In March 2021 they released an aqua and purple *Mix-Tape Volume 2* as part of their "Future of Sound Fest" outdoor festival with local artists.[62]

The impact of the creative idea led to a larger, tangible next step. In 2021, the members of the Factory Obscura collective turned their museum into an interactive exhibit centered on the mixtape. They describe the exhibit: "In a world of drag-and-drop, Factory Obscura has hand-crafted our own twentieth-century take on the classic audio autobiography: a grassroots playlist of emotions inspired by the music that made us who we are."[63] The visual marketing for the show features a turquoise blue cassette tape with a rainbow label and "the future is collaborative" in script.[64] Swirling tape surrounds a cartoon drawing of the museum building and the word mix-tape. A written description at the entrance to the museum exhibit in Oklahoma City reads, "You are about to immerse yourself in a 6,000 square-foot full-sensory art experience based on the classic American art form that is the Mixtape. [. . .] This Mix-tape is our hand-crafted auto-biography to you."[65]

This project reflects the emotive marketing feel of the twenty-first-century mixtape. The collective, collaborative project led by musicians to produce a tangible object expanded into a community-driven outreach program to connect people and emotions. The gift shop includes clothing, pins, stickers, patches, magnets, and cassette tapes all bedecked with mixtape imagery. A hand-drawn navy, pink, and turquoise cassette tape labeled "Mix-Tape/ Factory Obscura" is the predominant image.[66] Individual artists have added their own spin on the products available for sale. Artist Todd Clark, whose website includes many of the graphic design creations for Factory Obscura, has designed an additional sticker and print collection with individuals dressed in stereotypical 1980s clothing, but having analog tech instead of a head.[67] In one, a male character wears a pink and orange neon blazer, complete with rolled sleeves and has a large boombox for a head. Another incorporates a character in an orange and yellow patterned running suit with a bright blue Walkman for a head. He also has characters with a PC and a stereo for heads. Clark also created a holographic sticker with a pastel unicorn listening to a boombox.[68] The incorporation of memorabilia and the physical locations solidify the community aspect of mixtape culture.

Alongside creating community, mixtape also represents blending and combining disparate elements into something new. As with Brendan Leonard's memoir *The New American Roadtrip Mixtape* and Questlove's *Mixtape Potluck* cookbook, creative individuals have figured out how to combine the technostalgia of the mixtape with a new commodity. Beer and coffee, ubiquitous beverages in a world of micro-processing, need a strong marketing idea to stand out from the innumerable options on the market. A handful of companies have devised campaigns tied to the mixtape to capture customer attention.

Dogwood Coffee in Minneapolis, Minnesota sells bags of coffee beans called "Mixtape, Vol. . . ." In 2014 they sold Vol. 12, Guatemala & Colombia. In 2020 they sold Vol. 39 Colombia & Brazil, with other volumes released in between.[69] The description of coffee bean blends plays on the nostalgia of mixtape creation: "This blend is like one of the mixtapes you made for the person you really like-liked, but didn't know very well. It is balanced, a little bass-y and a little bright."[70] Buyers can also purchase a mixtape subscription, receiving a bag of beans every few weeks. The tag line for this subscription applies to musical nostalgia. It mentions listening to music on a Panasonic RX 5600LS, a classic boombox. Explaining how to set up a subscription, the text reads, "press play and boom, it's in your hands! [. . .] and you can adjust the levels or 'record over' at anytime."[71] This coffee adopts technostalgic wording while using coffee blends as a contemporary definition of a mixtape as a mix of disparate beans.

Like coffee, the excessive popularity of microbrewed beer requires a niche to attract consumer's attention. Multiple companies have prepared a mixtape beer in the past few years. A trio of breweries, including Nostalgia Brewing in Ohio, celebrated their one-year anniversary in early 2020 by making a beer called, "We Made You a Mixtape, Vol. 1." The face of the can is a full-sized black cassette tape with the name of the beer written on the title line.[72] Stoup Beer in the suburbs of Seattle created "Mixtape Romeo" beer. The website's description of the lager reads, "In the entire history of humankind, there has never been a more profound expression of love than the personalized mixtape. Hours of deliberation about which songs to share from your home tape collection followed by hours of tiny handwritten playlists with tiny hearts incorporated wherever possible."[73] Leaning into the metaphor of romance, the Romeo name fits with the description. Capitalizing on their imagery, they finish the description with the line, "Load it up, press play and enjoy."[74] Mixtapes are used by brewers as metaphors to capture the attention of beer drinkers. In a world saturated by options, any novel way of distinguishing a microbrewery can help sales.

Stone Brewing, an independent craft brewer in California produced the Stone Mixtape Ale Series in 2013.[75] Encouraged to try something new, the co-founders began adding unexpected blends to their ale which proved successful. Working with local restaurants, they have crafted five "Volumes" of unique mixtape ales which they describe as "Ultra rare." With names like "Belong to Where You Are, the Neighborhood Blend" and "RK & JM's Blend," the initials of the two individuals who worked together to produce the blend, these mixtape beers tap into a novel way to diversify merchandise.[76] By using "mixtape" as both a nostalgic term and a blending of unexpected ideas together to design a novelty, the brewery has expanded their niche in innovative ways.

Another craft brewery has taken the idea of mixtape as a visual recreation for their beers. Designing a wide variety of diverse cans, Grist House

Figure 8.2   Mixtape Mayhem Double IPA, Grist House Brewery. (Bailey Allegretti 2019 https://gristhouse.com/beer/) Image courtesy of Grist House and Bailey Allegretti, Design Creator.

Craft Brewery in Pittsburgh, Pennsylvania released the Mixtape Mayhem beer. Described as "Thoughtful and balanced, just like a perfect mixtape," this IPA came in a teal, yellow, and pink retro-colored can, covered with brightly colored diverse cassette tapes.[77] Each tape on the can has its own unique name from "Brew Day Mix" to "Don't Let Mom Find This" continuing the allegiance to the mixtape theme. One tape has the words "The Commonheart," the name of a popular local Pittsburgh band.[78] Bailey Allegretti, the Marketing Manager for the Brewery designed the label after chatting with an old friend about the mix CDs they made in high school. They decided playlists are "less genuine" than the mixes they made. With the conversation on her mind, Allegretti designed the can.[79] Grist House introduces new cans regularly as part of limited-edition runs. They announced the Mixtape Mayhem Double IPA on Twitter in October 2019 alongside three other original beers.[80] The Mixtape Mayhem beer sold out in less than a month.[81] For Grist House the name and design on the can is the appeal. Aside from the tagline description of the beer, which does weave mixtape into its phrasing, the brewery has little obvious tie to music. In this instance, the appealing visual imagery solidifies their niche; why not use bright mixtapes?

Mixtape creations, whether items conceived specifically as a reflection of the musical cassette, or ideas of mixtapes as a distinct blending have led to a disparate collection of consumable goods. In each of these inventions, marketing has played into the reminiscence of Gen X making musical mixes on cassettes to engage their customers. For other innovative outlets mixtapes have no tangible good. Instead, the idea is a marketing tool used to snare an audience.

Mixtape Campaign

The visual representation of the mixtape has solidified the role of this once physical artifact into a conceptual understanding of identity, friendship, connection, and nostalgia. Marketing campaigns recognize the nostalgic appeal of mixtapes and have found ways to incorporate them into advertising. In the summer of 2019 New Kids on the Block (NKOTB) announced its latest tour: The Mixtape Tour "with very special guests Salt-n-Pepa, Tiffany, Debbie Gibson, and Naughty By Nature."[82] New Kids on the Block, a quintessential boy band in the late 1980s and 1990s, helped to craft the current generation of boy band archetypes.[83] Their breakout album *Hangin' Tough*, including the title track song, cemented the group in the youth culture imagination. Their popularity coincided with the end of the twentieth-century mixtape era. The band performed until 2008 when newer, younger bands appeared, and New Kids' members moved on. By 2018, in the era of popular nostalgia tours,

New Kids benefitted and staged their own reunion tour. They wedded the entire framework of the tour around the concept of the mixtape.

On their website, NKOTB announced their Mixtape Tour as part of the thirtieth anniversary of Hangin' Tough.[84] In late 2018 they posted a marketing video which opens with a dual-cassette boombox, two hand-written mixtape cases, and NKOTB merchandise in the background.[85] A jewel case with a lined J-Card is the backdrop for clips of well-known videos for each of the artists on the tour. The mixtape imagery is clear in every second of the video. The same day, band members announced the special guests on *The Today Show*. Carson Daly, known to Gen X fans as the host of MTV's TRL (Total Request Live) from 1998 to 2003, interviewed the band, further solidifying the nostalgic tenor of the moment.[86] The set included a large screen designed to look like the spine of four cassette tapes which read "Mixtape Tour/New Kids on the Block/Mixtape Tour." Donnie Wahlberg described the tour, "We're creating a mixtape on tour every night, in every city."[87] The tours' guest performers walked on to applause and a short clip of their music. Introducing teen pop star Tiffany, Daly stated, "It wouldn't be the 80s pop mixtape tour without Tiffany."[88] Every minute of the interview plays into the nostalgia of a reunion tour for fans who remembered the band.

Merchandising for the tour built on the physical mixtape imagery. The predominant advertising image includes members of NKOTB standing on a cassette tape with handwritten song titles on the cover including "The Right Stuff" and "Hangin' Tough."[89] The spine of the cassette states in large red and black lettering "Mixtape Tour 2019." The guests appeared in primary color boxes to the right of the primary image. Promotional and retail items continued the theme. They sold a black tank top with the band and tour name emblazoned on a neon yellow and pink cassette tape. Collectible merchandise available with VIP sales included a small black zippered makeup bag designed to look like a cassette with a red sticker and the tour name in white.[90] Still shots of the concert show the band members dressed in all white standing in front of a large digital video screen. The image resembles a boombox with dual speakers and bright primary-colored equalizers.[91] The imagery and the accompanying merchandising and marketing remained true to form. The band reconnected to adult fans with retro artifacts and kitschy memorabilia.

To further solidify the concept, New Kids on the Block released the song "80s Baby" when they announced the Mixtape Tour. They described the song as "a truly epic, throwback track featuring their Mixtape Tour partners. The track, which appears on the thirtieth-anniversary re-release of the original *Hangin' Tough* album, 'takes listeners on a nostalgic yet refreshingly modern and fun ride through 80s song references and fresh verses'."[92] According to *People* magazine, they released the song, "to serve as a tribute to all the '80s ladies still jamming out to the beloved boy band."[93] It functions as an advertisement and a marketing jingle for the tour, as well as a walk down memory lane. Every lyric, which includes vocals by Naughty by Nature and Salt 'n' Pepa, harkens back to the 1980s, referencing popular dances like the moonwalk and the Smurf, and fashions like stonewashed, ripped jeans, and bangle bracelets. The video uses a retro 8-bit style concept reminiscent of early video games. Pop culture references to late-night TV ads, Star Wars imagery, Pac Man, and Mario side scrollers appear throughout.[94] The campy video continues the impression of a nostalgic era worth reminiscence grounded by the mixtape. Not merely advertising, the full line-up performed "80s Baby" as the final song on the setlist each night.[95]

In 2019 the New Kids on the Block Mixtape Tour encapsulated the current era of mixtape nostalgia. Directly connected to a pop culture band whose album appeared on cassette, LP, and CD, the marketing team responsible for putting together the tour solidified the retrostalgia for fans through the mixtape imagery. This representation pulls together thirty years of how mixtapes have been understood. From a format on which to create personalized compilations, to a nostalgic idea for a simplified past, to a marketing idea to pull in customers, the mixtape became a catch-all for New Kids on the Block fans. The collective memory of boy band fandom could be shared across generations. When the band rereleased the album for its thirtieth anniversary, correlating with the Tour and the merchandise they released the album on cassette.[96] A mixtape had become a reminiscence, a marketing strategy, and a metaphor for the past. New Kids on the Block capitalized on the campy retro appeal of a nostalgia tour and their fans embraced it.

In July 2019 KEXP, a Seattle-based, nonprofit, independent, community-supported radio station announced they would host "Mixtape Week" in late August. The station aimed to "celebrate the history of mixtapes and play selections from mixes submitted by listeners across all KEXP platforms, highlighting the memories, stories and emotions that go into constructing a mixtape."[97] John Richards, the Director of Programming and Morning Show host had had the idea for years. The week included a contest and several posts about mixtapes on the station website by various KEXP staff members. For the contest they expected a handful of mixtapes and received more than 400. A panel of KEXP DJs judged the contest submissions "for curatorial excellence, storytelling, creativity, and song sequencing."[98] Encouraged by the popularity, the station planned to repeat the event.

For Owen Murphy, Morning Show and Content Producer at KEXP, mixtapes are synonymous with playlists and DJ-curated radio shows. He believes Mixtape Week grew logically from what the station does every day to build community by, "curating a living mixtape."[99] He saw the event as sparking listener imagination, expanding the notion of DJs as the "people behind the mic who are having one-on-one conversations with each individual

Figure 8.3 KEXP Mixtape Week, 2019. (KEXP, 2019. https://www.kexp.org/mixtape/)
Image courtesy of KEXP.

listener."[100] Kevin Cole, KEXP's Chief Content Officer and Afternoon Show
host corroborated Murphy's description stating, "our DJs curate the music all
day long—no automated programming or algorithms are dictating what we
play. Each mix has a story. And whether it's a mixtape, a CD, a playlist, or a
radio broadcast, there's tremendous beauty in humans connecting with other
humans through music."[101] DJs at the station felt inspired by the mixtapes the
contestants had made: the format, the order of the songs, and the music they
incorporated. Among the KEXP submissions were old mixes individuals dug
out of their collections and brand-new mixes people made for the contest.[102]
Certain mixtapes exhibited a regional identity, sharing music specific to
one locality. Others reflected a historical document and reintroduced older,
nearly forgotten music to a new audience. One contestant sent the station five
separate mixtapes. The contest took a personal artifact and gave it increased
value through access to a large audience. Cheryl Waters, host of the KEXP
Midday Show, continued to play the mixes on her show after the contest
ended because she was so impressed with the ideas people had submitted.

   The physicality of the submissions played as important a role as the playlist. Murphy described a mix as "outsider art" which assumed a one-on-one
relationship because someone had made it for you and given it to you. As an
adolescent he created mixtapes because he wanted people to hear and love
new music as much as he did. Now he constructs Spotify playlists for his
family which are equally reverent because of the inherent meaning behind
the finished item. Nonetheless, he agreed the artwork and the time spent
curating a cassette tape subtly shifted the tenor of the item. Reviewing the

submissions for the contest when they arrived allowed him to see the artwork the contestants had included. For him, the personalized art was "so vital, so cool" and he said of the submissions "when [the artwork] was great, it was incredible."[103]

The winner of the contest, Jana Sturdivant, built a new mixtape for a friend on a cassette, only including songs that charted or were released in 1981. The mix included well-known bands like the Clash and Duran Duran next to lesser-known artists like Grauzone and Cleaners from Venus. She followed some of the archetypes of a mixtape, titling Sides A and B, Arts and Charts, respectively, and picking songs to fit within those categories. On the winner page, Sturdivant said, "I tried to pick a musical aesthetic [my friend] would enjoy but that I could tolerate listening to over and over as I mixed it."[104] This statement coincides with Murphy's perception of what makes mixtapes unique and special, "I loved when people were really creative. Sharing music with their friends and doing it in a unique way that's unique to them. That's what makes it great is that they're often unique to the person making them and who they're making them for."[105] In 2019, the KEXP mixtapes illustrated how crafting a compilation remains a relevant social interaction.

While KEXP did not specifically focus the week on nostalgia, a reflective attachment to the past appears in the shared stories. For the contest winner, a newly-constructed mixtape echoed a moment in time through older music. Staff members, who uploaded mixtapes on the station's website to promote the event, included descriptions like "I made this for my college boyfriend (who I was later married to for 20 yrs)."[106] and

As a kid of the 80s and 90s, I spent a ton of time listening to the radio in my room, always intently waiting for the moment when I'd need to run and hit record on my favorite songs. Inevitably, every single one of the songs on my mixtapes starts abruptly, and about 10 seconds in.[107]

Stacy McCauslin, a DJ Assistant, describes her mix as "still one of my most prized possessions."[108] One heartbreaking story about a friend who died ends, "The mix is the best reminder of him and our friendship."[109] A photograph of the tapes, all cassette-based and made pre-1995, accompanied each of these stories, complete with hand-written liner notes and hand-drawn artwork.

Dusty Henry, the Digital Content Manager for KEXP, wrote a longer piece for the station website. He begins, "I'm not sure if there's anything truer to the spirit of Mixtape Week than being awkward and weird about making someone a mix."[110] Henry admits he rarely reconsiders the mixtapes he made, which include seventy-plus digital playlists for his wife. Yet Mixtape Week caused him to look back and observe,

It's a curious experience, not unlike looking through an old photo album and seeing old haircuts and the way "things used to be." Beyond nostalgia, I've found not just a document of our relationship but revelations of what these mixes have taught me. Lessons I didn't know I was even learning.[111]

Thinking about a focused series of mixtapes for one individual allowed Henry to acknowledge shifts in his perception over time. Writing his "pseudo liner notes" for some of his mixes, he acknowledges, "If I'm being self-critical (welcome to my inner-voice, y'all) this is not the strongest mix I've made [. . .] But when you're making a mix for someone else, I now realize there's an aspect of removing a bit of yourself to make room for the other."[112] Henry's deep love for his wife permeates the analysis of his mixes. The music he includes ranged from Top 40 to punk. The mixes summarize his life, expressed through music. In this story, Henry articulates the power of the mixtape. Yes, it is about music. But it is more about the memory and the meaning. Mixtapes, whether recorded on a cassette in 1976 or curated on a streaming app, are personal. They signal the mixtaper and the recipient. Sentimental attachment is what makes a good mixtape.

Two of the blog posts on the KEXP site ponder how friendship shifts over time. "Scenes from Things You Missed: A Mixtape for My Dead Friend," by Martin Douglas analyzes a deep enduring friendship and the way they used music as an escape from difficult realties. After describing the mixes he made for his friend Que Linda, he outlines the structure he learned about how to make a mixtape. The second of his four takeaways is, "Every mixtape is a story. Therefore, sequencing is of the utmost importance."[113] The idea of a mixtape being more than a composite of unrelated songs reveals a truism for many mixtape aficionados. The songs are only as important as the story or emotion they are intended to convey. In a similar way Cyrus Despres, Director of Planning and Business Intelligence at KEXP, shares a story about reconnecting to friends through a collaborative mixtape. Each individual added songs to a Dropbox folder, building on the ideas and the songs submitted by the other two friends. Despres says of the endeavor, "Along with nurturing nostalgia, our song selections and emails were opportunities to reveal new parts of ourselves to each other. We were having a conversation through music."[114] He describes the finished work as a "personalized memoir." While the experience gave the friends an opportunity to reminisce, the sounds and emotions from the songs generated a new artistic work unique to those individuals and their sentimental bonds.

KEXP's Mixtape Week renewed excitement for mixtapes both among the station's listeners but also among the station's staff. Talking, writing, and thinking about mixtapes reconnected individuals to music and the emotional tie they had. The artistry of the covers and the creation of the compilations spoke to the DJs who enthusiastically re-aired the mixtapes they received. Rather than a purely nostalgic endeavor, many of the contestants connected to mixtapes anew in the twenty-first century. More than a marketing ploy, this event reinvigorated a discussion about the mixtape as a site of personal and collective memory.

Showcasing the physicality of a mixtape on a broadsheet, a theatre company invested an emotional appeal into their spring 2020 advertising campaign. Point Park University's Conservatory of Performing Arts, in Pittsburgh, Pennsylvania, decided to stage the world premiere of a new rock musical, *Pump Up the Volume*. Based on the 1990 cult film starring Christian Slater, the show tells the story of a small-town pirate radio DJ who broadcasts nightly for his high school classmates. The description of the new musical states, "Under cover of darkness, Mark bravely speaks truth to power—but when tragedy strikes, the powers-that-be make the hard-talking radio pirate their scapegoat."[115] For Point Park, the opportunity to participate in the formation of a brand-new musical appealed.[116]

When putting together the advertising campaign for the show, the production team contracted Steve Lowry of Blender Advertising. After reading the play and interacting with key figures involved in the production, Lowry aimed to design illustrations to intrigue viewers. Lowry and his partner's initial, and final, concept was a mixtape. For Blender Advertising, mixtapes represented a rejection of pop radio and "there was also something a little pirate-y about sharing music that we didn't buy or pay for."[117] Although there are no mixtapes in the show, the idea felt iconic. Lowry created a cracked cassette tape case image. The yellowed J-Card includes the words Pump Up the Volume handwritten horizontally in all caps with splatters of leaking ink. "World Premiere Musical" and the names of the production team appear below. The cover art reproduces a stylistic hand-drawn, handwritten cover, pervasive in original mixtapes.

Lowry and his partner both still have boxes of mixtapes and think *Pump Up the Volume*, "feels like the essence of mixtape culture. Your handwritten list of songs that represented you. [. . .] Because the tape was not for you alone in your room or your car—it was to be shared with your friends. It was a musical manifesto."[118] For the lead character and high school shock jock Mark, music is a way to express himself and to speak out against mainstream culture. In an interview on the twenty-fifth anniversary of the film's release, Kathy Nelson, the music supervisor for the film, described the movie as driven by music because "[Mark's] voice is the music. Because he doesn't talk, [. . .] it's almost that his character chooses to interact through the music he decides to play."[119] The first image in the original film trailer includes four cassette tapes piled atop a cassette player. Two of the cassettes, "Henry Rollins/Hard Volume" and "Soundgarden Louder Than Love" are

Figure 8.4   Pump Up the Volume Advertisement, Created by Blender, Inc. for Point Park University 2019–2020. (Blender Advertising/Point Park University, 2020. https://blenderadv.com/) Image courtesy of Point Park University and Steve Lowry, Image creator.

hand-labeled, noncommercial cassettes.[120] These tapes establish the genre of music and the character's relationship to DIY culture. When Lowry produced his image for the play, he wanted to conjure a feeling. The mixtape represented "A statement of your individuality, your style, and sometimes how cutting edge you wanted to seem to be."[121] That idea encapsulates the story of *Pump Up the Volume*. Using a mixtape to market a show, performed by young people, aimed at a cross-generational audience, coalesces the role of the mixtape. It represents emotional connection, nostalgia, and a collective understanding of anti-corporate youth culture tied to music.

From physical artifacts to marketing images for shows, the mixtape has expanded beyond a technostalgia for a cassette tape on which one can hear compilations of music. Cassette culture and the niche resurgence of music recorded on cassette does intersect with mixtape imagery, but the two are not exclusively interconnected. Artists, producers, and graphic designers have found an appeal in the visual representation of a cassette tape. The graphic representations of the blank cassette, with its personalized label and J-Card waiting for a playlist, embody the Gen X generation. Whether the mixtape image evokes nostalgia for the 1980s or is incorporated to describe an unconnected list of disparate ideas, it initiates thoughtfulness. Speaking to music producers, game designers, and graphic artists, every mixtape image began with a relationship with music and the cassette tape. When asked, each of these individuals spoke about making mixtapes in their past. They did not focus on nostalgia as the predominant reason for their contemporary designs. Instead, mixtapes, for these inventive individuals, represent sharing, connection, and joy. The mixtape products are not backward-looking nostalgic ties to the past. They are dynamic, lighthearted representations of a consumer culture audience who appreciates personal touches and retro analog imagery.

NOTES

1. Natalie Proulx, "Nine Teaching Ideas for Using Music to Inspire Student Writing," *New York Times* (May 10, 2018), https://www.nytimes.com/2018/05/10/learning/lesson-plans/nine-teaching-ideas-for-using-music-to-inspire-student-writing.html (Accessed September 21, 2020).

2. Geoffrey Sirc, "Serial Composition," in *Rhetorics and Technologies: New Directions in Writing and Communication*, ed. Stuart A. Selber, Studies in Rhetoric/Communication (Columbia: University of South Carolina Press, 2010).

3. W. F. Umi Hsu, "'The Mixtape Project' Assignment: Learning through Critical Making," http://beingwendyhsu.info/?p=742 (Accessed September 21, 2020).

4. Ibid.

5. Proulx.

6. Olivia Jean Hernández, "Mixtapes 101," in *Pop Con 2020—Mixtapes 101* (Virtual, September 4, 2020: Museum of Pop Culture, 2020). https://youtu.be/6vfz-B31rx-w (Accessed September 23, 2020).

7. Ibid.

8. Paul du Gay et al., *Doing Cultural Studies: The Story of the Sony Walkman* (London: Sage Publications Ltd, 2003), xv.

9. Ibid., 15.

10. Ibid., xiii.

11. Philip J. Deloria and Alexander I. Olson, *American Studies: A User's Guide* (Oakland: University of California Press, 2017), 43.

12. Alexander I. Olson, interview by Jehnie Burns, June 3, 2020, Phone Conversation.

13. Deloria and Olson, 294.

14. Ibid., 300.

15. Kevin Holt (GSAS'18) was an adjunct assistant professor in the Department of African American and African Diaspora Studies and Mellon Postdoctoral Fellow in African American Studies at Wesleyan University Walyce Almeida, "Community Scholar's Mixtape Museum Is an Ode to Hip-Hop," *Columbia News* (November 22, 2019), https://news.columbia.edu/news/hip-hop-music-mixtape-museum-commu nity-scholars (Accessed May 12, 2021).

16. The Mixtape Museum https://mixtapemuseum.org/ (website) (Accessed May 12, 2021).

17. Almeida.

18. Mixtape Museum, "The Mixtape Museum," Soundcloud, https://soundcloud .com/mixtapemuseum (Accessed May 19, 2021).

19. They also sold a range of items made from reclaimed cassette tape ribbon. Showcasing the quick turnover of pop culture, the array of items connected to cassettes and mixtapes available in 2015–2016 had disappeared from their website by 2019.

20. Jeff Klarin, *Cassette Player Future Fossil* (Uncommon Goods Catalog, 2014).

21. Ibid.

22. Ibid.

23. Jim Holodak, *Personalized Mixtape Doormat* (Uncommon Goods Catalog, 2020).

24. Uncommon Goods, *Personalized Mixtape Pillow* (Uncommon Goods Catalog, 2020).

25. Uncommon Goods, *Mixtape Glasses—Set of 6* (Uncommon Goods Catalog, 2013).

26. Cassie Tweten Delaney, "7 Mixtape Mixed Drinks: A Week of Cool Cocktails & Toe-Tappin' Tunes." The Uncommon Life: Uncommon Goods 2013 https://www.uncommongoods.com/blog/2013/7-mixtape-mixed-drinks/ (Accessed January 24, 2020).

27. Uncommon Goods, *Mixtape Glasses—Set of 6*.

28. Joel Johnson, @mixtapethegame (Instagram, June 5, 2019).

29. Joel Johnson, "Mixtape—The Song & Scenario Card Game," Kickstarter, https://www.kickstarter.com/projects/helpfundmixtape/mixtape-the-song-and-scenar io-card-game/description (Accessed July 13, 2020).

30. Joel Johnson, interview by Jehnie Burns, September 6, 2019, audio.

31. Breaking Games, "Mixtape," https://breakinggames.com/collections/check-o ut-our-hottest-new-games/products/mixtape (Accessed July 13, 2020).

32. Johnson.

33. Meghan LeVota, "KC-Made Card Game Mixtape Makes a 'Soundtrack for Your Life,'" August 26, 2016. https://www.startlandnews.com/2016/08/kc-made -card-game-makes-soundtrack-life/ (Accessed July 13, 2020).

34. Joel Johnson, *Mixtape, Kauffman 1 Million Cups* (1 Million Cups website May 27, 2015), 59:04 Video. https://www.1millioncups.com/kansascity/presentations /mixtape-229 (Accessed July 13, 2020).

35. Joel Johnson, *Mixtape* (Kansas City: Breaking Games, 2019). Board Game.

36. Elyssa Bezner, "Target Deals New Verse to KC-Born Mixtape Card Game; Players Could Pick Founder's Next Tune," *Startland News*, January 2, 2019.

37. Johnson.

38. Breaking Games.

39. Andrew Liszewski, "The Mixtape Will Live Forever through This Retroriffic Coffee Table," *Gizmodo* (May 24, 2012), https://gizmodo.com/the-mixtape-will-live-forever-through-this-retro-riffic-5913055 (Accessed July 13, 2020). Edward Moyer, "Classy 'Mixtape' Coffee Table Is One for the Jet (Cas)Set(Te)," *c|net* (May 31, 2012), https://www.cnet.com/news/classy-mixtape-coffee-table-is-one-for-the-jet-cassette/ (Accessed July 13, 2020).

40. Alessia Andreotti, "Technostalgia for the Cassette Tape," *Next Nature* (July 19, 2013), https://nextnature.net/2013/07/technostalgia-for-the-cassette-tape (Accessed July 13, 2020).

41. Ray Hu, "Things That Look Like Other Things: Mixtape Table by Jeff Skierka," *Core 77* (May 25, 2012), https://www.core77.com/posts/22544/things-that-look-like-other-things-mixtape-table-by-jeff-skierka-22544 (Accessed July 13, 2020).

42. Jeff Skierka, *Mixtape Table* (website & video: Jeff Skierka Designs, 2013).

43. Robert K. Elder, "Robert K. Elder: Digital Executive & Author," https://robelder.com/bio/ (Accessed September 1, 2020).

44. Running Press, "The Mixtape of My Life," Running Press, https://www.runningpress.com/titles/robert-k-elder/the-mixtape-of-my-life/9780762464074/ (Accessed September 1, 2020).

45. Anna Paige, "Former Billings Resident's Book Prompts Music Lovers to Explore the Soundtrack of Their Lives," *Billings Gazette*, July 20, 2018.

46. Ibid.

47. Robert K. Elder, *The Mixtape of My Life: A Do-It-Yourself Music Memoir* (New York: Running Press Adult, 2018).

48. Ibid.

49. Ibid.

50. Jenny Baker, "A Father's Day Gift Guide: Local Gift Ideas to Help You Think Outside the World's Best Dad Coffee Mug," *Winchester Star*, June 8, 2018.

51. Seth Pfannenschmidt, "Mixtape, in Garfield, Blurs the Lines between Music Venue, Bar and Art Gallery," *Pittsburgh City Paper*, March 2, 2016.

52. Brian Conway, "Mixtape and Black Forge Coffee Offer Music, Community Space and More," *Next Pittsburgh* (January 19, 2016), https://nextpittsburgh.com/city-design/more-than-just-music-at-pittsburghs-newest-mixed-use-venues/ (Accessed July 13, 2020).

53. Mixtape, "Mixtape," (Facebook, 2020). About page.

54. Jeremy, "Mixtape Pittsburgh Review—The Neighborhood Bar Garfield Needs," Discover the Burgh, https://www.discovertheburgh.com/mixtape/ (Accessed July 14, 2020).

55. Mixtape, "About Mixtape," Mixtape Pgh, https://mixtapepgh.com/about/ (Accessed July 14, 2020).

56. "Menus" Mixtape Pgh, http://mixtapepgh.com/menus/ (Accessed July 14, 2020).

57. Mixtape Pgh. "Lasonic Ghettoblaster." *Instagram*, August 31, 2019. https://www.instagram.com/p/B11qrwZBQlW/ (Accessed January 20, 2020).

58. Mixtape Pgh. "Memorex & Chartreuse." *Instagram*, March 21, 2019. https://www.instagram.com/p/BvSpfuFh0zI/ (Accessed January 20, 2020).

59. Mixtape closed in the summer of 2020 as a result of the COVID-19 outbreak.

60. "Our Mission" Factory Obscura. https://www.factoryobscura.com/meet#our-mission (Accessed May 1, 2021).

61. "How to Make a Mix-Tape" Factory Obscura. March 23, 2020. https://www.factoryobscura.com/news/2020/3/22/how-to-make-a-mix-tape (Accessed May 1, 2021).

62. "Mix-Tape Vol. 2 Cassette" Factory Obscura Shop. https://shop.factoryobscura.com/products/mix-tape-vol-2-cassette (Accessed May 1, 2021).

63. "Factory Obscura Presents Mix-Tape" Factory Obscura. On ShowClix https://www.showclix.com/event/factory-obscura-presents-mix-tape?_ga=2.86084952.1329353868.1616703496-952254359.1616177829 (Accessed May 1, 2021).

64. "Mix-Tape" Factory Obscura. https://www.factoryobscura.com/mixtape (Accessed May 1, 2021).

65. Brennan Barnes. "Virtual Tour of the Factory Obscura Art gallery in Oklahoma City," madwfilms.com https://www.factoryobscura.com/mixtape-360 (Accessed May 1, 2021).

66. "All Products" Factory Obscura Shop. https://shop.factoryobscura.com/collections/all-products (Accessed May 1, 2021).

67. Todd E. Clark. "Portfolio." Big Juicy Creative. https://bigjuicycreative.com/portfolio (Accessed May 1, 2021).

68. "All Products" Factory Obscura Shop.

69. Dogwood Coffee Co., "Mixtape Vol 12: Colombia & Guatemala," Dogwood Coffee Co., www.dogwoodcoffee.com/products/mixtape. "Mixtape Vol 39: Colombia & Brazil," Dogwood Coffee Co., https://www.dogwoodcoffee.com/products/mixtape-vol-39 (Accessed July 14, 2020).

70. "Mixtape Vol 12: Colombia & Guatemala."

71. "Mixtape Subscription," Dogwood Coffee Co., https://www.dogwoodcoffee.com/products/copy-of-bear-hug-espresso-subscription (Accessed July 14, 2020).

72. Ohio Craft Brewers Association, "Ohio Brewery News," Ohio Craft Brewers Association, https://ohiocraftbeer.org/ohio-brewery-news-1-31-2020/ (Accessed July 14, 2020).

73. Stoup Brewing, "Mixtape Romeo," Stoup Brewing, https://www.stoupbrewing.com/beer/mixtape-romeo-953.html (Accessed July 14, 2020).

74. Ibid.

75. Stone Brewing, "About Stone Brewing," Stone Brewing, https://www.stone-brewing.com/about (Accessed July 14, 2021); Brandon Hernandez, April 25, 2013, https://www.stonebrewing.com/blog/beer/2013/stone-mixtape-ale-series (Accessed July 14, 2020).

76. Brandon Hernandez.

77. Untappd, "Mixtape Mayhem: Grist House Craft Brewery," Untappd, https://untappd.com/b/grist-house-craft-brewery-mixtape-mayhem/3498919 (Accessed July 14, 2020).

78. Bailey Allegretti, interview by Jehnie Burns, June 9, 2020, email.

79. Ibid.

80. Grist House. Twitter Post. October 17, 2019, 11:03 AM. https://twitter.com/GristHouse/status/1184847388890062850 (Accessed July 14, 2020).

81. Grist House. Twitter Post. November 15, 2019. 12:35 PM. https://twitter.com/GristHouse/status/1195394985601966080 (Accessed July 14, 2020).

82. New Kids on the Block, "NKOTB Announce the Mixtape Tour 2019," https://www.nkotb.com/news/title/nkotb-announce-the-mixtape-tour-2019 (Accessed July 13, 2020).

83. They were one of the earliest bands to characterize individuals in the band with labels like, the bad boy, the quiet one, and the young one. Rolling Stone, "New Kids on the Block - 1989," *Rolling Stone* (May 5, 2011), http:/www.rollingstone.com/music/lists/the-top-25-teen-idol-breakout-moments-20120511/new-kids-on-the-block-1989-19691231 (Accessed July 13, 2020).

84. New Kids on the Block, "NKOTB Announce the Mixtape Tour 2019."

85. "2019 Mixtape Tour," https://www.facebook.com/watch/?v=696979487368443. Facebook Post (Accessed July 13, 2020).

86. "Carson Daly," IMDB, https://www.imdb.com/name/nm0004856/ (Accessed July 13, 2020).

87. The Today Show, *New Kids on the Block Announce Special Guests on Tour* (website 2018), 4:58. Video. https://www.today.com/video/new-kids-on-the-block-announce-special-guests-on-tour-1339176515847 (Accessed July 13, 2020).

88. Ibid.

89. New Kids on the Block, "NKOTB Announce the Mixtape Tour 2019."

90. Mercari, "NKOTB VIP Bags" (Posted October 13, 2019). https://www.mercari.com/us/item/m90711549421/ (Accessed July 13, 2020).

91. David Esquivel and Jason Kempin (photographer), "Here's What's Happening on New Kids on the Block's Mixtape Tour!," *Setlist* (May 17, 2019), https://www.setlist.fm/news/05-19/heres-whats-happening-on-new-kids-on-the-blocks-mixtape-tour-7bd6b650 (Accessed July 13, 2020).

92. New Kids on the Block, *80s Baby* (New Kids on the Block website 2019), Music Video, Video and description. https://www.nkotb.com/news/title/stream-80s-baby-now (Accessed July 13, 2020).

93. Brianne Tracy, "New Kids on the Block Give Fans a Behind-the-Scenes Look at Their Tour in '80s Baby' Music Video," *People* (June 6, 2019), https://people.com/music/new-kids-on-the-block-80s-baby-music-video/ (Accessed July 13, 2020).

94. New Kids on the Block, *80s Baby*.

95. Esquivel and Kempin.

96. Discogs, "New Kids on the Block—Hangin' Tough," https://www.discogs.com/New-Kids-On-The-Block-Hangin-Tough/release/13372440 (Accessed July 13, 2020).

97. KEXP, "Kexp Announces Mixtape Week: August 26–30, 2019," KEXP, https://www.kexp.org/read/2019/7/10/kexp-announces-mixtape-week-august-26-30 -2019/ (Accessed July 14, 2020).

98. Ibid.

99. Owen Murphy, interview by Jehnie Burns, January 17, 2020, audio.

100. Ibid.

101. KEXP, "Kexp Announces Mixtape Week: August 26–30, 2019."

102. The listenership of KEXP, while it averages around 35–40 years old, crosses generations and geographic region.

103. Murphy.

104. KEXP, "Get Ready to Hit Play August 26th–30th," https://www.kexp.org/ mixtape/ (Accessed July 14, 2020).

105. Murphy.

106. Athena Sears. KEXP, "Get Ready to Hit Play August 26th–30th."

107. Erin Waters. KEXP, "Get Ready to Hit Play August 26th–30th."

108. Stacy McCauslin. KEXP, "Get Ready to Hit Play August 26th–30th."

109. Jamie Alls. KEXP, "Get Ready to Hit Play August 26th–30th."

110. Dusty Henry to Mixtape Week, August 30, 2019, https://www.kexp.org/read /2019/8/30/liner-notes-endless-playlists-learning-love-deeper-and-stepping-outside -yourself-through-mixes/ (Accessed July 14, 2020).

111. Ibid.

112. Ibid.

113. Martin Douglas ibid., August 27, 2019. https://www.kexp.org/read/2019/8/27 /scenes-things-you-missed-mixtape-my-dead-friend/ (Accessed July 14, 2020).

114. Cyrus Despres ibid., August 28, 2019. https://www.kexp.org/read/2019/8/28 /mixtape-week-manchester-neverending/ (Accessed July 14, 2020).

115. Pittsburgh Playhouse, "Pump up the Volume: A New Rock Musical," Point Park University, http://www.pittsburghplayhouse.com/current-season/conservatory -theatre-company/pump-up-the-volume (Accessed May 11, 2020).

116. The production of the musical was cancelled because of the COVID-19 outbreak. Students had begun rehearsal and the University had begun marketing the show, but the final production never ran. BWW News Desk, "Pump up the Volume: A New Rock Musical to Have World Premiere at Point Park University's Pittsburgh Playhouse," *Broadway World* (2020), https://www.broadwayworld.com/pittsburgh /article/PUMP-UP-THE-VOLUME-A-NEW-ROCK-MUSICAL-to-Have-World -Premiere-at-Point-Park-Universitys-Pittsburgh-Playhouse-20200225 (Accessed May 11, 2020).

117. Steve Lowry, interview by Jehnie Burns, May 11, 2020, email.

118. Ibid.

119. Cam Lindsay, "Listening Hard: 25 Years of 'Pump up the Volume,'" *Vice* (August 24, 2015), https://www.vice.com/en_us/article/rmj9av/listening-hard-25- years-of-pump-up-the-volume (Accessed May 11, 2020).

120. Home Line Entertainment, *Pump up the Volume Trailer* (YouTube1990). https://youtu.be/xLDehtTqyig (Accessed May 11, 2020).

121. Lowry.

Conclusion

In 2019 Nick Hornby's *High Fidelity* got a reboot. The novel-turned-film became a television series. The co-writers of the new series gender-flipped the main character: Rob became Robyn, played by Zoë Kravitz. The executive music producer for the series, Questlove, helped to ensure the new series mixed the best combination of independent artists and old favorites. Da'Vine Joy Randolph played Cherise, the sidekick played by Jack Black in the film. Adding a Black female alongside Kravitz offered much-needed diversity to the show. In the new series, Rob has similar musical rules to the original Rob about how one makes a good compilation. However, there are no cassettes. There are playlists and Spotify and Instagram; the current-Rob's rule is she "won't settle for a playlist programmed by an algorithm."[1] As television critics reviewed the series, they played to the hype of a mixtape in their language. But their take on whether the mixtape remains relevant varies. A culture blog describes how writers "punch-up references, stretching the old mixtape idea to connect with a Spotify culture where 'bummer dude' playlists and jokes about Ariel Pink and Sufjan Steven take-up residence."[2] In this perspective, the mixtape needs an update or it won't resonate with the intended audience. In a *GQ* article titled "The Sexy Mixtape Is Dead and High Fidelity Can't Bring It Back," Sable Yong critiques the traditional mixtape's replacement, the Spotify playlist.

> Making a mixtape has long been heralded as an all-time Grand Gesture, romanticized by movies like the original John Cusack *High Fidelity*. And back in the pre-Spotify days, making one required not just thoughtful selection, but actual work, too. Copying music to cassette tape had to be done in real-time, and mix CDs involved creating some sort of album art as accompaniment. [. . .] But texting a link to a drag-and-drop Spotify playlist (even one that follows all of

Rob's rules) is a gesture that reads more like self-promotional spam. A link is too ignorable, too abstract to hold any real meaning.[3]

In her perspective, music remains important in a relationship, but not as a playlist. Instead, it must occur naturally. Despite her derision of the playlist, she loved the adaptation of *High Fidelity* because the soundtrack *"slaps."*[4] *The Atlantic* meanwhile has a different take on how *High Fidelity* has updated itself for the new generation. When Spencer Hornhaber writes, "Elitist condescension about musical preferences isn't cool anymore, but maybe—die-hard fans fear—obsessing and connecting over music are no longer cool either,"[5] he suggests music elitism does not have the same power it did in the 1990s. The characters in the new series are democratized because of the ease and ubiquity of finding music in the digital era. Unsurprisingly, the series has its own Spotify playlist, and Kravitz shared a full list of every song on her Instagram.[6]

Does the new generation of *High Fidelity* and its critics argue for the death of the mixtape? No. they argue the mixtape, as the stories throughout this book have shown, has undergone a transformation. Mixtape can be a synonym for playlist as some novelists have used it. It can be an organizing principle, as seen in memoirs. It can pull together the culturally specific use by hip hop artists to embrace the continued sampling freestyle music, or it can be an idea, with no tangibility remaining. The mixtape has not disappeared, it has morphed.

By 2020 the Gen X mixtape had lost its original definition as an item specifically made on an analog technology. It had moved from a part of new technology to an outdated idea to a cool retro kitsch item. Despite its continued dictionary definition of a recording, this version has become three overlapping but distinct ideas: a representation of a bond with another individual, a collection of unconnected ideas put together in a novel way, or retronostalgic kitsch imagery of a simpler moment. Merging these ideas with the contemporary strength of the hip hop mixtape as a fundamental aspect of rapper and DJs albums creates a diverse understanding of the term mixtape currently. All four of these definitions emerge from the original idea of a mixtape as a personal, anti-consumer means of recording and sharing music in the 1980s and 1990s.

The fascination with the mixtape extends past the English-speaking world. Peter Manuel's book *Cassette Culture: Popular Music and Technology in North India* was among the first scholarly books to think about how cassettes transformed the music industry outside of the English-speaking world and welcomed new voices into the fray.[7] David Novak's *Japanoise: Music at the Edge of Circulation* has continued the discussion about cassette culture internationally.[8] The German novel *This Is Not a Love Song* uses the mixtape as a plot point in much the same way as some of the novels discussed in this book.[9] The worldwide expansion of hip hop has led to the exportation of the mixtape concept internationally. Datpiff has pages of Spanish-language mixtapes as well as Arabic-language mixtapes. The Spanish-language website lamezcla.com lists "mixtapes" as one of the key links on their site.[10] A keyword search on Discogs shows more than 2,000 entries for both France and Germany. Type any language in front of mixtape on Soundcloud and a list of tracks and playlists will be generated.[11] The K-Pop world has incorporated the hip hop style mixtape as a self-released album to create a buzz for an artist or group. Understanding how other cultures have exported and understood the mixtape and whether it dovetails with both the personal Gen X mixtape and the hip hop mixtape is work that remains to be done. The intersection of music and youth culture to share ideas is not unique to the English-speaking world. The attentiveness to the death of a 94-year-old Dutch engineer showcases a single piece of this international discussion.

In March 2021 Lou Ottens, inventor of the cassette tape, passed away at the age of 94. Ottens' name resonated with American cassette culture junkies because of his central role in the documentary *Cassette: A Documentary Mixtape*. Ottens' unsentimental, wry humor about his own role in changing music made him an antihero in the world of analog nostalgia. But the attention paid to a Dutch engineer underscored the importance of the cassette and the CD (which he also had a hand in pioneering) across wide cultural groups. Journalist venues ranging from *PC Gamer* and the "engineering enthusiast" Hackaday website to *The Guardian* and *NPR* wrote eulogies of the man who changed music technology. While the article titles designated Ottens as the inventor of the compact cassette, the majority mentioned the mixtape in their discussion. Hackaday acknowledged the ubiquity of the cassette in part because they were the format "for teenage mixtapes on a Walkman."[12] The podcast "A journal of Musical Things" began their obituary stating, "If you've ever made an old-school mixtape, you owe everything to [Ottens].[13] Music Tech declared "The popularity of cassettes and the low cost of blank tapes also gave rise to mixtape curation and home taping, which can be seen as early forms of playlist creation and file sharing, respectively."[14] Their explanatory description suggests a younger audience not aware of the analog technology at its apex. *Cosmos Magazine* meanwhile added more definition of the mixtape than other obituaries. They wrote,

This news will resonate with a great many people, even though they didn't know Lou Ottens. That's because there was a time, way back in the 1970s and '80s, when one of the most earnest symbols of friendship, affection, and love, even, came in the form of a cassette tape—commonly known as "the mix tape."

People who made mix tapes were the precursors of today's DJs. They'd flip through stacks of vinyl records looking for songs, assembling playlists in ways that conveyed specific emotions. Their enabling item was the cassette tape: the physical destination of their playlist.[15]

As the obituaries suggest, Lou Otten's importance was not because of his name or job title, it was because he created a product that connected people.

Mainstream media also covered Otten's death and his role in making music personal and portable. *The Guardian* clarified, "Dubbing between cassette decks unleashed the creation of mix tapes, by which people curated and exchanged their own playlists. And with the coming of cassette players in cars, listeners could bypass radio completely."[16] Even *The Wall Street Journal* obituary which reflected on how the cassette made music portable, stated, "It was crucial in spreading the popularity of hip hop music. And it spawned the musical love letters known as mixtapes, decades before the digital playlist."[17] In an NPR article Zack Taylor, director of *Cassette* stated, "Cassettes taught us how to use our voice, even when the message came from someone else's songs, compiled painstakingly on a mixtape. So next time you make that perfect playlist on Spotify or send a link to share a song, you can thank Lou Ottens."[18] NPR also emphasized, "True to their do-it-yourself roots, cassette mixtapes have long been a favorite of punk and rock fans" emphasizing the continuation of cassette tapes tied to fans using mixtapes to curate and share songs.[19] They also connected the cassette tape to the hip hop ethos in which rappers and producers made mixtapes to "showcase their ability to chop up other music and create something new."[20]

Ottens' death pulled together the cross section invested in the cassette tape. From gamers to musicians to scientists, the cassette has transformed cultural musical exchange. And the understanding of that cultural exchange remains tied to the ability to craft personally curated playlists on the cassette. The mixtape rarely exists as a newly dubbed cassette tape, gifted from one individual to another. Instead, it has become a metaphor, an icon, a site of cultural memory. It exists as a two-dimensional drawing or an idea in marketing copy with a forty-year lineage tied to music, technology, popular youth culture, and art.

Since I began thinking about mixtapes as an object of study, I have received mixtape items from friends and family. There is a shelf in the living room with many of the items I have discussed in this book. I have a small and growing collection of cassette tape vinyl stickers. I have a package of blank mixtape greeting cards and locally created notecards with mixtapes stamped on the front. There is a metal tin of mixtape breath mints sitting on a coffee table that has never been opened. When we are out, my kids will point out cassette tape merchandise. I have purchased t-shirts from bands I follow specifically because of the cassette tape plastered across the front. I considered purchasing the NPR "In the Mix Kid's Tee" with teal, fuchsia, and yellow cassette tapes emblazoned on the front. The copy describes it as "Your favorite little NPR fan is sure to love this [. . .] t-shirt, even if he or she has never made their own mixed tape."[21] I follow Cassette Store Day on Facebook out of curiosity. I still buy my music on CD because I want a physical copy of everything I listen to. I have purchased cassettes from independent musicians who have put out their albums only on that format. And yet, I do not consider myself an avid fan of cassette culture.

As a Gen X teenager, poodle skirts and peace symbols predominated our junior high imagery. Retro was cool. And retro remains cool. I see my students wearing memorabilia from every era from the 1960s through the early 2000s. As a history professor they love to tell me about Woodstock but are surprised by how little they know about their own American history. When I asked my History of Music students to create a mixtape for their final project, complete with cover art, they all jumped in excitedly. Every student crafted a playlist of ten–fifteen songs. Some pulled together thematic ideas ranging from colors to seasons to a story about the rise and fall of a relationship. But, although I gave every student the option, not a single one took me up on creating an analog mixtape on cassette. Every mixtape I graded came complete with a Spotify Playlist or a list of YouTube links. By 2021 the cassette tape remains technostalgic and irrelevant in the mainstream, despite its slow and continued growth in the past few years. But the mixtape remains relevant, valid, and engaging, as a product, an idea, a metaphor, and an image.

NOTES

1. Dan DeLuca, "The New 'High Fidelity' and the State of the Music Geek in the Digital Age," *The Philadelphia Inquirer*, February 21, 2020.

2. John-Paul Shiver, "Staying In? Binge on Mixtape Romance 'High Fidelity,'" *48hills* (March 13, 2020), https://48hills.org/2020/03/staying-in-binge-on-mixtape -romance-high-fidelity/ (Accessed July 10, 2020).

3. Sable Yong, "The Sexy Mixtape Is Dead and *High Fidelity* Can't Bring It Back," *GQ* (February 20, 2020), https://www.gq.com/story/beware-the-playlist (Accessed July 10, 2020).

4. Ibid.

5. Spencer Kornhaber, "The New Rules of Music Snobbery: Hulu's *High Fidelity* Reboot Captures the End of Elitist Condesension and the Rise of Fervent Eclecticism," *The Atlantic* (March 2020), https://www.theatlantic.com/magazine/arc hive/2020/03/high-fidelity-hulu/605539/ (Accessed July 10, 2020).

6. Erica Gonzales, "Here's Every Song on *High Fidelity*, So You Don't Have to Shazam Every Scene: You're Welcome," *Harper's Bazaar* (February 27, 2020), https

://www.harpersbazaar.com/culture/film-tv/a30845138/high-fidelity-songs/ (Accessed July 10, 2020).

7. Peter Manuel, *Cassette Culture: Popular Music and Technology in North India* (Chicago: The University of Chicago Press, 1993).

8. David Novak, *Japanoise: Music at the Edge of Circulation*, (Durham: Duke University Press, 2013).

9. Karen Duve, *This Is Not a Love Song* [Dies ist Kein Liebeslied], trans. Anthea Bell (London: Bloomsbury Publishing, 2005).

10. La Mezcla http://www.lamezcla.com/home/ (Accessed May 18, 2021)

11. I tried Polish, Greek, Cajun and Portuguese.

12. Jenny List, "Rip Lou Ottens, Developer of the Compact Cassette and More," *Hackaday* (March 12, 2021), https://hackaday.com/2021/03/12/rip-lou-ottens-dev eloper-of-the-compact-cassette-and-more/ (Accessed May 18, 2021).

13. Alan Cross, "Ongoing History Daily: Rip Lou Ottens," *A Journal of Musical Things* (April 9, 2021), https://www.ajournalofmusicalthings.com/ongoing-history -daily-rip-lou-ottens/ (Accessed May 18, 2021).

14. Daniel Seah, "Lou Ottens, Inventor of the Cassette Tape, Dies at 94," *Music Tech* (March 11, 2021), https://www.musictech.net/news/lou-ottens-cassette-tape -dies-at-94/ (Accessed May 18, 2021).

15. Jeff Glorfeld, "End of a Musical Era (II): Lou Ottens," *Cosmos: The Science of Everything* (March 21, 2021), https://cosmosmagazine.com/people/culture/end-of -a-musical-era-ii-lou-ottens/ (Accessed May 18, 2021).

16. Michael Carlson, "Lou Ottens Obituary: Engineer Whose Invention of the Audio Tape Cassette Brought Benefits to Both Listeners and Performers," *The Guardian* (March 17, 2021), https://www.theguardian.com/music/2021/mar/17/lou- ottens-obituary (Accessed May 18, 2021).

17. James R. Hagerty, "Lou Ottens Led Team That Invented the Cassette Tape," *The Wall Street Journal* (March 12, 2021), https://www.wsj.com/articles/lou-ottens- led-team-that-invented-the-cassette-tape-11615556881 (Accessed May 18, 2021).

18. Bill Chappell, "Lou Ottens, Inventor of the Cassette Tape, Has Died," *NPR* (March 10, 2021), https://www.npr.org/2021/03/10/975598869/lou-ottens-inventor -of-the-cassette-tape-has-died (Accessed May 18, 2021).

19. Ibid.

20. Ibid.

21. NPR, "In the Mix Kid's Tee," NPR, https://shop.npr.org/products/in-the-mix -kid-s-t-shirt (Accessed December 2020).

Appendix A

Discography

Appendix A Discography of songs that incorporate "mixtape" by year of release (This list is accurate as of Summer 2020)

Song Title	Band	Album	Label	Year	Genre
Professor Booty	Beastie Boys	Check Your Head	Capitol Records	1992	Rap/Punk
Flute Loop	Beastie Boys	Ill Communication	Capitol Records	1994	Rap/Punk
R3Wind	Better than Ezra	Friction, Baby	Elektra	1996	Rock
Kate	Ben Folds Five	Whatever and Ever Amen	550 Music	1997	Alternative
I'd Rather Go Blind (Than See You With another Guy)	Paul Kelly	Words and Music	Vanguard Records	1998	Folk
Singing in my Sleep	Semisonic	Feeling Strangely Fine	MCA Records	1998	Alt. Rock
1989	Clem Snide	Your Favorite Music	Sire	2000	Country
Make Me a Mixed Tape	The Promise Ring	Electric Pink	Jade Tree	2000	Emo/hardcore
Mix Tape	Brand New	Your + Favorite + Weapon	Triple Crown Records	2001	Emo/Grunge
Sophia on the Stereo	The Benjamins	The Art of Disappointment	Drive-Thru Records	2001	Pop Punk
My Stereo's a Liar	Donots	Amplify the Good Times	BMG	2002	Rock
Mix Tape	Avenue Q soundtrack	Avenue Q Soundtrack	RCA Victor	2003	Broadway
My First Stereo	FM Static	What Are You Waiting For?	Compound Recording	2003	Pop Punk
Mixtape	Jim's Big Ego	They're Everywhere	Self-released	2003	Rock
Headphones	Hedley	Wild Life	Universal Music Canada	2004	Pop punk
This Island	Le Tigre	This Island	Le Tigre Records	2004	Electroclash
Compass and Square	Crime in Stereo	Explosives and the Will To Use Them	Brightside Records	2004	Hardcore Punk
I've Got Fives	Madison	For the First Time In Years . . . I'm Leaving You	Fidelity Records	2004	Rock
Mixtape	Butch Walker	Letters	Epic	2004	Glam Metal
Mixtape = Love	Viva Voce	The Heat Can Melt Your Brain	Full Time Hobby	2004	Indie Rock

City Noise	Scarling	So Long, Scarecrow	Sympathy For the Record Industry	2005	Noise Pop
Lost In Stereo	All Time Low	Nothing Personal	Hopeless Records	2009	Pop punk
Phoenix	Brooke White	High Hopes & Heartbreak	June Baby Records	2009	Indie pop/folk pop
Mixtape	Jimmy Eat World	Invented	DGC Records	2010	Alternative
Very Busy People	The Limousines	Get Sharp	Dangerbird Records	2010	Indietronica
Mixtape	Tift Merritt	See You On The Moon	Fantasy	2010	Folk
Mixtape	Jamie Cullum	The Pursuit	Universal Music	2010	Pop/jazz
Let It Ride	Automatic Loveletter	Truth Or Dare	Sony Music	2010	Rock
Stereo Hearts	Gym Class Heroes ft Adam Levine	The Papercut Chronicles Part II	Fueled By Ramen	2011	Alternative
Kaleidoscope	blink-182	Neighborhoods	DGC Records	2011	Rock
Sheena is a T-Shirt Salesman	Future of the Left	The Plot Against Common Sense	Xtra Mile Recordings	2012	Alternative
Tomorrow's Money	My Chemical Romance	Number One	Reprise	2012	Alternative
This is How We Roll	Florida Georgia Line	Here's To the Good Times - This Is How We Roll	Big Machine Records	2012	Country
Beach	San Cisco	San Cisco	Island City Records	2012	Indie pop/Folk pop
Boyz on the Hood	Adam Fears	Golden Gravel Road	Landstar Entertainment	2013	Country
That's My Kind of Night	Luke Bryan	Crash My Party	Capitol Records	2013	Country
If You Left Him for Me	Cody Simpson	Surfer's Paradise	Atlantic	2013	Pop- Australian
Impossible Things	98 degrees	2.0	Entertainment One	2013	Pop
Tape	Thurston Moore	The Best Day	Matador	2014	Alt/Indie
Freestyle	Lady Antebellum	747	Capitol Records	2014	Country
Perfect Storm	Brad Paisley	Moonshine In The Trunk	Arista Nashville	2014	Country

(Continued)

Appendix A Discography by year of release (These lists are accurate as of Summer 2020) (Continued)

Song Title	Band	Album	Label	Year	Genre
That's What's Up	Florida Georgia Line	Anything Goes	Big Loud Mountain	2014	Country
She Looks So Perfect	5 Seconds of Summer	5 Seconds of Summer	Capitol Records	2014	Pop punk
Chuck Wicks	Whatcha Got Girl	Turning Point	Blaster Records	2015	Country
Cool With That	Brett Kissel	Pick Me Up	Warner Music Canada	2015	Country
Mixtape	Lee Brice	Mixtape: 'Til Summer's Gone	Curb Records	2015	Country
Perfect Life	Steven Wilson	Hand. Cannot. Erase.	Kscope	2015	Progressive Rock
That's All I Need	Dirty Heads	Dirty Heads	Five Seven Music	2016	Alternative
Can't Be Replaced	Dierks Bentley	Black	Capitol Records	2016	Country
One More Time	Craig David	Following My Intuition	Insanity Garage	2016	Electronic pop
Things in my Jeep	The Lonely Island	Popstar: Never Stop Never Stopping - Official Soundtrack	Republic Records	2016	Soundtrack/Rap
I Like You That Way	Canaan Smith	I Like You That Way	Hump Head Records	2017	Country
Throwback	James Barker Band	Game On	Universal Music Canada	2017	Canadian Country
Too Young to Know	Jessie James Decker	Gold	Epic	2017	Country pop
Arisen my Senses	Bjork	Utopia	One Little Indian	2017	Singer/Songwriter
September Song	JP Cooper	Raised Under Grey Skies	Island Records	2017	Singer/Songwriter
Sisyphus	Clara Charron	Chai Tea Lattes	Pop of Color Records	2017	Singer/Songwriter
Isabelle	Vancouver Sleep Clinic	Therapy Phase 02		2018	Alternative
Kulfigur	Art Brut	Wham! Bang! Pow! Let's Rock Out!	Alcopop! Records	2018	Alternative

Radioland	Ashley McBryde	Girl Going Nowhere	Warner Music Nashville	2018	Country
Summer Fever	Little Big Town	(Single)	Capitol Records Nashville	2018	Country
Mixtape	Jens (Lekman)	(Single)	Universal Music	2018	Pop
Trust Fund Baby	Why Don't We	8 Letters	Atlantic	2018	Pop
Coffee and Cigarettes	The Night Game	The Night Game	Universal Music Group	2018	Rock
The Silence	Halestorm	Vicious	Atlantic	2018	Rock
You And I	Barns Courtney	404	Virgin EMI Records	2019	Alternative
Homemade	Jake Owen	Greetings From ...Jake	Big Loud Records	2019	Country
80s Baby	New Kids on the Block	Hangin' Tough (30th Anniversary)	Columbia	2019	Boy Band
UR Mixtape	Metronomy	Metronomy Forever	Because Music	2019	Electronic pop

Appendix B

Podcasts

Appendix B Podcasts that incorporate "mixtape" by year of release

Name of Podcast	Creator	Created in
Mixtapes	Loop	2005
Mixtape Sessions Master Class	DJ Adam Cruz	2010
Running Mixtapes by TO3Y	TO3Y	2012
Love. Play. House. Mixtapes	Love. Play. House.	2012
The Undacover Mixtapes	DJ Undacover	2014
Eric's VG Mixtape	Eric Mahler	2015
Mixtape Marketing Podcast	The Corporatethief Beats	2015
Mixtape Radio Show	Luca Guerrieri	2015
Mixtapes and Mixology	90.9 The Bridge	2016
Motivation Mixtape	audioBoom	2016
Outertone - Mixtape	Outertone	2016
The Black Joy Mixtape	Amber J. Phillips and Jazmine Walker	2016
The BS Mixtapes	Jasmine & Ceej	2016
The Emil Jay Mixtape	Emil Jay	2016
The Guilty Mixtape	The Guilty Mixtape	2016
The Mixtape Podcast	Fordy and Bolts	2016
CiTR—Mixtapes with Mc and Mac	CiTR & Discorder Magazine	2016
Comedian's Mixtape	Marc Williams	2017
Cross Fire Mixtape	Cross Fire Mixtape	2017
Earth's Mixtape	Mike, Roby, and Hannah	2017
Fantasy Mixtape	Fantasy Mixtape	2017
Marketing Mixtape	Scott Davis	2017
Medicine ReMixed	Medicine ReMixed	2017
Midlife Mixtape	Nancy Davis Kho	2017
Mixtape Rewind!	Mark Jeacoma	2017
Movie Mixtape	CJRU 1280 AM	2017
The Future Is A Mixtape	The Future Is A Mixtape	2017
The Nostalgia Mixtape	Tai and Christina	2017

(Continued)

Appendix B Podcasts (*Continued*)

Name of Podcast	Creator	Created in
This Broken Mixtape	Justin Lee and Jeff Woo	2017
This is Your Mixtape	Michael @ Megaphonic.fm	2017
Uncle Eddy's Mixtapes	The Farsighted Network	2017
TechCrunch Mixtape	Tech Crunch	2017
Mix Tape with a Chainsaw	Storyteller Matt	2017
Modern Mixtapes	Jackie and Tiffany	2017
_dj edge mixtapes	Rudy Valadez IV	2018
Cemetery Mixtape	Cemetery Mixtape	2018
Diary of a Mixtape DJ	DJ Rell	2018
Electro Mixtape	Huge Carter	2018
Jimmy & Dave's Mixtape Podcast	Dave Donahue, Jimmy Good	2018
KR Mixtapes	KR Mixtapes	2018
Maybach Mixtapes	DJ Maybach	2018
Millennial Mixtapes	Carl Nahigian & Mark Sarris	2018
Minimalist Mixtape	Joy Springer and Michael Springer	2018
Mixtape Mixtape! Podcast Podcast!	Julia R	2018
MixTape	Project Six19	2018
Mixtape Ambassadors	Jeff & Leo	2018
New Chat Mixtapes	DJ Pete Bodega	2018
Nostalgia Mixtape	Sama'an Ashrawi	2018
The Mixtapes Podcast	Brian Horace	2018
The Side Hustle Show: The Blogging Mixtape	Nick Loper	2018
The Side Hustle Show: The Freelancing Mixtape	Nick Loper	2018
The Village Mixtape	Well 'n Green	2018
Mixtape Assembly	Hartley Lloyd Pack	2018
BBC Music Introducing Mixtape	BBC Radio	2018
Mix Tape Mafia	Bean Bag Studios	2018
I Made You a Mixtape	Waking the Kraken	2019
Indie Mixtape	Uppercut	2019
Learn/Perform Mixtape	Laura Pasquini	2019
Lectionary Mixtape	Danierl Eisenberg	2019
Love Jawns: A Mixtape	Various	2019
Max Mixtapes	Max M	2019
Mixtape Memories	Matt Heart Spade & Jinners	2019
Mixtape Yearbook	Mixtape Yearbook	2019
The KayFay Mixtape	Kristen Farrah	2019
The Mixtape Marriage	Camille Lancaster	2019
The Thoughtfulness Mixtape	Doc & Company	2019
The Vancouver Mixtape	The Vancouver Mixtape	2019
Teenage Mixtape with Joel Dommett and Steve Dunne	Spirit	2019
Mixtapes	Bon Entendeur	2019

(*Continued*)

Appendix B Podcasts (*Continued*)

Name of Podcast	Creator	Created in
Mixtape	LO 41 Mixtape small group	2019
The New LoFi Mixtape	The New LoFi	2019
Mixtapes and Rollerblades	Erica Tourville	2019
Mistakes & Mixtapes	adrienne & orono	2019
Mixtapes by Marcelo C. Baez	Marcelo Baez	2020
The Meditation Mixtapes	Case Kenny	2020
FMB Mixtape Series—Feel My Bicep	Bicep	2020

Podcasts were available through either Google Play, Google LLC, 2020. https://play.google.com or Pocket Casts V.7.11.0 John W. Gibbons CEO, 2020. pocketcasts.com.

Appendix C

Kindle Books

Appendix C Kindle Books that incorporate "mixtape" by year of release

Title	Author	Year of Publication
Tiny Mix Tapes of the Soul: Four years of articles, essays, and confessions	Ken Napzok	2012
The Mixtape: An Urban Love Story	Paula M. Stinson	2013
Road Trip Mixtapes: Vegas, Red Bull, and Faith on a Detour	J. Churchill Morris	2013
The Family Mix: Essays on Family Life from Midlife Mixtape	Nancy Davis Kho	2013
Mix Tapes and Stuff	J. J. Lair	2014
The Mixtape: Side A	N'Jedi T'Challa	2015
The Devil's Mixtape	Mary Borsellino	2015
Mixtape Manifesto: A Pop Culture Confessional	SW Hammond	2016
Sunglasses, Mixtapes & Ministry: The Fly Chicks Go-To for Growing in Faith	Charisma Adams	2016
no crown, no title: a mixtape of tho(ugh)ts	Carla Aaron-Lopez	2016
The Mixtape (Special Edition)	Kenya Moss-Dyne	2017
The Startup Mixtape: The Guide to Building and Launching a High-Growth Tech Startup	Elliot Adams	2017
Mixtape: The Book	Ashton Lee	2017
Mixtape: A Collection of One-Act Plays	Adam Gaines	2017
My life as a mixtape (my life as an album Book 4)	LJ Evans	2018
Love Songs on a Mix Tape	Emeka Barclay	2018
TL;DR: A Redditwriters Mixtape Vol. 1	Joe Butler	2018
Remixed: The Poetic Mixtape	Kiara Benejan-Curry	2018
Made Marian Mixtape: A Made Marian Collection	Lucy Lennox	2019

(Continued)

Appendix C Kindle Books (*Continued*)

Title	Author	Year of Publication
Full Moon Mixtape (Tales of Urban Horror Book 2)	AJ Harper	2019
Holiday Mix Tape: A Modern Persuasion	Beau North & Brooke West	2019
Mixtape: How to Stop listening to the Recordings of Your Past	Kate Garnes	2019
You're Doing It Wrong: A Mixtape Memoir	Josh Gunderson	2019
Punk Charming: A Mixtape of Travel, Love and 80s Pop Culture	Laura Quinn	2019
Mixtape: A Bipolar Anthology: poems written before, during, and after some gnarly psychosis	Anthony Vizcarrondo	2020
Kitty's Mix-Tape	Carrie Vaughn	2020
The Mixtape to My Life	Jake Martinez	2020
The love deluxe mixtape	Alexandria House	2020
The Godchild 2: The Mixtape Years	Jymi Cliché	2020

These books appeared in searches of the Amazon Kindle Store Database in the summer of 2020. Kindle Store Amazon, "'Mixtape' Search,'" https://smile.amazon.com/s?k=mixtape&i=digital-text&ref=nb_sb_noss.

Bibliography

Adgate, Brad. "Podcasting Is Going Mainstream." *Forbes* (November 18, 2019). https://www.forbes.com/sites/bradadgate/2019/11/18/podcasting-is-going-main stream/#bbf1a9a1699d.

Adorno, Theodor W. *Introduction to the Sociology of Music*. Translated by E. B. Ashton. New York: The Seabury Press, 1976.

Almeida, Walyce. "Community Scholar's Mixtape Museum Is an Ode to Hip-Hop." *Columbia News* (November 22, 2019). https://news.columbia.edu/news/hip-hop-m usic-mixtape-museum-community-scholars.

Alonzo, Cristela. "A Mixtape Memoir: Cristela Alonzo and the Songs That Shaped Her Life." Interview by Kristen Carbrera. *KUT: Austin's NPR Station* (October 9, 2019).

Alonzo, Cristela. "Cristela Alonzo." http://cristelaalonzo.com/.

Alonzo, Cristela. *Music to My Years: A Mixtape Memoir of Growing up and Standing Up*. New York: Atria Books, 2019.

Amazon, Kindle Store. ""Mixtape" Search." https://smile.amazon.com/s?k=mixtape &i=digital-text&ref=nb_sb_noss.

Amoebite. "Vinyl Princess: Interview with Author Yvonne Prinz" (February 13, 2010). https://www.amoeba.com/blog/2010/02/amoeba-music/vinyl-princess-i nterview-with-author-yvonne-prinz.html.

Anderson, Ben. "Recorded Music and Practices of Remembering." *Social & Cultural Geography* 5, no. 1 (2004): 3–20.

Andreotti, Alessia. "Technostalgia for the Cassette Tape." *Next Nature* (July 19, 2013). https://nextnature.net/2013/07/technostalgia-for-the-cassette-tape.

Appadurai, Arjun, ed. *The Social Life of Things: Commodities in Cultural Perspective*, Cambridge Studies in Social and Cultural Anthropology. Cambridge: Cambridge University Press, 1986.

Apple Music. "St. Vincent's Mixtape Delivery Service." https://music.apple.com/us/ curator/st-vincents-mixtape-delivery-service/1002618148.

Arditi, David M. *"Freedom, Music, and the RIAA: How the Recording Industry Association of America Shapes Culture by De-Politicizing Music."* Blacksburg: Virginia Polytechnic Institute and State University, 2007.

Ashurst, Sam. "Guardians of the Galaxy: James Gunn's Trailer Breakdown." *Total Film* (February 19, 2014). http://www.totalfilm.com/features/guardians-of-the-gala xy-james-gunn-s-trailer-breakdown/star-lord-s-walkman.

Baker, Jenny. "A Father's Day Gift Guide: Local Gift Ideas to Help You Think Outside the World's Best Dad Coffee Mug." *Winchester Star*, June 8, 2018.

Barnett, Courtney. "Guest DJ Week: Courtney Barnett." Interview by Bob Boilen. All Songs Considered (August 17, 2017).

Basler, Moritz. "'New Stands of Beauty and Style and Taste'. Expanding the Concept of Camp." In *Quote, Double Quote: Aesthetics between High and Popular Culture*, edited by Paul Ferstle and Keyvan Sarkhosh. New York: Rodopi, 2014. https://eb ookcentral.proquest.com/lib/pointpark-ebooks/detail.action?docID=1686923.

Beauchemin, Molly. "St. Vincent Will Make You a Mixtape." *Pitchfork* (June 12, 2015). https://pitchfork.com/news/59936-st-vincent-will-make-you-a-mixtape/.

Bezner, Elyssa. "Target Deals New Verse to KC-Born Mixtape Card Game; Players Could Pick Founder's Next Tune." *Startland News*, January 2, 2019.

Bijsterveld, Karin, and José van Dijck, eds. *Sound Souvenirs: Audio Technologies, Memory and Cultural Practices*. Amersterdam: Amsterdam University Press, 2009.

Billboard. "Year-End Charts: Cast Albums." https://www.billboard.com/charts/year -end/2006/cast-albums.

Bir, Sara. "Mix Emotions: The Mix Tap, Cultural Touchstone of the Analogue Generation." Metro Publishing Inc. (June 22, 2005). http://www.metroactive.com/ papers/sonoma/06.22.05/mixtapes-0525.html.

Bitner, Jason, ed. *Cassette from My Ex: Stories and Soundtracks of Lost Loves*. New York: St. Martin's Press, 2009.

Blakemore, Erin. "A Brief History of Young Adult Fiction." *JSTOR Daily* (April 10, 2015). https://daily.jstor.org/history-of-young-adult-fiction/.

Bohlman, Andrea F., and Peter McMurray. "Tape: Or, Rewinding the Phonographic Regime." *Twentieth-Century Music* 14, no. 1 (2017): 3–24.

Book Trail, The. "Travel across the World with a Mix Tape and Jane Sanderson." https://www.thebooktrail.com/authorsonlocation/travel-with-a-mix-tape-and-jane -sanderson/.

Botstein, Leon. "Memory and Nostalgia as Music-Historical Categories." *The Musical Quarterly* 84, no. 4 (Winter, 2000): 531–36.

Bottomley, Andrew J. "'Home Taping Is Killing Music': The Recording Industries' 1980s Anti-Home Taping Campaigns and Struggles over Production, Labor and Creativity." *Creative Industries Journal* 8, no. 2 (2015): 123–45. doi:http://dx.doi. org/10.1080/17510694.2015.1090223.

Boucher, Timothy S. "Make Spotify Mix Tapes." *Medium* (September 2, 2017). https://medium.com/@timboucher/make-spotify-mix-tapes-15f473ef584b.

Box, Matthew. "Through the Magnavox Looking Glass: We Enter the Weird World of 'Limbo' with Writer Dan Watters." *Broken Frontier* (April 15, 2016). http:

//www.brokenfrontier.com/limbo-image-comics-dan-watters-caspar-wijngaard-in terview-review/.

Boym, Svetlana. *The Future of Nostalgia*. New York: Basic Books, 2008. eBook.

Bradley, Adam, and Andrew DuBois, eds. *The Anthology of Rap*. New Haven: Yale University Press, 2010.

Brainmonk. "Elbow Cassette Player." news release, 2017. http:/elbow.co.nf/img/ELBOW_PRESS.pdf.

Breaking Games. "Mixtape." https://breakinggames.com/collections/check-out-our-hottest-new-games/products/mixtape.

Brice, Lee. "Music." https://www.leebrice.com/#!/releases.

Bristow, Jennie. *Stop Mugging Grandma: The 'Generation Wars' and Why Boomer Blaming Won't Solve Anything*. New Haven: Yale University Press, 2019.

Brothers, Meagan. *Supergirl Mixtapes*. New York: Henry Holt and Company, 2012.

"Brucie B." Mixtapedia, http://www.mixtapedia.org/brucie-b.

Buckley, Sean. "We Destroyed a Collectible Doritos Bag to Get at Its Hidden Mp3 Player." *Engadget* (April 28, 2017). https://www.engadget.com/2017-04-28-we-d estroyed-a-collectible-doritos-mp3-player.html.

Bull, Michael. "The Auditory Nostalgia of iPod Culture." In *Sound Souvenirs: Audio Technologies, Memory and Cultural Practices*, edited by Karin Bijsterveld and José van Dijck, 83–93. Amsterdam: Amsterdam University Press, 2009.

BWW News Desk. "Lamb's Players' Mixtape Extends into Fourth Year, Now Thru 2/17." *Broadway World* (July 10, 2020). https://www.broadwayworld.com/san -diego/article/Lambs-Players-MIXTAPE-to-Extend-Into-Fourth-Year-110-217-20130109.

BWW News Desk. "Pump up the Volume: A New Rock Musical to Have World Premiere at Point Park University's Pittsburgh Playhouse." *Broadway World* (February 25, 2020). https://www.broadwayworld.com/pittsburgh/article/PUMP-U P-THE-VOLUME-A-NEW-ROCK-MUSICAL-to-Have-World-Premiere-at-Point -Park-Universitys-Pittsburgh-Playhouse-20200225.

Byrne, David. *How Music Works*. 1st ed. San Francisco: McSweeney's, 2012.

Campbell, Mikey. "Apple Invention Looks to Revive the Mixtape, with a Digital Twist." *Apple Insider* (August 6, 2015). https://appleinsider.com/articles/15/08/06 /apple-invention-looks-to-revive-the-mixtape-with-a-digital-twist?curator=Music REDEF.

Cargill, Angus, ed. *Hang the DJ: An Alternative Book of Music Lists*. New York: Soft Skull Press, 2009.

Carlson, Michael. "Lou Ottens Obituary: Engineer Whose Invention of the Audio Tape Cassette Brought Benefits to Both Listeners and Performers." *The Guardian* (March 17, 2021). https://www.theguardian.com/music/2021/mar/17/lou-ottens -obituary.

Carroll, Rachel. "'[S]He Loved Him Madly': Music, Mixtapes and Gendered Authorship in Alan Warner's Morvern Callar." Chap. 11 In *Litpop: Writing and Popular Music*, edited by Rachel Carroll, Adam Hansen, Stan Hawkins and Lori Burns, 187–99. New York: Taylor & Francis, 2016.

Cateforis, Theo. *Are We Not New Wave? Modern Pop at the Turn of the 1980s*. Ann Arbor: University of Michigan Press, 2011.

Caulfield, Keith. "Blue Swede's 'Hooked on a Feelin' Sales Soar Thanks to "Guardians of the Galaxy' Trailer." *Billboard* (February 2, 2014). https://www .billboard.com/articles/news/5915510/blue-swedes-hooked-on-a-feeling-sales-soar -thanks-to-guardians-of-the-galaxy.

Caulfield, Keith. "Exclusive: "Guardians' Soundtrack to Be Released on Cassette Tape." *Billboard* (October 20, 2014). https://www.billboard.com/articles/news/ 6289124/guardians-of-the-galaxy-soundtrack-cassette-tape.

Chang, Jeff. *Can't Stop Won't Stop: A History of the Hip-Hop Generation*. New York: Picador, 2005.

Chang, Justin. "Review: Edgar Wright's Exuberant 'Baby Driver' Is an Automotive Musical Like No Other." *Los Angeles Times*, June 27, 2017.

Chappell, Bill. "Lou Ottens, Inventor of the Cassette Tape, Has Died." *NPR* (March 10, 2021). https://www.npr.org/2021/03/10/975598869/lou-ottens-inventor-of-the -cassette-tape-has-died.

Chbosky, Stephen. *Perks of Being a Wallflower*. New York: Gallery Books, 1999.

Clark, Todd E. "Portfolio." *Big Juicy Creative* (2021). https://bigjuicycreative.com/ portfolio.

Cohen, Arianne. "Your Last-Minute Gift Plan: Make a Free Retromixtape Thanks to Apple." *Fast Company* (December 12, 2019). https://www.fastcompany.com /90446645/your-last-minute-gift-plan-make-a-free-retro-mixtape-thanks-to-apple.

Confino, Alon. "Collective Memory and Cultural History: Problems of Method." *The American Historical Review* 102, no. 5 (1997): 1386–403.

Conway, Brian. "Mixtape and Black Forge Coffee Offer Music, Community Space and More." *Next Pittsburgh* (January 19, 2016). https://nextpittsburgh.com/city-des ign/more-than-just-music-at-pittsburghs-newest-mixed-use-venues/.

Coontz, Stephanie. *The Way We Never Were: American Families and the Nostalgia Trap*. New York: Basic Books, 1993.

Corbett, John. *Vinyl Freak: Love Letters to a Dying Medium*. North Carolina: Duke University Press, 2017.

Craig, Steve, ed. *Men, Masculinity and the Media*. California: Sage Publications, 1992.

Cross, Alan. "Ongoing History Daily: Rip Lou Ottens." *A Journal of Musical Things* (April 9, 2021). https://www.ajournalofmusicalthings.com/ongoing-history-daily -rip-lou-ottens/.

Cudmore, Libby. "Debut Mystery from the 'Queen of the Mix CD'." Interview by Cat Acree. Book Page (February 2, 2016).

Cudmore, Libby. *The Big Rewind*. New York: William Morrow Paperbacks, 2016.

Cummings, Alex Sayf. *Democracy of Sound: Music Piracy and the Remaking of American Copyright in the Twentieth Century*. New York: Oxford University Press, 2013.

Cummings, Judy Dodge. *Hip-Hop Culture*. Minneapolis: Abdo Publishing, 2017. http://search.ebscohost.com/login.aspx?direct=true&AuthType=sso&db=nlebk &AN=1491310&site=eds-live&scope=site.

D, Mr. Davey. Breakdown FM. Podcast audio. Interview with Justo Faison: The History of Mixtapes. Accessed May 12, 2021, 2005. https://soundcloud.com/mr daveyd/breakdown-fm-intv-w-justo.

Dean, David. "Bree Housley: 'We Hope You Like This Song'." *Serial Optimist* (December 27, 2012). https://www.serialoptimist.com/conversations/bree-housley -we-hope-you-like-this-song-12104.html.

Delaney, Cassie Tweten. "7 Mixtape Mixed Drinks: A Week of Cool Cocktails & Toe-Tappin' Tunes." The Uncommon Life: Uncommon Goods 2013.

Dellinger, AJ. "The Art of the Mixtape Gets a Digital Makeover." *Daily Dot* (March 1, 2020). https://www.dailydot.com/debug/sharetapes-mixtapes/.

Deloria, Philip J., and Alexander I. Olson. *American Studies: A User's Guide.* Oakland: University of California Press, 2017.

DeLuca, Dan. "The New 'High Fidelity' and the State of the Music Geek in the Digital Age." *The Philadelphia Inquirer*, February 21, 2020.

Demers, Joanna. "Cassette Tape Revival as Creative Anachronism." *Twentieth-Century Music* 14, no. 1 (February 2017): 109–17.

Denton, Jack. "A Generation of Hip-Hop Was Given Way for Free. Can It Be Archived?" *Pacific Standard.* https://psmag.com/social-justice/a-generation-of-hip -hop-was-given-away-for-free-can-it-be-archived.

Despres, Cyrus. "Mixtape Week: Manchester Neverending." *Mixtape Week* August 28, 2019. https://www.kexp.org/read/2019/8/28/mixtape-week-manchester-never ending/.

Discogs. "New Kids on the Block—Hangin' Tough." https://www.discogs.com/New -Kids-On-The-Block-Hangin-Tough/release/13372440.

Discogs. "The Cassette Comeback, by the Numbers." *Discogs.* https://blog.discogs .com/en/the-cassette-comeback-by-the-numbers/.

Dlugacz, Adam. "Brand New: Your Favorite Weapon." *Pop Matters* (July 7, 2003). https://www.popmatters.com/brandnew-yourfavorite-2495835944.html.

Dodgson, Lindsay. "We Stop Discovering New Music at Age 30, a New Survey Suggests - Here Are the Scientific Reasons Why This Could Be." *Business Insider* (June 7, 2018). https://www.businessinsider.com/why-we-stop-discovering-new-music-around-age-30-2018-6.

Dogwood Coffee Co. "Mixtape Subscription." *Dogwood Coffee Co.* https://www.dog woodcoffee.com/products/copy-of-bear-hug-espresso-subscription.

Dogwood Coffee Co. "Mixtape Vol 12: Colombia & Guatemala." *Dogwood Coffee Co.* www.dogwoodcoffee.com/products/mixtape.

Dogwood Coffee Co. "Mixtape Vol 39: Colombia & Brazil." *Dogwood Coffee Co.* https://www.dogwoodcoffee.com/products/mixtape-vol-39.

Dormon, Bob. "Happy 50th Birthday, Compact Cassette: How It Stuck a Chord for Millions." *The Register* (August 30, 2013). https://www.theregister.co.uk/2013/08 /30/50_years_of_the_compact_cassette/.

Douglas, Martin. "Scenes from Things You Missed: A Mixtape for My Dead Friend." In *Mixtape Week.* KEXP, 2019. https://www.kexp.org/read/2019/8/27/scenes-th ings-you-missed-mixtape-my-dead-friend/.

Dowd, Timothy. "The Sociology of Music." In *21st Century Sociology: A Reference Handbook* edited by Clifton D. Bryant and Dennis L. Peck, 249–60. Thousand Oaks, CA: Sage, 2007.

Drew, Rob. "Mixed Blessings: The Commercial Mix and the Future of Music Aggregation." *Popular Music & Society* 28, no. 4 (2005): 533–51.

du Gay, Paul, Stuart Hall, Linda Janes, Hugh Mackay, and Keith Negus. *Doing Cultural Studies: The Story of the Sony Walkman*. London: Sage Publications Ltd, 2003.

Duve, Karen. *This Is Not a Love Song* [*Dies ist Kein Liebeslied*]. Translated by Anthea Bell. London: Bloomsbury Publishing, 2005.

Dyson, Michael Eric. *Know What I Mean?: Reflections on Hip-Hop*. New York: Basic Books, 2007. http://ebookcentral.proquest.com/lib/pointpark-ebooks/detail .action?docID=530375.

Edwards, Tim. *Cultures of Masculinity*. New York: Routledge, 2006. http://ebookcen tral.proquest.com/lib/pointpark-ebooks/detail.action?docID=201200.

Elder, Robert K. "Robert K. Elder: Digital Executive & Author." https://robelder .com/bio/.

Elder, Robert K. *The Mixtape of My Life: A Do-It-Yourself Music Memoir*. New York: Running Press Adult, 2018.

Eley, Craig. "Technostalgia and the Resurgence of Cassette Culture." Chap. 3 In *The Politics of Post-9/11 Music: Sound, Trauma, and the Music Industry in the Time of Terror*, edited by Joseph P. Fisher and Brian Flota. Ashgate Popular and Folk Music, 43–54. New York: Routledge, 2011.

Ellis, Bret Easton. *Less Than Zero*. United States: Vintage Contemporaries, 2010.

England, Lucy. "Apple Has Filed a Patent That Could Completely Reinvent the Idea of a Mixtape." *Business Insider* (August 6, 2015). https://www.businessinsider.co m.au/apple-files-patent-for-digital-mixtapes-2015-8.

Epstein, Eve, and Lenora Epstein. *X vs. Y: A Culture War, a Love Story*. New York: Abrams Books, 2014.

Esquivel, David, and Jason Kempin (photographer). "Here's What's Happening on New Kids on the Block's Mixtape Tour!" *Setlist* (May 17, 2019). https://www.set list.fm/news/05-19/heres-whats-happening-on-new-kids-on-the-blocks-mixtape-tour-7bd6b650.

"Exploring Mixtape and Hip Hop." *Discogs*, https://www.discogs.com/search/?q=m ixtape&type=all&page=2&genre_exact=Hip+Hop.

Factory Obscura. "Mix-Tape." (2021) https://www.factoryobscura.com/.

Factory Obscura Shop. "All Products" (2021) https://shop.factoryobscura.com/col lections/all-products.

Farsighted Blog, The. in *Uncle Eddy's Mixtapes*. 2020. https://farsightedblog.com/.

Feliciano, Stevie. "The Riot Grrrl Movement." New York Public Library, 2013. https ://www.nypl.org/blog/2013/06/19/riot-grrrl-movement.

"The 50 Best Rap Mixtapes of the Millennium: From Lil Wayne to Max B to Nicki Minaj, a Look at the Best Free Downloads, Tapes, and CD-Rs Released since 2000." *Pitchfork* (June 29, 2016). https://pitchfork.com/features/lists-and-guides /9908-the-50-best-rap-mixtapes-of-the-millennium/.

Frey, Michael. "Semisonic 'Singing in My Sleep'." *All Music Review*. https://www .allmusic.com/album/singing-in-my-sleep-us-mw0000048356.

Friedman, Skinny. "The Real Difference between a Mixtape and an Album." *Vice* (December 10, 2013). https://www.vice.com/en_ca/article/rmx446/the-real-diff erence-between-a-mixtape-and-an-album.

Frith, Simon. *Performing Rites: On the Value of Popular Music*. Massachusetts: Harvard University Press, 1996.

Frith, Simon. *Sound Effects: Youth, Leisure and the Politics of Rock 'N' Roll*. New York: Pantheon Books, 1981.

Fritzsche, Peter. "Specters of History: On Nostalgia, Exile, and Modernity." *The American Historical Review* 106, no. 5 (December 2001): 1587–618.

Futterman, Erica. "Literature's John Hughes: Rainbow Rowell on Her Love Affair with Music and Writing." *Buzzfeed* (July 15, 2014). http://www.buzzfeed.com/e ricafutterman/music-and-writing-sitting-in-a-tree#.byvE9NXEE.

Gasser, Nolan. *Why You Like It: The Science & Culture of Musical Taste*. New York: Flatiron Books, 2019.

Genius. *The History of Sound Clash Culture*. YouTube, 2017. https://youtu.be/ aASQlbktGkc.

Gilman, Greg. "'Guardians of the Galaxy' Becomes First Soundtrack in History without New Songs to Land No. 1 Spot." *The Wrap* (August 13, 2014). https://www.the wrap.com/guardians-of-the-galaxy-soundtrack-soars-to-no-1-on-billboard-200/.

Glennon, Mike. "Mixtapes V. Playlists: Medium, Message, Materiality." In *Sounding Out*. 2018. https://soundstudiesblog.com/2018/06/25/mixtapes-v-playlists-medium -message-materiality/.

Glorfeld, Jeff. "End of a Musical Era (II): Lou Ottens." Cosmos: The Science of Everything (March 21, 2021). https://cosmosmagazine.com/people/culture/end-of -a-musical-era-ii-lou-ottens/.

Gonzales, Erica. "Here's Every Song on High Fidelity, So You Don't Have to Shazam Every Scene: You're Welcome." *Harper's Bazaar* (February 27, 2020). https://www.harpersbazaar.com/culture/film-tv/a30845138/high-fidelity-songs/.

Grainge, Paul. "Nostalgia and Style in Retro America: Moods, Modes, and Media Recycling." *Journal of American & Comparative Cultures* 23, no. 1 (March 22, 2004).

Greene, Andy. "New Kids on the Block—1989." *Rolling Stone* (May 5, 2011). http:/www.rollingstone.com/music/lists/the-top-25-teen-idol-breakout-moments -20120511/new-kids-on-the-block-1989-19691231.

Hagerty, James R. "Lou Ottens Led Team That Invented the Cassette Tape." *The Wall Street Journal* (March 12, 2021). https://www.wsj.com/articles/lou-ottens-led -team-that-invented-the-cassette-tape-11615556881.

Halliday, Ayun. "Watch Lin-Manuel Miranda Perform the Earliest Version of Hamilton at the White House, Six Years before the Play Hit the Broadway Stage (2009)." *Open Culture* (March 4, 2019). http://www.openculture.com/2019/03/ watch-lin-manuel-miranda-perform-the-earliest-version-of-hamilton-at-the-white -house.html.

Harmon, Joshua. *The Annotated Mixtape*. Ann Arbor: Dzane Books, 2014.

Harrison, Anthony Kwame. "'Cheaper Than a CD, Plus We Really Mean It': Bay Area Underground Hip Hop Tapes as Subcultural Artefacts." *Popular Music* 25, no. 2 (2006): 283–301. https://www.jstor.org/stable/3877563.

Harrison, Anthony Kwame. *Hip Hop Underground: The Integrity and Ethics of Racial Identification*. Philadelphia: Temple University Press, 2009.

Hartlaub, Peter. "The Case for Cassettes: Still Bumping in 2017." *San Francisco Chronicle*, July 28, 2017.

Hartley, Karla. "Cast and Creators Recall the Birth of 'Avenue Q'." (November 22, 2017). https://stageworkstheatre.org/cast-and-creators-recall-the-birth-of-avenue-q/.

Hastings, Nick. "Get Your '80s on with Mixxtape, the Portable Music Player That Works Like a Cassette." *Digital Trends* (Jun 15, 2017). https://www.digitaltrends.com/home-theater/mixxtape-music-player-bluetooth-cassette-tape/.

Hebert, James. "The '80s Live! And So Does 'Mixtape,' Returning to Lamb's Players Theatre Nearly a Decade after Its Debut." *The San Diego Union-Tribune* (June 11, 2019). https://www.sandiegouniontribune.com/entertainment/theater/story/2019-06-11/the-80s-live-and-so-does-mixtape-returning-to-lambs-players-theatre-nearly-a-decade-after-its-debut.

Henry, Dusty. "Liner Notes for Endless Playlists: Learning to Love Deeper and Stepping Outside Yourself through Mixes." In *Mixtape Week*. 2019. https://www.kexp.org/read/2019/8/30/liner-notes-endless-playlists-learning-love-deeper-and-stepping-outside-yourself-through-mixes/.

Henseler, Christine, ed. *Generation X Goes Global: Mapping a Youth Culture in Motion*. New York: Taylor & Francis, 2012.

Herfenberger, L. "A Very JSTOR Daily Mixtape." https://daily.jstor.org/a-very-jstor-daily-mixtape/.

Hernandez, Brandon. "The Stone Mixtape Ale Series." *Stone Brewing*, 2013. https://www.stonebrewing.com/blog/beer/2013/stone-mixtape-ale-series.

Hernandez, Ernio. "Fantasies Come True: Broadway's Avenue Q Cast Recording Released Oct. 7." *Playbill* (October 7, 2003). https://www.playbill.com/news/article/fantasies-come-true-broadways-avenue-q-cast-recording-released-oct.-7-115590.

Hernández, Olivia Jean. "Mixtapes 101." In *Pop Con 2020*. Virtual: Museum of Pop Culture, 2020.

Hiatt, Brian. "Inside the 'Guardians of the Galaxy Vol. 2' Soundtrack." *Rolling Stone* (April 19, 2017). https://www.rollingstone.com/music/music-features/inside-the-guardians-of-the-galaxy-vol-2-soundtrack-123648/.

Hodgkins, Taylor. "Sides One and Two: Rob Sheffield's Love Is a Mix Tape and Me." *Medium* (2019). https://medium.com/@taylor.m.hodgkins/sides-one-and-two-rob-sheffields-love-is-a-mix-tape-and-me-7409dedbae89.

Hogan, Marc. "This Is Not a Mixtape." *Pitchfork* (February 22, 2010). https://pitchfork.com/features/article/7764-this-is-not-a-mixtape/.

Holden, Stephen. "The Pop Life." *The New York Times*, 1989.

Holodak, Jim. *Personalized Mixtape Doormat*. Uncommon Goods, 2020.

Home Line Entertainment. *Pump up the Volume Trailer*. YouTube, 1990. https://youtu.be/XmIr29myw7Q.

Hornby, Nick. *High Fidelity*. New York: The Berkley Publishing Group, 1995.

Hornby, Nick. *Songbook*. New York: Riverhead Books, 2003. Essay Memoir.

Housley, Bree. *We Hope You Like This Song" an Overly Honest Story About Friendship, Death, and Mix Tapes*. Berkeley, CA: Perseus Books Group, 2012.

Hsu, W. F. Umi. "'The Mixtape Project' Assignment: Learning through Critical Making." http://beingwendyhsu.info/?p=742.

Hu, Ray. "Things That Look Like Other Things: Mixtape Table by Jeff Skierka." *Core 77* (May 25, 2012). https://www.core77.com/posts/22544/things-that-look -like-other-things-mixtape-table-by-jeff-skierka-22544.

Huyssen, Andreas. *Present Pasts: Urban Palimpsests and the Politics of Memory*. Cultural Memory in the Present. California: Stanford University Press, 2003.

Image Comics. "Limbo #1." *Image Comics*, https://imagecomics.com/comics/rele ases/limbo-1.

Image Comics. "Limbo TP." *Image Comics*, https://imagecomics.com/comics/rele ases/limbo-tp.

IMDB. "Carson Daly." *IMDB*, https://www.imdb.com/name/nm0004856/.

Jeremy. "Mixtape Pittsburgh Review—The Neighborhood Bar Garfield Needs." *Discover the Burgh*, https://www.discovertheburgh.com/mixtape/.

Johnson, Chelsey. "Chelsey Johnson." http://www.chelseyjohnson.com/stray-city.

Johnson, Chelsey. *Stray City*. New York: Custom House, 2018.

Johnson, Joel. "Mixtape—The Song & Scenario Card Game." *Kickstarter*, https:// www.kickstarter.com/projects/helpfundmixtape/mixtape-the-song-and-scenario-ca rd-game/description.

Johnson, Joel. *Mixtape, Kauffman 1 Million Cups*. 1 Million Cups May 27, 2015. Video. https://www.1millioncups.com/kansascity/presentations/mixtape-229

JSTOR Daily. "JSTOR: Where New Meets Its Scholarly Match." *Ithaka*, https://daily .jstor.org/.

Kawaida, Michael. "Mixtapes: A Brief History of Hip-Hop's Ever Evolving Tool." *Hot New Hip Hop* (February 25, 2020). https://www.hotnewhiphop.com/mixtapes -a-brief-history-of-hip-hops-ever-evolving-tool-news.103882.html.

Kaye, Ben. "Guardians of the Galaxy Vol. 2 Soundtrack Coming to Vinyl and Cassette." *Consequence of Sound* (June 6, 2017). https://consequenceofsound.net /2017/06/guardians-of-the-galaxy-vol-2-soundtrack-coming-to-vinyl-and-casse tte/.

Kaye, Ben. "St. Vincent Pays Tribute to Prince on Her Beats 1 Radio Show—Listen." *Consequence of Sound* (February 15, 2017). https://consequenceofsound.net/2017 /02/st-vincent-pays-tribute-to-prince-on-her-beats-1-radio-show-listen/.

Kernfeld, Barry. *Pop Song Piracy: Disobedient Music Distribution since 1929*. Chicago: University of Chicago Press, 2011. https://ebookcentral.proquest.com/lib /pointpark-ebooks/detail.action?docID=3038271.

KEXP. "Get Ready to Hit Play August 26th-30th." https://www.kexp.org/mixtape/.

KEXP. "KEXP Announces Mixtape Week: August 26–30, 2019." *KEXP*, https://ww w.kexp.org/read/2019/7/10/kexp-announces-mixtape-week-august-26-30-2019/.

Kho, Nancy Davis. "Midlife Mixtape." https://midlifemixtape.com/.

Kiah, Amythyst. "Amythyst Kiah." Interview by Cindy Howes. *Basic Folk*, no. 54 (January 23, 2020). audio.

King, Eric. "Everything We Know About 'the Hamilton Mixtape'." *Billboard* (August 12, 2016). https://www.billboard.com/articles/news/features/7469389/eve rything-we-know-about-hamilton-mixtape.

Kirkpatrick, Marion. "Why a '70s Mixtape Propels the Plot of 'Guardians of the Galaxy'." *Billboard* (August 1, 2014). https://www.billboard.com/articles/news/ 6204544/guardians-of-the-galaxy-soundtrack-james-gunn.

Klarin, Jeff. *Cassette Player Future Fossil*. Uncommon Goods, 2014.

Knisley, Lucy. *Something New*. New York: First Second, 2016. Graphic Novel.

Knopper, Steve. "How Spotify Playlists Create Hits." *Rolling Stone* (August 15, 2017). https://www.rollingstone.com/pro/news/how-spotify-playlists-create-hits-200277/.

Komurki, John Z., and Luca Bendandi. *Cassette Cultures: Past and Present of a Musical Icon*. English Edition 2019 Benteli ed.: Switzerland: Deutsche Nationalbibliothek; Braun Publishing AG, 2019.

Kornhaber, Spencer. "The New Rules of Music Snobbery: Hulu's High Fidelity Reboot Captures the End of Elitist Condescension and the Rise of Fervent Eclecticism." *The Atlantic* (March 2020). https://www.theatlantic.com/magazine/ archive/2020/03/high-fidelity-hulu/605539/.

Kot, Greg. *Ripped: How the Wired Generation Revolutionized Music*. New York: Simon & Schuster, Inc., 2009.

KPBS. *Journey Back into the 80s with "Mixtape."* San Diego, 2011. YouTube video. https://youtu.be/fLMVJ5G6JZc

Laing, Dave. "Record Sales in the 1980s." *Popular Music* 9, no. 2 (1990): 235–6. http://www.jstor.org/stable/853504.

Lakshmin, Deepa. "Retrojam's Playlists Will Make You Nostalgic for Your Play-Doh Eating Days." *MTV* (February 2, 2015). http://www.mtv.com/news/2066209 /retrojams-playlists/.

Larson, Selena. "Retrojam Makes a Mixtape of All the Songs You Listened to as a Kid." *Daily Dot* (March 1, 2020). https://www.dailydot.com/upstream/retrojam-so ng-flashback/.

Laughey, Dan. *Music and Youth Culture*. Edinburgh: Edinburgh University Press, 2006. www.jstor.org/stable/10.3366/j.ctt1r1zxm.

Lena, Jennifer C. *Banding Together: How Communities Create Genres in Popular Music*. New Jersey: Princeton University Press, 2012.

Leonard, Brendan. *The New American Road Trip Mixtape*. USA: Semi-Rad, 2013.

LeVota, Meghan. "KC-Made Card Game Mixtape Makes a 'Soundtrack for Your Life'." *Startland News* (August 26, 2016). https://www.startlandnews.com/2016/ 08/kc-made-card-game-makes-soundtrack-life/.

Lindsay, Cam. "Listening Hard: 25 Years of 'Pump up the Volume'." *Vice* (August 24, 2015). https://www.vice.com/en_us/article/rmj9av/listening-hard-25-years-of -pump-up-the-volume.

List, Jenny. "Rip Lou Ottens, Developer of the Compact Cassette and More." *Hackaday* (March 12, 2021). https://hackaday.com/2021/03/12/rip-lou-ottens-dev eloper-of-the-compact-cassette-and-more/.

Liszewski, Andrew. "The Mixtape Will Live Forever through This Retroriffic Coffee Table." *Gizmodo* (May 24, 2012). https://gizmodo.com/the-mixtape-will-live-for ever-through-this-retro-riffic-5913055.

Lopez, Robert, and Jeff Marx. "Mix Tape." In *Avenue Q Soundtrack*: Masterworks Broadway, 2003.

MacGabhann, Brian. "Marketing Youth Culture." *Studies: An Irish Quarterly Review* 94, no. 374 (Summer, 2005 2005): 133–39.

Maira, Sunaina. "Youth." Chap. 64 In *Keywords for American Cultural Studies, Second Edition*, edited by Bruce Burgett and Glenn Hendler, 320. New York: NYU Press, 2014.

Manuel, Peter. *Cassette Culture: Popular Music and Technology in North India*. Chicago: The University of Chicago Press, 1993.

Marcus, Sara. *Girls to the Front: The True Story of the Riot Grrrl Revolution*. New York: Harper Perennial, 2010.

Menninghaus, Winfried. "On the 'Vital Significance' of Kitsch: Walter Benjamin's Politics of 'Bad Taste'." Chap. 2 In *Walter Benjamin and the Architecture of Modernity*, edited by Andrew Benjamin and Charles Rice, 39–57. Melbourne: re .press, 2009.

Meno, Joe. "'Hairstyles of the Damned' Puts Punk on the Page." Interview by Scott Simon. *Weekend Edition Saturday* (January 22, 2005).

Meno, Joe. *Hairstyles of the Damned*. New York: Akashic Books, 2004.

Mercari. "NKOTB VIP Bags." https://www.mercari.com/us/item/m90711549421/.

Meslow, Scott. "The Real DJ Behind the Baby Driver Jam You'll Be Humming All Summer." *GQ* (June 30, 2017). https://www.gq.com/story/kid-koala-baby-driver.

Mills, Ted. "Home Taping Is Killing Music: When the Music Industry Waged War on the Cassette Tape in the 1980s, and Punk Bands Fought Back." *Open Culture* (April 5, 2019). http://www.openculture.com/2019/04/home-taping-is-killing-music.html.

Miranda, Lin-Manuel. "Lin-Manuel Miranda on Disney, Mixtapes and Why He Won't Try to Top 'Hamilton'." Interview by Terri Gross. *Fresh Air* (January 3, 2017).

Mixtape Museum. "The Mixtape Museum." *Soundcloud*, https://soundcloud.com/ mixtapemuseum.

Mixtape. "About Mixtape." *Mixtape Pgh*, https://mixtapepgh.com/about/.

Mixtape. "Mixtape." Facebook, 2020.

Mixxim. "Mixxtape." https://mixtapeboss.com/products/mixxtape-1.

Mixxim. "Mixxtape." *Kickstarter*, https://www.kickstarter.com/projects/mixxtape/ mixxtape-the-cassette-reinvented.

Molanphy, Chris. *Hit Parade*. Podcast audio. The Lullaby of Broadway Edition 1hr 18 mins2019.

Molloy, David. "Baby Driver Is the Best Mixtape on Screen This Year." *The Brag* (July 10, 2017). https://thebrag.com/baby-driver-best-mixtape-screen-year/.

Moore, Ryan. *Sells Like Teen Spirit: Music, Youth Culture, and Social Crisis*. New York: New York University Press, 2010.

Moore, Thurston, ed. *Mix Tape: The Art of Cassette Culture*. New York: Universe Publisher, 2004.

Morgan, Marcyliena, and Dionne Bennett. "Hip-Hop & the Global Imprint of a Black Cultural Form." *Daedalus* 140, no. 2 (Spring 2011): 176–96. https://www.jstor.org /stable/23047460.

Morton, David. *Off the Record: The Technology and Culture of Sound Recording in America*. New Brunswick: Rutgers University Press, 2000.

Moyer, Edward. "Classy 'Mixtape' Coffee Table Is One for the Jet (Cas)Set(Te)." c|net (May 31, 2012). https://www.cnet.com/news/classy-mixtape-coffee-table-is -one-for-the-jet-cassette/.

Muncy, Julie. "Guardians of the Galaxy Is Leading the Unlikely Cassette Tape Revival" *Gizmodo*. (January 6, 2018). https://io9.gizmodo.com/guardians-of-the -galaxy-is-leading-the-unlikely-cassett-1821838451.

Munson, Ben. "Paul Simon: Graceland." In *Please, Vinyl Me*, edited by Emma Jacobs, 236–38: New York: Abrams, 2016.

Murray-Nag, Beatrice. "The Elbow Clip-on Cassette Player Is a Turntable Tonearm for Tapes." https://www.designboom.com/technology/elbow-casette-player-brain-monk-05-03-2017/.

New Kids on the Block. "2019 Mixtape Tour." https://www.facebook.com/watch/?v =696979487368443.

New Kids on the Block. "NKOTB Announce the Mixtape Tour 2019." https://www .nkotb.com/news/title/nkotb-announce-the-mixtape-tour-2019.

New Kids on the Block. *80s Baby*. New Kids on the Block, 2019. Music Video, Video and description. https://www.nkotb.com/news/title/stream-80s-baby-now

Newport Folk Festival. *Bonny Light Horseman// Tim Buckley*. Podcast audio. Newport Folk Podcast 21 mins 2020.

Newswire, PR. "Mixxtape Reinvents the Cassette." *PR Newswire*, https://www.prn ewswire.com/news-releases/mixxtape-reinvents-the-cassette-300953848.html.

Newton, Derek. "Higher Education Is Not a Mixtape." *The Atlantic* (January 27, 2015). https://www.theatlantic.com/education/archive/2015/01/higher-education -is-not-a-mixtape/384845/.

Nicholls, David. *One Day*. Vintage Contemporaries ed. United States: Vintage Books, 2010.

Norwood, Aubrey. "Why 2019 Will Be the Year of the Cassette (Again)." *Medium* (December 30, 2018). https://medium.com/@aubreynorwood/why-2019-will-be-th e-year-of-the-cassette-7f9fb91859a3.

Novak, David. *Japanoise: Music at the Edge of Circulation*. Durham: Duke University Press, 2013.

NPR. "In the Mix Kid's Tee." NPR, https://shop.npr.org/products/in-the-mix-kid-s -t-shirt.

The Obama White House. *Lin-Manuel Miranda Performs at the White House Poetry Jam, An Evening of Poetry & Music: The Spoken Word*. YouTube, 2009. https:// youtu.be/WNFf7nMIGnE

Ohio Craft Brewers Association. "Ohio Brewery News." Ohio Craft Brewers Association, https://ohiocraftbeer.org/ohio-brewery-news-1-31-2020/.

Owens, Skip. "The iPods of 'Baby Driver'." *Geek Dad* (February 12, 2018). https:// geekdad.com/2018/02/ipods-baby-driver/.

Paige, Anna. "Former Billings Resident's Book Prompts Music Lovers to Explore the Soundtrack of Their Lives." *Billings Gazette*, July 20, 2018.

Pappu, Sridhar. "'Baby Driver' Stirs Nostalgia for iPods." *The New York Times*, July 13, 2017, 4.

Pareles, Jon. "Cassette Singles: New 45's." *The New York Times*, September 2, 1987.

Passick, Adam. "The Magic That Makes Spotify's Discover Weekly Playlists So Damn Good." Quartz (December 21, 2015). https://qz.com/571007/the-magic-that-makes-spotifys-discover-weekly-playlists-so-damn-good/.

Peraino, Judith A. "I'll Be Your Mixtape: Lou Reed, Andy Warhol, and the Queer Intimacies of Cassettes." *The Journal of Musicology* 36, no. 4 (2019): 401–36.

Pérez, Celia C. "Celia C. Pérez Playlist." http://celiacperez.com/playlist.

Pérez, Celia C. "Celia Perez's New Novel 'The First Rule of Punk' Comes with Advice for Adolescents." Interview by Kelly McEvers. *All Things Considered* (September 1, 2017).

Pérez, Celia C. *The First Rule of Punk*. New York: Viking, 2017.

Peterson, James Braxton. *Hip Hop Headphones: A Scholar's Critical Playlist*. New York: Bloomsbury Academic, 2016. http://search.ebscohost.com/login.aspx?direct=true&AuthType=sso&db=nlebk&AN=1331575&site=eds-live&scope=site&custid=s7614884&ebv=EB&ppid=pp_1.

Pfannenschmidt, Seth. "Mixtape, in Garfield, Blurs the Lines between Music Venue, Bar and Art Gallery." *Pittsburgh City Paper*, March 2, 2016.

Pinch, Trevor, and Frank Trocco. *Analog Days: The Invention and Impact of the Moog Synthesizer*. Cambridge: Harvard University Press, 2002.

Pittsburgh Playhouse, The. "Pump up the Volume: A New Rock Musical." Point Park University, http://www.pittsburghplayhouse.com/current-season/conservatory-theatre-company/pump-up-the-volume.

Prinz, Yvonne. *The Vinyl Princess*. United States: Harper Collins, 2009.

Proulx, Natalie. "Nine Teaching Ideas for Using Music to Inspire Student Writing." *New York Times* (May 10, 2018). https://www.nytimes.com/2018/05/10/learning/lesson-plans/nine-teaching-ideas-for-using-music-to-inspire-student-writing.html.

Reilly, Nick. "R.E.M. Announce 40th Anniversary Reissue of Debut Single 'Radio Free Europe'." *NME* (May 18, 2021). https://www.nme.com/news/music/r-e-m-announce-40th-anniversary-reissue-of-debut-single-radio-free-europe-2943191.

Reynolds, Simon. *Retromania: Pop Culture's Addiction to Its Own Past*. New York: Faber and Faber, Inc, 2011.

RIAA. "U. S. Sales Database." 2021. https://www.riaa.com/u-s-sales-database/?fbclid=IwAR2-IuPU0w989pz0nuGsZflTrF3BFdK1C9FhpD3PfHg1CJTt4bs86UzPOvY.

Robertson, TR. "Mixtape—The Best of the 80's" Returns in Lamb's Players Theatre." *The Vista Press* (July 1, 2019). http://www.thevistapress.com/mixtape-the-best-of-the-80s-returns-in-lambs-players-theatre/.

Roffman, Michael. "Soundtrack to Baby Drivers Spans 30 Tracks and Multiple Decades." *Consequence of Sound* (June 2, 2017). https://www.latimes.com/entertainment/movies/la-et-mn-baby-driver-review-20170627-story.html?_ga=2.241958082.1551556259.1591026382-1270204586.1590782768.

Rogers, Jude. "Total Rewind: 10 Key Moments in the Life of the Cassette." *The Observer*, August 30, 2013.

Rose, Tricia. *Black Noise: Rap Music and Black Culture in Contemporary America*. Hanover, NH: Wesleyan University Press, 1994. http://search.ebscohost.com/login .aspx?direct=true&AuthType=sso&db=nlebk&AN=45315&site=ehost-live.

Rothman, Lily. "Rewound: On Its 50th Birthday, the Cassette Tape Is Still Rolling." *Time*, August 12, 2013.

Rowell, Rainbow. *Eleanor & Park*. New York: St. Martin's Press, 2013. Novel.

Running Press. "The Mixtape of My Life." *Running Press*. https://www.runningpress. com/titles/robert-k-elder/the-mixtape-of-my-life/9780762464074/.

Rys, Dan. "Mixtapes & Money: Inside the Mainstreaming of Hip-Hop's Shadow Economy." *Billboard* (January 26, 2017). https://www.billboard.com/articles/ columns/hip-hop/7669109/mixtapes-money-hip-hop-shadow-economy-mainstre am.

Rys, Dan. "The Evolution of the Mixtape: An Oral History with DJ Drama." *Billboard* (January 26, 2017). https://www.billboard.com/articles/columns/hip-hop /7669073/history-dj-drama-mixtape-evolution.

Rys, Dan. "The Roots' Black Thought on Lin-Manuel Miranda, Perseverance & 'The Hamilton Mixtape'." *Billboard* (November 30, 2016). https://www.billboard.com /articles/columns/hip-hop/7595776/hamilton-mixtape-the-roots-black-thought-on -lin-manuel-miranda.

Sanderson, Jane. "Mix Tape: Introduction." *Square Space*. https://janesanderson.com /books/mix-tape/.

Sanderson, Jane. *Mix Tape*. London: Transworld Publishers, 2020.

Sante, Luc. "Disco Dreams." *New York Review* (May 13, 2004), https://www. nybooks.com/articles/2004/05/13/disco-dreams/.

Sax, David. *The Revenge of Analog: Real Things and Why They Matter*. New York: Public Affairs, 2016.

Scholet, Nicole. "Hamilton Mixtape Unveiled at Vassar Reading Festival." *The Alexander Hamilton Awareness Society* (August 27, 2013). https://the-aha-soci ety.com/index.php/publications/articles/87-aha-society-articles/145-hamilton-mix tape-reading.

Seah, Daniel. "Lou Ottens, Inventor of the Cassette Tape, Dies at 94." *Music Tech* (March 11, 2021). https://www.musictech.net/news/lou-ottens-cassette-tape-dies -at-94/.

Selvin, Joel. "Music Store a Castle to 'Vinyl Princess'." *SF Gate* (December 26, 2009). https://www.sfgate.com/entertainment/article/Music-store-a-castle-to-V inyl-Princess-3277548.php#item-85307-tbla-1.

Semtex, DJ. "Street Dreams: How Hip-Hop Mixtapes Changed the Game." In Hip-Hop Raised Me *Medium*: Thames & Hudson, 2016. https://medium.com/cuepoint/ street-dreams-how-hip-hop-mixtapes-changed-the-game-40af79e8d953.

"Sharetape Puts a Modern Twist on the Physical Mixtape." *New Atlas* (February 12, 2013). https://newatlas.com/sharetapes-nfc-qr-mixtape/26202/.

Sheffield, Rob. *Love Is a Mix Tape: Life and Loss, One Song at a Time*. New York: Crown Publishers, 2007. Memoir.

Shelemay, Kay Kaufman. "Music, Memory and History: In Memory of Stuart Feder." *Ethnomusicology Forum* 15, no. 1 (June 2006): 17–37.

Sheth, Sarang. "Hello Cassette My Old Friend." Yanko Design (May 4, 2017). https://www.yankodesign.com/2017/05/04/hello-cassette-my-old-friend/.

Shiver, John-Paul. "Staying In? Bing on Mixtape Romance 'High Fidelity'." 48hills (March 13, 2020). https://48hills.org/2020/03/staying-in-binge-on-mixtape-romance-high-fidelity/.

Sirc, Geoffrey. "Serial Composition." In *Rhetorics and Technologies: New Directions in Writing and Communication*, edited by Stuart A. Selber. Studies in Rhetoric/Communication, 56–73. Columbia: University of South Carolina Press, 2010.

Skierka, Jeff. *Mixtape Table*. Jeff Skierka Designs, 2013. https://www.jeffskierkadesigns.com/portfolio-mixtape.html

Sklar, Monica. *Punk Style*. New York: Bloomsbury, 2013.

Sloan, Nate, and Charlie Harding. *Switched on Pop: How Popular Music Works and Why It Matters*. New York: Oxford University Press, 2020.

Sloane, Nikki, ed. "Nikki Sloane." Squarespace, https://www.nikkisloane.com/shop/mixtape-a-love-song-anthology.

Sloane, Nikki, ed. *Mixtape: A Love Song Anthology*. USA: Shady Creek Publishing, 2019.

Smith, Chris. "Forget Vinyl, Cassette Tapes Are the Musical Comeback Story of 2019." Trusted Reviews (August 2, 2019). https://www.trustedreviews.com/news/cassette-tape-comeback-3927671.

Smith, Courtney E. "Amazon Exclusive: A Q&A with Author Courtney Smith." Interview by Amazon Editorial Reviews (2011).

Smith, Courtney E. *Record Collecting for Girls: Unleashing Your Inner Music Nerd, One Album at a Time*. New York: Houghton Mifflin Harcourt Publishing Company, 2011.

Smith, Martin. "Are Universities Going the Way of Record Labels?" *The Atlantic* (July 7, 2014). https://www.theatlantic.com/education/archive/2014/07/how-universities-are-like-record-labels/374012/.

Smith, Mary. "How to Make a Mixtape for Someone." (June 3, 2018). https://arts.onehowto.com/article/how-to-make-a-mixtape-for-someone-12635.html.

Somerfield, Harry. "Music Gets Personal with New Tape Idea." *Orlando Sentinel*, March 19, 1988.

Sorrentino, Mike. "This Doritos Bag Plays 'Guardians of the Galaxy' Music." cnet (May 5, 2017). https://www.cnet.com/news/guardians-of-the-galaxy-vol-2-doritos-bag-soundtrack/.

Speer, Cindy. "Semisonic: Feeling Strangely Fine." *Pop Matters*. https://www.popmatters.com/semisonic-feeling-2496084000.html.

Spitznagel, Eric. *Old Records Never Die: One Man's Quest for His Vinyl and His Past*. New York: Plume, 2016.

Springsteen, Bruce. "Exclusive: The Complete Text of Bruce Springsteen's SXSW Keynote Address." *Rolling Stone* (March 28, 2012). https://www.rollingstone.com

/music/music-news/exclusive-the-complete-text-of-bruce-springsteens-sxsw-keyn ote-address-86379/.

Stone Brewing. "About Stone Brewing." *Stone Brewing*. https://www.stonebrewing .com/about.

Stoup Brewing. "Mixtape Romeo." *Stoup Brewing*. https://www.stoupbrewing.com/ beer/mixtape-romeo-953.html.

Strauss, Paul. "The Elbow Reinvents the Portable Cassette Player." *Technabob* (August 9, 2017). https://technabob.com/blog/2017/08/09/elbow-minimal-cassette -player/#ixzz6OWA8u9kf.

Styles, Harry. "Twitter Update." Twitter: @hsdaily, 2018.

Svetlik, Joe. "Dust Off Your Boombox, Mixxtape Is a Digital Music Player That Doubles as an Old School Cassette." *Trusted Reviews* (June 8, 2017). https://www .trustedreviews.com/news/mixxtape-is-a-cassette-shaped-music-player-that-plays- in-a-tape-deck-2950650.

Swirsky, Jen. "Review: Lee Brice's "Mixtape: 'Til Summer's Gone" EP." *Nashville Gab* (July 22, 2015). https://nashvillegab.com/2015/07/lee-brice-mixtape-til- summers-gone-ep.html.

Tactify. https://www.tactify.com/. 2020.

Taylor, Timothy D. *Strange Sounds: Music, Technology & Culture*. New York: Routledge Press, 2001.

Taylor, Zack. "Cassette: A Documentary Mixtape." 1:32: Gravitas Ventures, 2018. DVD 88 mins.

The Day the Mixtape Died: DJ Drama. Podcast audio. Louder Than a Riot 1:05 2020. https://www.npr.org/2020/10/27/928307301/the-day-the-mixtape-died-dj-drama.

"33 Things You Can Do with a Tape Recorder." *Tape Recording*, January 1966, 9–19.

Thompson, Ahmir "Questlove," Ben Greenman, and Lauren Schaefer. *Mixtape Potluck: A Cookbook: A Dinner Party for Friends, Their Recipes, and the Songs They Inspire*. New York: Harry N. Abrams Book, 2019.

Thomspon, Ahmir "Questlove". "Questlove on 'Hamilton' and Hip-Hop: It Takes One." *Rolling Stone* (September 28, 2015). https://www.rollingstone.com/culture/ culture-news/questlove-on-hamilton-and-hip-hop-it-takes-one-34370/.

Today Show, The. *New Kids on the Block Announce Special Guests on Tour*. October 8, 2018. Video. https://www.today.com/video/new-kids-on-the-block-announce-s pecial-guests-on-tour-1339176515847

Tracy, Brianne. "New Kids on the Block Give Fans a Behind-the-Scenes Look at Their Tour in '80s Baby' Music Video." *People* (June 6, 2019). https://people.com /music/new-kids-on-the-block-80s-baby-music-video/.

Trufelman, Avery. *Articles of Interest*. Podcast audio. Punk Style. MP3 Audio, 32:42 2018.

Truffaut-Wong, Olivia. "Sky Ferreira Switches It up in 'Baby Driver'." *Bustle* (July 11, 2017). https://www.bustle.com/p/who-plays-babys-mom-in-baby-driver-the-s inger-took-off-her-pop-persona-for-the-role-69511.

Uncommon Goods. *Mixtape Glasses - Set of 6*. Uncommon Goods Catalog, 2013.

Uncommon Goods. *Personalized Mixtape Pillow*. Uncommon Goods Catalog, 2020.

Untappd. "Mixtape Mayhem: Grist House Craft Brewery." Untappd, https://untappd .com/b/grist-house-craft-brewery-mixtape-mayhem/3498919.

van de Werff, Ties. "Technostalgia." Next Nature, https://nextnature.net/2010/07/ technostalgia.

Vanskike, Elliott. "A Very JSTOR Daily Mixtape: Volume 2." JSTOR, https://daily .jstor.org/jstor-playlist-mixtape-2/.

Vinyl Eyezz. *Make a Mixtape!* YouTube, 2017. https://youtu.be/POzBPM5YRJc.

Walsh, Jim. *Bar Yarns and Manic-Depressive Mixtapes: Jim Walsh on Music from Minneapolis to the Outer Limits.* Minneapolis: University of Minnesota Press, 2016.

Watters, Dan, and Caspar Wijngaard. "Get Stuck into 'Limbo with Caspar Wijngaard and Dan Watters [Interview]." Interview by Laura Sneddon (February 10, 2016).

Watters, Dan, and Caspar Wijngaard. "Interview: Dan Watters & Caspar Wijngaard Talk About the Musical Voodoo of Limbo." Interview by Chris Hayden (June 29, 2016).

Wavesfactory. "Cassette." https://www.wavesfactory.com/cassette.

Williams, Justin A. "'We Get the Job Done': Immigrant Discourse and Mixtape Authenticity in *the Hamilton Mixtape.*" *American Music* 36, no. 4 (Winter 2018 2018): 487–506.

Woodward, Afton Lorraine. "Tift Merritt: A Song for Every 'Mixtape'." *Review, NPR Music* (May 24, 2010). https://www.npr.org/templates/story/story.php?stor yId=127089755.

"Words and Music: Out 60 Favorite Music Books." Features, *Pitchfork* (July 11, 2011). https://pitchfork.com/features/lists-and-guides/words-and-music-our-60-fav orite-music-books.

Wright, Robin. "Audiotape Cassette." In *A History of Intellectual Property in 50 Objects*, edited by Claudy Op Den Kamp and Dan Hunter, 289–96. Cambridge: Cambridge University Press, 2019.

Yagoda, Ben. *The B Side: The Death of Tin Pan Alley and the Rebirth of the Great American Song.* New York: Riverhead Books, 2015.

Yong, Sable. "The Sexy Mixtape Is Dead and High Fidelity Can't Bring It Back." *GQ* (February 20, 2020). https://www.gq.com/story/beware-the-playlist.

Young, Alex. "Guardians of the Galaxy's Awesome Mix Vol. 1 Is Finally Being Released on Cassette Tape." Consequence of Sound (October 20, 2014). https://co nsequenceofsound.net/2014/10/guardians-of-the-galaxys-awesome-mix-vol-1-is- finally-being-released-on-cassette-tape/.

Zak, Albin J. *The Poetics of Rock: Cutting Tracks, Making Records.* Berkeley: University of California Press, 2001. https://ebookcentral.proquest.com/lib/point- park-ebooks/detail.action?docID=223044.

Zaleski, Annie. "35 Years Ago: The U.K. Launches the 'Home Taping Is Killing Music' Campaign." *Diffuser* (October 25, 2016). https://diffuser.fm/home-taping -is-killing-music-uk/.

Index

Page references for figures are italicized.

About the Author

Jehnie I. Burns is an associate professor who teaches European History, gender studies, and the occasional History of American Music course at Point Park University in Pittsburgh, Pennsylvania. She has served as director of the Core at Point Park, highlighting her investment in engaging students in general education. Her French history scholarship studying the Cité Universitaire has appeared in the *Journal of Contemporary European Studies*, *Migrance*, and *History of Education*.